I0023269

Thematic Guide to Biblical Literature

Thematic Guide to Biblical Literature

Nancy M. Tischler

GREENWOOD PRESS
Westport, Connecticut • *London*

Library of Congress Cataloging-in-Publication Data

Tischler, Nancy M.
Thematic guide to biblical literature / Nancy M. Tischler.
    p. cm.
  Includes bibliographical references and index.
  ISBN–13: 978–0–313–33709–3 (alk. paper)
  ISBN–10: 0–313–33709–8 (alk. paper)
  1. Bible and literature.   I. Title.
  PN56.B5T57   2007
  820.9′3822—dc22   2007000548

Reference —

British Library Cataloguing in Publication Data is available.

Library of Congress Catalog Card Number: 2007000548
ISBN-13: 978–0–313–33709–3
ISBN-10: 0–313–33709–8

First published in 2007

Greenwood Press, 88 Post Road West, Westport, CT 06881
An imprint of Greenwood Publishing Group, Inc.
www.greenwood.com

Printed in the United States of America

The paper used in this book complies with the
Permanent Paper Standard issued by the National
Information Standards Organization (Z39.48–1984).

10 9 8 7 6 5 4 3 2 1

pc
0 = 78788087

For Jim—
Big brother,
Great reader,
Good friend,
with enduring love.

Contents

Introduction

The Bible has one pervasive theme, the relationship between God and humankind. The great drama that moves from the Creation to the final days is more than literature. It is the basis of millions of peoples' beliefs over thousands of years. Especially in the West, the Bible's influence on the culture has been so deep as to make the world-view of scripture a basic assumption for literature.

As a consequence, the influence of biblical themes on Western literature is subtle and foundational. Even when the literature is a perversion of the original biblical concepts or a rejection of them, the influence remains. For example, even when the admonition to keep the Sabbath holy has largely disappeared from American life, it retains its echoes in literature. The lapsed Catholic F. Scott Fitzgerald sets the most depraved scenes of *The Great Gatsby* on a Sunday afternoon, making the depravity seem even darker. And the Loman family in *Death of Salesman* choose Sunday to wash their car. This is a deliberate violation of the commandment to keep the Sabbath holy, typical behavior of a family that appears to retain no clear memories of Judeo-Christian faith. Having replaced Christianity with the American Cinderella myth, the Lomans believe that love of one another and of success is sufficient to give their lives meaning. Biblical thinking is so intrinsically intertwined in our thinking that we find ourselves using biblical phrases, ideas, people, and stories as a natural part of our speech, even in a "post-Christian" world. They are deeply imbedded in our culture.

The other strong thread of influence in Western thought is Hellenism, which strongly contrasts with Hebraism. For this reason, I have included examples of well-known Greek stories and ideas to contrast the scriptural ones, showing the differences in tastes, morality, theology, and activity. This is particularly important in the study of the hero figure. The Greeks loved the beautiful body as well as the cultured mind. The Hebrews believed that faith in God was the beginning of wisdom and of virtue. Appearance is seldom mentioned in Bible stories.

Using these influences, with major focus on the Bible, I have tried to trace a few of the typical examples of the various biblical themes in English and American literature and occasionally in their European counterparts. In each chapter, a handful of individual works have detailed analysis for the purpose of demonstrating the continuing influence of biblical thought. The examples are by no means exhaustive, and the analyses are too brief to be fully satisfying; but they do provide samples of the transformation and persistence of the ideas through history.

I have approached this using the scriptural concept of typology. In other words, in scripture, all events point to one another in a mutually reinforcing manner. The New Testament writers considered the events and people and words of the Old Testament as types or foreshadowings of the further antitypes that were to come. These antitypes were the fully realized forms of the earlier figures. Thus, Paul considered Adam as a foreshadowing of Christ (Rom. 5:14), and Peter thought Christian baptism to be the antitype of God's salvation of mankind from the flood through Noah (1 Pet. 3:21; Frye, 78–79). These types then became the basis for much of Western literature, with Christ-figures too common to enumerate, and Eden innocence recurring in the imagination of every age.

Writers in the Western world, most of whom have been nurtured in the Judeo-Christian tradition, recognize and utilize the archetypes found in Scripture. Abraham, the father who is willing to sacrifice his beloved son for his faith, becomes a type of God-the-father, in the Christian Trinity. The Song of Solomon, a rich proclamation of sexual love, becomes a foreshadowing of Christ's love for his bride, the Church. The Royal Psalms are seen as an announcement of the coming of the Messiah.

These types, which are often parallel to types found in Greek and other cultures, often fall into patterns of revelation. Frye, in his book on this topic, *The Great Code*, describes seven phases: Creation, Revolution, Law, Wisdom, Prophesy, Gospel, and Apocalypse (Frye, 105–138). Because the Judeo-Christian view of existence is linear, moving from the beginning of time to the end of the world, I have ordered the chapters in a loosely chronological pattern, beginning with the stories of the Creation and ending with the Last Days. In between are a number of issues that involve the human interaction with the divine—fate and predestination, morality, love, worship, and so forth. There are many other themes that I might have included, themes such as dreams and visions, sacrifice, and salvation that the reader is free to explore for herself.

The segment of each entry that deals directly with scripture has few quotations but many citations, based on the assumption that the reader has a Bible for further study and thought. The citations are by no means complete; each chapter would require several volumes in order to provide an exhaustive account of the issues. Instead, the chapters explore only a few of the major ideas related to each topic. Some of the themes, like *love*, have hundreds of references in scripture.

For the literary parallels and influences, I have tried to select works by major authors that are well known and frequently anthologized. Although I began this study with careful attention to *The Bible as/in Literature*, a popular anthology by James S. Ackerman and Thayer S. Warsaw, I have used a number of others as well, quoting extensively from poetry. As a college teacher for half a century, I could not resist works that I enjoyed teaching students, even though they rarely appear in modern anthologies. Realizing that many of the readers would not have the poetry collections at hand, I have quoted entire poems when I thought them to be particularly relevant to the topic. Only a few exemplary literary works are included, usually with a modest effort to demonstrate how they echo, refute, or expand on biblical examples.

It was impossible to avoid overlaps: How can heroism be separated from war, or morality from sin? By using different examples and emphasizing different issues, I have sought to make the overlapping chapters mutually reinforcing and lively. Really powerful literature is never so didactic nor so simple as to be easily reduced to the formula, "The moral of this story is…. " Like scripture itself, the moral, or the theme, is often complicated by the circumstances and the characters involved. For example, the story of King David's adulterous affair with Bathsheba is not just about the violation of the marriage vow. It is also about murder, lying, abuse of power, and any number of other issues. Shakespeare's *King Lear* is not just a story of ungrateful children, who are failing to obey the commandment to honor their father. Such reductionist approaches do a disservice to the nuances of the play. The alert and sensitive reader must plow deeper and consider Lear's demands for flattery, his failure to rein in his own excesses, his abdication of responsibility, and other flaws in both him and his daughters. From the beginning of the play, we know he is misjudging the natures of his daughters and that his decision to divest himself of his authority is unwise and potentially tragic. The great writers all have this complexity, subtlety, power, and beauty that make them worth studying.

This book has been a pleasure to write. I have appreciated the people who were willing to look at chapters and give me advice, including my friend Kathy Adams; my pastor, Rev. David Hanson; and my tireless, meticulous, and wise editor, George Butler. I hope the essays help those teachers and students studying themes in scripture that also appear in other literature.

Creation

Readings

Genesis 1–3
Job 38
John 1
Lucretius, *On the Nature of the Universe* (50 B.C.)
John Milton, *Paradise Lost* (1667)
Mary Wollstonecraft Shelley, *Frankenstein* (1817)
Samuel Taylor Coleridge, *Biographia Literaria* (1817)
Percy Bysshe Shelley, *Defense of Poetry* (1821)
Robert Browning, "Abt Vogler" (1864)
Aldous Huxley, *Brave New World* (1932)

Introduction

> In the beginning God created the heaven and the earth.
> And the earth was without form, and void; and darkness was upon the face of
> the deep. And the Spirit of God moved upon the face of the waters.
> And God said, Let there be light: and there was light.
> And God saw the light, that it was good: and God divided the light from the
> darkness.
> And God called the light Day, and the darkness he called Night. And the
> evening and the morning were the first day. (Gen. 1:1–5)

The most famous lines in all of history are these opening words of the book of
Genesis. Their poetic form with the balance, repetition, and variation suggest that
this was once a creedal recitation among ancient peoples. Rich with meaning, the
first phrases establish that God was eternally present before the creation, that this act
marked the beginning of time. He created everything by fiat, by the sheer utterance
of the Word, and his Spirit, which "brooded over the waters," was an actor in the

creation event. Christians interpret these opening words as a description of Creation as the act of the Trinity (Father, Son, and Holy Spirit). This act of creation is echoed in the opening words of John: "In the beginning was the Word."

Writers and other artists are often fascinated by this creation story. The act of creation itself, whether out of the stuff of the writer's life or from some deep primordial rumblings, is in some ways parallel to God's action during the first week of the world. Whether the artist is a writer, painter, sculptor, or musician, the perennial dream is to create a work that transcends time. For every artist, this dream is frustrated: the manuscript is lost, the bowl is broken, and the note of music lingers on the air for less than a second. Many of the works of literature deal with this struggle to become more like God.

For scientists, who seek to discover the process of material creation and to replicate it, the puzzle is somewhat different. Medieval people thought the experiments of a Dr. Faustus to be a challenge to God. Marlowe's hero, in seeking to know everything, damns himself for eternity. In more recent times, with science's explosive progress, life's basic elements are now open to human manipulation. Both clergy and laypeople question how ethical it is to try to create human life artificially or to try to alter a fetus prior to birth. Writers have thought about these issues for at least two centuries. Genetic engineering, one of the great ethical dilemmas of the twenty-first century, reaches back to the very earliest verses in the Bible, challenging the very nature of God's creation of the fish, the birds, and the beasts, as well as man and woman.

Scripture

The first chapter of Genesis describes the sequence of creation as being rational, orderly, and good. Each of the six days of creation establishes a significant component of the world in which God finally placed mankind. The opening provides a summary of the first miracle: he created the heavens and the earth, which had no shape or light. On the first day, he created light, without which there could be no life, and by which time itself is calculated. He also gave names to the light and the darkness—*day* and *night*. (Later in Genesis, he delegated to Adam the task of naming the animals in the Garden.) On the second day, he created the firmament, which he called *Heaven*, the means by which he separated the waters, providing a second element for life. The waters below the earth provide springs and nourishment for plants and animals; the waters above the firmament bring the rains that revive the land. On the third day, he separated the waters from the land, thus providing dry land for his as yet uncreated creatures. On the land, he provided grass, herbs, fruit trees—the plant life that sustains his animate creatures. At each point, he provided the environment for life before bringing forth the creatures to inhabit it. On the fourth day, he set the sun, the moon, and the stars in the sky to provide regularity to light and darkness and the means for measuring time.

The passage opens with the repeated pattern of "And God said, Let there be ..." The change in the pattern with the beginning of animate life is interesting. Rather than creating these living things himself, he ordered the waters to "bring forth." Each section has a list of created items and includes the repeated judgment: "and God saw that it was good." It also contains a blessing and an admonition to "be fruitful and multiply." With the creation of the earth, he provided for "seed" so that the grass and the trees could multiply; but on the fifth day he commanded the lively creatures also to be fruitful.

The sixth day echoes the usual pattern, repeating the "bring forth" phrasing, this time saying "Let the earth bring forth the living creature after his kind, cattle, and creeping thing, and the beast of the earth after its kind: and so it was." The judgment, "it was good," is repeated, but not the blessing, perhaps saving this for the climactic scene of the day, which does include the blessing:

> And God said, Let us make man in our image, after our likeness: and let them have dominion over the fish of the sea, and over the fowl of the air, and over the cattle, and over all the earth, and over every creeping thing that creepeth upon the earth.
>
> So God created man in his own image, in the image of God created he him; male and female created he them.
>
> And God blessed them, and God said unto them, Be fruitful, and multiply, and replenish the earth, and subdue it: and have dominion over the fish of the sea, and over the fowl of the air, and over every living thing that moveth upon the earth. (Gen. 1:26–28)

This passage is so pregnant with implications that philosophers and poets over the ages have struggled with each word. The placement of man ("male and female") as the climactic segment, after the animals, and giving the human creature alone the "image of God" has led to long debate over whether humans are animals, whether men and women are equal, and what the nature of God's "image" is, whether it be male, female, or androgynous. Although the animal creations are "brought forth" from sky, water, or earth, the humans are not simply brought forth from the earth. They are God's individual and deliberately designed creation. The following chapter of Genesis speaks of God's forming them from the dust of the earth with his own hands.

On the one hand, the passage raises questions about the nature of the "dominion" that humans are granted over the rest of nature. On the other, it points to the bonds between humans and animals. The encouragement to "be fruitful" indicates that from the very moment of creation God expects humans as well as animals to reproduce.

The final day, the Lord rested. He blessed the seventh day, and "sanctified" it—thus providing the basis for the Sabbath and a precedent for worship of the Creator of the heavens and the earth.

These astonishing verses of Scripture, while portraying the act of creation itself, also portray God as the all-powerful creative force, with a delight in all the variety of life on his blessed earth. He plans for both the present, filling the earth with food, and for the future, providing for the propagation of the life he creates. He is also portrayed as a judging god, who decides whether things are "good." In the following scenes, when God speaks to these creatures and gives them directions and authority, this special relationship is reinforced. In the creation of man and woman, he proves himself a god capable of fellowship with these creatures who he made "in his own image."

Genesis 2 expands on the narrative of God's creation of humans: "And the Lord God formed man of the dust of the ground, and breathed into his nostrils the breath of life; and man became a living soul." The story of Adam in the Garden of Eden, of the naming of the animals and of the creation of Eve, evolve in an anthropomorphic narrative form, ending with the Temptation and Expulsion. The tone and form of the second chapter of Genesis are dramatically different from the first. Whereas the first chapter reads like a poetic creed that could be recited by a congregation of believers, the second chapter is a more prosaic tale, which might have told around the campfire This second telling became the narrative more frequently cited by poets and story-tellers over the ages. Sometimes it was as simple as African-American preachers, portraying God as a grandfatherly figure who walks with Adam in the cool of the day and talks with him (as pictured by James Weldon Johnson in *God's Trombones,* 1927). Sometimes it as complex as the poetic narrative of *Paradise Lost,* by John Milton (1667).

Whether in prose or poetry, in sermons or stories, this narrative is the key to much of Western thought and art.

Together, these chapters provide the basic presuppositions of most of Hebraic and Christian thought about the nature of God, of humans, of the relationship between the sexes, of human relationships with nature and animals, and of the structure of the earth, the heavens, and the seas. The first two chapters of Genesis also provide two concepts of creation: (1) God spoke the Word and things came into being by fiat out of nothing; (2) by forming, out of the dust of the ground, and breathing the breath of life into his nostrils, God made man a "living soul." In a parallel "making," he took a rib out of Adam and made Eve, the "mother of all living."

The physical, repeated act of creating new life physically, through birth, seedtime, and harvest, furnishes the rhythm of scripture. Suddenly, this rhythm is broken by the story of the Incarnation, found in the Gospels, when Mary realized that "she was with child of the Holy Ghost" (Matt. 1:18). In the various accounts of God's miraculous intervention in human history, we see the "begetting" of Jesus Christ, the "only begotten son" of God (John 3:16). John points back to the Genesis creation in his narrative of the new creation. He echoes the first chapter of Genesis with his first words, "In the beginning" before he describes the power of the Word. The "Word became flesh and dwelt among us" (John 1:14). As John says, Christ was born, "not of blood, nor of the will of the flesh, nor of the will of man, but of God" (John 1:12). In Genesis, God spoke, and things happen. In John, the Word actually becomes flesh and dwells among men.

Finally the Bible promises a New Creation for all believers. In the Last Days, all of God's chosen will become new creatures, casting off their dusty flesh and putting on the sparkling white garments of the blessed. Revelation is full of images of this promise. "And I saw a new heaven and a new earth: for the first heaven and the first earth were passed away; and there was no more sea" (Rev. 21:1).

For the Jews, the two accounts of Creation in Genesis 1 and 2 are central to their thought and expression. The "priestly" account in chapter 1 and the "Jahwistic" account in chapters 2 and 3 provide the model for the poetry and prose in much of Hebrew scriptures. The powerful opening of Genesis, with its various forms of parallelism, furnished both the poetic structure and the thematic substance for many of the Psalms. The second account in Genesis 2 and 3, furnishes a narrative form, with characters, setting, plot, and intrigue that provide the shape of many Biblical narratives to follow: limited use of dialogue, sparse language, little descriptive detail, and bold actions. The use of foreshadowing, the heavy sense of types that are repeated throughout history, is also typical of the way that scripture is crafted. These ancient Creation stories were probably held for centuries as oral traditions, faithfully remembered by the believers in Yahweh and recited to their children from generation to generation.

Other parts of the Old Testament, notably Proverbs and Job, add to our awareness of other ancient traditions hinted at in the Creation story. Some believe that there were many more of these tales of Eden that were part of the oral tradition, which were eventually excluded from the canon of sacred scripture.

A monologue in Proverbs, for example, in which Wisdom describes how she was present from the beginning, raises interesting questions:

The Lord possessed me in the beginning of his way, before the works of old.

I was set up from everlasting, from the beginning, or ever the earth was.

When there were no depths, I was brought forth; when there were no fountains abounding with water. (Prov. 8:22–24)

Some see this passage as a reference to the *Logos,* or the Word, repeated in the Gospel of John, where the Word is present at the Creation. Since Wisdom is portrayed as feminine, feminists see this passage as a reaffirmation of the female (or at least androgynous) nature of God. More traditionally, Wisdom was interpreted as a personification that Solomon used to sum up his discoveries. Wisdom, after all, was considered his primary claim to fame.

Christian apologists have interpreted Wisdom as Christ. Matthew Henry, the seventeenth-century Puritan biblical scholar said, "Wisdom here is Christ, in whom are hidden all the treasures of wisdom and knowledge." He goes on at some length to match this passage with attributes of Christ, including his allusion to "His agency in making the world. He not only had a being before the world, but he was present, not as a spectator, but as the architect, when the world was made." Henry justifies this interpretation by quoting numerous passages from the New Testament, including Eph. 3:9; Heb 1:2; Col. 1:16. The chief source for this interpretation is clearly John's Gospel, in which he states: "All things were made by him; and without him was not any thing made that was made. In him was life; and the life was the light of men" (John 1:3–4).

The book of Job provides yet another interesting insight into the Hebrew view of Creation. Poor Job has been trying to understand why he is being tormented, finally challenging the great plan of creation itself. God responds, in a voice from a whirlwind: "Where were you when I laid the foundation of the earth?" In a lyrical segment, God describes the days of creation, "when the morning stars sang together and all the sons of God shouted for joy." He lists with obvious delight in his own creativity the wonders of the word, including the Behemoth and Leviathan (Job 40–41).

After an extended and beautiful account of the amazing acts of Creation, poor Job is overwhelmed. He responds, "I have uttered what I did not understand, things too wonderful for me, which I did not know … I had heard of you by the hearing of the ear, but now my eye sees you; therefore I despise myself, and repent in dust and ashes."

In Revelation, John promises the coming of the New Creation, with a new heaven and a new earth after the first heaven and the first earth have passed away (Rev. 21). This vision of the future creation is splendid, with hope that there will be a new Jerusalem and a hope that in this new creation, there will be no more death and all our tears will be wiped away.

Literature

By contrast with many of the other creation stories of the ancient world, the book of Genesis is remarkable in several ways: God is distinct from his creation and his creatures. He exists prior to matter and creates the heavens and the earth out of nothing (ex nihilo); he creates by the power of his word rather than by making something out of pre-existent material. Yet he is also a maker, one who uses the matter he has created, shaping man of the dust, the woman of the rib. He orders the waters to bring forth moving creatures, and the earth to bring forth living creatures. This creation is not violent, random, or sexual like many primordial myths. It is logical, progressing toward the most complex creatures as the final act. It is also "good" and "blessed."

Other ancient peoples had myths to explain the creation of the world and of the human race. The Babylonian *Enuma Elish,* often referred to as the "Babylonian Genesis," praises Marduk, the god of Babylon. In this narrative, the creation is physical, sexual, violent, and chaotic. Apsu (the ocean) and Tiamat (primeval waters) lie together and eventually produce silt and slime, sky, earth, and heaven. In an extended and complex account of struggles, Marduk finally triumphs as the ruler of the earth.

Often in ancient myths, the primal creator is female, the creation is therefore a kind of birth, a begetting of the earth and all things in it. In the Old Babylonian myth (1750–1550 B.C.), for example, Nintu or Ninhursag, the goddess of earth, creates mankind. This is a plastic and generative creation, with both birth and shaping implied. The prayer to this wise goddess refers to her as the "mother-womb," the one who creates mankind. This prayer indicates that the first man is formed out of clay, yet is animated with blood. For the many who believed in this enormously popular faith, an earth mother became central figure. The mystery and thrill of fecundity and birth led many peoples of the Mid-east to worship the Great Goddess in her various forms, considering her the source of fertility in humans, animals, and in the soil. In the Bible, she most often appears as Ashtar, the goddess frequently tolerated by the Hebrews, who was worshipped in the "high places" amidst groves of trees. The worship often involved temple prostitutes and sexual acts, and may provide the key to understanding the story of the prophet Hosea and his delinquent wife, Gomer. Some commentaries see her as a temple prostitute, not just a straying wife.

By contrast, some of the later civilizations thought the physical part of creation to be a curse. The Gnostics, for example, believed that the primal creation of matter must have been performed by a lesser god, or an evil one since their God was too spiritual to dabble in fleshly and material creation. Their philosophy, which originated in Hellenistic Egypt in the second century A.D., was to have considerable influence on early Christian thought. Trismegistus, whose ideas were popular throughout the Greco-Roman world, had a dualistic vision parallel to that of the Zoroastrians. He considered matter evil and believed that gnosis, or saving knowledge, was essential to educate people regarding the true origin of their souls and their need to escape evil matter to return to pure light. Unlike the Jews and Christians, the Gnostics believed that God intended mankind to be immortal, not needing to "be fruitful and multiply."

The numerous ancient Greek and Roman myths are both lively and mutually contradictory. The Pelasgian Creation myth, for example (c. 3500 B.C.) shares the Near Eastern ideas of the creator rising out of chaos, the egg of creation being laid on the primeval waters, and the establishment of order with the controlling planetary powers. Many Greek myths are full of violence: divine forces battling one another, infanticide, castration, incest, treachery, and so forth. One generation follows another, with gods being cast into darkness by their children or adversaries. Some are allegorical, some seem to echo actual historical events in grotesque ways. By contrast, the Bible offers no biography of God, providing him with no ancestors and only one begotten son.

Hesiod's *Theogony* begins in a lyrical manner: "In the beginning, Euronome, the Goddess of All Things, rose naked from Chaos, but found nothing substantial for her feet to rest upon, and therefore divided the sea from the sky, dancing lonely upon its waves" (Sproul, 157).

The goddess is then impregnated by her son, a great serpent named Ophion, and lays the World Egg. The snake figure in this tale claims credit for the creation, leading to a sexual war with his wife-mother, who bruises his head and banishes him to the underworld.

This female creative force brings forth various elements through her union with other gods. In the Orphic myth of creation, Night, the Creatrix, lays a silver egg from which Love is hatched to set the universe in motion.

The creation of humans has less prominence in most of these other Near Eastern and Mediterranean stories than in Hebrew scripture. Most commonly, humans come from clay or dust. Egypt, Babylonia, and Greece all had such stories. In the Greek tale of Deucalion, he and his wife Pyrrha survive the great flood, finding mankind to have been obliterated. They are ordered to "throw the bones of your mother behind you." They interpret this to mean that they are to throw the "bones," or stones of Mother Earth behind them—from which rises up a new race of humans. This almost accidental creation of the race, without intent or purpose is quite different from the Hebrews' story of creation.

Not all the intellectuals among the Greeks and Romans approved of these mythic creation narratives. Some preferred a more orderly, scientific explanation. The Roman author Lucretius, born in the first century before the Christian era, found the mythic explanations of the universe and its creation less than satisfying. In his study of the ancients, he discovered the ancient Greek philosopher Democritus, who had later been interpreted by the philosopher Epicurus. For these writers, the structure of the universe was materialistic, with nothing beyond atoms and space. The mechanism for creation was motion, which produced change and evolution of life.

In *De Rerum Natura* (*On the Nature of the Universe,* c. 50 B.C.), a long, didactic epic poem, Lucretius explains that everything is material—including humans and the gods. Everything is born, flourishes, and will die, with its atoms dispersing to form new shapes. He reveals himself to be a close observer of nature, eager to dispel fear of the gods and fear of death. A blessed kind of relief comes over him as he realizes that nothing lasts forever, that he can rest content in a kind of stoic peace. He argues that nothing can be created out of nothing by divine power. All living things, animals and plants, spring up and develop from atoms in an orderly fashion, according to fixed laws of nature, and there is also a fixed natural limit to their growth. Only matter is indestructible. For Lucretius, this scientific certainty provides a sense of peace.

More often, writers of Western Europe have believed in supernatural creation. In fact, one of the first bits of scripture translated from the Latin into Early English (Anglo-Saxon) was the creation story in Genesis. This was considered a fundamental text for Christians. Medieval and Renaissance art is full of portrayals of the Creation itself (as in Michelangelo's fresco on the ceiling of the Sistine Chapel) and of Adam and Eve in the Garden of Eden. God, reaching out his hand to touch Adam, giving him the gift of life, as he cradles the uncreated Eve in his bosom, is a magnificent visual expression of Genesis.

In the Renaissance, the revival of classical literature and art led to a focus on human creativity, including God's gift of inspiration and talent. The prophets had noted that God is the potter, and we are the clay. The image of God in man, for the artist, is clearly the creative power. Plato characterizes the artist as an inspired mad-man, driven into a frenzy by the gods who use him to produce works of art. Homer and Virgil invoke the muses to give them the words for their epics. Christian writers have been more inclined to follow Milton's path and see themselves as inspired by God. Milton opens *Paradise Lost* with an invocation of the Holy Spirit:

Sing, Heavenly Muse, that, on the secret top
Of Oreb, or of Sinai, didst inspire
That Shepherd who first taught the chosen seed
In the beginning how the heavens and earth
Rose out of Chaos....
Instruct me, for Thou know'st; Thou from the first
Wast present, and, with mighty wings outspred,
Dove-like sat'st brooding on the vast Abyss,
And mad'st it pregnant.

(Milton, *Paradise Lost*)

The reader immediately notices Milton's blending of the scripture with pagan mythology here—the sexual creation, the heavens and the earth "rising" out of chaos. Milton's rendition in this epic poem of the creation of light is especially moving, undoubtedly enriched by his own blindness.

Hail, holy Light, offspring of Heav'n first born,
Or of th' Eternal Coeternal beam
May I express thee unblam'd? since God is light,
And never but in unapproached light
Dwelt from Eternity.

(Milton, *Paradise Lost*)

He goes on to describe those who dwell in darkness, including those damned souls who dwell with Satan in hell, ending with his delight in the celestial light that shines inward, irradiating the mind.

From the Renaissance on, writers, painters, and other artists became more introspective regarding their creative process. Considering themselves creators, much like God himself, they sought to understand the nature of creation, of the creator, and of the creative product. The eighteenth-century rationalists saw creation as a matter of shaping that which is generally known, "but ne'er so well expressed" in a suitable form (Pope, 140). Thus, the concern was with craftsmanship and form, not with the writer or painter himself or herself. Excess in emotion or in the presentation was considered bad form by writers like Alexander Pope, Jonathan Swift, or Dr. Samuel Johnson.

The Romantics, by contrast, saw themselves as the "unacknowledged legislators of the world," unique people who were divinely inspired, capable of seeing into the very heart of things. Percy Bysshe Shelley's famous *Defense of Poetry* (1821) portrayed the poet as "more delicately organized than other men, and sensible to pain and pleasure, both his own and that of others, in a degree unknown to them." He is "the author to others of the highest wisdom, pleasure, virtue, and glory, so he ought personally to be the happiest, the best, the wisest, and the most illustrious of men." Thus, this remarkable person must proclaim to the world the insights that he alone has discovered. "A poet is a nightingale, who sits in darkness and sings to cheer its own solitude with sweet sounds; his authors are as men entranced by the melody of this unseen musician, who feel that they are moved and softened, yet know not whence or why." The poetry rips off the veil of familiarity that hides the essence of the world's beauty from most folks.

The twentieth-century writer Arthur Koestler studied a large selection of creative people and examined their experiences. He determined that the act of creation involves visions, dreams, and inspiration. It appears to come from both without and within. This was certainly the case with Samuel Taylor Coleridge, whose methodology in writing is the subject of an interesting book by John Livingston Lowes, *The Road to Xanadu*. Lowes, after studying the books in Coleridge's library and the marginalia in this scholarly Romantic poet's handwriting, argues that Coleridge usually went through several stages in creation: (1) *the eagle's eye* (in which he read, watched, listened, and collected ideas), (2) *the deep well* (the storage of these images and ideas in his subconscious mind), (3) *the synthesis* (in which the images shifted, combined, were transformed within his mind without any act of will on his part), and (4) *the dredging* (the conscious act of bringing out those reshaped and transformed images and words out of the deep well and putting them on paper). Coleridge believed that, unlike the God of Genesis, humans cannot create ex nihilo. We need a basis for the work that we half create. Seeking to understand poetic inspiration, he did see the artist's role, like God's, as bringing order out of chaos. In the poet's case, the chaos was in his own mind and experience. The order was the work that he formed through his act of creation.

The nature of the so-called stuff of creation has been a perennial question. The neoclassicists acknowledged that they used existing materials as the basis for their writing. This was also true of Renaissance writers. Shakespeare took most of his tales from history. In Elizabethan times, originality was not considered a great virtue. By contrast, among the Romantics, the artist was thought to create a new thing. In addition, the art work that resulted had a kind of immortality denied to the artist himself or herself. Thus, the Grecian urn that Keats admires has its own life, far outlasting that of the anonymous potter and painter. Shakespeare said much the same thing in his sonnets, informing the Dark Lady to whom they were addressed that it was these poems that gave her beauty and his love for her a kind of immortality otherwise denied to the humans.

This permanence of the created object is only possible with some of the arts. A theatrical performance, if not recorded, lives only for the moment the actors tread the stage. The magic of the scene disappears as the curtain comes down. Also the musician, who sings or plays the perfect notes, has only the recollection of that experience as evidence of his artistic power. Robert Browning, a Victorian poet who was deeply concerned with art and music, wrote of the awareness of such impermanence in music. The poem "Abt Vogler" (1864) is written as a soliloquy of the German priest and musician of the same name; in the poem, Vogler extemporizes on a new kind of organ he has invented. This compelling poem accompanies the music of the organ, using parallel shapes in the lines and the rhythms.

At one point, Vogler considers the difference between himself and a painter, an architect, or a poet, who would have a creation left to contemplate, while his beautiful notes drift off, lingering only in his memory. He envies the semi-immortality of Solomon's Temple, which stood on the Temple Mount for the world to see, and lingered in the prophets' imagination for centuries thereafter. He then notes:

> But here is the finger of God a flash of the will that can,
>   Existent behind all laws, that made them and lo, they are!
> And I know not if, save in this, such gift be allowed to man,
>   That out of three sounds be frame, not a fourth sound, but a star,
> Consider it well: each tone of our scale in itself is naught,
>   It is everywhere in the world—loud, soft, and all is said:
> Give it to me to use! I mix it with two in my thought:
> And, there! Ye have heard and seen: consider and bow the head!

(Browning, "Abt Vogler")

His "palace of music" is quickly gone, but he sees his musical ability as an expression of God's power at work in him.

With the Industrial Revolution and the increased primacy of science over faith, a new awareness of human capability for extravagant experimentation arose. If scientists were to continue in their explorations, what would stop them from creating other humans or altering human nature? One nightmarish vision of such misbegotten human creativity is Mary Wollstonecraft Shelley's *Frankenstein* (1816). The ultimate ambition of the human, she believed, is to create life, a kind of hubris signaled by her subtitle, "The Modern Prometheus." In this long Gothic novel, she traces the lust for power that drives the scientist, Dr. Frankenstein, to create a mock-human who turns out to be a monster that the doctor cannot control. The creator can make him function physically, but cannot help him with his emotions or conscience. The poor forlorn monster seeks love and fellowship, like any other human, and finds instead that people flee at his approach. Indestructible by human means, the creature finally springs to an ice raft and "[is] soon borne away by the waves and lost in darkness and distance."

The mad dream of creating life has continued to intrigue many science fiction writers, who have played with the concept of test-tube babies engineered to match human ambitions. Aldous Huxley's *Brave New World* (1932) envisions a whole world created by such carefully engineered people. In the Central London Hatchery and Conditioning Center, eggs are fertilized and conditioned. For the lower castes (the Deltas and Epsilons), the eggs are forced to split into hundreds, even thousands of embryos, which then are treated against diseases and doused with enough chemicals to make them suitable for the tasks they will assume in life. The Alphas and Betas, shaped for managerial tasks, often are produced from a single egg, with no twins. All of these babies are predestined and conditioned from the bottle (the artificial womb) and then decanted (rather than being born). Paradoxically, in the midst of these "Alphas," and "Betas," Huxley's hero is the Savage, an abnormally normal man, who is a stranger in this "brave new world." The ironic title is taken from Shakespeare's *Tempest*.

This glimpse of a futuristic world of standardized, contented humans without free will or pain is grimly fascinating. At the time he wrote the book, Huxley assumed that such scientific advancements wouldn't be possible within six hundred years, given the developments in embryology, psychology, and behavioral sciences that the author saw about him. Unlike Frankenstein's monster, these creatures have no need for morality or anger or love. They learn to live without beauty, truth, or religion. Huxley saw this kind of life as the final humanistic triumph, where God had become unnecessary for human peace and happiness.

Dorothy L. Sayers, a writer and an essayist on religious topics, spent considerable time thinking about the creative process, setting down her ideas in her book *The Mind of the Maker* (1941). Drawing on St. Augustine's ideas regarding the role of the Trinity in the Creation, she speculated on the trinity of every act of creation. Quoting at length from her own play *The Zeal of Thy House*, about the building of a section of Canterbury Cathedral and the hubris of the architect who worked on it, she noted this trinity:

> For every work [*or act*] of creation is threefold, an earthly trinity to match the heavenly.
>
> First, [*not in time, but merely in order of enumeration*] there is the creative Idea, passionless, timeless, beholding the whole work complete at once, the end in the beginning; and this is the image of the Father.

Second, there is the Creative Energy [or *Activity*] begotten of that idea, working in time from the beginning to the end, with sweat and passion, being incarnate in the bonds of matter; and this is the image of the Word.

Third, there is the Creative Power, the meaning of the work and its response in the lively soul; and this is the image of the indwelling Spirit.

And these three are one, each equally in itself the whole work, whereof none can exist without the other: and this is the image of the Trinity. (Sayers, 37)

Conclusion

The nineteenth century was filled with scholarship that challenged a literal interpretation of Genesis's story of creation. A number of scholars began to deconstruct the language of the book, asserting that it was not the work of Moses or any one writer, but was drafted over centuries by a number of authors. This attack on the reliability of scripture came as Darwin's *Origin of the Species* appeared to call into question the Genesis record of creation, implying that evolution would not be the product of the famous first week, but of centuries. Nor was it the single act of God saying, "Let there be." Rather, Darwin proposed that creatures evolved, adapting to the environment, with the fittest attributes and animals surviving.

A famous court case arising out of this, the Scopes trial in Dayton, Tennessee (1925), involved some of the major figures of the time: Clarence Darrow, the attorney defending the young science teacher who had introduced the theory of evolution in his class; William Jennings Bryan, the attorney for the prosecution who was also a famous speaker and politician; and H. L. Mencken, who covered the story for the *Baltimore Sun*. Jerome Lawrence and Robert E. Lee turned the transcript of the trial into the play *Inherit the Wind*, which was quite popular on Broadway. The turning point in the trial is the admission that a "day" in the Genesis account may be more than twenty-four hours.

Needless to say, the debate continues among the Creationists, the Evolutionists, those who believe in Chaos Theory, the Big Bang, and Intelligent Design. As it turns out, the issues raised in the first chapters of Genesis (time and eternity, the nature of man, the role of woman, the nature of God, the persons of God, the means of creation) are among the liveliest subjects of literature and philosophy we have ever known.

See also: **Animals and Humans; Earthly Paradise; Last Days; Nature; Temptation and Sin.**

Bibliography

Ackerman, James S., and Thayer S. Warshaw. *The Bible as/in Literature*. Glenview, IL: Scott, Foresman and Company, 1971.

Browning, Robert. "Abt Vogler." In *Poems of Robert Browning*. Boston: Houghton Mifflin, 1956.

Calvin, John. *Institutes of the Christian Religion*. Trans., Henry Beveridge. Grand Rapids, MI: Wm. B. Eerdmans Publishing Company, 1989.

Coleridge, Samuel Taylor. *Biographia Literaria*. Online at http://www.gutenberg.org/etext/6081 (accessed September 12, 2006).

Foerster, Norman, and Robert Falk (eds.). *American Poetry and Prose*. Boston: Houghton Mifflin Company, 1960.

Graves, Robert, and Raphael Patai. *Hebrew Myths: The Book of Genesis.* New York: McGraw-Hill, 1964.

Henry, Matthew. *Commentary on the Whole Bible.* Grand Rapids, MI: Zondervan Publishing House, 1961.

Huxley, Aldous. *Brave New World.* Toronto, Ontario: Penguin Books, 1932.

Lowes, John Livingston. *The Road to Xanadu: A Study of the Ways of the Imagination.* Boston: Houghton Mifflin, 1927.

Lucretius, *On the Nature of the Universe.* London: Penguin Books, 1951.

Milton, John. *Paradise Lost.* In *The Student's Milton,* ed. Frank Allen Patterson. New York: Appleton-Century-Crofts, 1930.

Pope, Alexander. "Essay on Criticism." In *English Poetry of the Eighteenth Century,* ed. Cecil A. Moore. New York: Henry Holt and Company, 1951.

Sayers, Dorothy L. *The Mind of the Maker.* Westport, CT: Greenwood Press, 1941.

Shelley, Mary Wollstonecraft. *Frankenstein.* New York: Oxford University Press, 1969.

Shelley, Percy Bysshe. *Defense of Poetry.* In *Anthology of Romanticism,* ed. Ernest Bernbaum. New York: The Roland Press Company, 1948.

Sproul, Barbara. *Primal Myths: Creating the World.* San Francisco: Harper & Row, 1979.

Earthly Paradise

Readings

Genesis 2–3, 12:1–8
Joshua
Isaiah 2
Dante Alighieri, *Purgatorio* (1321)
Milton, *Paradise Lost* (1667), "Lycidas" (1637)
William Blake, *Songs of Innocence* (1789)
Aldous Huxley, *Brave New World* (1932)
William Golding, *Lord of the Flies* (1954)
Walker Percy, *Love in the Ruins* (1971)

Introduction

> And the Lord God planted a garden eastward in Eden; and there he put the
> man whom he had formed.
> And out of the ground made the Lord God to grow every tree that is pleasant
> to the sight, and good for food; the tree of life also in the midst of the garden,
> and the tree of knowledge of good and evil.
> And a river went out of Eden to water the garden; and from thence it was
> parted, and became into four heads.
> The name of the first is Pison: that is it which compasseth the whole land of
> Havilah, where there is gold;
> And the gold of that land is good: there is bdellium and the onyx stone.
> And the name of the second river is Gihon: the same is it that compasseth
> the whole land of Ethiopia.
> And the name of the third river is Hiddekel: that is it which goeth toward the
> east of Assyria. And the fourth river is Euphrates.
> And the Lord God took the man, and put him into the garden of Eden to
> dress it and keep it. (Gen. 2:8–15)

The earthly paradise described in Genesis is not set in any particular place: the
four rivers that run through it are on different continents. Most biblical scholars

believe that the original garden was in Mesopotamia, in the south of modern Iraq, an area that has been transformed into a wasteland in modern memory.

The beauty of this earthly paradise described in Genesis lies in both the natural splendor and the harmony among the animals, between humans and animals, between man and woman, and between man and God. Eden portrays a state of pristine purity before sin, evil, pain, and death entered the world.

In pagan literature, a vision of a Golden Age is parallel to this picture. The Greek pastoral poets polished and stylized the concept of a golden age in their songs of simple shepherds chasing young maidens, playing their flutes, and tending woolly lambs as they wandered among the flowers. This dream of an earthly paradise has reappeared frequently in literature, especially in more crowded and mechanistic cultures where the dream of pastoral harmony lingers on as a seductive contrast to the real world.

Eden has become the archetypal image of lost innocence, frequently interpreted as childhood. The Romantic poets were particularly enamored of the concept of the child as the real visionary, who loses his innocence and his bonds with nature as civilization closes in on him and he becomes an adult, blind to the mysteries of the natural world. For most of the English Romantics, the child running free in the woods is the very epitome of perfection.

For many others, who had less interest in nature and had no hope of recovering this lost world, the idea of a Promised Land or a Utopia became the replacement. The Promised Land, the homeland full of blessings from God, has remained the perennial dream of the Jews. For the Greeks, and many who were caught up in their ideas, the utopian vision was the ideal, a place where all people live in perfect harmony. For the true visionaries, who put no hope in this corrupt world, such as the prophets and Jesus, a heavenly Kingdom of God took shape, replacing the ancient dream of a return to Eden. In Christian thought, St. Augustine's *City of God* (426 A.D.) described the New Eden, the place of perfect bliss for those redeemed by the sacrifice of Christ.

For many moderns, such a dream of a heavenly reward has been replaced by a dream of new earthly paradise, a society perfectly designed for human happiness. Like Adam, who thought he could improve on God's plans by disobeying his rules and going his own way, socialists and other utopians think that they can fix the world by careful planning. Satan had proposed to Jesus that he turn stones into bread and provide for materialistic needs, a proposition that has interested planners all through the years. This "brave new world" built by humans determined to create a paradise on earth quickly turns into a nightmare in such novels as Orwell's *Animal Farm* or Huxley's *Brave New World*. Ironically, in these novels, God is no longer a necessary actor, and free will gradually fades away in the face of a "benevolent" totalitarian rule. The new designer sets himself up as the god who will make decisions rather than leave them to foolish humans. These dystopias are the ultimate fruit of humanistic logic, with man becoming the measure of all things.

Scripture

The Hebrews never lost the residual memory of this primeval paradise, a place between the rivers that was a so-called garden, where their ancestors lived in a happy state of nature, without labor or strife. For the ancients, a *garden* was a kind of park, a place with trees and vines and cultivated nature that served man's needs. By contrast, a *forest* was a wild place, full of frightening animals. This garden home was the paradise that Adam and Eve lost through their disobedience. In shattering this primal harmony, they entered a new land with forests and deserts, weeds and pain, hard work, and death.

The image of Eden is echoed in the later biblical descriptions of the Promised Land, a land "flowing with milk and honey." Canaan proved both a fulfillment of this dream and a disappointment. It had rich pastures and abundant resources, but it was also a land of cruel droughts and harsh winds and rugged mountains. The actual land that the Israelites settled was no Eden. Furthermore, it was no simple gift, like Eden. It took centuries and great labor for the Israelites to win this Promised Land, which was full of Canaanites who fought to keep their walled cities and their pagan gods safe from these nomadic peasants. Nonetheless, for the Israelites, it was home—a God-given place where they dreamed of living in peace, every man under his own olive tree, in perfect harmony with his family and his neighbors. It was ideally to be a place of earthly rest and contentment.

When Abraham heard the voice of God telling him to leave Mesopotamia and travel to this new land, he stepped out in faith, taking his family and his possessions with him. His son Isaac laid further claim to the land by digging wells and refusing to leave the land even to seek a wife. His sons continued to dwell in the land, leaving only when driven out by famine.

During the centuries of captivity in Egypt, the children of Israel kept this ancient memory of the Promised Land in their hearts. When free by God, under the leadership of Moses, they escaped the Pharaoh and began the long journey back to their long-hoped-for home. For 40 long years, they wandered in the wilderness, dwelling in tents as the Lord prepared them to take the land, giving them the Law, transforming them into a united people. Under Joshua, they finally crossed the Jordan and move from city to city, claiming the land that God had promised them. This bloody conquest, taking many years, was never quite complete.

The terms of the covenant under Joshua were clear: the tribes of Israel would retain the land only so long as they followed the law that God had given to Moses. They were warned not to bow down before the pagan gods or marry the women of the so-called nations that were around them. Before long, they had broken the covenant, each man "doing what was right in his own eyes." The history that follows, from Judges through the Kings, is full of examples of the broken covenant. Even their anointed rulers found wives among the pagans. Solomon and his descendants were infamous for their hospitality to the worship of foreign gods. Enemies attacked them from all sides, challenging their right to the land. Their dream of the Kingdom of God had died as they turned away from God's leadership and then as his regents on earth betrayed him.

It was therefore no surprise that the Israelites, like Adam and Eve, were once again cast out of their home. The story of the many invasions, the captivity, the violence, the cities under siege, and the kings killed are part of this long saga of the loss of their earthly dream. The remnant of the tribe did return from captivity, trying once again to establish Jerusalem as the Holy City, but even that effort was often thwarted.

As the dream of the Promised Land with its Temple grew dimmer, another hope rose among the Jews. Believing still that they were the children of the promise, they began to realize that the real kingdom would not be in this world. The prophets began to speak of an eternal kingdom, the Kingdom of God, and of a Heavenly Jerusalem.

Isaiah prophesies eloquently of the New Creation, a time when the Lord will return in all his glory, and the lion and the lamb will lie down together. In these powerful verses, the prophet revives in the Jews the ancient memory of Eden. The primal harmony between man and nature, between man and man, and between man and God will return in the Day of the Lord. Unlike Eden, however, this is not to be a simple garden or even a fertile and peaceable country, but it is to be the Kingdom of God, a world reigned over by the Prince of Peace. This promise of a New Creation, the City of God, dominates the opening section of Isaiah's vision.

Ezekiel's dazzling vision of the magnificent Temple far transcends the ruined but remembered glories of Solomon's Temple. As the reality of their own earthly kingdom diminishes, the Jews dream of citizenship in an eternal kingdom.

By the time of Jesus, the land promised to the Hebrews was under the iron fist of Rome, and even Herod's Temple was full of blasphemous activities. Christ emphasizes the kingdom that is to come, and outlines in the Beatitudes those astonishing attributes of the citizens of that kingdom: the meek, the poor in spirit, the mourners, the peacemakers, the persecuted—all the blessed children of God (Matt. 5). Like Joshua, Jesus invites his followers, the true citizens, to cross over and enter, and finally to possess the Promised Land, which has been made ready for them since the world was made (Matt. 25:34–40).

This theme of the coming of God's peaceable kingdom is sprinkled throughout the epistles. Hebrews (4:11, 6:11), for example promises a Sabbath rest awaiting the people of God. Romans 8:15–17 explains that believers are God's children and his heirs, the Christians now becoming the chosen people, the heirs under the New Covenant. Philippians 3:20–21 names believers the citizens of heaven, and 1 Peter 1:4; 2:9–10 emphasizes the inheritance of Christ's followers will never wither. This "chosen race" and "dedicated nation" will not perish.

In the book of Revelation, John envisions a "new heaven and a new earth" with the "holy city, New Jerusalem, coming down from God out of heaven" (Rev. 21). Centuries later, after the destruction of Herod's Temple and the decline of Rome, this became an even more compelling idea. This vision, which St. Augustine traces in more detail, has some of the components of Eden, but belongs to a far more sophisticated and complex time. It is a new creation, not a re-creation of Eden. Humans cannot return to primal innocence or to this magical land, still guarded by the fiery Cherubim. They must learn to live as best they can east of Eden until "Thy kingdom come."

Literature

Although he believed in the literal existence of the Garden of Eden, St. Augustine also argues for the symbolic significance:

> The life of the blessed; in its four rivers, the four virtues of prudence, fortitude, temperance, and justice; in its trees, all useful knowledge; in the fruits of the trees, the holy lives of the faithful; in the tree of life, that wisdom which is the mother of all good; and in the tree of the knowledge of good and evil, the experience that results from disobedience to the command of God. (St. Augustine, *The City of God*, 287)

Augustine read the Genesis narrative as an allegory of the Church, prophetic of what was to be in the future. His interpretation opened the door to a general understanding of the Garden of Eden as the state of innocence that all individuals and groups know at the beginning, before they exercise their free will and fall into sin and damnation.

Paradise stories are common in Europe, the Orient, Central and North America, and Polynesia. Among the most famous is the one Hesiod includes in his *Theogony*. It speaks of the five ages of man:

> The gods, who live on Mount Olympus, first
> Fashioned a golden race of mortal men;
> These lived in the reign of Kronos, king of heaven,
> And like the gods they lived with happy hearts
> Untouched by work or sorrow. Vile old age
> Never appeared, but always lively-limbed,
> Far from all ills, they feasted happily.
> Death came to them as sleep, and all good things
> Were theirs; ungrudgingly, the fertile land
> Gave up her fruits unasked. Happy to be
> At peace, they lived with every want supplied.

(Hesiod, *Theogony*, in Sproul, 157)

Hesiod then describes the subsequent ages: the silver, the bronze, and the iron. This decline from the Golden Age contrasts with the biblical view that Eden innocence lasted only briefly. The Fall of mankind was quick and final, not a gradual decline. The people thousands of years later bear the same scars of sin that Adam and Even recognized as they were driven from the Garden. Cain's murder of Abel soon after made clear that humankind have inherited Adam's fallen nature and bear the mark of Cain.

Hesiod's Golden Age is also different from the Hebrews' earthly paradise in that God cast the humans out of Eden and placed his angels to guard against a return. For Hesiod, there is no such garden; the race from this remarkable time continue to live "hidden in the ground" as benevolent spirits who protect people from harm. Hesiod records the Greek belief that each succeeding race is shaped afresh by the gods. For the Hebrews, creation was a single dramatic occurrence by one God.

Typically, Christian literature of the Middle Ages followed the path laid out by the Church Fathers. Like Augustine, Dante assumes that the Earthly Paradise is both a reality and a symbol. Having taken his poet through the horrors of Hell, Dante moves quickly to the second section of *The Divine Comedy*, "Purgatorio." He begins the difficult climb of the seven-story mountain, where the Christians' sins are explained, punished, and expunged.

Virgil finally leads the poet to the "seventh stair" and resigns his office as mentor. This wise and prescient pagan writer is not allowed to linger in the Earthly Paradise or ascend into Heaven. At this point in his story, Dante must pass through the cleansing flames and become "lord" over himself, with his own miter and crown. Having passed the flaming swords of the Cherubim who guard the gate, he enters the sacred wood, enjoying the delicate air and gentle breezes. Dante describes this place of eternal peace where God made "man good, and for good, set him." Explaining the parallel classical vision of a golden age, he writes:

> Those men of yore who sang the golden time
>   And all its happy state—maybe indeed
>   They on Parnassus dreamed of this fair clime.
> Here was the innocent root of all man's seed:

Here spring is endless, here all fruits are, here
The nectar is, which runs in all their rede.

(Alighieri, *Purgatorio*, 293)

In the Earthly Paradise the poet (his *persona* in the poem) is purified from all earthly corruption before entering into Heaven. The elaborate role of virtues and vices in *Purgatorio*, the complex theological discourses on the nature of sin and contrition, and the allegory portraying the central doctrines of the Church that he witnesses at his most ecstatic moment, all point to Dante's careful study of the Church Fathers. These honored saints and scholars, like St. Augustine, had explored the potential meanings of Eden.

For Dante, the real "home" or "promised land" for the saints is not in Eden. It is in Heaven, where they will dwell in eternal bliss in the presence of God. This joy transcends the perfect physical comforts of Eden. Now the believer is thrilled that God allows him or her to choose good over evil, obedience over selfishness, service over pride. As he describes the "rest" finally available for the saints, he proclaims, "His will is our peace"—an echo of Augustine.

Some cynical writers of the seventeenth century came to propose, jokingly, that Eden was lost with the advent of Eve. The seventeenth-century writer Andrew Marvell, in "The Garden," said: "Two paradises 'twere in one, / To live in paradise alone." For this English poet, the glory of Eden was the solitary delight in nature:

Such was the happy garden-state,
While man there walked without a mate;
After a place so pure and sweet,
What other help could yet be meet!
But 'twas beyond a mortal's share
To wander solitary there.

(Marvell, "The Garden," 751)

Milton did not agree with his contemporary. For him, Eve's presence enriched the delight of life in the garden. In *Paradise Lost*, he describes her charm and sweetness as she gathers a perfect medley of foods for the meal the first couple to share. In their bower of bliss, their nuptial grove, they are in perfect harmony—largely because of her gentle subservience. For Milton, this golden-haired beauty is the ideal companion, considerate, coy, submissive, modest, and chaste. She is everything that Milton dreamed of before his own troubled marriage. Only when Eve steps out of her role, seeks more knowledge and independence, does she ruin Eden for them both.

In Books IV and V, Milton describes the Adam and Eve, their love for one another and for God, their activities, and their surroundings. He includes a catalogue of trees and flowers that sounds like the idyllic English countryside: laurel and myrtle, roses, violets, hyacinths, and so forth. This description echoes many of the Elizabethan pastoral poems in which the shepherd and his nymph cavort over the green hills among the woolly lambs, enjoying the delights of the springtime. Milton himself wrote the pastoral poem "Lycidas," an elegy much admired by Shelley and Keats. The form derived from the classics, where authors from both Greek and Roman cultures used the supposed innocence of the simple life as a reminder of their legendary Golden Age.

The pre-Romantic poet William Blake, a great fan of both Dante and Milton, recognized in their poetry the divine inspiration that he felt deep within himself. In his work as a printer and an engraver, he illustrated many of their works, including the *Divine Comedy*. He drew heavily on their ideas for his far simpler poems, which have their own charm and power. *The Songs of Innocence* (1789) capture the child-like innocence of Eden, with the pastoral tone of shepherds and sheep. Among the more famous of these are "The Lamb" and "The Tiger," both poems of creation:

> Little lamb, who made thee?
> Dost thou know who made thee?
> Gave thee life, and bid thee feed,
> By the stream and o'er the mead;
> Gave thee clothing of delight,
> Softest clothing, woolly, bright;
> Gave thee such a tender voice,
> Making all the vales rejoice?

> (Blake, "The Lamb," 114)

In this deceptively simple little lyric, Blake reminds the reader of Adam's role as name-giver in Eden, the innocence of the creatures in this Earthly Paradise, as well as the lamb's subsequent role as the sacrifice for human sins, the symbol of Christ's sacrifice. Blake envisions Eden as the essence of primal unity, a condition natural to young children, whom he sees as not yet fallen. Eden becomes, for him, a state of mind that innocent children reflect briefly. It is lost forever as humans mature, know evil, choose sin, and become alienated from one another and from nature. This is a clear change from the Calvinistic emphasis on total depravity, which involves the child as well as the adult. Jean Jacques Rousseau had preached this at about the same time that Blake was writing his poetry and may have influenced his thought.

William Wordsworth, a Romantic poet who inherited many of the same ideas as Blake, also saw the child as innocent. He thought that we come to earth "trailing clouds of glory" from heaven, which is our home. In the introduction to his "Ode on Intimations of Immortality," he insists that "dream-like vividness and splendor which invest objects of sight in childhood" provide "presumptive evidence of a prior state of existence." He admits that this tempting concept of an ideal place of prior-existence derives from Platonic philosophy. As he opens the ode, he quotes an earlier poem that hints at this philosophy of pre-existence and natural goodness: "The Child is Father of the Man; / And I could wish my days to be / Bound each to each by natural piety." In the long poem, he describes his youthful days and his vivid sense of nature:

> There was a time when meadow, grove, and stream,
> The earth, and every common sight,
>   To me did seem
>   Apparelled in celestial light,
> The glory and the freshness of a dream.
> It is not now as it has been of yore;—
>   Turn whereso'er I may,
>   By night or day,
> The things which I have seen I now can see no more....
>   But yet I know, wher'er I go,
> That there hath passed away a glory from the earth.

> (Wordsworth, "Ode: Intimations of Immortality from
> Recollections of Early Childhood," 232)

Like Blake, Wordsworth in poem after poem equates childhood with Eden innocence and adulthood with life "east of Eden." "The Prelude" is one of his fullest portrayals of this growth of the poet's mind—a long autobiographical poem filled with beautiful descriptions of nature and mystical moments. For the Romantics, the lively imagination of youth, which declines with age, is evidence of the divine image that resides in the child.

This Platonic faith in a perfect world from which we descend, which we recollect from time to time in visions, and to which we will ultimately return is hardly biblical. As opposed to this cyclical view of life, the Hebrews understood history and individual experience to be linear. Humans had once lived in the garden of perfect innocence. The fall of human kind was once and for all, not a delightful metaphor for the state of mind shared by all children, lost once again in each lifetime. The Romantics were drawing on Greek thought and Rousseau's notions of man's basic goodness for their doctrine of human virtue.

Like their British contemporaries, Americans of the nineteenth century were also tempted by this vision of idyllic youth. Turning away from the stern Calvinistic doctrine of total depravity, they came to believe in the basic goodness of humans. It is very difficult to look at the sweet face of a child and perceive behind that apparent innocence an ingrained human depravity. In fiction and in popular thought, a new veneration for motherhood, children, and domestic tranquility developed the theme of the home as a kind of man-made Eden. This sentimental cult of domesticity replaced the tough old Hebrew Eden.

The child in the garden became an image of primal innocence. Harriet Beecher Stowe uses a series of domestic images, both black and white, to make her case against slavery in *Uncle Tom's Cabin* (1850). The children in her novel instinctively know that slaves are people, not just possessions, and are far more likely to feel the pain of those who are abused.

James Fenimore Cooper portrays the primitive American forests with the Indians and the wild animals as a lost paradise in books like *The Deerslayer* (1841) or *The Last of the Mohicans* (1826). By contrast, the more orthodox Christian writer Nathaniel Hawthorne sees the forest as a place of danger and temptation. In *The Scarlet Letter* (1850), it is in the woods, in an Edenic setting, that Hetty and her lover commit adultery. When they succumb to the temptations of this "natural" paradise, they open the door to a life of anguish for them both.

In books such as *Huck Finn* and *Tom Sawyer*, Mark Twain loves to portray the boys of his remembered youth, playing innocent pranks, running wild in nature, enjoying a carefree world as young noble savages. But he does show that Huck Finn and Nigger Jim each has his own problems. Even youth is not simple or without its briars and nettles. The automatic cruelty that the white boys show to their black friend, who is a slave, reveals that no world is without the shadow of sin. Twain's comic parody of Adam and Eve in the Garden of Eden (*Adam's Diary, Eve's Diary*, 1904), brings a modern sensibility to a primeval scene. He (like Andrew Marvell) presumes that the harmony is broken by the introduction of woman into the garden.

Even Emily Dickinson saw Eden as childhood innocence, though with enriched insights. In her poem "Eden Is That Old-Fashioned House," she asserts that Eden is also the here and now. It is the place we dwell everyday without suspecting our abode, "until we drive away." As a later writer, Thomas Wolfe was to say, "You Can't Go Home Again." The simple, carefree, thoughtless days of youth, or even the more mature moments with family and friends may never be regained. The doorway is locked, the house demolished. Dickinson's vision of Eden, sounding suspiciously like a New England house, is the life of the moment, appreciated only when lost.

This perennial dream of a place where humans live in perfect harmony with one another and with nature (and sometimes with God) has haunted the literary imagination. It has served as the basis for numerous utopian writings, from Plato's *Republic* to Huxley's *Brave New World* (1932). Refusing to believe that Eden is lost, dreamers repeatedly design their own earthly paradises according to principles of their own devising. Readers of Thomas More's *Utopia* or Orwell's *Animal Farm* can easily see how a man-made utopia quickly evolves into a dystopia—a nightmare community, like that in George Orwell's *1984*. Moderns, drawing on the nineteenth-century dream of the innocent natural man, assume that they can eliminate sin from their new creation. In the twentieth century, we have come to see that no socialist republic or planned community can address the enormously complex world set in motion in the original Eden.

The modern Southern novelist Walker Percy laughs at this humanistic arrogance in his spoof on planned communities of modern America, *Love in the Ruins* (1971). The central character, a mad doctor who is a lineal descendant of Thomas More, is a rare breed, a Roman Catholic in the South. He and his wife and child live in Paradise Estates, in a perfect home. But as soon the child dies, the wife runs off with a pagan Englishman to discover "Higher Truth," and Dr. More finds himself in an abandoned Holiday Inn, in the middle of an asphalt jungle, with a cluster of displaced persons. He knows deep in his heart that all this is foreordained, a result of the fall and of his own daily lapses.

A far more sinister portrayal of "paradise" is chronicled in William Golding's *Lord of the Flies* (1954). After his experience in World War II, Golding, appalled at man's inhumanity to man, wrote this fearful tale. He begins the book with an airplane wreck that strands a group of school children on a paradisiacal deserted island. The children, of various ages and physiques, have been evacuated from British schools (one a choir school). Unlike the character Robinson Crusoe, with his strong sense of concern for survival and his need to build a civilization in the wilderness, these young boys see little reason for order or thought for the future. The warm climate and plentiful supply of fruit make their days a delight. Soon, however, they go their own thoughtless, egocentric ways, eating green fruit, using the whole island as their toilet, accidentally setting the woods on fire. They become enamored by the hunting and killing of wild pigs, which prompts a series of primitive rituals: dancing and chanting around a fire, blood-sacrifice to a pig-idol, and finally ritual murder. Their "chief" represents the very worst of human nature, more vicious than the animals he kills, as gross in his tastes as the "Lord of the Flies" (Beelzebub), the idol to whom he sacrifices.

The island itself is idyllic, but the boys eventually burn the whole surface, destroying their own food supply. They are finally rescued from their Eden paradise, just as they have rendered it unlivable. Golding is unwilling to allow even their rescue to represent any form of redemption, pointing out in his notes that the rescuer is himself a member of the Navy, part of a destructive force that is also intent on hunting and killing in a far larger way. As is noted in the comments at the end of the book, Golding describes the theme of *Lord of the Flies* as:

> An attempt to trace the defects of society back to the defects of human nature. The moral is that the shape of a society must depend on the ethical nature of the individual and not on any political system however apparently logical or respectable. The whole book is symbolic in nature except the rescue in the end where adult life appears, dignified and

capable, but in reality enmeshed in the same evil as the symbolic life of the children on the island. The officer, having interrupted a man-hunt, prepares to take the children off the island in a cruiser which will presently be hunting its enemy in the same implacable way. And who will rescue the adult and his cruiser? (Golding, *Lord of the Flies*, 315)

These gloomy words point to a common modern horror scenario—a fallen world, a lost Eden, but no story of redemption.

Conclusion

One of the most famous, and frightening, of all modern novels is Aldous Huxley's *Brave New World* (1932). Based on the patterns Huxley saw developing in his world, the advances of science, the fixation on comfort and security, the willingness to forego freedom for a benevolent totalitarian regime, the vulgarization of popular culture, and the obsession with perpetual youth, he envisions where it is all leading. He sets his "brave new world" some 600 years in the future, in the "year of Our Ford." This is the earthly paradise that would be the twentieth century's fondest dreams.

Setting his sterile, urban Eden well into the future, Huxley projects a precisely managed paradise, with all activities from birth to death carefully monitored. By fitting people for the essential tasks of the society, he sweeps away all unhappiness and frustration. By providing a pill for every pain, a solution for every problem, he frees his happy little world from disease, sorrow, loneliness, confusion, and all forms of discontent. Even death is efficiently and pleasantly managed with the chemical components of the body retrieved for re-use.

In stark contrast, he allows his main characters a vacation at a "Savage Reservation," full of filth, disease, anger, passion, and violence. Here, people are born, not decanted. Rather than retaining their youth until the very moment of their death, they grow fat, old, and ugly. They have families that they love and hate, feel jealous when others steal their husbands. They get drunk and suffer painful hangovers. And they have their wild worship services that mingle Christian and Indian elements in a kind of grotesque and bloody mysticism.

All of this "savage" behavior is avoided in the trivial world of Huxley's perpetual adolescents, where people have ready access to food, attractive clothing, entertainment ("feelies" and television), sex (without pregnancy or limits), drugs (soma, which has only pleasant narcotic effects with no painful after-effects). They never need to think for themselves or work on the tough issues of life. They venerate "Our Ford," and have "Orgy-porgies," which end in group sex, to replace worship services.

Imagining the ideal paradise often transforms the product into a dystopia—a nightmare. At the time he was writing the novel, Huxley was aware of the advent of the Communists, the Nazis, and other "planners" who promised their followers a heaven on earth. They dreamed of universal prosperity, perfect peace, and found instead massive slaughter and brutal deprivation. While projecting human desires into a universal system produces delight for some (principally the planners), it becomes a straight jacket or a concentration camp for others. All of the projected utopias, including Brook Farm, Robert Owen's sanctuary of chatter, Upton Sinclair's Helicon Hall eventually failed, often ending in scandal. Sinclair Lewis in his enormously popular novel about the potential for a fascist takeover of the United States, *It Can't Happen Here* (1940), has a character named Jessup who is skeptical of nostrums of both left and right, believing finally that "There is no Solution, there will always be envy and inefficiency." Humankind is too diverse for any earthly paradise designed by the minds of humans.

This makes the story of Eden all the more impressive. Here were all the flora and fauna living with the first humans in perfect harmony. Scripture teaches that perfection on earth is shattered by the sinful human heart, that we should expect such perfect bliss, not on earth, not even in Jerusalem, but in Heaven, when we finally come to dwell with God.

See also: **Animals and Humans; Creation; Nature; Government and Politics.**

Bibliography

Alighieri, Dante. *The Divine Comedy.* Trans., Dorothy L. Sayers. New York: Basic Books, 1973.

Ashe, Geoffrey. *Behind the Dawn: A Search for the Earthly Paradise.* New York: Henry Holt & Co., 1993.

Augustine, St. *City of God.* Trans., Gerald G. Walsh, Demetrius B. Zema, Grace Monahan, and Daniel J. Honan. New York: Image Books, 1958.

Blake, William. "Songs of Innocence." In *Anthology of Romanticism,* ed. Ernest Bernbaum. New York: The Roland Press Company, 1948.

Boies, Jack. *The Lost Domain.* New York: University Press of America, 1983.

Dickinson, Emily. "Eden Is That Old-Fashioned House." In *The Bible as/in Literature,* ed. James S. Ackerman and Thayer S. Warshaw. Glenview, IL: Scott, Foresman and Company, 1971.

Golding, William. *Lord of the Flies.* New York: Berkley, 2003.

Heilbroner, Robert L. *The Worldly Philosophers: The Lives, Times, and Ideas of the Great Economic Thinkers.* New York: Simon and Schuster, 1999.

Hesiod. *Theogyny.* In *Primal Myths: Creating the World,* ed. Barabara Sproul. San Francisco: Harper & Row, 1979.

Huxley, Aldous. *Brave New World.* Toronto, Ontario: Penguin Books, 1932.

Marvell, Andrew. "The Garden." In *The Oxford Book of Seventeenth Century Verse.* Oxford: Clarendon Press, 1951.

Milton, John. *Paradise Lost* and "Lycidas." In *The Student's Milton,* ed. Frank Allen Patterson. New York: Appleton-Century-Crofts, 1930.

Morris, William. *Stories from the Earthly Paradise (Told through the Ages).* London: George G. Harrap, 1906.

Percy, Walker. *Love in the Ruins.* New York: Farrar, Straus, and Giroux, 1971.

Nature

Introduction

> The heavens declare the glory of God; and the firmament showeth his handiwork. (Ps. 19:1)

The psalmist was not the only one to marvel at God's handiwork, the creation of the heavens and the earth (Ps. 8:3; 19:1–3; 24:2; Jer. 27:3; Gen. 1). The great Reformist John Calvin spoke of nature as the book of God's creative power, evidence of the Creator's awesome imagination (Calvin, 154). To have created the enormously complex and diverse range of plants and animals, to have structured the world so that these creations might be self-sustaining, self-propagating, and balanced in the whole network of other creatures, was a dazzling *tour de force*.

Genesis 1 describes the pattern of creation and details a few of the creatures, climaxing with the creation of man (male and female) in the image of God. Genesis 2 tells how God gave humans the role of caretakers, with dominion over the animals and the task of assigning them names. The Garden of Eden is simply the setting for the drama of the Fall, not aparticipant in the disastrous human actions—except for providing the fruit of the forbidden tree. Some, however, believe that all of nature fell from its original ideal state when Adam and Eve were cast out of the garden. A part of the result of the Fall was that humans would face nature as an adversary—full of thorns and thistles, hard ground, and snakes. This is not the harmonious, happy garden in which the first couple made their first home.

This particular idea is illustrated in Daniel Defoe's popular novel *Robinson Crusoe* (1719). Unlike the noble savages that populated much of eighteenth-century literature, Crusoe's man Friday is a simple native on the island where Crusoe is shipwrecked. Frightened of the neighboring cannibals who are planning his death, Friday is grateful that Crusoe saves him and is willing to serve as Crusoe's servant. When tutored in the concepts of Christianity, Friday proves to be an eager learner. Defoe makes it clear that the Christian faith is not innate. The religion must be taught to the heathen by a person who has received the basic tenants of the faith from some teacher at home and at church. Friday can make no theological sense of the Book of Nature that stands before him until he has been instructed in the faith of his new master. Nature, after all, includes both the abundance of food and water on the one hand, and savage men eager to eat their enemies on the other.

Defoe's novel encapsulates some of the central philosophic and theological arguments regarding the interaction among God, humans, and the natural world: What is our relationship with nature? Are we the guardians, the opponents, or the beneficiaries of the fruits of nature? Does nature have any moral component or any lessons that may be learned by humans? What are our obligations to our environment?

Scripture

For the most part, scripture uses nature as a background for the events of the human actors. On occasion, a violent eruption of some sort—a drought or a flood—may bring nature into the foreground. For instance, in the story of Noah and his ark (Gen. 6–9), we see God's use of the rain and the flood waters to punish rebellious humans. We also see his concern for the animals and his promise of protection of Noah and his descendants. Although they suffer the consequences of human evil, breeding stock of every sort of creature are carefully preserved by God's direct orders and Noah's laborious obedience. The plants that are swept away by the flood replenish themselves afterwards, as we see as the olive leaf is growing again on the olive tree. The natural symbol of the rainbow serves as the seal of God's promise to humans that this is the last of such universal catastrophes.

Although scripture deals with the violence of nature, the extremes seen as catastrophes by humans do not define nature. God is the master of the storms and the lightening, the floods, the droughts, and the earthquakes. Jesus demonstrates his own divinity when he quiets the storm on the Sea of Galilee. In the Bible, neither Hebrews nor Christians worship nature itself or confuse nature with God. When the psalmist proclaims, "I will lift up mine eyes unto the hills," he adds that his strength comes from God, who made Heaven and Earth (Ps. 121). It comes from the Lord, who "shall preserve thee from all evil: he shall preserve thy soul. The Lord shall preserve thy going out and thy coming in from this time forth, and even forevermore." In scripture, nature is not presented as an entity to be personified or worshipped.

Although God set his order into the very fabric of nature, he interrupts or manipulates these regular rhythms from time to time for purposes of his own divine providence, producing miracles. Such spectacular events often are so precisely timed that they can hardly be explained by "natural" events. Although an earthquake or a tidal wave might well explain the parting of the Red Sea, it is God who chooses the perfect moment for this to occur. Sometimes he interrupts the natural movement of the sun and stars, making the sun stand still for Joshua, or using a star over the stable in Bethlehem to guide the wise men to the Christ child. The miraculous healings by the prophets, the saints, Christ, and his apostles appear to combine natural and supernatural events. Some healing may be purely psychological, some cannot be explained by anything but supernatural intervention—such as bringing Lazarus back to life. For Jews and Christians, God is an active participant in human history, not simply a great watchmaker who created the world, set it in motion, and then closed the door on events, locking up his shop and leaving nature to run automatically to the end of time.

In the Bible, nature is God's good creation, but of less importance than humans. In some primitive faiths, God is to be found in nature: animists discover God-like characteristics in such things as rocks and mountains. Animists often take this a step further by creating an image or selecting a special mountain or a tree or a rock that becomes the object of veneration. The temptation to worship Ba'al, the god of thunder and storms, for instance, or to build Ashteroth's temples in high places among groves of trees was lamented by the prophets. King Solomon's openness to the worship practices of his many wives, including worship "in high places," eventually divided the kingdom and undercut the undergirding faith in Jehovah as the one and only god. The Egyptians found evidence of the sacred in cats, beetles, snakes, flies, fish, and so forth. Many of the ancients venerated bulls as symbols of fertility. This may well explain the worship of the Golden Calf.

While animists turn nature into god, pantheists find God everywhere in nature. Pantheists and some Transcendentalists are inclined to see God in the hills and clouds and trees. The Romantic English poet William Wordsworth comes close to this pagan concept in his poetry, recommending "Let Nature be your teacher!"

> One impulse from a vernal wood
> May teach you more of man,
> Of moral evil and of good,
> Than all the sages can.

> (Wordsworth, 190)

The Jews, even in their most nature-soaked imagery, never confused God with his creation. In Hebrew scripture, God is clearly separate from nature.

This is not to say that the writers of scripture were blind to the beauties and liveliness of nature. The book of Job is a virtual catalogue of nature imagery, as is the Song of Solomon. The curious catalogue of attributes of the "fair" beloved, for example, has lines like this:

Behold, thou art fair, my love; behold thou art fair; thou hast doves' eyes within they locks: thy hair is as a flock of goats, that appear from mount Gilead.

Thy teeth are like a flock of sheep that are even shorn, which came up from washing, whereof every one bear twins, and none is barren among them....

Thy temples are like a piece of a pomegranate within thy locks ...

Thy two breasts are like two young roes that are twins, which feed among the lilies.

Until the day break, and the shadows flee away, I will get me to the mountain of myrrh, and to the hill of frankincense. (Song of Sol. 4:1–6)

Jesus reveals his awareness of natural splendor when he tells his followers not to worry about clothes and food. Pointing to the wildflowers on the hillside, he comments, "Consider the lilies of the field, how they grow; they toil not, neither do they spin: And yet I say unto you, That even Solomon in all his glory was not arrayed as one of these. Wherefore, if God so clothe the grass of the field, which today is, and tomorrow is cast into the oven, shall he not much more clothe you, O ye of little faith?" (Matt. 6:28–30). He speaks of the foxes and the birds, lamenting even the fall of a sparrow. The natural world, the fields and flowers, the Sea of Galilee with its winds and waves, the hills and the wilderness are all part of his story. He walks everywhere, from one end of Israel to the other, stays in the desert for over a month, is baptized in the Jordan River, and frequently climbs the long path to Jerusalem. Even after the Crucifixion, the resurrected Christ walks along the road of Emmaus with his disciples and cooks fish for friends on the shore of the Sea of Galilee.

Though nature provides the background for the New Testament narratives, it affords no guidance for the way a person should live his or her life. Paul, reminding the Corinthians of the Fall, speaks of the "natural man." He tells the Corinthians (1 Cor. 2:14), "But the natural man receiveth not the things of the Spirit of God: for they are foolishness unto him: neither can he know them, because they are spiritually discerned." This message is echoed several other places. The natural man is the person who lacks the spiritual discernment that comes with the Holy Spirit: the capacity to know spiritual truth beyond the innate powers of the untutored human. Nature alone, Wordsworth's views notwithstanding, cannot teach people the way to either the good life or salvation.

Literature

The Greeks, like the Hebrews, loved nature without losing their focus on the humans in the foreground. While the Hebrews spoke frequently of the hills, the Greeks loved the "wine-dark sea." Homer's epic similes often picture wild animals and tame ones in pastoral settings: He compares his warriors to ferocious lions, uses the painting on Achilles's shield to describe oxen plowing fields back home. He loves the "rosy-fingered dawn." Like other Greeks, he personifies forces of nature—the winds, the perils of the sea. They become monsters like Scylla and Charybdis, or the Sirens, or simply minor gods. The sea itself is controlled by the god of the sea, Poseidon (called *Neptune* by the Romans), just as the sky is controlled by Zeus and the underworld by Hades. These gods are limited to their own sphere of activity. They can neither create nor destroy the sea. By petitioning the winds, they might whip up waves to punish or reward humans.

This imagery contrasts sharply with the Hebrews' view of God as the creator and sustainer of the universe, omnipotent and omniscient. As he thunders out his majestic response to Job, he reveals his power to raise up the waters and tear down mountains, set rocks in their place, appear in the midst of a whirlwind, or speak from a burning bush. At no point do the Hebrews turn nature into a god to be adored.

Early English poetry is full of references to nature, but usually as an adversary. When Beowulf goes to the mere (a body of water, perhaps a lake) to challenge Grendel's mother, he does not stop to admire the scenery. Instead, he dives into the icy waters and challenges this grotesque monster in her native habitat. In shorter sea poems such as "The Wanderer" or the "Seafarer," the persona (or speaker of the poem) complains of numb feet and "the wail of the wild gale." Rather than admiring the birds, he describes the "piercing cry of the ice-coated petrel" and "The storm-drenched eagle's echoing scream" (quoted in Lieder, Lovett, and Root, 48–51).

These are poems written by people who have seen the ferocity of wind and wave. They are not by romantic adventurers in love with the "wine-dark sea." The poetry also reflects a different, Nordic climate, where the weather is not friendly to seafarers. The poems that have survived from this era were transcribed and transformed by monks, who provided an overlay of Christian piety not fully intrinsic to the poetry itself. After describing the agony of the seafarer's life, the poem suddenly switches to a praise of God's blessings:

> But fairer indeed are the joys God has fashioned
> Than the mortal and mutable life of the world.

The poet then continues to tie all of this observation of the seafarer's life into the Christian's life and to God's good creation, sometimes with interesting juxtapositions (like God and fate):

> Firmer is fate, greater is God,
> Than the thoughts of man can ever imagine.
> Let us muse in our hearts on our heavenly mansions,
> Thitherward planning our pilgrimage,
> Seeking the way of the blessed stronghold
> Of life and joy in the love of the Lord

> ("The Seafarer," in Lieder, Lovett, and Root, 48–51)

For these early English poets, life on earth was a constant struggle against cruel nature; for them the heavenly mansions were the ultimate image of a warm and welcoming home.

By Chaucer's time, the images of nature became more benign. Chaucer quickly sketches the April showers and flowers, the "smale foweles" that "maken melodye" as background for his springtime pilgrimage to Canterbury, These details of nature are used to set the tone for the pilgrims and their tales, encouraging the reader to share in the good feelings that springtime brings to most people. The Seafarer, by contrast, hears in the song of the birds a call to return to the sea and to the rugged life.

Shakespeare uses nature in much the same manner as Chaucer. In his plays, the natural setting often establishes background for actions and the mood for human activity. One of the most famous scenes in all of Shakespeare's plays is the heath scene in *King Lear*. The old king shouts at the wind as he vents his rage and sorrow at the perfidy of his daughters and his despair for his own life. The storm is a perfect reflection of his own wild state of mind.

This remarkable playwright often captures human emotions in his setting: trag- edies are often placed in bleak, gloomy places, often in the dead of winter. The bitter cold of *Macbeth* echoes the coldness of the hero's heart. Comedies are more usually in mid-summer or springtime, when all of nature is coming to life and love is in full bloom.

Later, many Gothic writers repeat this strategy. They seem to assume that most evil deeds are plotted by candlelight on dark wintry nights; Arthur Conan Doyle fills his stories with fog and gloom, a suitable background for the crimes to be solved by Sherlock Holmes. The writers of romances know that love stories blos- som with the springtime. This use of nature as a mirror of human moods has been called "pathetic fallacy," the notion that nature somehow sympathizes with human activities.

As life in England grew more urbane and comfortable, writers like Thomas Gray became increasingly sentimental about nature. Living in London during the Indus- trial Revolution, this gentle scholar much preferred to retreat to smaller towns and cherished untrammeled nature. His most famous poem is "Elegy Written in a Country Churchyard," a celebration of life close to nature. In language replete with poetic diction that is hardly "natural," he considers the "rude forefathers of the hamlet" whose graves are in the churchyard, where they "sleep" under the elms and yews. This poem implies that the simple life of the yeoman is happier than that of educated city folk who follow the "paths of glory"—which we know " lead but to the grave."

Artists of the period, like Turner and Constable, began to paint canvasses of idyllic landscapes, with tiny human figures dwarfed by the vast expanse of nature's splendor. Beautiful clouds, gorgeous sunsets, waterfalls, banks of flowers, magnifi- cent trees are all indications of a new respect for "sublime" nature. Nature is fre- quently described, during this period, to be the teacher to humans. William Blake contrasts these lovely bucolic scenes with the "dark Satanic mills" of the growing cities. As people grew more civilized, they lamented the loss of their close ties with nature, though they enjoyed all of the benefits of the Industrial Revolution.

The English Romantic poets love Nature (now personified and capitalized) as a transcendent power, capable of healing and teaching humans. William Wordsworth writes about his beloved Lake District when on a walking trip with his sister, Doro- thy, in the summer of 1798. "Lines Composed a Few Miles above Tintern Abbey" is a long, blank-verse poem describing the poet's return to a scene along the Wye River, a place he enjoyed as a young lad. He describes the actual landscape before him in moving terms, almost as if he were painting it:

> These waters, rolling from their mountain-springs
> With a soft inland murmur.—Once again
> Do I behold these steep and lofty cliffs,
> That on a wild secluded scene impress
> Thoughts of deep seclusion ...
> These plots of cottage-ground, these orchard-tufts,
> Which at this season, with their unripe fruits,
> Are clad in one green hue, and lose themselves
> 'Mid groves and copses.

Note the "sublime" quality of wild landscape in this scene he describes, typical of the taste for wild nature during the late years of the eighteenth century.

The poet has lived in towns and cities, where the very memory of these scenes provided for him "sensations sweet" and brought memories of pleasure and a tranquil restoration—even a kind of mystic experience:

> that blessed mood
> In which the burden of mystery,
> In which the heavy and weary weight,
> Of all this unintelligible world,
> Is lightened.

In such moments, Wordsworth insists that "we see into the life of things."

He recalls his youth in these hills, when he enjoyed the "coarser pleasures" and bounded about like a young animal. He also remembers a second phase of his life, when he was thrilled with the colors and forms of nature—a kind of aesthetic appetite and delight. But in his later years, he has come

> To look on nature, not as in the hour
> Of thoughtless youth; but hearing oftentimes
> The still, sad music of humanity.

In this third phase of his nature-experience, the writer's persona has discovered a "presence," "a motion and a spirit," that impels thinking things and rolls through all things. This would appear to imply a pantheistic concept of a God-spirit found throughout nature. Wordsworth does acknowledge that the poet himself "half-creates" the experience of the natural world, recognizing in it "the language of the sense" and discovering there "the nurse,/ The guide, the guardian of my heart, and soul/ Of all my moral being." In the final section, he also speaks of his sister, his "dearest Friend," who has helped him to see and to remember. He pronounces a very beautiful benediction on her:

> Therefore let the moon
> Shine on thee in thy solitary walk;
> And let the misty mountain winds be free
> To blow against thee.

> (Wordsworth, "Lines Composed a Few Miles above
> Tintern Abbey," 191–193)

The final lines of the poem return to the opening, reminding the reader that Wordsworth and his sister are standing on the banks of the river before this lovely scene, as worshipers of Nature.

The poem is moving, personal, detailed, and emotional, full of insights into Wordsworth's own experience. It also provides clear evidence that he is more Greek than Hebrew in his response to the natural world. As he says, he would rather be a "Pagan suckled in a creed outworn" than one who misses the delights of nature. The worshipful quality of the poem's tone, the choice of words suggesting veneration, reinforces this theme.

In stark contrast, Gerard Manley Hopkins, another English writer who delighted in the natural world, was much more clearly a Christian. He was a Jesuit, a learned and complicated man, who sang his songs of praise to God the Creator, not to Nature. In "Pied Beauty," he exclaims,

Glory be to God for dappled things—
    For skies of couple-color as a brinded cow;
        For rose-moles all in stipple upon trout that swim; …
Landscapes plotted and pieced—fold, fallow, and plow;
    And all trades, their gear and tackle and trim.
All things counter, original, spare, strange;
    Whatever is fickle, freckled (who knows how!)
        With swift, slow; sweet, sour; adazzle, dim;
He fathers-forth whose beauty is past change:
    Praise Him.

                        (Hopkins, "Pied Beauty," 930)

He lists a dazzling selection of the amazing things that are "counter, original, spare, strange; Whatever is fickle, freckled … /swift, slow; sweet, sour; adazzle, dim." God, who "fathers forth" this incredible variety of unique life, is a God "whose beauty is past change." He concludes this brief poem with the simple line: "Praise Him." Like the Psalms, the poem is built on a parallel listing of attributes. He creates this prayer of praise in a verse form akin to Old English, full of alliteration and accented syllables, not relying on rhythm and rhyme. Even though Hopkins's poem shares the poetic form of scripture, his content, a listing of startling diversity, makes this quite unlike most Bible passages, with the possible exception of Job. It is much more personal and modern. Although the Jews knew their animals well, the way farmers, fishermen, and shepherds are bound to know the fish, the sheep, and the goats, they did not discuss the beauty of "brindled cows" or "moles on trout."

In another of his poems that has the general structure of a sonnet, Hopkins makes a somewhat different point about nature and its creator. The poem "God's Grandeur" points in a more traditional way to nature as God's book, or as evidence of his creative power:

The world is charged with the grandeur of God.
    It will flame out, like shining from shook foil;
    It gathers to a greatness, like the ooze of oil
Crushed. Why do men then now not reck his rod?

In deliberately antique words, Hopkins notes that humans fail to pay attention to the message richly expressed in nature, flashing out here and there. Rather, humans have trod through one generation after another over paths, losing through the repetition their amazement at this incredible splendor. Their feet no longer have touch with the soil "being shod."

But even though man, with his cities and buildings and busy ways, ignores God's remarkable power and creativity, the freshness of "deep down things" continues and morning returns:

Oh, morning, at the brown brink eastward, springs—
Because the Holy Ghost over the bent
    World broods with warm breast and with ah! bright wings

                   (Hopkins, "God's Grandeur," 929)

Notice how, in this final tribute to the Holy Spirit, Hopkins captures the delightful surprise of the flash of wings of the dove. In these last lines, he recalls the biblical description of the creation, where the spirit of God broods over the waters. We also see in it the wonderful moment of Jesus's baptism by John the Baptist, when the dove descends and the heavens open, and God speaks. Hopkins, who knows both scripture and nature, can capture the wonder of a moment, the silver flash of a fish or the sudden glimpse of a scarlet wing on a bird; he can make us feel anew the delight of individual natural splendors, using this thrill to give thanks to the God who created it.

America, like England, has produced many lovers and worshippers of nature. The contemporary writer Annie Dillard has caught the wonder of God's creation in much the same way that Hopkins did a century earlier. Her description of her own experiences in the natural world, *A Pilgrim at Tinker Creek* (1974) can make the reader gasp in amazement. She loves, as did Hopkins, the idiosyncratic and startling moments that have touched her, the sudden disappearance of a frog or the pitiful crippling of a butterfly. In her work, she draws on a long heritage of nature writers, including such essayists as Henry David Thoreau, who also chronicled his own close observations at Walden Pond.

A better known and more prolific writer in the nature tradition is Walt Whitman, who wrote at the time of the Civil War. In one of his more philosophical poems, "Song of Myself," a child asks this simple question: "What is the grass?" Rather than limiting his response to the tight quatrains that Blake employed with such power in response to such apparently simple questions, Whitman takes a free-verse, American path. He rambles on loquaciously, letting his thoughts wander far and wide. Among the multitude of answers he proposes are these:

I guess it must be the flag of my disposition, out of hopeful green stuff woven.
Or I guess it is the handkerchief of the lord,
A scented gift and rembrancer designedly dropped,
Bearing the owner's name someway in the corners...
Or I guess it is a uniform hieroglyphic,
And it means, Sprouting alike in broad zones and narrow zones,
Growing among black folks as among white,
Canuck, Tuckahoe, Congressman, Cuff, I give them the same, I receive them the same.
And now it seems to me the beautiful uncut hair of graves.
All goes onward and outward, nothing collapses,
And to die is different from what anyone supposed, and luckier.

(Whitman, "Song of Myself," *Leaves of Grass*, 205)

For Whitman, nature may be the sign of God's creation, or it may be the sign of unending life. He accepts both answers.

The Naturalists, on the other hand, have a far darker and flatter view of the natural world. They personify nature, seeing it as a malevolent god, or at least a disinterested one. In a Darwinian universe, "red in tooth and claw," they watched nondescript men and women strive valiantly to make life have meaning, to act heroically. In the end, they are doomed—like the ants on the burning log in Ernest Hemingway's *A Farewell to Arms*. Stephen Crane, one of the most articulate of this group of writers, published only two slender volumes of verse. In one, he included this brief, cruel poem:

A man said to the universe:
"Sir, I exist!"

"However," replied the universe,
"The fact has not created in me
A sense of obligation."

(Crane, "A Man Said to the Universe," in *Foerster and
Falk, 877*)

In Stephen Crane's short story "The Open Boat," we see the blank and uncaring ocean beat against the men in the small craft. This nineteenth-century American writer wrote a report in very realistic detail about the experience of four men who survived the sinking of the steamer *Commodore*, only to be tossed on the sea for some time in an open boat. The captain is hurt and unable to help row; the oiler, the cook, and the correspondent are the main crew. They have a little water but no food when they find themselves within view of land off the coast of Florida. In their shared effort to survive, they form a "subtle brotherhood" not uncommon among those who go down to the sea in ships.

Gradually, they discover that one hope after another is dashed: they cannot row close enough to shore to swim the rest of the way, there is no "refuge" or lighthouse that will help them; the people on shore who spot them do not realize they are in trouble. They think the seamen are just waving a friendly greeting. The refrain finally becomes, in the words of an un-named narrator: "If I am going to be drowned, why in the name of the seven mad gods who rule the sea, was I allowed to come thus far and contemplate sand and trees?" They rage at the clouds, which are as oblivious of them as the sky, the sea, and these people on shore.

Crane sums up the vision of the story clearly: "When it occurs to a man that nature does not regard him as important, and that she feels she would not maim the universe by disposing of him, he at first wishes to throw bricks at the temple, and he hates deeply the fact that there are no bricks and no temples." He wants to confront some personification of this complacent universe, but "A high cold star on a winter's night is the word he feels that she says to him. Thereafter he knows the pathos of his situation." Nature is no benevolent mother figure. The universe is simply indifferent to mankind, not cruel or treacherous or wise—"She was indifferent, flatly indifferent."

The end of the story reinforces the theme of meaninglessness. The ones saved and the one lost have not been foreshadowed. Their fates are not determined by their wisdom, strength, or hard work. What happens, happens. In some ways, this is the natural outcome of the Deists' view of William Paley's watchmaker God in *Natural Theology* (1802). Combined with Darwin's theory of evolution, where only the "fittest" survive, the gloomy concept emerged that the world grinds the weak and sensitive creatures into extinction. Or, as the world-weary writer of Ecclesiastes said centuries earlier, the Lord makes rain to fall on the just and the unjust. He also follows this up with, "All is vanity under the sun." The theme has not really changed.

A more cheerful view of nature appears in Willa Cather's Midwestern stories, such as "Neighbor Rosicky" and *O, Pioneers!* (1913). This turn-of-the-century American writer describes vividly the western plains with their fierce winters and thrilling springs, the battle of men and women to bring a living out of the soil. She also describes the toll the land takes on the people who dare to farm this great and fertile land. Her immigrants, from Bohemia and other eastern-European regions, are realists who love their farms and realize that the work of the farmer is full of day-to-day challenges. The rewards for their hard labor are potentially enormous, but these rewards do not typically include the arts or the other niceties of life. Cather shows that human planning and persistence are essential in this long and loving battle to make a living out of nature.

Some Americans have found that they are doomed to lose this perennial battle with nature. John Steinbeck describes one family's response to the devastations of the Dust Bowl, a prolonged drought that hit the mid-west in the 1930s. The opening chapter of *The Grapes of Wrath* (1939) is one of the most powerful descriptions of dust storms ever written. The Joads are driven from their farm in Oklahoma by the winds and the dust, joining the Oakies and Arkies and others who seek the green pastures of California. Like the ancient Hebrews headed for Egypt, these immigrants find themselves virtual slaves in the new territory. As migratory workers, following harvest, they too seek primarily to survive as a family. For Steinbeck, the hope lies in the solidarity of the people—in farm labor unions and in human sympathy. He expects and finds no divine intervention. At the end of the day, California is not a promised land for these poor wanderers.

An interesting parallel work about farmers is Pearl Buck's *The Good Earth* (1931), an immensely popular story of a Chinese farmer and his family. Like the Joads, Wang Lung is also forced from the land by drought. Faced by desperate times, he takes his aged father, his wife, O-Lan, and his children to the nearest city, hoping to find work, food, and prosperity. This family soon discovers that they are strangers in this new terrain, marked by their poverty and their speech. They survive by hard labor and begging, seeking always to return to their land, which they consider the ultimate hope for themselves and their prosperity.

By "luck" they find the means to return and prosper, living out their lives according to their own principles, praying occasionally to gods they barely credit. For this family, Christianity is the alien idea of a naked man suffering on a cross, incompatible with their culture and understanding. Wang Lung believes in the land itself, which is the very real source of his hope. In his love of material prosperity, he gradually loses sight of the richness of his life—especially the blessing of his hard-working and devoted wife. Only after he has taken a second wife and O-Lan is dying does he come to understand that she, like the land, has been the key to his happiness. The sad ending of the narrative comes as Wang Lung himself faces death, knowing that his educated sons will leave the land, sell it, and forget their roots.

Pearl Buck, the daughter of Presbyterian missionaries, born and raised in China, was American by heritage and education. In her most famous novel, she captures the simple peasants' lives in China and their confusion of fate, luck, and faith. They need something beyond themselves to account for the catastrophes of nature, but find their many idols as helpless as the petitioners who kneel before them.

America's Southern writers have tended to be more mystical in their approach to nature. For many of them, the land is God's gift, lent to humans "for the time being." The history of the region is written on the blood-soaked earth, marking every tree and hill. In novels such as *Absalom, Absalom!*, the Southern writer William Faulkner mocks the arrogance of those men who believe they can "own" nature. Thomas Sutpen's hundred acres in northwestern Yoknapatawpha County, which he got from the Chickasaws, was never really his any more than it had been theirs. The land will remain long after the man dies and is buried. His great effort to make "Sutpen's Hundred" a permanent legacy ends with catastrophe and futility. *Absalom, Absalom!* (the title taken from David's lament over his beloved son) is the story of this monumental struggle to dominate the land and his own legacy.

A number of Faulkner's stories deal with nature. *The Bear* is an excellent study in human interaction with nature, with the white man stealing it from the Indians, shedding the blood and sweat of slaves on it, stripping the land of its forests, and trying to claim it for his posterity. The small band of hunters at the center of the story are closer to the real appreciation of nature's mysteries than most, enjoying the democracy of the campfire, respecting the power and dignity of their prey, laughing at the idiosyncrasies of their dogs.

Another of his tales, the novella *Old Man* (in the book *Wild Palms*), tells of an actual flood of the Mississippi River, the lives it swept away, the human stories it uncovered. For a short time, the Tall Convict sees the world outside of the penitentiary, the patterns of life and death, the struggle for survival. Faulkner had a strong sense of humans' relationship with the land. He understood obsession with the land—people loving it too much, being to greedy to own it, or fighting too hard to subdue it. To the very end, Faulkner found nature a source of affection, comedy, power, and wonder.

Another Southerner, Flannery O'Connor, also loves to include details of nature in her writing, and sees much of the foolishness of humans as they proclaim their "ownership" of the land. Unlike Thomas Gray, she has no faith that working on the land can make a person more honest or happy. Her farm people are realistically portrayed: they are middle-class property-owners, poor white migratory workers, and African American laborers, all trying to make their claims on the land, which inevitably belongs to the Lord. They have dominion only so long as they have life and strength.

This is the clear point at the conclusion of O'Connor's story "The Displaced Person." The old lady who is so land-proud, referring constantly to "my place," finds herself deserted by everyone but the priest, who labors on explaining Catholic doctrine to her. In the story "A Circle in the Fire," some mischievous boys from the inner-city come to a farm where the persnickety owner claims the woods, the fields, the barn, the house as "my place." They argue, when she is out of sight, that "it don't belong to nobody," and prove it by riding her horses, washing in her trough, and finally setting "her" woods on fire. O'Connor was very clear on her theology: humans are not the possessors of nature, only its stewards for the time being.

Jane Smiley, a contemporary American author, pushes harder on the idea that humans are assigned the role of caretakers of nature—not just dominators. Adam and Eve were told to care for the Garden of Eden. In her novel about farm life in the Midwest, *A Thousand Acres*, she takes the same idea that Faulkner explored in *Absalom, Absalom!*, but she blends the health of the people with the health of the land. The violation of the one produces illness and death in the other. For many people who are concerned with the fragile ecosystem of the earth and the need for harmony between civilization and the environment, Smiley is a lively and convincing spokesperson. She is, however, more in love with the created world than she is concerned with its Creator.

Conclusion

Much of the twentieth century's view of humans and nature is summed up in one of its most influential poems, T. S. Eliot's *The Wasteland*. This long free-verse poem draws liberally on scripture for its inspiration, especially on the world-weary tone of the book of Ecclesiastes and the alienated imagery of Ezekiel. Presenting his persona as a kind of twentieth-century prophet, Eliot echoes Ezekiel in his "Son of man" address.

He opens the poem with a satirical contrast to the opening of *The Canterbury Tales*. Instead of happy pilgrims heading off on pilgrimages at the first sign of spring, he sees April as the "cruelest month." Then he lays out the basic structure of his poem in these lines:

> What are the roots that clutch, what branches grow
> Out of this stony rubbish? Son of man,
> You cannot say, or guess, for you know only
> A heap of broken images, where the sun beats,
> And the dead tree gives no shelter, the cricket no relief,
> And the dry stone no sound of water. Only
> There is a shadow under this red rock,
> (Come in under the shadow of this red rock),
> And I will show you something different from either
> Your shadow at morning striding behind you
> Or your shadow at evening rising to meet you;
> I will show you fear in a handful of dust.

(Eliot, *The Wasteland*, 948)

In this brief passage, Eliot reminds us of the rootlessness of most moderns; their failure to produce good fruit; their confused and broken images, which have none of the coherence and immediacy of the Hebrews'; the lack of "shelter" for the wanderers in the wilderness, with no stone that breaks open to offer sweet water (as with Moses in the Exodus); the need for protection from fear in the shadow of a great rock (Christ and his Church); and fear of being reduced—like Adam and Job—to dust from which we came.

Eliot echoes Ezekiel's vision of the Valley of the Dry Bones—a title some have used for Western culture in the twentieth century:

> The hand of the Lord was upon me, and carried me out, in the spirit of the Lord, and set me down in the midst of the valley which was full of bones,
> And caused me to pass by them round about: and behold there were very many in the open valley; and, lo, they were very dry.
> And he said unto me, Son of man, can these bones live? and I answered, O Lord God, thou knowest.
> Again he said unto me, Prophesy upon these bones, and say unto them, O ye dry bones, hear the word of the Lord,
> Thus saith the Lord God unto these bones; Behold I will cause breath to enter into you, and ye shall live. (Ezek. 37:1–5)

The message in Ecclesiastes is even clearer, using the natural world as a reflection of spiritual dryness:

> Remember now thy Creator in the days of thy youth, while the evil days come not, nor the years draw nigh, when thou shalt say, I have no pleasure in them;
> While the sun, or the light, or the moon, or stars, be not darkened, nor the clouds return after the rain....
> And the doors shall be shut in the streets, when the sound of the grinding is low, and he shall rise up at the voice of the bird, and all the daughters of music shall be brought low;
> Also when they shall be afraid of that which is high, and fears shall be in the way, the almond tree shall flourish, and the grasshopper shall be a burden, and desire shall fail: because man goeth to his long home and the mourners go about the streets;
> Or ever the silver cord be loosed, or the golden bowl be broken, or the pitcher be broken at the fountain, or the wheel broken at the cistern.

Then shall dust return to the earth as it was: and the spirit shall return unto God who gave it.

Vanity of vanities, saith the preacher, all is vanity. (Eccles. 12:1–8)

Eliot, in his richly resonant poem, has blended much of modern learning, the decline of religious orthodoxy, the sense of despair in a century full of prosperity and moral decay, into an image that is scriptural, natural, and powerful: We live in a sterile world waiting for rain, a wasteland. In the Bible, the desert is usually a place for meditation, prayer, fasting, and mortification of the flesh. The image of the waste-land, though terrifying for the reader who sees only the sterility and dreariness of the scene, is rich with resonance for the Bible reader, who knows that the sojourn in the desert is the prelude to the prophetic ministry that follows.

And so the long, rich story of humans and nature continues. Whether viewed as the book of God's handiwork, the gift of God's love, or a trust in our hands, nature is more than background for us. In our concrete jungles, we sense our alienation from the natural world; we hunger for closer communion with it; we fear damaging it; and we are overwhelmed by our gratitude for the changing seasons, the flowers, the plenitude of creatures that surround our lives and enrich them. The writers who are able to revive this spirit of wonder in us deserve our gratitude.

See also: **Animals and Humans; Creation.**

Bibliography

Buck, Pearl. *The Good Earth.* New York: Washington Square Press, 2004.

Calvin, John. *Institutes of the Christian Religion.* Trans., Henry Beveridge. Grand Rapids: Wm. B. Eerdmans Publishing Company, 1989.

Cather, Willa. "Neighbor Rosicky." In *American Poetry and Prose,* ed. Norman Foerster and Robert Falk. Boston: Houghton Mifflin Company, 1960.

Crane, Stephen. *The Open Boat.* In *American Poetry and Prose,* ed. Norman Foerster and Robert Falk. Boston: Houghton Mifflin Company, 1960.

Defoe, Daniel. *Robinson Crusoe.* New York: Aerie Books, 1988.

Dillard, Annie. *Pilgrim at Tinker Creek.* New York: HarperCollins, 1995.

Eliot, T. S. "The Wasteland." In *American Poetry and Prose,* ed. Norman Foerster and Robert Falk. Boston: Houghton Mifflin, 1960.

Fairchild, Hoxie Neale. *Religious Trends in English Poetry* (6 volumes). New York: Columbia University Press, 1968.

Faulkner, William. *Absalom, Absalom!* New York: Library of America, 1990.

Gray, Thomas. "Elegy Written in a Country Churchyard." In *British Poetry and Prose,* Vol. I, ed. Paul Robert Lieder, Robert Morss Lovett, and Robert Kilburn Root. Boston: Houghton Mifflin, 1950.

Hemingway, Ernest. *The Old Man and the Sea.* New York: Charles Scribner's Sons, 1952.

O'Connor, Flannery. *Collected Works.* New York: Literary Classics of United States, 1988.

Steinbeck, John. *The Grapes of Wrath.* New York: Penguin Books, 2002.

Thomas, Keith. *Man and the Natural World: A History of the Modern Sensibility.* New York: Pantheon Books, 1983.

Untermeye, Louis, ed. *Modern British Poetry: Mid-Century Edition.* New York: Harcourt, Brace and Company, 1950.

Whitman, Walt. "Song of Myself." In *The Treasurey of American Poetry.* New York: Barnes and Noble Books, 1993.

Wordsworth, William. "Lines Composed a Few Miles above Tintern Abbey." In *Anthology of Romanticism,* ed. Ernest Bernbaum. New York: The Roland Press Company, 1948.

Animals and Humans

Readings

Genesis 1–2, 8
Geoffrey Chaucer, *The Canterbury Tales* ("The Nun's Priest's Tale") (c. 1400)
Jonathan Swift, "A Modest Proposal" (1729), *Gulliver's Travels* (1726)
Alexander Pope, *An Essay on Man* (1733–34)
William Blake, *Songs of Innocence* (1789), *Songs of Experience* (1794)
Samuel Taylor Coleridge, *The Rime of the Ancient Mariner* (1798)
George Orwell, *Animal Farm* (1945)
Ernest Hemingway, *The Old Man and the Sea* (1952)
Annie Dillard, *A Pilgrim at Tinker Creek* (1974)

Introduction

> And God said unto them, Be fruitful, and multiply, and replenish the earth,
> and subdue it: and have dominion over the fish of the sea, and over the fowl
> of the air, and over every living thing that moveth upon the earth. (Gen.
> 1:28)

Many of the ancient people's creation myths involve a giant serpent or various
sorts of monsters. *The Enuma Elish*, the most famous of the ancient Near Eastern
texts, tells of Tiamat, "our mother":

She has made the Worm,
the Dragon
the Female Monster
the Great Lion
the Mad Dog
the Man Scorpion

(*The Enuma Elish*, in Sproul, 91)

This "Old Hag, the first mother" produces a hideous bunch of "serpents with cutting fangs, chock-full of venom instead of blood, snarling dragons wearing their glory like gods," but she creates nothing that she or any of the other gods consider "good." The contrast with Genesis could not be more stark.

Even in God's magnificent response to Job's wailing, the monstrous animals mentioned have splendor:

> Behold now behemoth, which I made with thee; he eateth grass as an ox. Lo now, his strength is in his loins, and his force is in the navel of his belly. He moveth his tail like a cedar: the sinews of his stones are wrapped together. His bones are as strong as pieces of brass; his bones are like bars of iron. He is chief of the ways of God: he that made him can make his sword to approach unto them. (Job 40:15–19)

The description of the sea creature of comparable size, the leviathan, is also spectacular, and also marked by the usual observations in the biblical Creation narrative: that God created him, that he is under God's control, and that man is by no means his equal in power:

> Canst thou draw out leviathan with a hook? or his tongue with a cord which thou lettest down? ... Will he make many supplications unto thee? Will he speak soft words unto thee? Will he make a covenant with thee? Wilt thou take him for a servant for ever? Wilt thou play with him, as with a bird? Or wilt thou bind him for thy maidens? ... Behold, the hope of him is in vain: shall not one be cast down even at the sight of him? None is so fierce that dare stir him up: who then is able to stand before me? (Job 41:1–10)

Animals were seen as God's creatures, created even before man and woman. Sometimes, humans have seen animals as enemies, sometimes as pets, sometimes as ancestors, and sometimes as co-inhabitants of planet earth. The question of the relationship between humans and the animals was raised in the earliest biblical traditions: the need to have dominion over the animals, to encourage them to multiply and replenish their species, and to name them. Later, east of Eden, animals were used for sacrifice, for food, for clothing, and for help in labor.

In literature, animals have often taken on personalities of their own. Sometimes they become the actors in fables. Aesop, like the author of Proverbs, saw moral lessons to be taught by animals. As attitudes toward animals have changed over time, and as people have become more sensitive to the understanding, suffering, and affection displayed by animals, arguments have arisen over their "rights" and our respect for them.

Scripture

One of the first issues raised in Genesis is what relationship God ordained between humans and animals. What does "dominion" mean in God's clear instructions to Adam? As God tells Job centuries later, humans cannot dominate the monstrous animals of the world—the crocodile and the rhinoceros, the whale and the elephant. Even so, this theme of dominion and of God's special place for the human is repeated in the Psalms:

> What is man, that thou art mindful of him? and the son of man, that thou visitest him?
>
> For thou has made him a little lower than the angels, and hast crowned him with glory and honor.

Thou madest him to have dominion over the works of thy hands; thou has put all things under his feet:
    All sheep and oxen, yea, and the beasts of the field;
    The fowl of the air and the fish of the sea, and whatsoever passeth through the paths of the seas.
    O Lord our Lord, how excellent is thy name in all the earth! (Psalm 8:4–9)

This famous psalm sets forth the basis for the Great Chain of Being, the concept that all of creation is ordered like a series of links, with humans somewhere between the animals and the angels, and with God at the pinnacle of all creation. In the eighteenth century, when this concept became powerful among the writers, Alexander Pope considered the Great Chain of Being foundational to his world view. He saw a chain stretching from earth to heaven, with the instinctive creatures at the bottom, the reasoning ones in the higher regions. He was delighted at the idea of the plenitude of this great panoply of life:

Above, how high progressive life may go!
Around, how wide! how deep extend below!
Natures ethereal, human, angel, man,
Beast, bird, fish, insect, what no eye can see,
No glass can reach, from infinite to thee;
From thee to nothing.

In this famous poem, Pope explains that the role of humans is to submit to their position. To seek more than God ordains is to violate the order of the universe. As Pope admonishes his impatient audience:

The bliss of man…
Is not to act or think beyond mankind;
No powers of body or of soul to share,
But what his nature and his state can bear.
Why has not man a microscopic eye?
For this plain reason, man is not a fly

(Pope, *An Essay on Man*, 815)

Animals, which fall below humans in this chain, should remain subjected to their superiors. This theme of the great chain of being was to linger in the human imagination over the centuries, shaping not only the view of kings as divinely ordained for their role, but also the relationship between man and beast as established from the beginning by God. It is clear from the book of Genesis that humans were designed to be both masters and stewards of the earth, responsible for its replenishment as well as its fruitfulness.

Another segment of the Creation narrative indicates that animals, like humans, fell from primal innocence with the transgression of Adam and Eve. The Lord turned on the serpent at that point, saying to it: "Because thou hast done this, thou art cursed above all cattle, and above every beast of the field" (Gen. 3:14). From this time forth, humans and beasts are set at enmity with one another, with mankind wearing animal skins and eating animal flesh. In the earliest recorded sacrifice, Abel's animal offering is preferable to the grain that Cain offers to God. The first murder is precipitated by God's preference for Abel's sacrifice, the "firstlings of his flock and the fat thereof" (Gen. 4:3).

Some argue that animals were included in Noah's covenant with God, who was concerned with the preservation of every living thing of all flesh, and arranged for Noah to take the animals into the Ark two by two. Curiously, this covenant that God offers Noah after the flood includes the warnings that fear and dread will now replace the primal harmony, and that "every moving thing that liveth shall be meat for you." God tells Noah that "fear of you and the dread of you shall be upon every beast of the earth, and upon every fowl of the air, upon all that moveth upon the earth, and upon the fishes of the sea; into your hand are they delivered" (Gen. 9:2). This Noahic covenant explicitly includes the entire animal kingdom; God seals it with the rainbow, promising that "the waters shall no more become a flood to destroy all flesh."

Genesis also provides another hint at the dominant position of humans over animals—the right to name them (Gen. 2:19). This authority reveals the lordship of Adam. In his book *Adam's Diary*, Mark Twain laughs at this obligation. He doubts that Eve would have allowed her husband to choose all the names, and would have snatched the role from her spouse. As he portrays the scene in his comic extracts from *Adam's Diary*, "I get no chance to name anything myself" (quoted in Ackerman, 29–35).

In his impressive study of Western views of nature, *Man and the Natural World*, Keith Thomas devotes considerable space to the concern for nomenclature. Eventually, the scientists took control over this naming task, replacing the popular names for the animals developed over thousands of years with Latin ones, fixing them so that people might study animals more carefully and with more universal understanding. Before the Renaissance, the lively art of naming animals was an accepted part of humans' creative activity. People gave species and individual animals names that marked their role and their relationships. Unfortunately, older literature, including scripture, often includes names that have long since disappeared from usage, making it difficult to picture what a *leviathan* or a *behemoth* is in modern terms.

Scripture most often pictures animals helping humans, carrying their burdens, supplying their food, clothing, and shelter, serving humankind with their skins, their milk, their meat, and their labor. Humans have domesticated many types of animals, feeding and caring for them in return for their labor. A wide variety of animals are mentioned in scripture, both domestic and wild. In early times, the domestic beasts lived under the same roofs as their masters. Some must have been close enough to be seen as pets—as mentioned in Nathan's parable regarding a pet lamb. The very closeness between men and animals encouraged affection and consideration that carried over into customs.

The law of Moses is quite detailed on the protection of the animals that live in the midst of the people. The ox threshing the grain is not to be muzzled. Domestic animals are not to be mistreated or stolen or maimed or sexually abused. They are to share the Sabbath rest with their masters. Leviticus is filled with specific rules and regulations about the proper treatment of all God's creatures.

Wild animals are a different matter. Shepherds must protect their flocks from lions, which lurk by the side of the road and threaten humans and beasts. Samson does not hesitate to kill a lion that he meets along the path. Nor does he hesitate to abuse foxes, which often damage the crops. (Actually, Samson proves more destructive than the little foxes. He turns against his enemies and burns their crops by setting fire to the foxes' tails.) Animals are loved or feared according to their role in human activities. Scripture is not sentimental about animals, nor does it confuse animals with humans by attributing proper names and individualized personalities to them.

Farmers, who know they must kill their cattle or sheep, are reluctant to become too affectionate with them. The massive sacrifices recorded in scripture, with hundreds of animals slaughtered in a day, point to the unsentimental stance of both clergy and laymen. Although it is important the sacrificial animals be without blemish, it is not important that they be loved.

The scriptural tradition uses animal imagery for humans, but keeps the two levels of creation quite separate, with animals invariably in the background. The imagery of the Bible testifies to the close observation of the people's habits and traits of animals. Although we "like sheep have gone astray," no one literally thinks of humans as sheep or sheep as humans. When John the Baptist calls Herod a "fox," he uses the term as an image, not as a literal fact. And when Satan is said to lurk by the side of the road like a "raging lion," no one considers this is meant literally. The prodigal son, when he eats the pigs' food, realizes how low he has sunk and decides it is time to return to his father, repent, and serve him henceforth. Animals may be companions and helpers and sources of sustenance, but not on the level with humans.

Literature

Only twice in scripture do animals speak (the serpent in the Garden of Eden, and the donkey in the story of Balaam). By contrast, the fables of Greek writer Aesop use numerous loquacious animal characters to portray human foibles. This fable tradition continued among the Romans and into medieval literature. Chaucer's comic rooster, Chanticleer, (in "The Nun's Priest's Tale") and the popular French character Reynard the Fox are famous examples of talking animals.

In this tradition, Carmen Bernos de Gasztold includes "The Prayer of the Cock," in the lively collection of poems *Prayers from the Ark* (1962). Here, a "cocky" rooster foreshadows Chanticleer. He tells God not to forget that "it is I who make the sun rise" (de Gasztold, 67). In related poems included in this charming collection, the other animals who traveled on the ark with Noah are also characterized by human traits, the will-o-the wisp quality of the butterfly, the plodding faithfulness of the ox.

A number of modern writers have mined the folklore tradition of children's fairy tales, with little pigs, bears of various sizes, and big bad wolves for adult entertainment and edification. One of the most delightful modern versions of these stories that build on the fairy tale tradition is E. B. White's *Charlotte's Web*, the story of a group of farm animals and a spider.

Notably, the much more serious and satiric novel by George Orwell, *Animal Farm* (1945), uses pigs, horses, sheep and other creatures to explain the underlying history of the Russian Revolution and the rise of Communism. In this book, the animals, having overthrown the farmer, quickly assume dominant or subordinate roles according to their nature, their wits, and their malevolence. The pigs, being the smartest of the animals, grab the authority while the sheep, the dumbest, bleat helplessly and follow mindlessly. The hard-working horses do their unthinking duty, plodding along, puzzled but faithful.

Scripture does draw on the traits of certain creatures to demonstrate traits and activities that appear parallels to those of human. Thus, we see the busy and productive ants and bees of Proverbs. The bestiaries of the Medieval period, drawn from both the Bible and later Church literature, present animals as more flatly symbolic of human qualities, often turning them into icons that can be read as precise equivalents.

Thus, the dog has come to represent fidelity (thus the name "Fido"), the raven is considered an omen of death, and the dove has become a symbol of peace. Statuary and paintings frequently employed animals to identify biblical characters or saints. The most famous of the animal-loving saints was the gentle twelfth-century Italian St. Francis of Assisi, whose devotion to his "brother" animals became legendary. He is usually portrayed with an animal by his side or in his arms, typically a wolf and a lamb (Ferguson, 121).

Jonathan Swift, an eighteenth-century writer and the Dean of St. Patrick's Cathedral in Dublin, used the scriptural divide between animals and humans to reinforce the brutality of the English in their treatment of Irish peasants. In his fierce satire "A Modest Proposal" (1729), he proposes using the Irish children as if they are lambs, since the landlords already treat the families as little more than livestock. Employing shocking imagery from animal husbandry and a dry and rational tone, he suggests ways in which the Irish babies might "contribute to the feeding and partly to the clothing of many thousands." The viciousness of his proposal, and his sardonic intent are telegraphed by such statements as references to "landlords, as they have already devoured most of the parents, seem to have the best title to the children." He protests that he has nothing to gain from his modest proposal: "I have no children by which I can propose to get a single penny; the youngest being nine years old, and my wife past child-bearing."

Swift is perhaps best known for his imaginative tale of Gulliver, whose travels took him to the lands of the Lilliputians (where the people were tiny in comparison with Gulliver); and from there to the Brobdingnabs (where they were enormous); from this voyage to the Houyhnhnms (where the rulers were horses); and finally to a series of places, including Laputa (where eccentric scholars were in charge). The animals in Lilliput are so tiny and Gulliver so enormous that all of his physical needs became disgusting and animalistic. By comparison, the animals are dainty and genteel. His decision to put out a fire by urinating on it, for instance, outrages the whole community. By contrast, when he is among the Brobdingnabs, even cats and mice can tyrannize him. He is frightened of all the animals in this monstrous land and has to be treated as a pet by his mistress, who puts him on her bosom to protect him. This leads to vivid descriptions of his revulsion at the animal qualities of the human body—the oil pouring out of her pores, the smells that overwhelm tiny Gulliver. A giant bird eventually carries him out of the country, thereby concluding this chapter of the book.

The most fascinating of his travels for its revelation of the animalistic quality of humans is the trip to the Houyhnhnms, where rational and honorable horses are the rulers and Yahoos (ape-like creatures) are the despised lower beings. Here the Great Chain of Being is reversed, with the human gazing with adoration at the superior horses. Gulliver becomes enamored of the decency of these animals and is hideously embarrassed to be viewed as a Yahoo. When he returns home, Gulliver is shocked to find that his family and friends look very much like Yahoos. He ends his days disgusted with his own family, spending most of his time in the stables, talking to his horses.

William Blake, a mystic and a pre-Romantic, who was also born in the eighteenth century, takes a simpler and more direct approach to nature. Like many of the Romantic writers, he loves animals. He sees in these creatures a mirror of God's mighty power and infinite creativity. In his poem "The Lamb," he asks the creature, "Little Lamb, who made thee?" Using biblical language that echoes the Twenty-third Psalm, Blake asks:

[Who] Gave thee life, and bid thee feed,
By the stream and o'er the mead.

In the second stanza, he answers for the lamb:

> Little Lamb, I'll tell thee:
> He is called by thy name,
> For He calls Himself a Lamb,
> He is meek, and He is mild;
> He became a little child.

(Blake, "The Lamb," Songs of Innocence, 1028)

Invoking the image of Christ as one with the Creator, Blake here proves himself more orthodox than many of his followers. Then, in a later poem, he poses the same question of the tiger with all his sinister and beautiful power.

> Tiger! Tiger! burning bright
> In the forests of the night,
> What immortal hand or eye
> Could frame thy fearful symmetry?

He ponders the creative process, the "dread hand" that wielded the hammer, anvil, and chain that made such a magnificent, but deadly creature. Using the phrasing of Job, one of Blake's favorite books of scripture, he wonders about this Creator God:

> When the stars threw down their spears,
> And watered heaven with their tears,
> Did He smile his work to see?
> Did He who made the Lamb make thee?

(Blake, "The Tiger," Songs of Experience, 1030)

Is the God who is the source of innocent beauty also the source of evil? Did he proclaim both the lamb and the tiger "good" on their day of creation? These rhetorical questions, posed in simple and forthright lines, make these twin poems a powerful expression of one of our most basic puzzles: did God create evil? Using increasingly complex imagery in "The Tiger," Blake mirrors the very complexity of the mental process of conceiving cruelty and the twisting of the heart. The combination of this brutality with great beauty is even more puzzling. Certainly, the tiger is one of God's most beautiful and fearful creatures.

Other Romantic writers, such as Wordsworth and Shelley, tend to idealize nature, often personifying it or turning it into a mystical experience. Shelley, for example, addresses the skylark, transforming the bird into the very image of the poet. As it sings on its flight toward heaven, it becomes more a disembodied voice than a real bird. The speaker of the poem begins: "Hail to thee, blithe Spirit!" He then goes on to insist, "Bird thou never wert." In his emotional response to the song of a bird, he transforms the creature into an image of himself. He is less interested in the actual bird than in his own emotional and philosophic response to it.

John Keats, by contrast, believes that the poet must have "negative capability," the capacity to see and respond to forms around him without identifying with them. He can enjoy the sounds of the grasshopper and the cricket, delighting in the "poetry of earth," without losing his objectivity (cf. "On the Grasshopper and Cricket"). In his famous "Ode to a Nightingale," he records his delight at the song of a nightingale. In responding to the "happy" song of the bird, he imagines the many generations that have heard this same song, turning the bird into an image of immortality, much like art:

> Thou was not born for death, immortal Bird!
>   No hungry generations tread thee down;
> The voice I hear this passing night was heard
>   In ancient days by emperor and clown:
> Perhaps the self-same song that found a path
>   Through the sad heart of Ruth, when sick for home,
>   She stood in tears amid alien corn.

(Keats, "Ode to a Nightingale")

He ends the ode with a return to reality, wondering at his reverie: "Was it a vision, or a waking dream?" he asks, while noticing that the music has ended. More of a realist than some of his fellow Romantics, Keats tends to return to reality after his flights of fantasy.

The Romantics, who often returned to classical and medieval literature for their inspiration, loved Gothic monsters. Both Keats and Samuel Taylor Coleridge (a somewhat earlier Romantic poet) wrote of blended human-animal creations. Both developed poems about a lamia, a mythic figure that was part snake, part woman. Coleridge uses this concept in "Christabel"(1798), a long poem in which the woman exhibits curious tendencies to hiss and clutch at other people. (He notes that the "lady's eyes they shrunk in her head, / Each shrunk up to a serpent's eye.") In his introductory note about this "tale of witchery," the author explains the lamia character: "Geraldine, of course, is a supernatural spirit of evil, a lovely woman and yet a scaly serpent" (Coleridge, 169).

When Keats wrote his "Lamia" poem, he indicated that he found the inspiration in Burton's *Anatomy of Melancholy*, where Philostratus tells a story about a young philosopher entrapped by his love for this fantastic creature. Classical literature is full of such half-human monsters, some half bulls, some half goats, some half horses. The transformation of humans into alien shapes is the subject of Ovid's famous collection, *The Metamorphoses*. Such legendary creatures as the basilisk (half cock and half snake), which could kill at a glance; the phoenix, a mythical bird which lived between three hundred and five hundred years, burning itself on a funeral pyre and then rising from its own ashes; or the unicorn, a small animal the size of a kid, with a single horn in the center of its forehead, which could be caught only by being trapped by a virgin—these were the delight of medieval and later writers.

Such fabulous monsters are not like those that populate Revelation. St. John's beasts, sometimes coming out of the sea to dominate the land are closer to the vicious were-witch in *Beowulf*. There is nothing seductive about Grendel or his mother. For the medieval world, most of the monsters were symbols of evil, the spawn of Cain, most often portrayed as denizens the infernal regions. They appear as gargoyles on the cathedrals and in the hideous portrayals of the gaping mouth of hell in medieval art.

Modern myth writers, such as C. S. Lewis and Tolkien, use their animal figures as both diabolic monsters and as blessed saviors. The most famous of the latter is Lewis's portrayal of Aslan, the noble, golden lion in his novel *The Lion, the Witch, and the*

Wardrobe (1952). The lion has a long and impressive history as a symbol. In scripture, it is often the fearful wild animal, but also a symbol of strength and beauty. The "Lion of Judah," David, is famous for his courage in battle. Generally, the lion stands for power, majesty, courage, and fortitude. Ferguson notes that "Legendary natural history states that young lions are born dead, but come to life three days after birth when breathed upon by their sire. Thus the lion has become associated with the Resurrection, and is the symbol of Christ, the Lord of Life" (George Ferguson 1966, 21).

In *The Chronicles of Narnia*, Lewis also uses other animal figures, including the gentle beaver family. Lewis is firmly in the Romantic tradition, to which he adds biblical motifs and a strong sense that the imagination is a gift from God. Much of his technique is parallel to children's fairy tales, using animals according to popular views of their traits, interweaving fabulous stories of magic and wonder with moral themes.

Coleridge was also a Christian and a mystic. His poem *Rime of the Ancient Mariner* (1798) is full of Christian symbolism. The killing of the albatross by the Ancient Mariner brings a curse on the ship. The other seamen hang the dead bird about his neck as a sign of his guilt and their obligation to pay for his sin:

And I had done a hellish thing,
And it would work 'em woe;
For all averred, I had killed the bird
That made the breeze to blow.

The moral of this extended ballad is expressed in the Mariner's final words to the Wedding Guest, who has listened to the riveting tale:

Farewell, farewell! but this I tell
To thee, thou Wedding-Guest!
He prayeth well, who loveth well
Both man and bird and beast.
he prayeth best, who loveth best
All things both great and small'
For the dear God who loveth us,
He made and loveth all.

(Coleridge, 159)

One of the most famous fish tales of all time is Herman Melville's *Moby-Dick* (also known as the *Leviathan*, 1851). Although the white whale is the subject of this philosophical novel, it is less a real fish than a symbol. This mythic creature haunts the imagination of the ship's skipper, Ahab, and proves a source of dread for all the crew of the *Pequod*. The monomaniacal quest for this giant whale takes Ahab toward insanity, and finally to death. The final scene shows Moby-Dick, harpooned by Ahab, who is ensnared by the harpoon line. The ship has capsized, and the skipper is carried off in the wake of the whale, following relentlessly in death as he did in life. The whale has been identified by critics as Evil, God, Fate, Primal Good, Accidental Malice, Blood Consciousness, Nature, and so forth (Pops, 725).

The careful study of animals has marked much of the advancement of science in the modern world. With Darwin's epoch-making volume *The Origin of Species by Means of Natural Selection, or the Preservation of Favoured Races in the Struggle for Life* (1859), the possible role of animals as ancestors of humans has dominated Western thought.

All through the nineteenth century, the debate regarding humans' descent from "hairy quadrupeds, arboreal in their habits" (or apes) shocked and intrigued writers. The additional concept of the survival of the fittest, or natural selection, led a writer like Alfred, Lord Tennyson to surmise that nature is "red in tooth and claw." Evolutionary theory implies that only the most brutal of the animals and people have survived, and that God has little role in the whole process. In fact, there is no need for God at all, unless the modern notion of an Intelligent Designer might involve a God who guides this complex process of evolution. Darwin's book turns the idea of the Great Chain of Being on its head, eliminating the Creator, the sense of a rational plan and order to the animal kingdom, and any obligation among the creatures in this chain to serve or nurture the others. If anything, it opens the door for Nietzsche's Super-man, the proper end of evolution.

One of Doris Lessing's story of life in South Africa, entitled "A Sunrise on the Veld," mirrors this Darwinian view of her small world. While the young boy stands and watches a buck with a broken leg being devoured by ants, he is horrified that he cannot interrupt this natural process. At the end, he laments, "Yes, yes. That is what living is."

The dog stories of Jack London often have some of this harsh survival quality. The animals are portrayed as capable of ferocity and of heroism, depending on their environment. A dog like White Wolf, can respond to the brutality of the dog fight, the life in the wild, or the affection and concern of a loving human. He is simply an animal that is shaped by his environment. The dog has the characteristics of both parents, the wild wolf and the domesticated husky. London, however, cannot resist a touch of Romantic sentimentality in making the dog capable of loyalty and love.

The American author Ernest Hemingway, one of the twentieth century's most popular writers, often presents a post-Darwinian view of man and nature. He loves to tell stories of bull fights in Spain and game hunts in Africa. His close observation of nature combines with a delight in the contest, even a pleasure in the bloody victory. The one who survives might be the strongest, or perhaps the cleverest.

The Old Man and the Sea, one of Hemingway's last novels, a short one the size of a novella, tells of an old fisherman going too far out to catch a fish that proves too big for the old man's failing strength and for his tiny boat. The fisherman is not a religious man, and sees the giant fish in realistic terms. It is not as intelligent as he is, so he can outsmart it. Yet he has respect for the fish's power and the determination to live. This is no mystical *Moby Dick*. The prey is never more than a fish, though it becomes "brother fish" after two days and nights of struggle. Returning to the biblical theme of man's domination over nature, the old man plans to kill the fish for his own food and upkeep. The actual killing is quick, not the least bit sentimental. And the subsequent fate of the carcass, which is attacked by sharks, is handled with realism as well. The giant bone structure amazes those back on the shore, but no one turns it into a monument. At the end, it is "now just garbage waiting to go out with the tide." Hemingway and his fisherman admire the beauty of the sea creatures without personifying them, worshipping them, or citing them as indication of God's glory.

Another American writer, Annie Dillard, brings a scientist's love of detail and diversity to her precise descriptions of nature. She even takes time to study insects, amphibians, as well as fish. She finds genuine joy in the splendor that "breaks forth" in nature. In *Pilgrim at Tinker Creek*, she writes of her own experiences, in the tradition of Thoreau's *Walden: of Life in the Woods* (1854). Her close attention to such creatures as butterflies and frogs, and her thrilling insights shock us into larger awareness of the complexity and power of nature. She sees nature as transcendent, leading the thoughtful student to a glimpse of God's power.

This approach is quite different from those who have revived the worship Mother Nature, rejecting the whole biblical narrative of creation. Some modern environmentalists and feminists praise that ancient fertility goddess, the Great Mother, and see humans as nothing more than animals who need to return to *Nature* (personified and capitalized) in order to find the key to life and satisfaction.

By contrast, orthodox Christian writers, often Roman Catholic ones, like Flannery O'Connor, have chosen to study nature as God's handiwork, finding richer insights than Hemingway's or the environmentalists'. O'Connor lived on a farm in Georgia, studied the people around her, and raised "peafowl." In her pleasure with her peacocks, Flannery O'Connor makes much the same point that Gerard Manly Hopkins made a century earlier—that the peacock, when he spreads his wings in an elegant display and turns around for all to see the brilliant eyes in the vivid background, is a reminder of the Holy Spirit and the Glory of God. In her essay on "The King of Birds," she notes that even a simple black woman, when first confronted with this glory, exclaimed, "Amen! Amen!"

Conclusion

Over the years, the battle of the Bible has circled around the ideas that humankind were put on earth to have dominion over nature and to tend to it. The managers of the natural environment see animals as being at our service—as food or labor or companionship. The environmentalists accept an obligation to preserve and to cherish all the species of life granted to us. In either case, there is no confusion about the significance of animals. Unlike the modern ethicist Peter Singer, the majority of Western people have placed animals lower than humans. Singer calls this "Speciesism"—a privileged position awarded to the humans at the expense of the animals. He sees no reason to consider humans of more value than apes.

For many artists, the ultimate dream for humans and animals is the "Peaceable Kingdom." The vision of St. Francis of Assisi, where the animals were perceived as our brothers, is reinforced by the annual gathering of the animals in Christmas crèches. Isaiah says it best, when he dreams of a time when the whole of nature, including the animals, will be free of the curse set upon them in Eden:

> The wolf also shall dwell with the lamb, and the leopard shall lie down with the kid; and the calf and the young lion and the fatling together; and a little child shall lead them.
>
> And the cow and the bear shall feed; their young ones shall lie down together; and the lion shall eat straw like the ox.
>
> And the sucking child shall play on the hold of the asp, and the weaned child shall put his hand on the cocatrice' den.
>
> They shall not hurt nor destroy in all my holy mountain; for the earth shall be full of the knowledge of the Lord, as the waters cover the sea. (Isa. 11:6–9)

See also: **Creation; Nature.**

Bibliography

Blake, William. *Songs of Innocence* and *Songs of Experience*. In *British Poetry and Prose*, Vol. I., ed. Paul Robert Lieder, Robert Morss Lovett, and Robert Kilburn Root. Boston: Houghton Mifflin, 1950.

Chaucer, Geoffrey. *The Canterbury Tales*. New York: Modern Library, 1994.

Coleridge, Samuel Taylor. "Christabel" and *The Rime of the Ancient Mariner.* In *Anthology of Romanticism,* ed. Ernest Bernbaum. New York: The Roland Press Company, 1948.

deGasztold, Carmen Bernos. *Prayers from the Ark.* In *The Bible as/in Literature,* ed. James S. Ackerman and Thayer S. Warshaw. Glenview, IL: Scott Foresman and Company, 1971.

Dillard, Annie. *Pilgrim at Tinker Creek.* New York: HarperCollins, 1995.

Enuma Elish. In *Primal Myths: Creating the World,* ed. Barbara C. Sproul. San Francisco: Harper and Row, 1979.

Ferguson, George. *Signs and Symbols in Christian Art.* New York: Oxford University Press, 1966.

Hemingway, Ernest. *The Old Man and the Sea.* New York: Scribner, 1952.

Keats, John. "Ode to a Nightingale." In *Anthology of Romanticism,* ed. Ernest Bernbaum. New York: The Roland Press Company, 1948.

Lessing, Doris. *African Laughter.* New York: HarperCollins, 1992.

Lewis, C. S. *The Lion, the Witch and the Wardrobe.* New York: HarperEntertainment, 2005.

London, Jack. *White Fang.* New York: Athaneum, 2000.

Lovejoy, Arthur O. *The Great Chain of Being: A Study of the History of an Idea.* New York: Harper and Row, 1960.

Melville, Herman. *Moby-Dick.* Nineola, NY: Dover Publications, 2003.

Orwell, George. *Animal Farm.* New York: Harcourt, Brace, Jovanovich, 1983.

Pope, Alexander. "Essay on Man." In *British Poetry and Prose,* Vol. I., ed. Paul Robert Lieder, Robert Morss Lovett, and Robert Kilburn Root. Boston: Houghton Mifflin, 1950.

Pops, Martin Leonard. "Herman Melville." In *The Reader's Encyclopedia of American Literature,* ed. Max J. Herzberg. New York: Thomas Y. Crowell Company, 1962.

Sproul, Barbara C. *Primal Myths: Creating the World.* San Francisco: Harper and Row, 1979.

Swift, Jonathan. "A Modest Proposal." In *British Poetry and Prose,* Vol. I., ed. Paul Robert Lieder, Robert Morss Lovett, and Robert Kilburn Root. Boston: Houghton Mifflin, 1950.

———. *Gulliver's Travels.* New York: Crown, 1980.

Thomas, Keith. *Man and the Natural World: A History of the Modern Sensibility.* New York: Pantheon Books, 1983.

Twain, Mark. *Adam's Diary.* In *The Bible as/in Literature,* ed. James S. Ackerman and Thager S. Warshaw. Glenview, IL: Scott Foresman and Company, 1971.

Temptation and Sin

Readings

Genesis 2–3
Psalm 1
Jonah
Job
Dante Alighieri, *The Inferno* (1321)
Christopher Marlowe, *The Tragical History of Doctor Faustus* (c. 1590)
John Milton, *Paradise Lost* (1667)
Voltaire, *Candide* (1759)
Johann Wolfgang von Goethe, *Faust* (1790)
Nathaniel Hawthorne, *The Scarlet Letter* (1850)
Fyodor Dostoyevsky, *Crime and Punishment* (1866)
Robert Penn Warren, *All the King's Men* (1946)
Flannery O'Connor, "A Good Man Is Hard to Find" (1955)
Philip Booth, "Original Sequence," from *Letters from a Distant Land* (1957)
C. S. Lewis, *The Screwtape Letters* (1942)

Introduction

> This is an evil among all things that are done under the sun, there is one
> event unto all, yea, also the heart of the sons of men is full of evil, and
> madness is in their heart, while they live, and after that they go to the dead.
> (Eccles. 9:3)

Neither the Jews nor the Christians ignore evil. For them, evil is part of existence
on earth, not an illusion, not a coequal deity. They admit frankly that bad things
do indeed happen to good people. Quite often, this evil that befalls humans comes
as a result of wrongful actions. Sometimes, calamities come without any apparent
reason.

In the realm of natural disasters, earthquakes, tornadoes, fires, hurricanes, floods and droughts come to both the just and the unjust. They wipe out whole cities, innocent children as well as sinful old men. Philosophers have explained our universal experience of pain and death by observing that the earth is not designed for human comfort. Beyond our species, it is home to many other fauna and flora. The design of the universe is not circumscribed by our needs and desires.

Deists believe that God, being good and perfect, must have created the best of all possible worlds. They cite the idea of the Great Chain of Being, which provides for the plenitude of nature, making no special allowances for human well-being. Voltaire's attack on this theory, which he considered simplistic, forms the basis for the great comic novel *Candide* (1759). The young man in the story, Candide, has a tutor, Dr. Pangloss, who subscribes to this line of thought and explains away all of life's vicissitudes by assuming that everything happens for a purpose in this "best of all possible worlds." A British writer of the same period, Alexander Pope, took the philosophy more seriously, citing it as an explanation for his own life of suffering. In *An Essay on Man* (1733–34), he assured his readers that God made humans exactly right for the role they play in this symphony of life. Both Pope and Voltaire wrote eloquently of this philosophy, which became popular in the eighteenth century, and then faded before the much darker view of the naturalists, who were more Darwinian in their view of the malevolence of nature and the hopelessness of humans.

Others have posited that God allows natural catastrophes on earth to test humans. Most people become stronger, better, wiser as a result of such testing—if they survive it. Some believe that God brings disaster on cities or floods regions because of the sins of the locals, just as he did in the time of Noah and Lot. This view appears to be contradicted by both scripture and logic.

Other theories of evil exist in secular and philosophic writings, including the idea that sin, pain, sickness, and catastrophe do not really exist. They are simply figments of the imagination. Most people tend to believe in the reality of their suffering and the presence of evil, though they may disagree on the causes and the cures.

A major cause of evil is the perversity of the human heart. Even when circumstances are comfortable, humans often do cruel and brutal things to one another. They cheat their friends, lie to their families, desert their children, abuse their wives, betray their husbands, murder their neighbors. They take their own talents and pervert them, turning their bodies to repositories for all manner of drugs and diseases. Both sacred and secular literature are full of examples of sinful behavior.

For most Jews and Christians, such evil is explained by people turning away from God, refusing to follow his guidance. In scripture, evil is not a force, but an absence of good. As John expresses it in the opening lines of his Gospel: "And the light shineth in darkness, and the darkness comprehended it not" (John 1:5).

If God is seen as light, evil is nothing more than shadow—the absence of light.

Scripture

The forbidden tree in the Garden of Eden is the Tree of the Knowledge of Good and Evil. Since Adam and Eve already know good, their deliberate exercise of free will results in the choice to know evil. And so they do. From this act of disobedience in the Garden of Eden flows all the evils of the world. The fruits of the sin travel beyond this moment: the first couple are thrust out of Eden, and forced to live in a world of pain, hard work, and broken relationships. Their easy converse with God comes to an end as they are cast out of the Earthly Paradise.

They also discover death. As Philip Booth notes in his poem "Original Sequence," "Time was the apple Adam ate." What the first couple do not realize is that by eating of the tree of the Knowledge of Good and Evil, they miss the opportunity to enjoy the Tree of Life. As Booth notes, by biting into the apple, they "wound the clock." By eating from the Tree of Knowledge, Adam and Eve are expelled from Eden: "And the Lord God said, Behold, the man is become as one of us, to know good and evil, and now, lest he put forth his hand, and take also of the tree of life, and eat, and live forever: Therefore the Lord God sent him forth from the garden of Eden" (Gen. 3:22).

From this moment forward, the ground which humans have been doomed to till for their food is cursed, indicating, according to some commentators, that humans will find nature inhospitable, explaining the devastation of natural disasters. Living "east of Eden," humankind are to know pain, sweat, and tears. Their own child becomes a murderer and an outcast. The continued disobedience explains the vast destruction caused by the Flood of Noah. It also is the justification for the devastation of Sodom and Gomorrah, cities which are known for their cruelty and perversion. For the ancient Jews, all suffering seemed to derive from sin, either the individual's sin, the community's, or from the sin of their ancestors. They understood that God had his hand in history, guiding floods and droughts, bringing plagues of locusts on the Egyptians. Sometimes, in a more benevolent mood, he provided water for his followers and manna from heaven for the faithful.

Scripture deals with several levels of evil behavior among humans: error, sin, and transgression. Error is a simple misunderstanding, which, if followed to its logical conclusion, perverts the moral values and the life of the person. Joshua, for instance, sometimes thinks he understands how to proceed with warfare without first turning to the Lord in prayer before he acts. This could result in catastrophes, as in the case of the failure to take the city of Ai on the first try. The good man may commit an error, be forgiven, and correct it without continued sorrow.

Sin, however, is more fearful. It is the violation of the law of God, or a failure to follow that law. (Crime, which is a violation of human law, often overlaps with sin, as in the case of perjury, theft, or murder.) The sinner can repent, change his behavior, seek forgiveness through prayer and sacrifice, and put himself into conformity with God's will. Peter, who denies his Lord when challenged by strangers, knows that he is wrong. When the cock crows the third time, he realizes that he has sinned and he weeps for shame, acknowledging his guilt for this betrayal of his good master. He falls away briefly, but is soon forgiven and restored, becoming one of the leaders of the early Church. This is the case of a decent man who shows signs of weakness, yet is restored to the community of believers and to his relationship with God.

The transgressor is one whose evil is of a different magnitude. In this case, the action is deliberate and determined. Psalm 1 speaks of such people as the "scornful." They damage their own souls and cause collateral damage to those around them. The evil-doer may even attack the law itself and the God who gave it to humans. Knowing the law, preferring one's own path, and scoffing at any who would stand in their way, the transgressors challenge God. Pride, the preference for one's own will over God's, is at the heart of transgression. Without a complete transformation of character, this evil-doer stands damned for eternity. Such is apparently the case of Judas, who knows Jesus and deliberately chooses to betray him, never turning back to seek forgiveness. His is an example of apostasy, ending in death and damnation.

For most of the Old Testament, sin and suffering appear to be yoked. The sinner can expect God's judgment as a result of the sin. The psalmist admonishes the believer to avoid bad company: not to walk in the counsel of the ungodly, to stand in the way of sinner, or to sit in the seat of the scornful (Psalm 1). This simple message outlines types of depravity, caused largely by turning away from the godly path. The first action is to go along the erroneous road with the person giving ungodly advice, causing the listener to forget God's rule that he must obey the law of Moses, turning neither to the right nor to the left. The second action is to stop and become entangled with the person of sinful actions, not just the one meditating on the wrong things. And the third action is to settle down with those who sneer at the true believers. This pattern takes the pilgrim from a simple act of mistaken fellowship to a deliberate act of evil.

The Proverbs are full of such advice to the unwary, especially young people, who are easily ensnared by bad company, either male or female. Most of the warnings are to young men who need to recognize the traps that evil places along their path through life.

Although the prophets frequently proclaim that Israel's and Judah's tragic circumstances are a result of their sinful ways, suffering and sin are not inevitably linked in scripture. Sometimes, an evil nation is allowed to triumph over the more righteous victim. Sometimes, the good man is killed. Morality and decency are not always rewarded on this earth, nor is evil always punished. The author of Ecclesiastes is bitter in his cynical judgment of the vanity of all human life. The good person is no more likely to win a life of sunshine and happiness than the evil one. Justice must often wait for the world to come.

When Jesus is asked who had sinned to cause the fall of the Tower of Siloam and the deaths of the 18 people there, he indicates that divine justice is not always so easy to determine. In this case, the accident was not a punishment for their bad behavior (Luke 13:4). Nor did he agree that the blind man he healed had been born blind because of his or his parents' sins (John 9:1). Nonetheless, good behavior, morality, and godliness are usually rewarded by peace of mind and blessedness.

One of the strongest rejections of this clear cause-and-effect relationship between sin and suffering is the Book of Job. When Job's friends suggest that this good man is suffering for his iniquities, he rejects their arguments. He insists that, if he is weighed in the balance, God will see his integrity. He has given to the poor, acted justly in matters of business, been faithful to his wife, his family and his Creator. Finally, taking his case directly to God, he complains that he is being punished without reason and demands an explanation. It is then that the voice out of the whirlwind thunders the series of rhetorical questions that puts an end to his complaints.

> Who is this that darkens counsel by words without knowledge?
> Gird up your loins like a man,
>   I will question you, and you shall declare to me.
> Where were you when I laid the foundation of the earth?
>   Tell me if you have understanding. (Job 38:1–4)

And on God goes, challenging poor, frightened Job with a series of unanswerable questions, not pausing for a response. At one point, he demands of Job: "Will you condemn me that you may be justified?" Job clearly wants to blame God for his own misfortunes. When the speech comes to an end, Job responds meekly and with full acceptance of his inadequacy:

> I know that thou canst do all things,
>   and that no thought can be witholden from thee …

Therefore have I uttered that I understood not,
    things too wonderful for me, which I knew not....
I had heard of thee by the hearing of the ear,
    but now mine eye seeth thee;
therefore I abhor myself,
    and repent in dust and ashes. (Job 42:1–6)

This ancient story about the justice of human suffering begins and ends with the mystery of God's will. Beyond human knowledge, God works his divine purpose. We here on earth know only the landscape of pain and death. Joy and blessedness come when God so wills—as he does at the end of Job's story. As Richard Eberhart says, "God does not live to explain" (quoted in Ackerman, 284).

In scripture and in literature, we see many instances of temptation to sin. Usually, the sinner, motivated by the desire for wealth or power or physical pleasure or some other perceived "good," rationalizes the violation, steps over the moral barriers, and enters the land of sin.

One of the great Psalms of David chronicles his desolate mood after he has succumbed to the temptation of Bathsheba, both to claim her as his concubine and then to have her husband murdered. He writes poignantly:

Out of the depths have I cried unto thee, O Lord.
    Lord, hear my voice: let thine ears be attentive to the voice of my supplications.
    If thou, Lord, shouldest mark iniquities, O Lord, who shall stand?
    But there is forgiveness with thee, that thou mayest be feared. (Psalm 130)

At the end of the psalm, David turns from his individual sin to general iniquity, pleading that Israel be forgiven.

This particular distress of King David involves at least three of what are later to be called the "Seven Deadly Sins": lust, sloth, and avarice. As the tale is recorded in 2 Samuel 11, it "came to pass ... at the time when kings go forth to battle.... David tarried still at Jerusalem." David has won the respect and love of his people by his prowess in battle. Now, in the springtime when his men are off fighting, he chooses to linger in his splendid court, watching his neighbor's wife bathing on the roof of the next home. He "sent messengers and took her; and she came in unto him, and he lay with her." He plans on keeping this adultery a secret, but then she returns with the chilling words: "I am with child."

It is at this point that David compounds the sin, turning it into a conspiracy to commit murder. He orders Bathsheba's husband Uriah to return home in hopes of convincing him that he is the father of the child. But Uriah's faithfulness to his role as a warrior keeps him from his wife's bed. Then David finds himself moving into still deeper evil, ordering that Uriah be placed in the front of the fighting so that he will be killed.

At the end of this time, Bathsheba mourns for her husband. And when the mourning is past, David sends a servant to fetch her to his house; she becomes his wife, and bears him a son. It is clear that David believes that he and his paramour have won the day: their deception has succeeded and they are blessed with a child. Their punishment comes quickly. First Nathan the prophet uses a parable so that David convicts himself of his sin. Nathan prophesies that David's house will face evils as a result of this sin. Then the child dies, as Nathan has warned. All of David's repentance and fasting are to no avail. At the end of this terrible time, when the child is dead, "David arose from the earth, and washed, and anointed himself, and changed his apparel, and came into the house of the lord and worshipped" (2 Sam. 11:26–27; 12:1–20). The cycle of temptation, sin, repentance, and redemption is complete.

An earlier scene of temptation and sin occurs after Joshua defeats Jericho. God dictates the terms of conquest of that Canaanite city, insisting on *harem*, the total destruction of all the people, goods, and animals (except for one friend who has helped them and for the metal which belongs to God). Achan, one of his warriors, cannot resist a beautiful cloak imported from Babylon—a thing of special beauty. Nor can he resist the gold and silver which he has found. Taking these items to his tent, he buries them. The clear violation of the covenant, brings a curse down on all of Israel. For the sin of one man, all are punished. When Joshua falls on the ground, begging God to send them back if He does not plan to give them victory, he discovers that one of his own men has brought this curse on them. Led finally to Achan, he confronts the man, who confesses: "It is true. I have sinned against the God of Israel" (Josh. 7:20). After this confession, Joshua orders that Achan be stoned to death and his family and possessions be burned—just as God had ordered for the whole of Jericho.

Sin is no light concern in the Old Testament. It involves not only the individual but his family, his tribe, and his whole nation. In this case, it is a specific violation of the covenant and an act of blasphemy, for he has stolen that which was dedicated to God.

In the New Testament, the great story of temptation is that of Jesus in the wilderness (Matt. 4:1–11). This remarkable dialogue pits Jesus against Satan. In this narrative we see the different types of sin that confront humans and the good man's battle against each. For 40 days, paralleling the Israelites 40 forty years in the wilderness, Jesus fasts and prays in anticipation of his ministry. At the end of that time, Satan comes to him three times, first suggesting that he prove that he is the Son of God by turning the stones into bread. It would be a natural temptation for the hungry man to accept this challenge and find this comfort by eating a piece of bread. Jesus responds: "Man shall not live by bread alone, but by every word that proceedeth out of the mouth of God."

The second temptation is set on the pinnacle of the Temple. Satan challenges him to prove that he is the Son of God by casting himself down, ironically quoting scripture: "for it is written, He shall give his angels charge concerning thee: and in their hands they shall bear thee up, lest at any time thou dash thy foot against a stone." Jesus refuses to "tempt the Lord," even though such a dramatic event would certainly proclaim his deity and bring followers to him in droves.

The third, and in some ways the most serious, temptation is set on a high mountain, with the kingdoms of the world before Jesus. Satan offers to give him all things if he will fall down and worship him. This temptation Jesus rejects scornfully, "Get thee hence, Satan: for it is written, Thou shalt worship the Lord thy God, and him only shalt thou serve" (Luke 4:1–13).

Jesus chooses to follow a humble path of ministry, gathering his disciples one-by-one, teaching them by word and deed, living quietly, walking among the crowds, and performing his miracles all over Galilee and beyond. Regardless of the gentle nature of his teachings and his life, his incendiary ideas lead Jesus into confrontations with authorities and to the death usually saved for a criminal. Here is the supreme example of the good man facing the unjust suffering and death.

In pagan literature, the death of Jesus on the cross would be labeled a "tragedy." It has all the potential for a classical tragedy, with the suffering of the good man, and a man's gentle response to unwarranted persecution. In this story of the final week, the supplication that God "take this cup from me," the arrest, the beatings, the trials, the brutal path to Gethsemane, his anguish as he is nailed to the cross and set between two thieves, we have the stuff of tragic drama. When Jesus cries out "It is done," we seem to have the climax of the episode. But in this case, death is not the end. After the burial and the three days in the grave, Christ rises again, first showing himself to the women at the tomb and then to his disciples and others. He talks with them, walks with them, eats with them. They reach out and touch his resurrected body before he is lifted up into heaven. This is not the way tragedies end.

The Christian story is therefore not tragedy in the classical sense. It is not the tale of a death of a good (though flawed) man who ends in disaster and death, but rather it is the dramatic account of a perfect man who chooses to suffer and die for the salvation of sinners. In the end, he is resurrected and goes to sit on the right hand of God. For the Christian, death is not the end, for Death itself is dead. It is for this reason that Dante called his great poem of the afterlife *The Divine Comedy*. In it, Dante follows the path of Christ from his descent into Hell, through the days on earth to his heavenly home—a happy conclusion to the suffering.

Literature

For the Greeks, *tragedy* had a very different meaning. According to Aristotle's *Poetics*, a tragedy is the story of a pre-eminently good man (sometimes a woman) who has a tragic flaw, usually *hubris*. This sin of pride leads the man or woman to challenge Fate and bring about his or her own downfall. Thus, Oedipus tries to escape his Fate, the prediction that he will murder his father and marry his mother, not realizing that the people who raised him are his adoptive parents. Meeting a man as arrogant as he at the "place where the three roads met," he challenges and kills the king of Thebes, whom he later discovers to be his father. He then visits the kingdom from which the king came, marries the widowed queen, who turns out to be his natural mother, and only learns the truth of his life and the irony of his prophesy much later.

Oedipus's response to the full recognition of his deep evil, performed unknowingly, is to put out his own eyes and wander as a pariah until he dies. His suffering serves as an expiation for his thoughtless actions and for his challenge of Fate. Ironically, by seeking to do good, he inadvertently does evil. Although the plays about Oedipus are powerful, they hardly teach a lesson for the common person. The role of Fate here seems to remove the responsibility from the hero and muddle the moral of the myth.

Contrast this concept of tragedy with the Christian "divine comedy," which assumes a place of judgment and justice after death. If death is the end of existence, then dying is indeed a tragedy. If the hero is also noble and falls from great heights, the tragedy seems even more frightening. In Aristotle's view, the audience's recognition of their own lives in the dramatic presentation should cause them fear and pity, thus producing a *catharsis*—a purging of the emotion by watching the great man or woman brought low.

The greatest of all stories involving the tragic fall is the tale of Lucifer. The Evil One, also called Satan and Mephistopheles, makes only a few appearances in scripture. Isaiah tells us of his fall when Lucifer led the rebellion of the angels. Job tells of his daily activities. The Gospels reveal his strategies for winning souls to his side. Disguised as the serpent in the Garden of Eden, he discloses his techniques: lying to Eve, tempting her to eat of the forbidden fruit, and scurrying off when God approaches.

In secular literature, Satan appears only rarely as the personification of evil. Dante sees him as the monster with three faces at the very core of hell, which was formed by his great fall. In darkness and icy cold, he gnaws at the three humans who symbolize the very worst of human sins, the betrayal of a benevolent master: Judas, Brutus, and Cassius. This is the region of Traitors, called *Judecca* after Judas. Judas himself is the betrayer of God, Brutus and Cassius the betrayers of Caesar, a symbol of human society or the Roman Empire. In Dante, Satan is passive and hideous, not an active or attractive force (Alighieri, 289).

Christopher Marlowe's Mephistopheles is a milder, more human image of a lesser Satan, who is intent on cheating Dr. Faustus out of his immortal soul. Only after the agreement is signed in blood does he reveal that hell is here and now for the lost sinner. Goethe, who drew heavily on Marlowe's play to write his own poetic drama two centuries later, sees Mephistopheles as a genteel man about town. Both authors tell the story of the famous alchemist whose hunger for knowledge overpowered his judgment. The story has been retold in various forms through the years, especially in American films and plays, where the satanic figure is a shrewd bargainer offering the willing victim whatever pleasures he desires in return for his soul.

Not all writers assume that evil is obvious or ugly. Milton presents his Lucifer with vestiges of his previous splendor still lingering about him. He is still a proud and beautiful angel, though fallen. And he proves he is still a charismatic leader who can stir up his demonic troops. Some critics later complained that, by modeling his Satan on Prometheus, Milton makes a Greek hero of him.

C. S. Lewis characterizes his demonic figure in *Screwtape Letters* as a subordinate demon in a bureaucratic world. He is comic in his frustration, eager to blame others for his failure to pervert the desires of the new Christian. Unlike Milton, Lewis portrays most evil as trivial and subversive, not heroic and robust. After watching the Nazis being sentenced at the Nuremberg Trials, Hannah Arendt spoke of the "banality" of evil. These war criminals explained their slaughter of millions of Jews by whining that they were simply following orders.

The melodramatic efforts to personify evil came to a climax among the Gothic writers of the Romantic era. In stories like *Dracula, The Monk, Frankenstein,* and *Dr. Jekyll and Mr. Hyde,* the authors create monstrous figures of supernatural fearfulness. Exaggerated descendants of Milton's Satan, they are more powerful, more sinister, more hideous than natural sinners. They lurch across the frozen tundra, drain the blood from their victims' necks, transform themselves by chemical means into villains one day and saints the next. They are designed to frighten and horrify the reader, not necessarily to reform sinners.

Robert Louis Stevenson's Mr. Hyde is a Victorian gentleman, who dabbles in evil, drinking a potion to turn himself into Dr. Jekyll. This thriller is based on the idea of a double personality, part good, part evil. In the end, evil dominates the poor man, rendering him unable to return to his previous goodness.

Even Oscar Wilde, a brilliant end-of-the-century writer known largely for his dissipated life and comic plays, wrote a dramatic cautionary tale of the effects of sin. In *The Picture of Dorian Gray* (1890–91), his hero breaks every possible rule while remaining handsome and young physically. In the meantime, his magical portrait grows more and more grotesque until the point when the man seeks to destroy the painting and stabs himself instead, dying a disgusting and ugly old reprobate. The story is a variation of the Faust legend, with a curse placed on the portrait that brings forth a Mephistolean figure, who lures Dorian into a profligate life. His pursuit of pleasure and vice, the new Hedonism of the period, and his refusal to repent at the end point to his eternal damnation.

The legacy of Gothic literature has carried over in America with the stories of Edgar Allan Poe, who loved the crumbling mansion, the mad villain, and the helpless victim. This damned hero of his tales may be haunted by perverse hungers, ancient wrongs, or unnatural appetites for mutilation and bestiality. Modern horror stories continue to delight readers, such as those who read of Steven King's characters torture one another as they reveal their true, depraved selves.

Some of these writers were influenced by the discovery of the savage cultures that Joseph Conrad wrote of so powerfully in his *Heart of Darkness* (1902). In this voyage into the darkness of the African continent and the human heart, Conrad reveals the innate desire to dominate and destroy. The central figure in the story, Kurtz, establishes himself as a god with the natives and reduces them to slavery as he brutally raids the area in search of ivory. His hut is surrounded by severed heads that suggest his vicious techniques for control. This journey into evil is often interpreted as a statement of specific evils of the time, including the colonization of third-world countries by the European powers. Scenes of temptation are the basic stuff of literature. The will to satisfy the ego or the appetites invariably clashes with the clear understanding of the will of God for the person.

In *Crime and Punishment*, Dostoyevsky presents a brilliant psychological analysis of the mind of a man determined to transgress the law. We have Raskolnikov, a bright young university student who is fixated on the idea that certain exceptional men have the right to make their own laws, to kill, to steal, to do as they choose. Napoleon is his model, a man who killed vast numbers of people and yet is celebrated as a hero, not a murderer. Assuming he is one such exceptional man, Raskolnikov. chooses a pawnbroker to murder and rob, plotting the action precisely. He carries it out in a feverish, compulsive burst of activity, finding several problems along the way, including the sudden entrance of the pawnbroker's sister. He takes an axe along under his coat, kills both women in a bloody scene, and escapes without being noticed. From that point to the end of the book, he deals with his guilt and confusion: he is unable even to count the money he has stolen and hides the bag of loot rather than using it for the purposes he intended. He becomes obsessive about discovering what others know about the crime, acts suspiciously when questioned by the police, comes close to admitting his guilt to several people.

He finally chooses to tell the whole story to a young woman, a prostitute he has come to adore as a kind of saint, Sonia. She is horrified, but does not turn against him. She insists he must repent that he has sinned by shedding blood, regardless of his insistence that the old woman was nothing but a "louse," a worthless creature. Sonia tells him he must go the police, confess, and expiate his sin. She promises to leave her life of prostitution, take the money she has suddenly acquired by a gift, and go with him if he is sent to Siberia.

He confesses to the police, faces a trial, makes no excuse for his violent action, and accepts his punishment. After serving some time in Siberia, with gentle Sonia living nearby as his own private saint, he is redeemed by love. "They were renewed by love; the heart of each held infinite sources of life for the heart of the other." As Dostoyevsky notes, "Life had stepped into the place of theory." Raskolnikov now begins reading the New Testament looking first at the story of the raising of Lazarus. This is his own resurrection from the dead.

Flannery O'Connor makes this point over and over in her short stories of the twentieth-century American South. A Roman Catholic, she tells her stories in a country accent flavored with sardonic wit. Her matrons are church-going middle-class women, who believe that most people are essentially "good." In "A Good Man Is Hard to Find," she reveals the silliness of this assumption by confronting the shallow, chattering grandmother with a murdering thug. When the family leaves the straight road for the byway that the grandmother wants, they end up with an accident: the hidden cat jumps out of the cage, the father veers off the road, and the family is scattered all about the ditch. Soon another car approaches—one that looks like a hearse. Out of it come three men, one of whom is the "Misfit." As scripture has admonished, the family should have been suspicious of the "lion" that lurks beside the path, but they believe in foolish bromides about the essential decency of country folks. The grandmother insists, "I know you're a good man. You don't look a bit like you have common blood. I know you must come from nice people!"

The escaped convicts take the family into the woods two-by-two to shoot them. Meanwhile, the old lady prattles on to the Misfit. He turns out to have a clearer idea of Christianity than she does.

> "Jesus was the only One that ever raised the dead," The Misfit continued, "and He shouldn't have done it. He thrown everything off balance. If He did what He said, then it's nothing for you to do, but throw away everything and follow Him, and if He didn't, then it's nothing for you to do but enjoy the few minutes you got left the best way you can—by killing somebody or burning down his house or doing some other meanness to him. No pleasure but meanness." (O'Connor, 152)

When the grandmother replies idiotically, "Why you're one of my babies," he simply shoots her, insisting she needs that, but ending, "It's no real pleasure in life."

O'Connor rarely explains her enigmatic and abrupt stories, using our shocked reaction to force us into a radical reconsideration of our own assumptions. In this story, we also find ourselves annoyed by the prattling grandmother, but comforted by the idea that she means well. The stark notion that Satan lurks by the side of the road like a raging lion seems ridiculous in twentieth-century rural Georgia. But there he is in all his viciousness. As it turns out, Red Sammy, the owner of the barbeque place is right in his assertion that "a good man is hard to find."

We are all "conceived in sin and born in iniquity." This particular biblical phrasing comes from the cynical lips of another Southern character—Willy Stark, the politician at the center of Robert Penn Warren's masterpiece, *All the King's Men*. Willy confides in his friend that his early training at a Presbyterian Sunday School has helped him in politics. Beginning with the basic assumption that all people are sinners, even those who seem most distinguished and virtuous, he tells his associate, "There is always something." Unfortunately for Willy, he is a believer in total depravity without the follow-up of contrition and hope of redemption. He believes in himself, not in God, making of himself a petty tyrant (to do good as he sees it) and making of his useless son an idol. The story is based on the career of Huey Long, the famous political force in Louisiana during the Depression. Eventually, everything good in his life—his marriage, his son, his dream of helping poor people, his friendships, and his own integrity—become twisted. A man who starts out hoping unselfishly to help the people of his state becomes a living symbol of the sinister corrupting force of absolute power and the inherit evil in the heart of mankind.

Conclusion

Disasters such as floods and hurricanes and tsunamis and earthquakes in scripture are often attributed to God. Certainly the plagues that struck Egypt are the handiwork of God as is the plague that decimates the army of Sennacherib, who are intent on attacking Jerusalem. The scripture's use of God-generated disasters is usually connected with some refusal to bow to God's will—such as the uncivilized treatment of the visiting angels in Sodom and Gomorrah or the Pharaoh's refusal to let God's people go. Some attribute such actions as the parting of the Red Sea, the opening of the waters of the River Jordan, or the fall of the walls of Jericho to God's use of natural forces—tidal waves or earthquakes.

In secular literature as in the sacred, the more subtle and realistic vision of evil comes in the form of "normal" people behaving badly. The everyday sins of lust, covetousness, anger, pride, jealousy, and greed can consume a person, twisting a once noble mind into a sick and degraded one.

In scripture, the Evil One constantly struggles for domination, but God remains in control. People repent of their sins, pray for forgiveness, and try to reform their lives. In older literature, this is the most frequent pattern, even in monstrous Gothic tales. The monsters appear, as in the Book of Revelation, and seem to prevail for the time being. The Whore of Babylon or the Beast out of the Sea or the Antichrist may seem to be triumphant, but God is the final victor, making all things right at last.

See also: **Creation; Good People; The Hero; The Journey of Life; Nature; War.**

Bibliography

Ackerman, James S., and Thayer S. Warshaw. *The Bible as/in Literature.* New York: Scott, Foresman and Company, 1976.

Alighieri, Dante. *The Divine Comedy.* Trans., Dorothy L. Sayers. New York: Basic Books, 1973.

Bonhoeffer, Dietrich. *Creation and Fall: Temptation.* New York: Macmillan Publishing Company, 1959.

Booth, Philip. "Original Sequence," from *Letters from a Distant Land.* In *The Bible as/in Literature,* ed. James S. Ackerman and Thayer S. Warshaw. New York: Scott, Foresman and Company, 1976.

Dostoyevsky, Fyodor. *Crime and Punishment.* Trans., Constance Ganett. New York: Modern Library, 1994.

Goethe, Johann Wolfgang von. *Faust.* Trans., George Madison Priest. Chicago: Encyclopoedia Britannica, 1955.

Hawthorne, Nathaniel. *The Scarlet Letter.* Belmont, CA: Fearon Education, 1991.

Hick, John. "The Problem of Evil." In *The Encyclopedia of Philosophy,* Vol. 3. New York: Macmillan Publishing Company, 1967.

Lewis, C. S. *The Screwtape Letters.* New York: Macmillan, 1961.

Lovejoy, Arthur. *The Great Chain of Being: A Study of the History of an Idea.* New York: Harper and Row, 1936.

Marlowe, Christopher. *The Tragical History of Doctor Faustus.* In *Typical Elizabethan Plays.* Ed., Felix Emmanuel Schelling and Matthew Wilson Black. New York: Harper and Brothers Publishers, 1949.

Milton, John. Paradise Lost. In *The Student's Milton,* ed. Frank Allen Patterson. New York: Appleton-Century-Crofts, 1930.

O'Connor, Flannery. "A Good Man Is Hard to Find." In *Collected Works.* New York: Literary Classics of United States, 1988.

Speiser, E. A. *Genesis: A New Translation.* The Anchor Bible. Garden City, NY: Doubleday, 1979.

Voltaire. *Candide.* New York: Modern Library, 2002.

Warren, Robert Penn. *All the King's Men.* San Diego, CA: Harcourt Brace Jovanovich, 1990.

God's Love, Humans' Response

Readings

Introduction

> For God so loved the world, that he gave his only begotten Son, that
> whosoever believeth in him should not perish, but have everlasting life.
> (John 3:16)

God is love. Love is an essential part of his personality. It was his motive in the Creation. It was also the reason for allowing his creatures free will, the choice of loving him in return. It was love that led him to chastise his children, to protect them, to perfect them, and to redeem them.

Because of love, God chooses Abraham, blesses Israel, and gives his Son to save the world. The Incarnation and the redemption of humankind are evidence of his love. In return, he expects that humans will love him, honor him, and obey him. The relationship between the Creator and his creations has been difficult from the very beginning. Abraham bargains with God for the salvation of Sodom and Gomorrah;

Jacob wrestles with God; Moses pleads that God choose someone else to lead the Hebrews out of Egypt, Jonah tries to talk him out of saving Nineveh; and even Jesus begs him to "take this cup from me." Desiring that the love mankind feels for him be freely given, he allows humans to have free will. This introduces both obedience and disobedience, forgiveness and anger, shame and humility into human reaction to this incredible gift. The Bible is the account of this great love story.

Scripture

God's love for humans is both collective and personal. Only three times does God express his love for an individual: with Solomon (2 Sam. 12:24, Neh. 13:26); and the Messiah (Isa. 48:14). He also says, at the moment of Jesus's baptism by John the Baptist, "This is my beloved Son, in whom I am well pleased" (Matt. 3:17). Paul says of David's calling by God, "I have found David the son of Jesse, a man after mine own heart, which shall fulfil my will" (Acts 13:24). The love he feels for David and Solomon may well be symbolic of his love for his people, Israel. Like his erring people, these monarchs do not deserve the love and blessings he lavishes on them.

God's love for Israel is not based on their faithfulness or any virtue he discovers in this people. He chooses them before they even exist, from the foundations of the earth. He cherishes them, saves them from slavery, teaches them his law, nurtures them, and leads them in their battle for the Promised Land. One of the great miracles of all time is God's preservation of this people. Long after the Sumerians, Assyrians, Canaanites, and all the others have disappeared, the Jews have survived. They are well aware of this unfailing love, which the psalmist proclaims fills the earth and "reaches to heaven" (Ps. 33:5, 36:5).

The prophet Hosea reveals that God's love of Israel is like the love of a husband for a wife, even when she breaks faith with him. The phrasing of the first commandment given to Moses is startlingly personal. He tells his beloved people:

> I am the Lord thy God, which have brought thee out of the land of Egypt, out of the house of bondage. Thou shalt have no other gods before me. Thou shalt not make unto thee any graven image, or any likeness of any thing that is in heaven above, or that is in the earth beneath, or that is in the water under the earth. Thou shalt not bow down thyself to them, nor serve them; for I the Lord thy God am a jealous God, visiting the iniquity of the fathers upon the children unto the third and fourth generation of them that hate me; And showing mercy unto thousands of them that love me, and keep my commandments. (Exod. 20:2–6)

He speaks to them like a jealous husband protecting his wife from temptations by other men. In spite of Israel's disobedience, God tells his wayward and adulterous people, "I have loved you with an everlasting love" (Jer. 31:3). Even when they break the covenant with him, he forgives them again and again.

Nonetheless, the other side of his remarkable love for his people is his fierce wrath at them when they offend him and at those who seek to lead the Hebrews astray or hurt them. The Psalms are full of the wrath of God, and at the gratitude of the psalmist when this wrath destroys Israel's tormentors. The enemies of Israel are seen as the enemies of God, well deserving their slaughter. God also threatens to love this chosen people no more (Hos. 9:15), perhaps meaning that he will cease to be their God if they cease to honor him. In spite of this threat, God has continued to love Israel with an "everlasting love."

In the Incarnation, God reveals his love even more fully. The term "beloved" or "only-beloved" is used only in references to Christ: "The Father loveth the Son and hath given all things into his hand" (John 3:34). John, the Gospel writer most consumed by the inspired love of God, notes: "For God sent not his Son into the world to condemn the world; but that the world through him might be saved" (John 3:17). In these quotations we see the broadening of God's love beyond Israel to include the "world."

His love is nonetheless quite personal. Jesus notes that God the Father is concerned for each individual and knows the very hairs on our heads. The psalmist says that the Lord has known him from the womb, that he knows his going out and his coming in. It is a love that is deeper than a mother for her children (Isa. 49:15; 66:13).

The appropriate human response to such *agape*-love is worship of God and love of fellow human beings. When a lawyer among the Pharisees asks Jesus, "Master, which is the great commandment in the law?" Jesus responds: "Thou shalt love the Lord thy God with all thy heart, and with all thy soul, and with all thy mind. This is the first and great commandment, And the second is like unto it, Thou shalt love thy neighbor as thyself" (Matt. 22:35–39). In this response, Jesus is quoting the Old Testament. In the midst of the listing of laws concerning neighbors runs the constant refrain: "Hear, O Israel: The Lord our God is one Lord; And thou shalt love the Lord thy God with all thine heart, and with all thy soul, and with all thy might" (Deut. 6:4–5). This is the great obligation of God's creatures—to love him with all their power.

Occasionally, the psalmist expresses something of this ideal response of the human to the love of God, panting and thirsting after God, noting that love is better than life itself. In Psalm 43:2, the psalmist proclaims "with my whole being I thirst for God." The singer is thrilled with the unfailing love of God, which is as wide as the heavens. For him, the worship in the temple serves to reenact the story of God's true love for his people (Ps. 48:9). This powerful response of the believer to God's bounty and his faithfulness provides a model for the community. At the same time, the God portrayed in the Psalms is sometimes a fearsome God, full of anger at Israel and at Israel's enemies. His power and majesty require that his people bow down before him, praise him, and acknowledge his gracious gifts. He is not just another person, not just a king, but the creator, sustainer, guardian, and judge of all mankind. His people realize they must approach his holy presence with awe as well as affection.

God requires that those who love him worship him and obey his law. The covenant that God establishes with Moses continues under the leadership of Joshua, whose task is to settle his people in the Promised Land. God blesses his people with this land on the condition that they remain faithful to him. Joshua is told that he must obey the law that God gave Moses, not turning to the right or to the left (Josh. 1:7) in order to receive God's promises. He and his people are to enjoy God's guidance and blessing only so long as they keep their covenant with their Lord.

They soon forget their obligations to their loving and generous Father, turning to the pagan idols that lure them into the very worship so clearly forbidden in the first commandment. The proliferation of burnt offerings and regulations as a substitute for a "broken and a contrite heart" proves abhorrent to God. He seeks the full-hearted love of humans, not ritual actions of worship. The worship is intended to serve as an outward symbol of their awe, gratitude, shame, and faith. The prophets warn the Jews that this pretence of worship, no matter how lavish, is no substitute for loving God with all their hearts.

Jesus provides a living, human example of the kind of perfection that God asks humans to seek. He also reveals a glimpse of the face of God, telling his disciples that if they have seen him, they have seen the Father. As a manifestation of God's love, Jesus lives a life filled with acts of compassion, healing, and teaching. The Beatitudes are full of advice for deeper love among humans, a humble view of self. In his gentle acceptance of suffering and death, Jesus reveals himself as the "Suffering Servant," a willing sacrifice revealing God's love for humankind.

We are admonished to become "perfect," in the image of God and of his son. Jesus explains this more precisely:

> But I say unto you, Love your enemies, bless them that curse you, do good to them that hate you, and pray for them that despitefully use you, and persecute you; That ye may be the children of your Father which is in heaven; for he maketh his sun to rise on the evil and on the good, and sendeth rain on the just and on the unjust. For if ye love them which love you, what reward have ye? Do not even the publicans the same? … Be ye therefore perfect, even as your Father which is in heaven is perfect. (Matt. 5:44–48)

Having been forgiven countless times by a long-suffering God, humans are expected to show their love of God by forgiving their neighbors, and enemies, "seventy times seven."

The commandment that the early Church accepts in response to God's loving gift to them, is to worship him and to love one another. They are expected to be recognized by their love. Seeing themselves as partners in the New Covenant, replacing Israel as God's chosen people (Gal. 6:16; Eph. 5:25), they accept the obligation to teach the whole world of God's immortal love.

At the center of the Christian message is *agape*-love, the love of God, whose unfathomable love for the world is beyond human understanding. The New Testament is full of admonitions to love, explanations of specific circumstances requiring love, encouragement for those who have showered love on their fellow Christians, and expressions of the overflowing love that the apostles feel for their God and mankind. When Peter sees the resurrected Christ, Jesus asks him, "Do you love me?" Peter protests that he does. The third time Jesus repeats the question, Peter is hurt and protests, "Lord, you know all things; you know that I love you." Then Jesus commands him, "Feed my sheep" (John 21:17).

For the disciples and apostles, the leaders of the early Christian Church, their obligation is clear. They must mirror the love of Christ by feeding their flocks, being kind and gentle to those they lead, and proclaiming the great love of God to the entire world. The Revelation of John takes this epic of God's love into the future, ending with the Bridal Feast of the Lamb, the consummation of the love story between God and humans first introduced in Genesis.

Literature

The Bible's great drama of a loving God in a continuing relationship with his creation is quite different from the central narrative of other religions. The Greeks had a goddess of love, Aphrodite, who was chiefly responsible for physical attraction. Beautiful and faithless, she loved a few of the gods and a few humans, but proved selfish and peevish in most of her affections. She was not the goddess of marriage or of sexual power, nor was she the goddess of fertility. Demeter, Hera, and Eros had their roles in encouraging affection and bringing it to fruition. None of these gods loved all of humanity. The Greek gods did not create or sustain life; their involvement in affairs on earth was motivated by jealousy or spite more often than by love. The *Iliad* and the *Odyssey* are both full of evidence that different gods had favorites on earth, whom they helped in their activities, but none (other than Prometheus) felt a generalized love or even sympathy for humankind.

The Greeks responded to this family of gods, by choosing to worship the gods of their own cities, the gods they thought to be powerful enough to be useful, or those who for some reason favored them. They felt no special obligation to love either the gods or one another.

The Greek vocabulary of love was both extensive and specific. The Greeks had words for heterosexual, homosexual, parental, filial, conjugal, fraternal, patriotic, and other kinds of love. Rather than *agape,* the love of God, most were associated with *eros* or *philos,* physical attraction or friendship. Unfortunately for those trying to analyze these variant forms of love, both Greek literature and Greek translations of the Bible tend to use these terms in overlapping ways, often appearing in the same work with variant meanings.

In his justly famous *Symposium,* Plato pictures a group of friends gathering to eat and drink and talk about love. Socrates leads the discussion, making sure that the topic is carefully defined and described. Others give examples that reveal their own personalities and lives, providing opportunities for colorful stories and arguments as they tease one another. Because the speakers are friends and lovers, the discussion begins with the love of attractive young men. It then moves beyond the appealing individual to the concept of the ladder of love. For Plato, human love begins with attraction on a physical level, moves up the ladder to a love of wisdom and immortality, dropping off the lower rungs of the ladder as the aspirant climbs upward. Beginning with a desire for a specific beautiful person, love becomes increasingly spiritual. Love then aspires to ideal beauty and wisdom and goodness, which are within reach at the highest rung of the ladder.

For Plato, the realm of the ideal is without personality or specificity. Unlike the very personal God of both Jews and Christians, he venerates abstract Ideals—the Good, the True, the Beautiful. It is therefore impossible to speak of "God's love" in this context, since there is no specific god capable of feelings about individuals or groups. Plato's abstractions cannot walk in the garden in the cool of the day with his beloved Adam, inviting his love in a gentle manner.

This is directly contrary to the Hebrew concept of God's love, which is revealed in history and touches individual lives. God is not an abstraction in Judeo-Christian thought. Literary expressions of this concept came, at first, through the confessional and meditative literature of the saints and mystics.

Augustine, a fourth-century North African scholar, who was converted to Christianity and became one of the finest early spokesmen for the faith tells the story of his spiritual journey in his *Confessions* (c. 397). Augustine, who like many Christian philosophers was interested in Platonism, uses Plato's ladder of love to describe his own path to God. He begins his ascent of the ladder with selfish love, intending to please no one but himself. This hedonistic part of his autobiography is the section most often discussed by readers, who find his vivid revelations of his youthful adventures read like a novel. He writes of knowing that in his youth he causes sorrow to his beloved mother, who is a dedicated Christian; but he is reluctant to repent of his lust and self-indulgence. The death of a friend turns his attention to the love of his fellow men, leading him to organize a small group of fellow Christians who would live together in charity, sharing their belongings. Although this idea comes to nothing, it leads him to increasingly unselfish love. As one scholar explains his transformation, "Through self-knowledge he learned to look upon the eternal light and ultimately came to the complete love of God." He describes this in the tenth book of the *Confessions*. "The fruit of this love was knowledge of the divine. Whereas for Plato and Philo cognition led to love, for Augustine it was love that led to cognition" (Boaz, 92). As Augustine explains, in this great autobiography, he could not rest until he rested in God. He was to find peace only by complete submission to God's will, the ultimate act of love.

Other medieval saints left records of their great love of God and of the lives that they lived in response to his call. One eleventh-century British hermit and saint, Godric of Finchale, tells his story to Reginald of Durham, who records it for later generations to contemplate. It is an amazing tale of a merchant who enjoys the world's delights. Finally convinced of his own dark sins, he feels forced to confess them and commit his life to God. He lived for sixty years at Finchale as a hermit.

This remarkable story interested a modern writer, Frederick Buechner, who wrote a fictionalized account, based on Reginald's record. In *Godric* (1980), the old hermit describes his colorful life in his own words, opening with the astonishing admissions that he has only five friends, and two of them are snakes—Tune and Fairweather. The words sound medieval, smacking of Anglo-Saxon, as do the adventures. His confession of his various sins show that he is forced to live apart because of his very real temptation by the world, the flesh and the devil. As he tries to make sense of his chaotic life, he finds that his love affair with God has proven as confusing and relentless as it did for the old Patriarch Jacob. His powerful love of God and his need to be with him finally brings him to this desolation and peace.

Many of the mystics of the early medieval Church wrote sermons, prayers, and meditations that were sometimes saved, copied, and passed around. The most famous of these early works was a gentle little book by Thomas à Kempis, which was made public anonymously in 1427. Called *The Imitation of Christ*, it was immediately a popular work, with many manuscript versions produced over the next few years. Even today, it is available in over fifty languages and remains the most popular of all religious books next to the Bible. Thomas was a member of a religious order known as the Brothers and Sisters of the Common Life. Consumed with the love of God, he was eager to show that love through his imitation of his Lord and Savior.

This book reveals something of his struggle to achieve perfection. It encourages the disciplines of monasticism: the solitude, the simple life, the sexual purity, the time in prayer and devotion. The form is neither autobiographical nor confessional. It is more a meditation, sometimes a sermon, sometimes a prayer, and in one extended section, a dialogue between a disciple and Christ. He has clearly chosen the contemplative path rather than the active life, searching for the Kingdom of God that is within him. He focuses his heart entirely on the eternal things and on his powerful love of God. His delight in the Communion, where he feels united with Christ, captures the mystery of the experience. The reader can easily see that he discovers personal transformation in the imagery of Christ as the groom, the Church as the bride, and the wedding feast of the Lamb as the consummation of their love. His passion for Christ is profound, moving readers centuries later to reconsider their own lives.

Dante drew upon the experience and ideas of a number of earlier saints and contemplatives in his dazzling symphony of divine love, *The Divine Comedy* (1321). In this vision of a universe in which love literally does "make the world go 'round," as the soul grows closer to God, the sense of lightness, joy, and blessedness increases. By the time the pilgrim approaches the very presence of God, there is no jealousy, no anger, no memory of wrongs on earth. The hungers of the flesh have disappeared in the sheer delight of being with God.

Such mystical experiences lend themselves to diaries, autobiographies, and essays. They only occasionally appear in *belles lettres* or popular literature. To a certain extent, the Reformation did invite writers to speak openly about their love affairs with God, their shame at their failures and sins, and their need for forgiveness. The mystical moment was no longer the exclusive property of the recluse who spent his years in a cave or monastery. Every believer might expect to see this blinding light of God's grace during his progress toward the Eternal City.

This became the basis for one of the first English novels, *The Pilgrim's Progress* (1678). Even before Bunyan revealed his own pathway to salvation in *Grace Abounding to the Chief of Sinners* (1666) his spiritual autobiography, others had opened up the English public to such private matters. Like earlier confessions, this narrative describes the inner life of the converted sinner, the fearful visions that torment him on his path to salvation, his spiritual conflicts, and finally his conversion by the grace of God and baptism in 1653. Neither this book nor *Pilgrim's Progress* would have been possible without the preparation of the reading public by earlier writers who left records of their spiritual autobiographies.

In English literature, public devotional materials became popular in Elizabethan times, with the Protestant concern with soul-searching. One of the most talented and prolific of the Elizabethan writers was Edmund Spenser, who wrote romances, love songs, allegories, and sonnets. Two of his "hymnes" touch on the subject of love, one earthly ("An Hymne in Honovr of Love") and the other divine ("An Hymne of Heavenly Love," 1598). Both are written in rhyme royal, a complex pattern of seven-line stanzas, rhyming ABABBCC. The first five lines are iambic pentameter, the final two are tetrameter. It is a form used by Chaucer, Shakespeare, and others. In this long poem, Spenser begins with a prayer to God parallel to an invocation to the muse:

> Love, lift me up upon thy golden wings
> From this base world vnto thy heavens hight,
> Where I may see those admirable things,
> Which there thou workest by thy soueraine might.

He then goes on to lament, like so many of the reformed sinners, that he wrote so much "lewd" literature in praise of "that mad fit which fooles call loue." He attributes this concentration on eros as a youthful folly, and now turns to "heauenly prayers of true love." He traces the history of heavenly love from eternity, before the world was created, including the Fall of mankind and the "deep wound" of the Crucifixion.

His ode to the "blessed well of love," Christ, who has given everything for humans, is followed by an invitation to love God "with all thy hart, with all thy soule and mind." The final stanzas assure the believer that

> Then shalt thou feele thy spirit so possest,
> And rauisht with devouring great desire
> Of his deare selfe, that shall thy feeble brest
> Inflame with love, and set thee all on fire
> With burning zeale, through every part entire,
> That in no earthly thing thou shalt delight,
> But in his sweet and amiable sight.

(Spenser, "An Hymne of Heavenly Love," 376)

The final two stanzas complete this thought with assurances that life on earth will be blessed by eternal bliss when the sinner has turned his eyes toward God's great love. Spenser wrote his *Four Hymns* late in his life, largely because of his concern for his early misuse of his talent. As one critic notes, he drew on "Christian myth, Calvinistic theology, and a big body of Platonic and Neo-Platonic lore" from a variety of Renaissance writers (Rollins and Baker, 332).

Some of the finest poetry of the seventeenth century captures this *agape* love, the intense love of God. The Metaphysical poet John Donne began his own poetic career by deifying love, writing songs to his mistress and later to his beloved wife with clearly religious titles, like "The Relic," or "Love's Deity." When he settled down later in life to become a respected clergyman, serving as the Dean of St. Paul's Cathedral, he wrote his "Holy Sonnets," which rank among the finest sonnets in English. In them, he often speaks directly to God, asking that God teach him "how to repent" or begging God to "batter" his heart. The tone is that of a lover to his beloved, fierce in its intensity, complex in its imagery. In many of his poems, he shows a combination of wit and sincerity unusual in religious poetry. For example, in "A Hymn to God the Father," he begs God's forgiveness for his repeated sin, using a play on his own name to proclaim:

> Wilt thou forgive that sin through which I run,
>> And do run still, though still I do deplore?
> When thou hast done, thou hast not done,
>> For I have more.
> Wilt thou forgive that sin which I have won
>> Others to sin, and made my sins their door?
> Wilt thou forgive that sin which I did shun
>> A year or two, but wallowed in a score?
> When thou hast done, thou hast not done;
>> For I have more.
>
> I have a sin of fear, that when I have spun
>> My last thread, I shall perish on the shore;
> But swear by thyself that at my death thy Son
>> Shall shine as he shines now and heretofore;
> And having done that, thou hast done;
>> I fear no more.

> (Donne, "A Hymn to God the Father," 487)

A somewhat simpler poet of the metaphysicals was George Herbert, who was also a minister struggling with his faith. He wrote very personal poems portraying his love for God, two of which are excellent examples of *agape*-poetry. In "Love," he dramatizes his meeting with God, presenting God as a welcoming host, and his soul as a guilty stranger:

> Love bade me welcome; yet my soul drew back,
>> Guilty of dust and sin.
> But quick-eyed Love, observing me grow slack
>> From my first entrance in,
> Drew nearer to me, sweetly questioning,
>> If I lacked anything.
>
> "A guest," I answered, "worthy to be here."
>> Love said "You shall be he."

"I, the unkind, ungrateful? Ah, my dear,
    I cannot look on Thee!"
Love took my hand and smiling did reply,
    "Who made the eyes but I?"

"Truth, Lord; but I have marred them, let my shame
    Go where it doth deserve."
"And know you not," says Love, "who bore the blame?"
    "My dear, then I will serve."
"You must sit down," says Love, "and taste my meat."
    So I did sit and eat.

(Herbert, "Love," 489)

In this simple dialogue, Herbert provides a lovely invitation to the Lord's Supper, with an explanation of God-the-Creator, and God-the Redeemer naturally expressed in the welcoming statements of God or Love.

The pre-Romantic poet most concerned with God's love and his nature was William Blake, a mystic who loved the scripture, and the works of Dante and of Milton. He tended to write in superficially simple four-line stanzas, using natural images and expressions, but with troubling and complex ideas. His poem on "The Clod and the Pebble" is a good example of his view of types of love, one completely focuses on God's generous love of humans, and the other on love of self:

"Love seeketh not itself to please,
Nor for itself hath any care,
But for another gives its ease,
And builds a Heaven in Hell's despair."

So sung a little Clod of Clay,
Trodden with the cattle's feet,
But a Pebble of the brook
Warbled out these metres meet:

"Love seeketh only Self to please,
To bind another to its delight,
Joys in another's loss of ease,
And builds a Hell in Heaven's despite."

(Blake, "The Clod and the Pebble," 1030)

In these twelve lines, carefully balanced with contrasting ideas, Blake uses the biblical images of maleable clay and unyielding rock to show how life on earth can be turned to heaven or hell by the kind of love one chooses. On the one hand is *agape* love, mirroring God's love for his creatures. On the other is *eros*, a selfish love that requires the sacrifice of everything from the beloved for the gratification of greedy lover.

Among the finest examples of poems that speak of human love of God and God's love of humans are those that have been set to music, including many of the hymns written from the seventeenth century to the present. The hymns of Isaac Watts, or Charles and John Wesley, or William Cowper use language of everyday life to express an intense passion. Like the Psalms on which many of them are based, they speak of such topics as "Love Divine, All Loves Excelling," "How Great Thou Art," or "Amazing Grace" with deeper feeling than the printed word alone can demonstrate.

A few modern plays also capture some of this sense of *agape*-love. The story of Gideon, as told by Paddy Chaefsky is a good example of the reluctant hero, carried through to the end by God's guiding hand and love. Another reluctant hero is Thomas à Becket in Eliot's *Murder in the Cathedral*. Knowing that he is doomed to die at the hands of the king's men, he nonetheless returns to England, to Canterbury, to his pulpit. From there he preaches his final sermon on St. Stephen's Day, a sermon honoring the loving sacrifice of martyrs for God.

As Thomas explains martyrdom to his congregation, he notes:

> A martyr, a saint, is always made by the design of God, for his love of men, to warn them and to lead them, to bring them back to His ways. A martyrdom is never the design of man; for the true martyr is he who has become the instrument of God, who has lost his will in the will of God, not lost it but found it, for he has found freedom in submission to God. The martyr no longer desires anything for himself, not even the glory of martyrdom. So thus as on earth the Church mourns and rejoices at once, in a fashion that the world cannot understand; so in Heaven the Saints are most high, having made themselves most low, seeing themselves not as we see them, but in the light of the Godhead from which they draw their being. (Eliot, *Murder in the Cathedral*, 199)

Thomas's love of his congregation and his God are so intense that none of the tempters in the play can dissuade him from his goal.

As we can see, many of the richest examples of this *agape* love tend to be in poetry, a form that lends itself to expressions of mystery and praise. Occasionally, however, a novel has surfaced that captures something of the same quality. Leif Enger, a young native of Minnesota, has won praise for his astonishing novel *Peace Like a River* (2001). Jeremiah Land, an unlikely hero who has been preserved by a miracle in the midst of a whirlwind, loves the Lord more than he loves his own children. A saint, as well as a handyman, he believes that his children, especially his son Reuben, whom he commands to breathe his first breath on earth, are his most precious possessions on earth. When the oldest of them commits a crime in defense of his family, Jeremiah prays for his soul and responds to his enemies with gentleness and love. He argues with the Lord, even wrestling with him through the night, before agreeing to help the authorities search for this boy and beg him to face his punishment for manslaughter. When the story ends with a shoot-out, as a result of this first transgression by his son, Jeremiah and Reuben are both shot. A mystical death scene ends with Jeremiah pleading with God to take his life rather than his son's.

This remarkable man's willingness to follow the Lord's guidance as he chases his prodigal son across the frozen Northwest, his gentle words in the face of wrath, his constant reliance on God's grace and mercy, his gratitude at the provision of sustenance and safety, and his final sacrificial death make him the model for "the mind of Christ." It is astonishing to find such a message at the heart of a modern shoot-'em-up Western.

Conclusion

Popular literature is not a likely place to discover *agape* love. Novels and plays are far more likely collection of erotic tales. Rather, the great diaries of the saints, the devotional literature of the ages, the magnificent music of the Psalms and of the church—these are the natural expressions of the very personal feeling of the human love of God, and the amazing love of God for individual humans.

See also: **Friends and Family; The Hero; Love and Marriage.**

Bibliography

Alighieri, Dante. *The Divine Comedy*. Trans., Dorothy L. Sayers. New York: Basic Books, 1973.

Augustine, St. *The Confessions*. Grand Rapids, MI: Baker Books, 2005.

Buechner, Frederick. *Godric*. New York: Atheneum, 1980.

Bunyan, John. *Grace Abounding to the Chief of Sinners*. New York: Penguin Classics, 1987.

———. *The Pilgrim's Progress*. New York: Pocket Books, 1957.

Blake, William. "The Clod and the Pebble." In *British Poetry and Prose*, vol. I, ed. Paul Robert Lieder, Robert Morss Lovett, and Robert Kilburn Root. Boston: Houghton Mifflin, 1950.

Boaz, George. "Love." In *The Encyclopedia of Philosophy*, vol. 5, ed. Paul Edwards. New York: Macmillan, 1967.

Donne, John. *Holy Sonnets*. In *The Renaissance in England: Non-Dramatic Prose and Verse of the Sixteenth Century*, ed. Hyder E. Rollins and Herschel Baker. Boston: D.C. Heath and Company, 1954.

———. "A Hymn to God the Father." In *British Poetry and Prose*, vol. I, ed. Paul Robert Lieder, Robert Morss Lovett, and Robert Kilburn Root. Boston: Houghton Mifflin, 1950.

Eliot, T. S. *Murder in the Cathedral*. In *The Complete Poems and Plays: 1909–1950*. New York: Harcourt, Brace & World, 1952.

Enger, Leif. *Peace Like a River*. New York: Atlantic Monthly Press, 2001.

Günter, W., and H. G. Link. "Love." In *The New International Dictionary of New Testament Theology*, vol. 2, ed. Colin Brown. Grand Rapids, MI: Zondervan Publishing, 1986.

Herbert, George. "Love." In *British Poetry and Prose*, vol. I, ed. Paul Lieder, Robert Morss Lovett, and Robert Kilburn Root. Boston: Houghton Mifflin, 1950.

Kempis, Thomas à. *The Imitation of Christ*. New York: Dorset Press, 1986.

Plato. *The Republic and Other Works*. Trans., B. Jowett. New York: Anchor Books, 1989.

Spenser, Edmund. "An Hymne of Heavenly Love." In *The Renaissance in England: Non-Dramatic Prose and Verse of the Sixteenth Century*, ed. Hyder E. Rollins and Herschel Baker. Boston: D.C. Heath and Company, 1954.

Friends and Family

Introduction

> This is my commandment, That ye love one another, as I have loved you.
> Greater love hath no man than this, that a man lay down his life for his
> friends. (John 15:12–13)

We humans have a natural affinity for those who contribute to our comfort or our prestige, who mirror our appearance, tastes, or attitudes, or who make us feel valuable. We say that we "love" our animals, our possessions, our children. It is even easy to love our neighbors and friends, if they are of the same tribe, faith, and heritage. Jesus advises his disciples to love one another, as he has loved them. But he also expands this, telling them to go beyond the love of those who love them (Matt. 5:43–44). Loving a "neighbor" when he is a Samaritan may be harder. Loving one's enemy goes against both common sense and our fallen nature.

Philos, the love of fellow humans, has no parallel term in Hebrew, which instead uses *aheb* or *ahabah* to describe a variety of loves. *Philos* can describe the love of a child, the love of a husband or wife, the love of a young woman, or even the love of savory meat in a stew. It is an all-encompassing kind of love. Usually, however, we consider this general love of other humans quite distinct from the love we feel for God (*agape*) or the love we feel for a sexual partner (*eros*).

Especially in literature, the various forms of love overlap or change, with the friend becoming an object of erotic desire, the wife becoming a good friend, and God becoming the hunger of the writer's heart. A work like Dante's *Divine Comedy* is a great example of the manifold varieties of love. The love of God, the love of the good earth, the love of other people, the perverse love of self, the possessive love of children, the distorted love of country—these are the motivating forces for the whole world. At the center of it all is God's incredible love of humankind.

Scripture

God looks down at the man he has created and placed in the Garden of Eden and realizes that he is not meant to be alone. From the beginning man is a social creature. At first, it is the family that is the social center, and the love is directed toward relatives. Even within this first family, the worm is hidden in the apple. Eve is not content to be tempted alone, nor is Adam willing to accept the blame for his own iniquity. Cain is not content to acknowledge that his brother's sacrifice is more pleasing to God than his own and be happy for Abel. After he has murdered the brother he should have loved, Cain refuses to repent of his sin. The scripture tells of a son (Jacob) tricking his father and his brothers into selling their younger sibling (Joseph) into slavery, and a brother raping his own sister (Amnon and Tamar).

Yet, even with these glaring exceptions, love within the family is presented in both the Old and New Testaments as the ideal pattern for life on earth. In fact, the relationship of God to humans is presented in terms of a loving family headed by a stern, but loving father. Jesus presents God this way frequently, and speaks of him as "abba," a familiar form for *father*, like our "daddy."

In the Bible, the love of fellow humans derives from an awareness that we are all created in the image of God. Even the earliest laws, both the natural law and the God-given law, emphasize the distinctiveness and value of human life. The concern for the shedding of human blood, the law of retaliation, the concern for women and children are all indications that humans are precious. The law of Moses, with the protections of life, property, and family, provides a path to building a harmonious and loving community of believers. The Ten Commandments forbid murder, theft, adultery, false accusation, and even coveting of one's neighbor's possessions. The provision of the Sabbath rest and the dietary restrictions reveal a consideration for human health.

These rules and regulations point to healthy and loving homes with respect for fathers and mothers, proper treatment of children, loyalty of husbands and wives to one another, and hospitality for visitors. As the psalmist says, the ideal is a table around which the loving family sits in harmony, the wife like a fruitful vine, and the children as numerous as the shoots of the olive tree (Ps. 128:3).

In fact, the love of brothers or sisters for one another is expected, making the betrayal of one brother by one another, as with Cain and Abel or Jacob and Esau, worse than a normal sin. Such betrayal is a violation of the family. Where members of the family are particularly generous to one another, as Abram is to Lot and Joseph is to his brothers, the forgiving and open-handed man is portrayed as praiseworthy.

Many of the stories in scripture go far beyond this basic concern for the survival of the human race. The intense love Abraham and Sarah feel for Isaac, and Hagar's agonized fear for the life of Ishmael are two examples of love that goes well beyond the simple animalistic concern for a child. These children represent the future of the family, the closest thing that the Jews of this period knew of immortality.

Certainly the story of Ruth and Naomi is presented as ideal, a love transcending the requirements of the mother-in-law, daughter-in-law relationship. Ruth's love for Naomi is more important in her life than the love of her own father and mother, foreshadowing her most famous descendant, Jesus, whose love also reaches beyond the bonds of blood. Ruth chooses to go with her mother-in-law to an alien land and live among strangers rather than follow the customs of her own country. Boaz's generosity to Ruth exceeds even this, but is undoubtedly a response to the demonstration of love he sees in these women and his own attraction to this appealing young woman.

Scripture's first great portrayal of a friendship outside the family is that of David and Jonathan. Tested by difficult times, these young men find their shared friendship more important than even their love of family. Jonathan serves as David's protector at Saul's court and gives him warnings of dangers. When Jonathan is killed by the Philistines, along with Saul, David mourns for him, weeps, and proclaims without embarrassment that this love is deeper than the love of a man for a woman.

The repeated command of love in the Law of Moses extends beyond friends and family. The Israelites are commanded to welcome the strangers in their midst, show them hospitality, and treat them with dignity. They are told, "Thou shalt love thy neighbor as thyself" (Lev. 1:18). This is followed by the rationale behind this command: "I am the Lord."

Jesus takes this law of love and expands on it. Our love of God, who first loved us, should lead us into forgiveness of our brother and love of our fellow humans. He demonstrates this love through his regular teaching of God's forgiveness of the sinners, his many acts of healing, and his sacrifice on the cross for other humans. Even hanging from the cross, Jesus shows love for his mother, his disciples, the criminals hanging on either side of him, and even his executioners.

After the death and resurrection of Jesus, his disciples are bound together by their love of Jesus and their devotion to spreading the new faith. Although Jesus admonishes them to love one another, they do not always heed this message. Two of them argue for preference in his kingdom, misunderstanding his message, and one of them betrays him.

When Jesus's mother and brothers, in an act of love, seek to bring him back to Nazareth, to keep him safe from the threats they see in his ministry, he denies their blood-claim on him. "These are my brothers," he says of the disciples. His followers, not his kin, are his new "family." After that, both his mother and his brother James appear to follow him and listen to his teachings. The disciples and the "women," his numerous followers from Galilee, all seem to live in harmony his leadership. Jesus widens the circle of love to include not only his mother, but other women as well. Mary's lavish gift of oils to anoint his feet reveals her delight at his generous acceptance of her. The numerous comments of Mary and Martha during his sojourns at their home suggest that they also are close friends as well as followers.

At his death, his followers continue to pray together, expecting his return. Their loving bond becomes an example for the early Church, which is considered the "Bride of Christ." In 1 Corinthians 13, Paul elaborates to the Corinthians the nature of the love they should have for one another: bearing all things, believing all things, never failing, not greedy, not easily provoked, thinking no evil. This generous love of fellow believers extends to the gentiles as well as the Jews. In his parable of the Good Samaritan, Jesus makes explicit that this love of neighbor transcends not only family and fellow believers, but even nationality.

Peter, who resists any outreach to the gentiles at first, becomes convinced that nothing that God calls *clean* may be considered *unclean* by humans (Acts 10: 9 ff). In a vision, he learns this hard lesson, thereafter opening his heart to the fellowship of these previously-offensive fellow believers. At the Council of Jerusalem, he leads the group that allows gentiles to become Christians without first becoming Jews.

Paul soon takes this inclusive message into the European world, making friends there among a group long considered by the Jews to be beyond the pale. Although he reaches out to thousands of people in his ministry, Paul also has his close personal friends, including Priscilla and Aquila, with whom he shares a home and work as a tent-maker for an extended period of time. His letters also signal a fondness for John, Mark, Silas, and Barnabas, who traveled with him, and numerous others to whom he sends his regards.

Scripture emphasizes that the love that was once based on attraction or affection, such as the love one has for one's children or best friends, can be enriched and deepened by the awareness that they are bearers of God's image. The message of scripture also enlarges this love so that the whole human race becomes a loving family, all the children of God.

Literature

In secular literature, the dysfunctional families, twisted friendships, and incestuous longings are at least as common as portrayals of happy families. Much of literature deals with the absence from the family, the isolation of the wanderer or the outcast, the hunger for a faithful friend in a busy city, the loneliness of the hero. Happy families and faithful friends are rarely the stuff of great literature.

Curiously, war, the very antithesis of love, often breeds loving tales. The violent Achilles creates a loving little "family" of sorts in his tent with Chryseis and Patrocolus. Even in a story as old as Homer's chronicles of the fall of Troy and the voyage of Odysseus, the longing for home and family is palpable. Homer portrays his Trojan hero, Hector, with his loving wife and child in a charming scene that precedes his final battle. Odysseus spends ten years of tortuous travel in his determination to return home to Ithaca, to his wife and son.

Much of Greek tragedy is based on a betrayal of trust, particularly betrayal by a member of the hero's own family. These tales of the murder of the husband by his adulterous wife (Agamemnon and Clytemnestra) or a mother by her son (Clytemnestra and Orestes), or a father by his son (Oedipus) reveal what Aristotle considered the best possible ingredients for tragic drama. Confused families, lonely children, angry parents, and isolated old people continue to be the stuff of literature, even in modern times.

The Greek concept of *philos* tends to be quite different from the biblical one. The classical Greek ideal of noble warriors, aristocrats fighting side by side in defense of their city or their honor, breeds a kind of manly love quite alien to the Hebrews'. The Greeks considered homosexual love a natural part of the soldier's life. In *The Iliad*, Achilles' love for Patrocolus is deeper than his love for the young woman who shares his tent. Out of love for his friend and concern for his friend's honor, Patrocolus puts on Achilles's armor and goes into battle. When Patrocolus dies in battle, Achilles mourns him in extravagant and extended ceremonies, far exceeding those of David for Jonathan. In *The Iliad*, mourning the beloved involves laments, funeral games, a funeral pyre, and a pledge of revenge. This relationship became the Greek ideal of love.

Socrates, in Plato's *Symposium,* explains this intense love of comrades. For him, the greatest human love is that shared by fellow warriors willing to risk their lives for one another. This, in fact, becomes a staple of war stories throughout the history of litera- ture. For the Israelites, such love would have been an outrage. The law of Moses clearly prohibits sexual relations between men, threatening transgressors with death.

The shared experience of warriors has always built strong friendships, strength- ened by shared danger, reliance on one another, as well as extended absence from women and family. The heightened emotions in the face of death press warriors toward intense personal relationships. Among the Greeks, the love of youth and the veneration of the body (not to mention the absence of any laws forbidding homosex- ual acts) probably increased the temptation to move from close friendship to physical expressions of love or even *eros*—a passionate attachment to another man.

In literary history, notwithstanding the Greek model, bands of brothers were often chaste and idealistic, as appears to be the case in some of the Knights of the Round Table. The basic idea of chivalry, with the knights clustered around the great leader, was mod- eled on the host of angels who gathered around God, "the Lord of hosts," enthroned in Heaven. In some ways, they mirrored Christ's disciples, joined together around a com- mon leader, sharing a religious faith, devoting their lives to a shared quest.

In *Henry V,* Shakespeare describes the troops in the English camp preparing for war against the French. Harry walks among them on the night before their big battle, cheering them up, telling them that "Tomorrow is Saint Crispian" and will long lin- ger in their memories as a special time:

> This story shall the good man teach his son,
> And Crispin Crispian shall ne'er go by,
> From this day to the ending of the world,
> But we in it shall be remembered—
> We few, we happy few, we band of brothers,
> For he today that sheds his blood with me
> Shall be my brother....
> And gentlemen in England now abed
> Shall think themselves accursed they were not here,
> And hold their manhoods cheap whiles any speaks
> That fought with us upon Saint Crispin's Day.

> (Shakespeare, *Henry V,* IV, iii)

World War I brought together many talented, articulate, and attractive young men to fight in the trenches of France. In his survey of that time, Paul Fussell explains the deep relationships that resulted in a sort of temporary homosexuality:

> Given this association between war and sex, and given the deprivation and loneliness and alienation characteristic of the soldier's experience—given, that is, his need for af- fection in a largely womanless world—we will not be surprised to find both the actual- ity and the recall of front-line experience replete with what we can call the homoerotic. (Fussell, 272)

This sublimated or chaste form of love for fellow warriors is marked by references to "charm" or "innocence" or simply "good looks."

This tendency toward homoerotic love was exaggerated by the aesthetes at Oxford in the late nineteenth- and early twentieth-century period, encouraging a cultural trend which derived in large part Greeks' view of male love as the highest form of human feeling. W. H. Auden, who shared in the experiences of the period, says in *The Age of Anxiety*, "In times of war even the crudest kind of positive affection between persons seems extraordinarily beautiful, a noble symbol of the peace and forgiveness of which the old world stands so desperately in need" (quoted by Fussell, 170).

Somewhat similar loving relationships among men are apparent in sea stories. Herman Melville's *Billy Budd* (c.1891), for example, has also a distinctly homoerotic tone. Aboard the ship, with its all-male crew, all eyes are fixated on the handsome sailor. The motivation for Clegg's hatred of this angelic young man seems to be a kind of twisted desire. The way the other men watch, admire, and lament the death of Billy all point to a special kind of love they feel. They memorialize this in their songs after his death.

Women have traditionally had quite different kinds of friendship. Outside of convents or girls' schools, most women have been restricted in their close relationships to family and close neighbors. Like Ruth and Naomi, they have loved and supported one another in their daily lives without commentary. We know little about the daily lives or friendships of women through the ages until the advent of the novel. From the Renaissance forward, women's experiences have become more visible and women have become more articulate in describing them.

Among the finest literary examples of this exploration of women's relationships are the novels of Jane Austen. Her heroines usually include a coterie of sisters, relatives, or friends with whom they discuss their joys and sorrows, most often related to marriage possibilities. The closeness of the relations, the openness of the exchanges, and the depth of the love of sisters is impressive in books such as *Pride and Prejudice* (1796) or *Sense and Sensibility* (1811), In *Emma* (1815), we see the devotion between a father and daughter that finally enlarges to include a husband and son-in-law.

In Austen's case, the religious element is minimal. There is little indication that this love has any basis in faith. In fact, the very spokesman for Christianity in her novels is often a pompous clergyman, useful primarily for presiding over marriages, baptisms, and funerals. His own behavior rarely mirrors Christian love either to his brothers in Christ or his choice of a bride.

Emma is a good example of her delicate exploration of family love. Emma's deep affection for her aged father seems to destine her for a life of spinsterhood. She cannot consider leaving him and "cleaving" only to another man. The ideal man who enters her life, properly named Mr. Knightly, has a fatherly regard for her and a genuine respect for her father and for her love for the old gentleman. He watches her behavior with concern, showing little of his affection until the very end of the story, when he joins this household rather than requiring that it be torn asunder by marriage. Thus, *eros* can enter Emma's life without losing her other great need for *philos*.

In American literature, Louisa May Alcott captures something of the same genuine friendship among sisters and neighbors in her classic *Little Women* (1867). Actually, this literary interest in innocent friendships proved very strong in the nineteenth-century novels of Mark Twain, James Fenimore Cooper, and others who portray friendships among boys and girls, or young adults. They are often pictured as innocents in Eden before the Fall. Those who twist such friendships are seen as the serpent in the Garden.

Arthur Miller frequently uses this kind of boyish good fellowship in his plays, with young men involved in sports, work, or war, revealing close friendship for one another. Willy Loman, in *Death of a Salesman* (1948), considers his own popularity to be a mark of success and has great hopes for his son Biff, the handsome young athlete in his home. The crowd of youngsters who gather around Biff when he is the high school football hero delights his dad. Some of the friends of both father and son prove remarkably loyal, even when they grow up while the Loman men all remain perennial adolescents. Although it is very important to Willy and his boys to be "well liked," they show little self-sacrificial love for others. The characters are reluctant to use the term *love*, preferring the superficial term *liked*. The father loves one son far better than the other, betrays his wife in casual adulteries, and lies to his few friends. The favorite son quickly turns against his father and is soured on the world. The boys have a kind of companionship in their promiscuity and braggadocio, but not much more than a superficial love for one another or for their parents.

More often, especially in the later years of the twentieth- and early years of the twenty-first century, writers have sexualized this friendship-love, making it an expression of homosexuality. An interesting example of this is Tennessee Williams's play *Cat on a Hot Tin Roof* (1958), one of the first American dramas to deal openly with gay themes. The hero of the play is Brick, a handsome though crippled young man who is married to Maggie, a bright, attractive, and "catty" young woman. They once shared the friendship of Skipper, an athlete who played football with Brick in college and afterwards. Because they relished their close ties in the locker room and on the field, they try to go into business together, but find that maturity and marriage have become barriers to their closeness. One night, Skipper proposes a physical relationship with Brick, winning from the innocent friend a horrified rebuke. Shortly afterwards, Skipper commits suicide, leaving Brick a legacy of anguish and sexual confusion. He blames Maggie for Skip's death and has turned against her, refusing to sleep with her. His father, Big Daddy, who is tolerant of homosexual love, and who loves his favorite son, Brick, far more than the good, but dull, son Gooper, blames Brick for Skipper's death.

The point-of-view of the drama is sympathetic to homosexual love—a "deep, deep friendship" that may flower into physical expression. It is clear that Williams laments Brick's revulsion at the very idea of homosexual love, which turns his "pure" love of Skipper into something "dirty." In a depressing commentary on the play, Williams states that he does not believe that people can change. Even sadder is his analysis of the Maggie-Brick marriage: "He will go back to Maggie for sheer animal comfort, even if she did not make him dependent on her for such creature comforts as only a devoted slave can provide. He is her dependent. As Strindberg said: 'They call it love-hatred, and it hails from the pit" (Tennessee Williams, *Where I Live*, 73).

Williams, who was an avowed homosexual, often punishes his heroes for their "love." In numerous of his plays, this grandson of an Episcopal minister may be reflecting the Old Testament punishment for a man sleeping with another man "as with a woman"—death by stoning. For the most part, his stories and plays that deal with this theme end in tragedy.

Another twentieth-century Southerner, William Faulkner, describes another quality of friendship. In his portrait of a hunting party in "The Bear," he shows how men of various professions and different races can gather around a campfire and tell stories, laugh at one another's jokes, review the day's activities, and prepare for the day to come. These friendships, some of which date back to childhood, are the enduring relationships in a difficult world—clearly one of God's most merciful gifts to human beings. He is saddened by the ritual of the young man's "coming of age" in the South, often marked by racial awareness and the separation of good friends.

A number of modern novels deal with love within families and among friends. Marilynne Robinson's *Gilead*, for example, is a love letter from a father to his son.

The memories of the dying pastor linger on his long relationship with another pastor, his life-long friend, who has shared all of his joys and sorrows. He also is near death at this point. Their shared love of his friend's renegade son binds them in even deeper bonds of sympathy and fear. Like Faulkner's characters, in the long friendships that are built on shared experiences, confidences, and faith, these old men have a very special gift.

One of the sweetest family stories to come out of recent times is David James Duncan's *The Brothers K* (1992). Each of the brothers in the story (as in Dostoyevsky's novel on which it is based) follows a different spiritual path. In a family with an agnostic baseball player for a father and a fanatic Seventh Day Adventist for a mother, one son becomes a Buddhist, one a radical atheist, and one a true believer. Yet all these people learn to love and respect one another. Their hardships unite them as does their love of their father and admiration for his talent. Finally, the need to rescue the saintly Irwin, the only faithful Christian among the children, from the madness of the Vietnam War and his subsequent treatment for "insanity," brings them together in loving and self-sacrificial scenes. The death of the father further cements this eccentric domestic group, allowing the survivors to work out their individual salvation while growing in their love for one another.

The novel, which is told from the child's point-of-view, is a sweet and loving story that blends some of Dickens' love of children and hunger for close families with Dostoyevsky's philosophic investigation of religion.

Confused families, lonely children, angry parents, and isolated old people are the basic materials of modern literature. At the same time, new family configurations, with cohabiting friends, gay lovers, adopted children are increasingly replacing the old sets of blood relations. Our world is filled with isolated people who feel rootless and unloved. The hero is often a lonely outsider, who is searching for the kind of love and acceptance Robert Frost describes in "The Death of a Hired Man." Home is the place, when you have to go there, they have to take you in—a place of unconditional love.

Conclusion

In his interesting essay on friendship "The Four Loves," C. S. Lewis pays tribute to the delights of sharing time with good friends. As he notes in the essay, many movements in literature, religion, and politics have begun with deep conversations among friends. In literature, the Romantics were especially noted for their close friendships that enhanced their understanding and enriched their poetry (e.g., Wordsworth and Coleridge, Shelley and Byron). Among the twentieth-century writers, the most famous group of friends was the Inklings, the Oxford group which included Tolkien, Lewis and his brother, among others. They shared an orthodox faith, a love of learning, a fascination with the Middle Ages, and a delight in good conversation. Their afternoons in Lewis's rooms at Oxford, with a good fire burning in the hearth as they talked, laughed, and shared a glass of sherry or a cup of tea proved enriching for them all. Lewis commented that, after one of their members died, the meetings were never quite the same. The complex web of relationships, with one man's wit or memories triggering reactions in another was lost when the whole group was not present.

Dorothy L. Sayers, among others, longed to join this group, but was excluded primarily because of her gender. She did find her best friendships among fellow believers, including Charles Williams, who encouraged her in much of her work.

In her translation of *The Song of Roland,* Sayers points out the importance of Roland's love for Oliver. And in her notes to her amazing translation of *The Divine Comedy,* she shows how love motivates Dante's journey into the afterlife: love brings his guides to his service; love (or its absence) determines the whole geography of hell, purgatory, and heaven; love is the key to the bliss of paradise. When Dante arrives at the final moment, faced with a revelation of God, he loses his capacity for speech:

> High phantasy lost power and here broke off;
>> Yet, as a wheel moves smoothly, free from jars,
>> My will and my desire were turned by love,
> The love that moves the sun and the other stars.

(Alighieri, Paradise, 347)

In this final vision of paradise, all love somehow merges into a blinding light: the love of God, the love of fellow humans, and the desire to unite as "one flesh."

See also: **God's Love, Humans' Response; Love and Marriage; War.**

Bibliography

Alighieri, Dante. *The Divine Comedy.* Trans., Dorothy L. Sayers. New York: Basic Books, 1973.

Austen, Jane. *Emma.* New York: Popular Publishing, 2001.

DeRougemont, Denis. *Love in the Western World.* Trans., Montgomery Belgion. Princeton, NJ: Princeton University Press, 1983.

Duncan, David James. *The Brothers K.* New York: Bantam Books, 1996.

Frost, Robert. "The Death of a Hired Man." In *Modern American Poetry,* ed. Louis Untermeyer. New York: Harcourt, Brace and Company, 1950.

Fussell, Paul. *The Great War and Modern Memory.* New York: The Oxford University Press, 1975.

Günter, W., and H. G. Link. "Love." In *The New International Dictionary of New Testament Theology,* vol. 2, ed. Colin Brown. Grand Rapids, MI: Zondervan Publishing House, 1986.

Homer. *The Iliad.* Trans., Robert Fagles. New York: Penguin Books, 1998.

———. *The Odyssey.* Trans., Robert Fagles. London: Penguin Books, 1996.

Lewis, C. S. "The Four Loves." In *The Inspirational Writings of C.S. Lewis.* New York: Inspirational Press, 1960.

Melville, Herman. *Billy Budd, Sailor and other Stories.* New York: Penguin Books, 1986.

Miller, Arthur. *Death of a Salesman.* In *Arthur Miller's Collected Plays.* New York: Viking Press, 1957.

Plato. *The Symposium.* In *The Republic and Other Works.* Trans., B. Jowett. New York: Anchor Books, 1989.

Robinson, Marilynne. *Gilead.* New York: Picador, 2006.

Shakespeare, William. *Henry V.* In *Shakespeare: Major Plays and the Sonnets,* ed. G. B. Harrison. New York: Harcourt, Brace and Company, 1948.

Tischler, Nancy. *Tennessee Williams: Rebellious Puritan.* New York: Citadel Press, 1960.

Williams, Tennessee. *Cat on a Hot Tin Roof.* In *The Theatre of Tennessee Williams,* vol. 3. New York: New Directions, 1971.

———. *Where I Live: Selected Essays.* New York: New Directions, 1978.

Love and Marriage

Readings

Song of Solomon

Geoffrey Chaucer, *The Canterbury Tales* (1400)

Miguel de Cervantes Saavedra, *Don Quixote* (1615)

Edmund Spenser, "Epithalamion" and "Prothalamion" (1596)

Christopher Marlowe, "The Passionate Shepherd to His Love" (1599)

Sir Walter Raleigh, "The Nymph's Reply to the Shepherd" (1600)

William Shakespeare, *Sonnets* (1609), *Romeo and Juliet* (1597), *A Midsummer's Night's Dream* (1596), *Antony and Cleopatra* (1608)

T. S. Eliot, *The Wasteland* (1922)

C. S. Lewis, *Till We Have Faces* (1956)

Introduction

> And the Lord God said, It is not good that man should be alone; I will make him a help meet for him. (Gen. 2:18)

Human sexuality is considered one of the most precious elements of God's creation. In the creation story, God orders his creatures to go forth and "multiply." The obvious and practical purpose of this generative power of all living creatures is to allow the continuation of their species. It allows humans to become small creators. The significance of the "seed" of the man is emphasized regularly, even sealing the covenant with Abraham. The mark on his flesh, circumcision, signals that Abraham's body belongs to God, who has blessed his seed and promises that his descendants will be as numerous as the sands of the desert. God says to Abraham, "Look now toward heaven, and tell the stars, if thou be able to number them: and he said unto him, So shall thy seed be" (Gen. 15:5).

From Genesis to Revelation, the human expression of sexual love blessed by God is a permanent and fruitful relationship in marriage. Eve is immediately seen by

Adam as "bone of my bones, and flesh of my flesh." The narrator follows this with, "Therefore shall a man leave his father and his mother, and shall cleave unto his wife and they shall be one flesh" (Gen. 2:23–24). This union of a man and a woman in a committed relationship, centered in a home and blessed with children becomes the basic social unit of human society, providing stability, security, and continuity. In this repeated human experience, Eros, or the climactic bonding of lovers, is tamed and shaped into the most complete form of union with another human being. When love is absent, Eros is simply animalistic lust. When representing enduring love as well as sexual hunger, it is one of God's richest blessings.

New Testament scripture cites two other kinds of love: *agape* and *philos. Eros* is a term not used in the Bible except in Greek translations from the Hebrew. *Agape* is the love of God; *philos*, the love of one's fellow human, while *eros* is passionate sexual love. The New Testament writers avoided this third term because it had become associated with the mystery religions. These popular cults in Greco-Roman culture were intended to unite the participant with the godhead in a physical manner, producing a sensual ecstasy, leaving moderation and proportion far behind (Günter and Link, 538). Although the Hebrew God frequently refers to his people in terms of a bride, and Christ speaks of himself as a bridegroom, the gross physical aspects of the pagan sexual practices of their neighbors never became part of the worship of the Jewish and Christian God.

Nonetheless, of these three kinds of love, *eros* has proven to be the most popular in literature and in life.

Scripture

Many writers have assumed that the sin of Adam was caused by his love of Eve, not by hunger for the fruit of the Tree of the Knowledge of Good and Evil or by his pride that led him to put his own will over that of his Creator. Scripture argues against this concept of sex as the original sin. Rather, sexual union is implied at the Creation with God's admonition to his creatures to "Be fruitful and multiply" (Gen. 1:22, 28). In fact, it is partly the abuse of human sexuality, along with the willingness to disobey the Lord, that leads to the fall of Eve, the temptation of Adam, and the alienation from God. Some argue that Eve lures Adam to transgress and eat the apple, knowing that he can not resist her. Others assert that her assumption of the leadership role leads them both into sin This series of actions leads to further actions and reactions: the lies they tell to God, and the expulsion from the Garden of Eden. Some theologians believe that Adam may have been present at Eve's temptation. In that case, his sin is his failure to dissuade her from deliberate disobedience of God. In any case, his willingness to take the fruit from her hand and join her in the transgression makes him equal in her guilt.

The extensive list of marriages of the patriarchs that punctuate the book of Genesis and the record of the births of the various children provide ample testimony regarding the importance of marriage and sexual relations. Only occasionally does scripture indicate that the marriages are based on love. The long partnership of Abraham and Sarah certainly sounds like a loving one. When Isaac first sees Rebekah, he forgets his sorrow for his recently departed mother and takes his new bride into his tent, clearly delighted with her. Jacob may not love Leah as much as he does Rachel, but she does produce a host of children for him. He is willing to work 14 years for the woman he really loves, and mourns her death in childbirth a few years later.

The main point of the traditional marriage is not a consummation of love, but a fortification of the family. Love often comes after marriage. In the New Testament as well as the Old, the obligations of both the husband and wife involve the marriage bed and the production of children. C. S. Lewis may be correct in his essay on Eros, describing traditional marriage:

> Most of our ancestors were married off in early youth to partners chosen by their parents on grounds that had nothing to do with Eros. They went to the act with no other "fuel," so to speak, than plain animal desire. And they did right; honest Christian husbands and wives, obeying their fathers and mothers, discharging to one another their "marriage debt," and bringing up families in the fear of the Lord. (Lewis, 262)

Though most marriages in scripture are arranged, love is clearly indicated as a significant component in the relationships of Ruth and Boaz, David and Bathsheba—and many others. It is unfair to see the Patriarchs' love of their wives as little different from their love of their oxen, their sheep, and their farm implements—loved because they belong to them. Solomon, who considers marriage a clever device for building alliances with other countries, seems to have little interest in love. His marriage to hundreds of women may be a sign of his impressive lust or of his even more impressive political ambitions. Ironically, the great love poetry in scripture, the Song of Solomon, is attributed to this cynical collector of women.

The marriage covenant becomes an important component of Hebrew society, guarded by law and custom. The purity of the wife is essential to ensuring that the children produced by the couple are the man's seed, worthy of his careful attention. The unfaithful wife might be punished for her iniquity by being stoned to death. God often speaks to the Hebrews as if they are his bride, in an exclusive covenant with him, and suffering for his jealousy when they go "whoring after other gods."

Hosea's prophesies are an extended metaphor based on this covenant relationship. This Old Testament prophet in the final days of Israel's apostasy writes of his own troubled marriage, extending this private experience to Israel, which he characterizes as an unfaithful bride. Hosea loves his adulterous wife, Gomer, so fiercely that he repeatedly forgives her for her infidelity and redeems her. His love for this wanton wife makes an ideal image of God's merciful forgiveness for his beloved Israel. This blend of *agape*-love with *eros* is an incredibly powerful statement of God's "everlasting love."

Of all the poetry and prose of scripture, the "Canticles," the "Song of Songs," or the "Song of Solomon" is the greatest celebration of physical love between a man and a woman. This extended poem (or perhaps collection of poems), is sometimes a dramatic dialogue between lovers and sometimes a dramatic monologue, with one lover absent. This famous paen to earthly love is thought to have been written by or about Solomon, early in his reign, though some scholars insist it was composed many years later. In its literal form, the book is a love song of the shepherd-king and a Shulamite maiden. It is a difficult work to summarize, with abrupt transitions and ambiguity regarding speakers' identity and a confusing narrative line. There are choruses of the "Daughters of Jerusalem," and The New International Version of the Bible prints it as a drama, with indications of when the Beloved, the Friends, or the Lover speaks. The structure is circular, with much of the opening repeated in the closing lines, signaling that it is a mood piece rather than a love story.

In many ways, it is like other ancient love poetry of Egypt, Babylon, and Sumer, where religious ceremonies sometimes involved a "sacred marriage" (Carr, 285–286).

All of these collections share the love-song motif, have exchanges between lovers, and describe the adornment and physical charms of the woman. Like all love poetry, the dominant theme is the desire of the lovers to cling to one another in erotic embrace. The language of the Song of Solomon is typical of the Near East, with references to parts of the body, perfumes, ornaments, and royalty. The missing element here, curious for a book of scripture, is any reference to God. Although this is usually considered a wedding song, even references to marriage are not clear. Ironically, these very omissions have encouraged later readers to interpret the book as an allegory of God and Israel or of Christ and his Church.

Whichever interpretation the reader chooses, the book is replete with explicit and lusty sexual imagery. It begins with the invitation: "Let him kiss me with the kisses of his mouth: for thy love is better than wine." The reason that the Shulamite maiden is designated as the beloved is clarified in 1:5: "I am black, but comely, O ye daughters of Jerusalem." The maiden's invitation to her lover, who is called a shepherd at the beginning and Solomon later, is full of unusual imagery, comparing her beloved to a company of horses, his cheeks to rows of jewels, his neck with chains of gold, and his whole being to a bundle of myrrh, a cluster of camphor. Rather than choosing items that have parallel appearance and connotations, the singer chooses items that are expensive, cherished, and sweet-smelling. She compares herself to the "rose of Sharon, and the lily of the valleys" and remembers with delight her lover's embraces. In Western literature, this woman's song of invitation is unusual, as is her catalogue of her lover's physical attributes.

His response, which is somewhat more in conformity with accepted courtship rituals, is also full of peculiar imagery: her hair is like a flock of goats, her teeth like a flock of sheep, her lips like a thread of scarlet, her neck like the tower of David full of shields, and her breasts like two twin roes. The lover follows this curious catalogue with an invitation to come from Lebanon to Jerusalem, comparing his beloved to a "garden enclosed ... a spring shut up a fountain sealed" (4:12).

Although the book does not specifically mention marriage or faith, it does designate the beloved as "bride" and "sister." Most scholars assume that it is an *epithalamion*, a hymn in celebration of marriage. Carr sums up his view of this as a non-sequential set of episodes: "the Song celebrates human sexuality as a fact of life, God-given, to be enjoyed within the confines of a permanent, committed relationship. This is no passing fling. What is celebrated here is total dedication to the beloved other, a permanent obligation gladly assumed." Pointing to the original promise in the Garden of Eden, he notes that these "two creatures, opposites, yet alike, 'suitable' for each other, male and female made in the image of God, celebrating and fulfilling their God-given desires. Freely and openly they give to each other, because they have been given freely" (Carr, 294–295).

Many of the phrases and images of the Song of Solomon appear in love literature of Western Europe and beyond. The imagery changes, but the theme of the virgin as a walled garden beset by the little foxes, the elaborate celebration of her physical splendor, and his passionate desire for her are themes that reappear frequently.

The Christian tradition, though encouraging stable marriages, tends to treat passion with somewhat more reserve. Most of the New Testament elevates love of God and of fellow humans to the highest position, using sexual love as a metaphor. This may well be a result of Jesus's failure to marry. Although Christ attends a wedding at Cana before he begins his ministry, he never has the comforts of a wife and children.

The bond between Jesus and his disciples is *philos*, not *eros*. Even the women who follow him, including Mary Magdalene, accept him as a teacher and savior.

Recent scholars have sought to alter this traditional interpretation, pointing for their evidence to the *Gospel of Mary Magdalene*. Elaine Pagels has written extensively on the sexual relationship she believes existed between Mary and Jesus. The best-selling novel *The Da Vinci Code*, by Dan Brown (2003), projects this Gnostic supposition into an involved plot that involves the Roman Catholic Church. In the book, he depicts the Roman Catholic Church as scheming for centuries to hide the "fact" of the marriage of Jesus and Mary, as well as the child supposedly produced by these alleged lovers.

In this long tradition of writers and myth-makers seeking to give Christ a sex-life, Nikos Kazantzakis's *The Last Temptation of Christ* (1955) proves one of the most thoughtful. He assumes that, since Jesus was fully human as well as fully God, that Jesus must have been tempted to leave the cross and enjoy marriage, sex, and family. In the novel, when Jesus prays in the Garden of Gethsamane, this temptation to have a family is part of his pleading with God. Since none of this is supported by the Gospels or the early Christian writers, orthodox Christians have traditionally ignored or decried such theories as fictions.

Paul actually discourages the early Christians from marriage, unless they "burned with passion" and cannot control themselves (1 Cor. 7:9, NIV translation). For him, marriage is a diversion from the more pressing calling of evangelizing the world. Understanding that most folks are not willing to become "eunuchs" for Christ, he does provide some loving counsel for husbands and wives, based on mutual love and submission. His preference for the celibate life led many of the early Christians to believe that the only path of the saint was the way of negation, of meditation and isolation, and that the rejection of family life was the way to show their love of God.

The book of Revelation concludes with the wedding feast of the Lamb, when Christ will come again and take the Church to be his bride. In this beautiful scene, Jesus invites all believers, to join in this joyous celebration:

> And the Spirit and the bride say, Come. And let him that heareth say, Come. and let him that is athirst come. And whosoever will, let him take the water of life freely. (Rev. 22:17)

Literature

The Greeks most certainly recognized the power of Eros. She was the instigator of the Trojan War. It was jealousy as much as anger that motivated Clytemnestra to kill her husband. Lust was certainly the reason Phaedra destroyed her marriage, her step-son, and herself. The Greeks realized that the power of sexual desire causes reasonable men and women to behave as if they are possessed. The Greek comedies are full of sexual innuendo; their comic actors wore enormous artificial phalluses to emphasize their lusty nature. The dramas, produced at the time of the Great Dionysius, were in fact part of a great fertility festival. They honored Dionysus, the god of wine, usually ending the festivities with a drunken orgy.

The lyric writers of Greece also celebrate human love and sexuality. Like King Solomon, the classical writers of Greece and Rome wrote pastoral romances that celebrate the love of a shepherd for his beloved. This charming pretence that sophisticated gentlemen are transformed into simple shepherds pursuing lovely nymphs across the fields allows poets to combine love, nature, youth, and beauty in their lyrics. Like the Song of Solomon, these pastoral poems are full of springtime imagery, woolly sheep, and green pastures. Flowers abound, often as symbols of mutability, encouraging the young woman to "Gather ye rosebuds while ye may/ Old Time is yet a flying."

For the Greeks of the fifth century B.C., the love of one man for another was presented as the ideal expression of sexuality. In Plato's *Symposium,* Socrates leads his attractive young friends in a discussion on the nature of Love that begins with physical attraction but rises to a union of a far more spiritual nature with Ideal Beauty. The funniest part of this symposium is Aristophanes' description of the "original" nature of Love, based on a comic notion of creation. He hypothesizes that we were once yoked creatures, with two heads, four arms, four legs, partially female and partially male (though some were all male or all female). Due to some violation of the gods' orders, the ruling deities split humans into half-beings. We humans therefore go through life searching for our other half—usually the opposite sex, but sometimes of the same sex. This explains the hunger to clasp one another and hold one another as close as possible, to return to our original state of existence. Interestingly, this comic myth has some ideas that parallel the Genesis view of marriage as creating of the two beings "one flesh."

By the late Middle Ages, romantic love had become a popular theme in literature. The "romances," those delicate little tales of adventure in which knights save their beloved ladies from dreadful dangers, charmed aristocratic audiences. Based on the courtly love tradition that flourished during the Crusades and thereafter, they are best known from the Arthurian legends. Such stories as "Sir Gawain and the Green Knight" draw on the elaborate courtesy owed to the "lady" and the obligation of the courtier to sing about his love but forbear his pursuit of the actual woman. In most cases, he is nothing more than a troubadour or a lowly knight, and she is married to the king, his master.

Some of Chaucer's *Canterbury Tales* are examples of the genre. The stories in this famous collection of medieval literary forms vary from courtly romances to bawdy fabliau. "The Miller's Tale" is one of the livelier of the comic stories told by the pilgrims. It is a travesty of the romance, reduced to the lust of common folk and their subsequent common actions. The silly lover in this story is a fool, tricked into kissing the buttocks of his rival. The "lady" plots with another young clerk to outwit her old husband and enjoy a night of extramarital sex with her "lover." At the end, no one is badly hurt, the intrigue is revealed, and the neighbors have a good laugh.

By contrast, Chaucer's Knight tells a prim story of idealized love which echoes some of the imagery of Song of Solomon. Set in ancient Greece, it employs the devices of medieval romances. He pictures the beloved Emilia with her long yellow hair, sitting in the enclosed garden gathering flowers, weaving a garland for her head. Needless to say, she immediately becomes the love object of the knight Palamon when he is imprisoned in a tower. He cries out at this vision of loveliness:

Prison was not the reason for my cry.
For I was hurt just now, pierced through the eye
Right to the heart; the wound is killing me.
The beauty of that lady whom I see
There in that garden wandering to and fro,
Made me cry out; she's cause of all my woe.
I don't know if she's woman or goddess,
But it is really Venus, I would guess.

(Chaucer, "The Knight's Tale," 29)

This exaggerated emotion and pseudo-veneration of the lady, putting her on a pedestal, is quite unlike the approach of King Solomon, who has no doubt that his beloved is thoroughly human. Another scene in "The Knight's Tale" makes explicit the young knight's devotion to Venus, the goddess of love, to whom he pledges his devotion. Even so, there is no hint of the kind of sexual delights that are so clear in the Song of Solomon.

The story tracks the extended conflict between two friends, both of whom are enamored of the same woman, ending with the death of the rival and the marriage of the lovers. Even the narrator comments that the story ends "at last," and is acclaimed by the group as "noble." There is no hint of sensuality in the story, which is full to overflowing with honor and proper conduct. For this genre, the dance of courtship is more important than the passionate embrace.

Courtly love was based in part on worship of Venus, and in part on the veneration of the Virgin Mary, who had become an idealized figure of the perfect, eternally virginal female. Like the Virgin, women of high estate were also portrayed as spiritual beings, enthroned far above base, sensual men, to be adored from afar. This chivalric love, which elicited extraordinary poetry written by such sonneteers as Plutarch, is an ideal love, never to be consummated. In fact, the woman that is the object of the knight's adoration is often married to someone else. The lovelorn suitor sings songs in her honor, fights battles for her glory, but never expects to share her bed. The stylized imagery of her beauty (rose-red lips, pearly teeth, golden hair) has no clear relationship to her actual appearance. The love itself is often described as a form of sickness.

The Renaissance Spanish writer Miguel de Cervantes uses his comic masterpiece *Don Quixote* (1615) to mock these courtly romances with their exaggerated imagery. A scarecrow of a man, of the wrong age, the wrong appearance, the wrong class, Don Quixote undertakes a quest for adventure, making believe his armor is satisfactory, his poor hack of a horse is a magnificent steed, and that he is a true knight of the medieval tradition. His grotesque celebration of a local wench whom he barely knows, as the love of his life, is a delightful spoof on the Petrarchan love tradition. While Don longs for his beloved and beatific Dulcinea, the real neighboring peasant woman is crude and lusty. Sancho Panza, his short, fat partner in chivalry, who rides on a donkey at his side, has a wife and a family while Don has only his dreams of beauty and adventure.

Shakespeare also makes fun of this artificial fashion of love-making in his sonnets, especially the one that begins, "My mistress' eyes are nothing like the sun." He portrays his dark-haired beauty as being far more human than the usual object of the courtly lovers, and his love as being far more real. Although some of his plays toy with the fantasies of courtly love, most of them present the real stresses and stains of marriage, showing both men and women as fully human. His later plays and his tragedies often reveal the complex interplay of emotions in a realistic picture of affection between the sexes.

Romeo and Juliet is full of idealized love, elegant speeches, and melodramatic gestures. The scene that follows the secret wedding of Romeo and Juliet, for example, is a triumph of love poetry. The pain of separation the lovers know, and their final death scene also echo the moods expressed in both the Song of Songs and of Petrarchan love poetry. Like the romances, his early plays often idealize the love of the beautiful maiden and the handsome young man (or sometimes the somewhat older duke) who are clearly intended for one another.

In *A Midsummer Night's Dream*, Shakespeare takes a comic approach to love. On the one hand we have the wedding ritual for Theseus and Hippolyta. We also have the argument between the king of the fairies and his queen over her insistence on keeping a little "changeling boy." Lysander and Demetrius are both in love with Hermia, who loves one but is doomed to marry the other. Hermia's friend Helena is in love with Demetrius, who is determined to marry Hermia, who does not love him. And then we have crude tradesmen, who are acting out the ancient tale of Pyramus and Thisbe. The comedy of love is capped by the enchanted Queen Titania's love for the crude Bottom, who is magically outfitted with the head of a donkey. It is clear that Shakespeare thinks love is both blind and foolish. The impossible story is a scramble of love affairs that Shakespeare delights in ensnarling still further, before he provides some recognitions to the lovers, bringing them all to a satisfactory conclusion.

As we might expect, his tragedies picture love and lust somewhat differently. *Macbeth* shows both love and manipulation, with Lady Macbeth sharing her husband's ambition and facilitating murders in order to achieve their common goals. Hamlet is outraged that his beloved mother has forgotten his father so quickly and is willing to fall into bed with his uncle, whom he suspects of foul play.

One of the most love-saturated of his plays is *Antony and Cleopatra*. The famous lovers are willing to risk their reputations, their political power, and finally their lives for their love of one another. This is a story of adultery on the international stage. Cleopatra, Queen of Egypt, is a world famous beauty, who has also been mistress to Caesar. When she first appears, floating down the Nile on a gorgeous barge, she dazzles her Roman guest. While he lavishes his attention on her, falling victim to her temptations, others back in Rome plot against them both. He does break away long enough to return to Rome to rebuild his relationship with Octavius by marrying his sister, but soon returns to his Egyptian mistress, thereby angering his new wife and his fellow rulers.

Cleopatra is willing to play Antony for her advantage and her country's, even accompanying him to battle and encouraging him to challenge Octavius to a duel. He loses his followers, his prestige, his authority—all for "this false soul of Egypt." Yet he loves her and she him to the very death. Each of them commits suicide, he by falling on his sword, she by the bite of an asp smuggled into her rooms and held to her breast for that purpose. Caesar, recognizing the depth their destructive but irresistible love, orders them buried in the same grave.

Antony's beautiful speeches describing Cleopatra's beauty and her charm are among Shakespeare's greatest tributes to the power of erotic love. The story line, however, is a cautionary tale of the destructiveness of illicit love, that ruins marriages, loyalties, and finally destroys the lovers.

One of the most poetic of the Renaissance writers, Edmund Spenser, sought to copy the style of the classical celebration of marriage in his poems "Epithalamion" and "Prothalamion." Replete with poetic diction and classical references, the poems are lovely examples of Renaissance style. He speaks of the "Flocke of Nymphes" carrying flowers to the wedding bower, includes a prayer for the blessing of the marriage, and ends with a double wedding. The prothalamion (a prelude to the wedding) is dedicated to specific members of the court on the occasion of their marriage. His other "nuptial hymn" or "Epithalamion" also has its share of nymphs, minstrels, and groomsmen. The bride's description combines Petrarchan and biblical imagery: "goodly eyes lyke Saphyres," a "forehead yvory white," cheeks "lyke apples which the sun hath rudded," a breast "like a bowle of creame uncrudded," and a "snowie neck lyke to a marble towre." He also echoes the Psalms in his movement toward the "temple gates" where the wedding is to take place. The attention to the ceremony is explicitly religious and spiritual, making clear that this is not a celebration of eroticism but of marriage—unlike the Song of Solomon. The poem takes the couple into the evening, when the wedding guests have left and the couple enjoy the "bridale bowre and geniall bed" "without blemish or staine."

The poetry of the seventeenth century is full of love, lust, and psychology of sex. It clearly follows in the tradition of Greek pastorals. Christopher Marlowe wrote the lyrical song of "The Passionate Shepherd to His Love":

> Come live with me and be my Love,
> And we will all the pleasures prove
> That hills and valleys, dales and field,
> Or woods or steepy mountains yields.
>
> And we will sit upon the rocks,
> And see the shepherds feed their flocks
> By shallow rivers, to whose falls
> Melodious birds sing madrigals.
>
> And I will make thee beds of roses
> And a thousand fragrant posies,
> A cap of flowers, and a kirtle
> Embroidered all with leaves of myrtle.

> (Marlowe, "The Passionate Shepherd to His Love")

The song uses the next three more stanzas, to describe the gown, the slippers, the belt, and the other bits of dress they will glean from the pretty lambs, the straw, the ivy, and other natural contributors. The easy rhymes, regular rhythm and total absence of real descriptions of the natural world make this a totally artificial seduction song, celebrating youth and springtime.

Sir Walter Raleigh, taking the point-of-view of the older, more world-weary lover, responds to this song with his own:

> If all the world and love were young,
> And truth in every shepherd's tongue,
> These pretty pleasures might me move
> To live with thee and be thy Love.

He goes on to note that Time drives flocks to other fields, rivers rage, winter comes, flowers fade, and the "honey tongue" soon proves to hide a "heart of gall."

> Thy gowns, thy shoes, thy beds of roses,
> Thy cap, thy kirtle, and thy posies,
> Soon break, soon wither—soon forgotten,
> In folly ripe, in reason rotten.

His final stanza is a sad acknowledgement of the evanescent quality of both youth and love:

> But could youth last, and love still breed,
> Had joys no date, nor age no need,
> Then these delights my mind might move
> To live with thee and be thy Love.

> (Raleigh, "The Nymph's Reply to the Shepherd")

The Renaissance in England was a splendid period for erotic love poetry. John Donne wrote some of the very best. He was willing to break the rules of poetry and challenge the traditional usage of religious language to express the depth of his passion for his beloved. "The Canonization," for example, is thoroughly unorthodox in thought and expression, beginning, "For God's sake hold your tongue, and let me love." This is hardly the standard opening of a love song.

Another of his metaphysical poems contains a particularly grotesque image. "The Flea" presents the concept of the physical blending of the two lovers' blood, the insect having bitten them both. "This flea is you and I, and this/ Our marriage bed, and marriage temple is." Only a Metaphysical poet, in love with fresh imagery that will break traditional molds would have attempted such a ludicrous thought.

Donne is also capable of extremely delicate expressions, as in "A Valediction Forbidding Mourning."

> Our two souls therefore, which are one,
> Though I must go, endure not yet
> A breach, but an expansion,
> Like gold to airy thinness beat.

> (Donne, "A Valediction Forbidding Mourning")

A later seventeenth-century Metaphysical poet, Andrew Marvell, was also a witty and thoughtful poet of love. His passion occasionally shines through, though his carefully controlled verse forms and clever turns of phrase make poems like "To His Coy Mistress" more witty than passionate. For example, look at this couplet:

> The grave's a fine and private place,
> But none, I think, do there embrace.

In this, he answers her coyness by his challenge to consider the short life of youth and the approach of death, ending with more emotion than he demonstrates in much of the earlier part of the poem:

> Let us roll all our strength and all
> Our sweetness up into one ball,
> And tear our pleasures with rough strife
> Thorough the iron gates of life:
> Thus, though we cannot make our sun
> Stand still, yet we will make him run.

> (Marvell, "To His Coy Mistress")

The Romantics and Victorians saw a return to a Medieval view of women as either virgins or sluts, therefore to be adored or abhorred and abused. The hero (if he is a righteous man) carefully controls his passions and their expression. Love is the great motivating force in most of the Victorian novels. The careful calibration of love in Jane Austen's stories of young women searching for suitable mates gave way to great gusts of passion in stories by Charles Dickens, Thomas Hardy, Charlotte and Emily Brontë, and many others. By this time, young people were more free than they had ever been to choose mates according to their affections rather than relying solely on parental arrangements. The romantic tale therefore took on new excitement, and the narratives presented new threats to women increasingly liberated from the protections of the older societies.

T. S. Eliot, whose love of tradition led him back to the scripture and to the classics, uses the image of wedded bliss as an ironic counterpoint to his scenes of stale marriages, failed seductions, and meaningless affairs. When poor J. Alfred Prufrock tries to attract a woman, she replies, "That is not it at all, / That is not what I meant at all" (Eliot, "The Love Song of J. Alfred Prufrock"). He acknowledges that he is not likely to hear the mermaids singing to him—though he has heard them. He is too old and too tired to be tempted.

When the typist, in *The Wasteland* is visited by the carbuncular clerk, he sees that the "time is now propitious":

> The meal is ended, she is bored and tired,
> Endeavours to engage her in caresses
> Which still are unreproved, if undesired.
> Flushed and decided, he assaults at once;
> Exploring hands encounter no defence;
> His vanity requires no response,
> And makes a welcome of indifference.

When he leaves, she looks at herself in the mirror, barely aware that he has departed:

> Her brain allows one half-formed thought to pass:
> "Well now that's done: and I'm glad it's over."

> (Eliot, *The Wasteland*)

In *The Wasteland*, the Thames does not flow with flowers toward the wedding scene, but carries along its waters nasty scraps of modern life. Unlike the deep sense of distress that the betrayed woman feels in eighteenth-century novel *The Vicar of Wakefield*, these women are trivial and bored. They see sex as nothing more than a game of chess. In the eighteenth and nineteenth centuries, "When lovely woman stoops to folly and learns too late that men betray," nothing can "soothe her melancholy" and no art "can wash her sin away." For the Victorian maiden, once fallen, she had no means to recover her virtue or redeem herself. She must die to be forgiven. The modern citizen of the wasteland world, walking through London's dirty streets, drinking with friends in the bars, indulging in meaningless sex, there is no shame. Her liberation frees her from the after effects of "folly," but also insulates her from the rich experience of erotic delight known to King Solomon and his beloved.

C. S. Lewis, in his retelling of the myth of Psyche and Cupid, *Till We Have Faces*, analyzes the various faces of love. In the beginning, the narrator, Orual, loves her sister in a familial and nurturing way, making Psyche the center of her life. When Psyche is sacrificed as the bride of the Brute, however, and becomes a transformed woman, Orual's love turns to an envious and possessive form of Eros. She threatens to kill herself and thinks of killing Psyche rather than allowing her sister to live in the embraces of this shadowy creature—even though Psyche is abundantly pleased with her marriage. In the third phase, she comes to understand a deeper and more caring sort of love, in which she identifies with the suffering of her sister. As she comes closer to her own understanding of God's love and mystery, she begins to understand the deep joy that Psyche experienced in her brief time as a wife.

Conclusion

Sexual love has become the great subject of modern literature. In more recent times, the love between women, between men, between women and men have all been explored in excruciating detail. Films, television shows, plays, poems, songs, short stories, and novels consider every possible nuance of human relationships. For all the explicit detail and freedom, the rich human joy in the marriage bed usually is missing. Unlike the scripture, which admonishes the lover not to arouse or awaken love "until it so desires," the modern writers focus on arousal. No longer enclosed in a garden, reserving the sexual pleasures for the marriage, the modern lover diminishes the delights by making them everyday activities, unaccompanied by love or commitment.

See also: **God's Love, Humans' Response; The Hero; Friends and Family; Women as Heroes.**

Bibliography

Carr, G. Lloyd. "Song of Songs." In *A Complete Literary Guide to the Bible,* ed. Leland Ryken and Tremper Longman III. Grand Rapids, MI: Zondervan Publishing House, 1993.

Cervantes Saavedra, Miguel de. *Don Quixote.* Trans., P. A. Motteaux. New York: Knopf, 1991.

Chaucer, Geoffrey. *The Canterbury Tales.* New York: Modern Library, 1994.

de Rougement, Denis. *Love in the Western World.* Trans., Montgomery Belgion. Princeton, NJ: Princeton University Press, 1956.

Donne, John. "A Valediction Forbidding Mourning." In *British Poetry and Prose,* vol. I, ed. Paul Robert Lieder, Robert Morss Lovett, and Robert Kilburn Root. Boston: Houghton Mifflin Company, 1950.

Eliot, T. S. "The Love Song of J. Alfred Prufrock" and *The Wasteland.* In *The Complete Poems and Plays: 1909–1950.* New York: Harcourt, Brace & World, 1952.

Günter, W., and H. G. Link. "Love." In *The New International Dictionary of New Testament Theology,* vol. 2, ed. Colin Brown. Grand Rapids, MI: Zondervan Publishing House, 1986.

Lewis, C. S. *The Allegory of Love: A Study in Medieval Tradition.* New York: Oxford University Press, 1958.

———. "The Four Loves." In *The Inspirational Writings of C.S. Lewis.* New York: Harcourt Brace Jovanovich, 1960.

———. *Till We Have Faces.* New York: Harcourt Brace Jovanovich, 1980.

Marlowe, Christopher. "The Passionate Shepherd to His Love." In *British Poetry and Prose,* vol. I, ed. Paul Robert Lieder, Robert Morss Lovett, and Robert Kilburn Root. Boston: Houghton Mifflin, 1950.

Marvell, Andrew. "To His Coy Mistress." In *British Poetry and Prose,* vol. I, ed. Paul Robert Lieder, Robert Morss Lovett, and Robert Kilburn Root. Boston: Houghton Mifflin, 1950.

Pagels, Elaine. *The Gnostic Gospels.* New York: Random House, 1979.

Raleigh, Sir Walter. "The Nymph's Reply to the Shepherd." In *The Renaissance in England: Non-dramatic Prose and Verse of the Sixteenth Century,* ed. Hyder E. Rollins and Herschel Baker. Boston: D.C. Heath and Company, 1954.

Shakespeare, William. *Antony and Cleopatra, A Midsummer's Night's Dream,* and *Romeo and Juliet, Sonnets.* In *Shakespeare: Major Plays and the Sonnets,* ed. G. B. Harrison. New York: Harcourt, Brace and Company, 1948.

Spenser, Edmund. "Epithalamion" and "Prothalamion." In *The Renaissance in England: Non-dramatic Prose and Verse of the Sixteenth Century,* ed. Hyder E. Rollins and Herschel Baker. Boston: D.C. Heath and Company, 1954.

Trawick, Buckner B. *The Bible as Literature: The Old Testament and the Apocrypha.* New York: Barnes and Noble Books, 1970.

The Hero

Readings

Joshua
Judges 6–8
Homer, The *Iliad* and the *Odyssey* (c. 800 B.C.)
Plato, *Socrates' Apology* (c. 390 B.C.)
Aristotle, *Poetics* (c. 320 B.C.)
William Shakespeare, *Macbeth* (1605)
John Milton, *Samson Agonistes* (1671)
A. E. Housman, *A Shropshire Lad* (1896)
Vachel Lindsay, "Samson" (1917)
T. S. Eliot, "The Love Song of J. Alfred Prufrock" (1917), *Murder in the Cathedral*
    (1917)
Harper Lee, *To Kill a Mockingbird* (1960)
Paddy Chayefsky, *Gideon* (1961)
Tom Wolfe, *The Bonfire of Vanities* (1987), *A Man in Full* (1998)

Introduction

In the beginning, God. (Gen. 1:1)

For unto us a child is born, unto us a son is given: and the government shall
be upon his shoulder: and his name shall be called Wonderful, Counselor, The
mighty God, The everlasting Father, The Prince of Peace. (Isa. 9:6)

The real hero of all of scripture is God himself—God the Father and Creator in
the Old Testament, God the Son in the Gospels, and God the Holy Spirit in the book
of Acts and the Epistles. The Bible, the "greatest story ever told," is the epic drama
of God's relationship to his new creation, humankind. It tells of men's and women's

breach of trust, of God's guidance, punishment, forgiveness, and the ultimate sacrifice of His own son for the redemption of humans.

Since the story of the mighty acts of God is told from the point-of-view of humans, it tends to focus on the creatures rather than the creator. Still, behind and above all is the hand of God. The books of the Bible reveal the nature of God bit by bit, limited to what humans can see and understand. For Christians, the climax of this narrative of the hero is in the Incarnation, when the Word is made flesh and dwells among us.

By contrast, human heroes are limited by time, space, and power. The heroes are those extraordinary creatures who rise to the top in a particular historical setting, serving as both a mirror and a lamp for the values of that society. The hero, who is revered by a community, whether he be a warrior, a lover, a leader, an orator, a philosopher, a politician, a cowboy, a detective, a boxer, a doctor, or a fireman, tells us what matters to that group of people. Reflecting the greatest aspirations and fears, while also offering an image of the path to triumph, this figure has traditionally embodied the ideals of the community.

By tracing the characteristics that such heroic figures as Abraham, Jacob, Joseph, Moses, Joshua, or Samson exhibit, we can understand much of the culture from which they spring. The transformation from the fatherly Abraham to the warrior Samson, and then to King David portrays the changing needs of the Hebrews. In the later days of Israel's painful history, the prophets became the heroes, reflecting the hunger for spiritual certainty. All of these are left in the dust as the New Testament proclaims the heroism of Jesus the Christ, a fulfillment of many of their prophesies of the Messiah.

Scripture

As described in the Old Testament, the earliest of the Hebrew heroes are simple men, intent on surviving, preserving their families, and serving their God. Though they may also be handsome, the scripture does not elaborate on the appearance of Abraham, Isaac, or Jacob. Joseph is attractive enough to tempt his boss's wife, but scripture does not provide any description of him. Appearance is significant in Hebrew scriptures only when it proves intrinsic to the story. Sarai (later Sarah) is so beautiful even at 80 that she presents a threat to her husband's safety. Wherever the tribe of Abram (later Abraham) goes, the kings want her, forcing Abram to pretend she is his sister. Later, when Jacob meets Rachel, he loves her at first sight, and is sorely disappointed that he is paid for his first seven years of labor by the hand of Leah (of the weak eyes). Notice that in the Hebrew stories, the female's beauty is more important than the male's. We know that Saul was a large man, that Stephen looked like an angel when he was dying, but further description is absent. Even Jesus is not described physically.

We are probably to assume that all of these men looked like the other Hebrews: dark hair and eyes, sunburned skin, beards, and clothing common to other men of their class. Only when the usual Hebrew dress is replaced, suited with armor or stripped to a loin cloth of camel's hair, or embellished with a coat of many colors, is clothing worth mentioning.

It is rather their personalities that differentiate them, usually hinted at in terse passages: Ishmael grows up to be like a wild ass; Esau is hairy and loves hunting; Jacob is a smooth man, who dwells in tents. None of the Patriarchs have the brutality of an Achilles, but Jacob and Joseph are as clever as Odysseus. Jacob in particular is something of a trickster, willing to join his mother in cheating his impetuous brother Esau out of his patrimony. When his father-in-law, Laban, turns the tables on him, tricks him into an unwelcome marriage, Jacob bides his time, finally building his family, winning the bride of his heart, and making himself a fortune before returning the favor. Even when he returns to his own country and to a meeting with his long-estranged brother Esau, Jacob is careful in his approach and conniving in his response. He trusts no one.

Joseph is more sheltered than his father was. The favorite son, he is pampered and clever; but he proves himself more of a good man and a forthright one, not willing to lie or cheat others. His harmless tricks serve the purpose of testing his brothers, not hurting them. He is a man to be trusted and loved. He is also forgiving, though clear-sighted in what his brothers have done to him. His love for his family is tinged with an understanding of their potential for deceit. The Hebrews love leaders who are shrewd, protective, and foresighted. They also admire men who have close relationships with God, who are visionaries, dreamers, planners.

With the Exodus, the hero becomes somewhat different. Moses has something of the Greek quality of the hero in his miraculous birth and preservation, as well as in the secret of his Hebrew identity while he is being raised as an adopted child of the Egyptian royal family. He is a man of culture and wealth, an aristocrat. He is also a violent man early in his life, killing the overseer to save one of his own people. His flight into the wilderness and his adventures there, have something of the flavor of Greek stories. But his motives and experiences are clearly Hebrew. He becomes a shepherd, marries and has two sons, meets God face-to-face, and feels the call to return to Egypt and bring his people to freedom.

He relies on God's power, not his own skill as a warrior, a leader, or even an orator. He is not eloquent enough to plead the case of the Hebrew slaves on his own: God provides his more fluent brother, Aaron, to serve as his spokesman. Nor is he much of a warrior during the Exodus. He leads the mass of Hebrews, but relies again on God to deal with the thundering chariots of the Pharaoh. He and his sister Miriam lead the people in singing a song of triumph as they cross over the Red (Reed) Sea on dry land and see the Pharaoh's men and horses overwhelmed by the walls of water.

On his journey through the wilderness, taking his people home to the Promised Land, which none of them have ever seen, he prays for food, for water, for guidance. With God's help, he provides them the means to survive and the Law that would guide them throughout their history. Confronted by tribes of hostile foreigners, Moses turns onto other paths, sometimes allowing his men to fight, but never serving as a warrior himself. He holds his hands up imploring God's power during the battle against the Amelekites, but does not engage in the fighting. By this time, he is an old man, not a hot-blooded young warrior. He is a hero whose strength lies in his close relationship with a powerful God.

Up to this point, most of the leaders are old men, father-figures to their tribe. They accumulate wealth along the way, but still live in tents or huts much of their lives. Except for Moses, they are not accustomed to luxuries or education. Abraham may come from a wealthy family, but we meet him only as he strikes out to become a nomad. Shepherds, without a settled place to live, are tough, protective, thoughtful men. Their day-to-day life is rarely chronicled, a generation might pass in a single verse of scripture. Not courtiers or warriors, they are a hard, shrewd people who love their families and their God, tell their children the ancient stories of Adam and Eve in the Garden of Eden, of Noah's flood, of Abraham's visit with the angels, of the near-sacrifice of their progenitor Isaac, of the providential escape from Egypt. In these stories told around the campfire, discussed over meals, repeated generation after generation, they preserve the memories of their forefathers, and assure that they have a great destiny as the chosen people of God who are to live in the Promised Land.

At the death of Moses, another kind of leader is needed by the Hebrews. This time, God chooses the warrior Joshua to take his people into the Promised Land, to capture it, and to settle it. Joshua has been a close associate of Moses, standing with him when others have defected. An old man by the time he becomes a leader, he is a faithful follower of the Law, a believer in the Covenant between God and the Hebrews.

The time has come for battle, a series of wars against the far stronger indigenous peoples of Palestine. The Canaanites have fortified cities with great walls. The giant Philistines have iron chariots. By contrast, the Hebrews are still a nomadic, stone-age people, using wooden spears, flit-tipped arrows, and slingshots, the weapons they have used against predatory beasts that attack their flocks. They are not prepared for the more sophisticated iron-age people they now confront. But by shrewd devices, clever strategies, and divine intervention, they win the land. First Jericho, that ancient city, sees its wall tumble down and its people massacred. Then one city after another is overwhelmed by these fierce nomads. Fighting a holy war for the land their God has promised them, they gradually take Canaan. (Historians argue about the details, suspecting that the Hebrews infiltrated the Canaanite communities during a long period, even intermarrying, not always waging war against them.)

When the land is settled, the Hebrews continue to need warrior-leaders. The Judges are combined fighters and judges. These charismatic leaders settle arguments and unite some of the tribes for battle against threatening forces. The various tribes sometimes choose men of physical power, but are generally more interested in leaders who combine faith and simple wisdom.

Gideon (Judg. 6–8), a simple man of God, is such a leader. He is a farmer, not a fighter, first introduced in scripture threshing grain in the winepress to avoid the spies of the Midianites, marauders who swoop down to rob farmers at harvest time. Gideon, one of the earliest of the judges, is a reluctant hero. Rather than eagerly agreeing to lead the charge against his foes, he tests God with a miracle involving fleece, dew, and dry ground. When the spirit of the Lord comes upon him, he speaks in a great voice, drawing men to him in great numbers from almost all the tribes of Israel. By following the Lord's leadership, he employs a strategy of placing lamps in jars, blowing trumpets, and scaring the Midianites into a rout. The Lord shows him the way to select the best warriors by watching the way the men drink from a stream. He then takes his sturdy little band to fight the enemy.

When he is successful in his massacre of the Midianites, his people offer him kingship, but he declines. He acknowledges God's kingship instead. His only unwise move is the decision to melt down the Midianites' golden trinkets and make of them a gold ephod, which becomes an object of worship among the Israelites. His reward for his faithful service is a large group of wives, who bear him seventy sons. Unfortunately, his oldest son slaughters all his brothers, fearing they will challenge his power.

Gideon is a modest man of God, faithful in his service, one of the finest of the judges. He protects his people, returns to his plow, and seeks no renown for his heroism. Paddy Chayefsky, a modern American playwright, adapts this biblical story in the 1961 Broadway play, *Gideon*. He pictures him as a common man who had uncommon experiences. Chayefsky chooses to emphasize the transformation of his character as the spirit of the Lord came upon him, changing his voice, his relationships, and his view of himself. He assumes that Gideon would be tempted to accept the kingship, and would want to wear the golden ephod. Once seen as the "donkey" of his clan, he is transformed into a "wild ox" by the end of the story. It would be hard for anyone to remain modest and humble when acclaimed as the savior of his people.

Unfortunately, the play is badly flawed by the ending, which diminishes the God who gives Gideon this opportunity at heroism. When the playwright waxes philosophical, the angel (who is the God-figure) sounds silly rather than profound. Chayefsky does capture something of the comic nature of this gentle man forced into a role he would never have chosen for himself, only to become a leader respected and feared by the multitudes. His arguments with God are hardly heroic. Rather, he does everything he can to escape becoming a hero.

Samson (Judg. 13–16) is a natural hero, marked from birth to be special. He is celebrated for his great strength, which is enhanced as the spirit of God comes upon him from time to time. Unfortunately, his combined power, ungoverned lust, and uncontrollable rage frequently land him in tangled situations. His lust leads him to Philistine women, who are in league with the enemy. When tricked or betrayed, he is as furious as the Greeks' Achilles, and lashes out at those men he considers guilty, generally ignoring his own errors or the perfidy of those women who betrayed him. Eventually, he finds himself blinded, bound, shorn of his long hair, and tied to the pillars of the temple of Dagon in a pagan land. In a final moment of anger and hunger for retribution, with the renewed empowerment of the sprit of God, he pulls the temple down on his enemies and God's.

Samson's chief motive appears to be his own pleasure, until the final scene, when he pulls down the pillars of the temple, praying that he be allowed to sacrifice his own life to avenge the Philistines "for one of my two eyes." He never attacks the women who betrayed him or repents of his own careless lust. He is said to have "judged" for twenty years, but scripture makes no mention of a single judicial act on his part. He is a brute, killing a lion with his bare hands, scraping honey out of a carcass for his delight, setting the foxes' tails on fire and sending them through the crops to burn the fields, destroying olive trees, and killing his wife's vicious kinsmen and Philistine tormentors.

Samson is hardly a typical Hebrew hero. Of all the figures in scripture, he is the one most like the Greeks' Achilles of the *Iliad*, whose wrath is one of the themes of the epic. Rather than serving as a model, Samson stands, as do many of the figures in the book of Judges, as an admonitory example. His adventures teach the Hebrews why they should not marry outside of their faith. The Hebrews are not interested in personal heroism, but in the survival of the tribe. Samson is heroic because he slaughters Philistines, God's more persistent enemies.

The hero-as-family-man is more typical of scripture passages. David weeps when forced to kill his own son Absalom. Although a warrior, capable of killing or ordering others killed, he loves his family in spite of their betrayal. The Hebrew patriarchs are the best representatives of this tradition. Genesis presents one story after another of the preservation of the seed of Abraham. Even when Joseph has been sold into slavery by his brothers, he forgives them and brings them to Egypt to ensure the survival of the family of Jacob.

The kings, who follow the Judges, are often warriors, slaying their thousands and their "tens of thousands." At this point, the Israelites become more like the other peoples around them in their concept of the hero, wanting the big, strong, courageous leader who can keep them safe. In some sense, this continues to be the image of the ideal hero for the Jews. As they are captives of one foreign power after another, they dream of a Messiah king—one who will preserve them as a people.

Jesus must have been a real shock for those looking for a militant hero, a king who would lead his people in rebellion against the Romans. Rather than a handsome young man riding majestically on a horse and brandishing a sword (like Alexander the Great), Jesus rides into Jerusalem on the foal of a donkey and preaches peace. He refuses to defend even himself or to allow his disciple Peter to fight on his behalf. He tells Peter that his kingdom is not of this world, that those who live by the sword will die by the sword.

In the New Testament, the gentle hero becomes the spiritual warrior. As the saint willing to be martyred, the Messiah willing to be sacrificed, this heroic figure transforms the whole concept of the *hero*. We see the fresh vision in the Gospels, where Jesus constantly stands strong, while admonishing his disciples to avoid violence. Blessedness comes with purity, meekness, and peacemaking, not setting foxes' tails on fire or slaying the Philistines with the jawbone of an ass or chasing foreign women. For those of his disciples who are eager to lead an insurrection against Rome, this must have been a disappointment. Choosing to die rather than to fight, Christ displays a courage prophesied by the prophets.

For John the Baptizer, Stephen or Paul or Peter, the path of the saint takes a kind of inner strength that others come to admire and seek to emulate. They eventually face martyrdom, but in their shed blood, the faith triumphs and others come to believe. For Paul, "fighting the good fight" or "running the race" or "wrestling" are spiritual activities, in which the Christian brings glory, not to himself, but to God.

Literature

A. E. Housman, an English poet who wrote in the late nineteenth and early twentieth century, captured something of the ancient Greek and the modern American notion of the hero. For many who train for or who love to watch the Olympic games, sports are a great source of satisfaction. The life of the athlete is marked by formalized rules and challenges of strength like those men face in war, sacrificing self for the greater good of the team, as well as perseverance, discipline, and endurance. Like the ancient Greeks, we tend to love the young, handsome hero of the football field, the basketball court, or the track. Running for his own glory and that of his town or country (as in the Olympic Games), he is lionized for a time, and then forgotten. Housman's poem "To an Athlete Dying Young" captures something of the irony of this young fellow who has had his 15 minutes of fame:

> The time you won your town the race
> We chaired you through the market place;
> Man and boy stood cheering by,
> And home we brought you shoulder high.

"Luckily" for this young man, he dies young, before he wears his honors out and is forgotten by the very folk who have cheered so heartily:

> Today, the road all runners come,
> Shoulder-high we bring you home,
> And set you at your threshold down,
> Townsman of a stiller town.

> (Housman, "To an Athlete Dying Young,"
> in *A Shropshire Lad*, 935)

Still wearing the champion's garland of laurel on his golden curls, he remains a hero rather than becoming a "has-been."

Housman's gentle, lyrical poem captures the Greek adulation of youth and beauty and physical prowess, very different from the Hebrew ideal of the old man, clever, and empowered by God. When the Greeks conquered Palestine under the leadership of Alexander the Great, they brought their zeal for athletics with them, building stadia in the major cities, even in Jerusalem. The young Hebrew men were sorely tempted to join in the gymnasium activities, running the foot races, throwing the discus, and swimming in the pools, soaking in the hot baths, and luxuriating with the rub-downs with olive oil, which the Greeks relished. This athletic hero figure, whom Paul employs in his imagery of racers and wrestlers, was antithetical to the Hebrew concept of true heroism. For the Hebrew, the man to be admired was the protector of his people, the follower of his God.

The figure of the athletic hero has a long history in Greek culture. The very choice of the warrior-hero Achilles as the central figure in the *Iliad* idealizes the savage fighter: brutal with his enemies, supernatural in power (Achilles' mother is a goddess), and jealous of any attack on his proud name. Achilles is a good musician and a loyal friend to his tent-mate, Patrocolus (probably even a lover). He is an aristocrat attended by servants, and he expects to make full use of those women conquered in battle. When Agamemnon ruthlessly takes the woman who is Achilles's booty from the war, he believes himself to be publicly humiliated, and refuses to fight until she is returned. His refusal to engage the enemy leads to the death of his friend, and then to the death of a host of other people. He knows that, when he once again joins the fray, he will be trading a long, uneventful life for a brief, heroic one. Eventually, he chooses heroism and death. Bigger than life, Achilles is violent and relentless—the perfect warrior for a primitive world.

Another type of Greek hero described by Homer, Odysseus, the epic wanderer of the *Odyssey*, is an older man. Although beloved of some of the gods (and hated by others), he is all human. Having fought with valor in the Trojan War, and led his men in the violent conquest of the city of Troy, he is tired and ready to return to Ithaca. He has been away from his wife, Penelope, for 10 years and wants to take his men back to their homeland. His tortuous journey, with contrary winds and strange adventures, leads him to exotic lands of Lotus Eaters, one-eyed monsters, and gracious hosts. It also leads through many temptations, some of which can prove fatal to members of his crew—such as sailing between Scylla and Charybdis, resisting the song of the Sirens. He is a mature, wily man, a strong wrestler, a good leader, a loving husband and father, but a man easily tempted by other women, and by adventures. He is known for his ability to twist the truth when it suits his purposes, for his handsome appearance, and for his clever tricks.

Centuries later, the Greeks honored yet another kind of hero, Socrates, an ugly old man, but a gentle and thoughtful philosopher. Socrates, whose story is told by his disciple Plato, acts as the "gadfly" of Athens, stirring up troubles among the rulers and those who think themselves wise. Eventually, his enemies bring him to trial before the Aeropagus, giving him the choice of leaving the city as an exile or dying of hemlock. The old philosopher chooses to die rather than leave his beloved Athens. In his "Apology," Socrates sets out the themes of his life, his delight in walking about with his friends talking of the Good, the True, and the Beautiful. He explains his preference of death to exile or silence. As he insists, "The unexamined life is not worth living."

These three types of heroes that we see in Greek culture, the physical man, the shrewd man, and the thoughtful man, are typical of many people's literature. In the famous survey of the hero in mythology, *The Hero with a Thousand Faces*, Joseph

Campbell outlines the stages in the hero's life, from the supernatural birth, to the great adventure, to the predestined death. He also considers the hero-as-warrior , as lover, as tyrant, as saint, and as savior of his people. Not all of these categories relate easily to the Hebrew heroes, who were historical figures, not mythic creations.

In other cultures, the brute warrior continued to dominate the imagination of savage peoples who admired the strong man, the protector of his people. Siegfried in *The Nibelungenlied,* and even the strong woman Brunhilde, spring from this hunger for security. In England, the Old English hero Beowulf can also wrestle water monsters to their death In the epic poem *Beowulf* (c. 675–725), this young warrior can use a sword, but does not really need one. He wrestles Grendel, a cannibal-ogre, to protect his uncle Hrothgar's mead hall and his fellow thanes. He subsequently swims to the bottom of the sea, where Grendel's mother lives, coming out at night only to terrorize and murder. He tries to kill her with his trusty sword, but is again forced to rely on his great strength to win glory.

At the same time, in Christian countries, the ideal man was supposed to be the sacrificial saint of the New Testament, who sought to conform to "the mind of Christ." The many martyrs of early Christian times testify to the willingness to die rather than fight. With the advent of Islam and the rapid conquest of large parts of Asia, Africa, and Eastern Europe for Allah, Christians saw their faith challenged and abandoned the ideal of pacifism.

A new kind of hero was required, one who would fight for his faith. In France, Roland (in the *Song of Roland,* c. 1100) was a warrior in the army of Charlemagne, fighting the Moslems, who were surging up from Spain, threatening France. In much of Europe, this new hero was the Crusader. The Crusades lasted from 1095–1272. This series of assaults on the Moslems for the conquest of the Holy Land involved England along with the Christian countries of the continent. The Crusades introduced the codes of knighthood and chivalry into England and transformed British literature. Although this Christian warrior, like Joshua, was a warrior who fought for God and the Holy Land, seeking to cleanse the land of the pagan forces, he was very different from this simple old Hebrew. This Christian soldier was handsome and young, idealistic, a great lover and a great fighter. He fought for his king and his beloved, rode out on a beautiful steed, dressed in full armor, with a spear in one hand and a banner in the other. He became the new romantic hero.

This period spawned numerous *Romances,* so-named because they were originally written in "Romance" languages, those deriving from Latin. These were action-packed stories of knights going off to war, or setting out on some great quest. For the Arthurian heroes, the quest was for the Holy Grail. The knights of the Round Table were quite different from the martyred Stephen or the evangelical Paul. They were elegant aristocrats who sought adventure and romance. A rare example of the pure hero, with the sweetness of a Christ figure is Sir Gawain, who appears in the famous alliterative verse tale "Sir Gawain and the Green Knight," or Sir Gawayne and the Grene Knight" (c. 1375). Sir Gawain accepts a challenge from a wildly unlikely mysterious green visitor to King Arthur's court, spends a year in fulfilling the terms of the agreement, faces and resists temptation, and finally is punished for one small failure. His abject repentance marks his sensitivity and faithfulness. It all proves to be a test of his purity.

This story reveals the transition from the epic, primitive, simple-minded hero we have in Beowulf. The new hero is sophisticated, chivalrous, sympathetic to the feelings of others, emotional, and curiously feminized. The emphasis on his chivalrous behavior toward the women of the court and his rejection of offers to enjoy the brutality of the hunt suggest a new softening of the masculine ideal for the society.

In much of Western history, as in world history generally, the warrior in full battle gear has been considered the great hero. He is portrayed in statues, paintings, and literature. In later years, he is revived in Tennyson's Arthurian poems and more recently in the epic *Lord of the Rings*, which has echoes of both Arthur's knights and Beowulf's mead hall associates.

Shakespeare draws on this popularity of the swashbuckling hero in some of his history plays. His more heroic kings are admirable largely because of their prowess in battle. The thrill of combat, the excitement of risking life, the love of comrades, and the exaltation of victory makes this the most memorable time of a man's life. Most of Shakespeare's histories and tragedies take advantage of this intensification of emotion, involving on-stage battle scenes.

The battles may have drawn the crowds to see his plays, but the rationale for the heroic gesture gives shape and purpose to his plays. Shakespeare clearly differentiates between Henry, who is fighting for his people, and Macbeth, who is fighting for himself. In the early scenes of *Macbeth*, the protagonist is indeed a hero, but in the later ones, he becomes a villain. Not just fighting and winning, but fighting for the right cause, is central to the concept of heroism. This amazing author sees human conflicts with such realism that he refuses to portray his characters as simply good or bad.

Macbeth is so consumed with ambition, the hunger for power and glory, that he never bothers with idealistic justification of his fights. Unlike young David, who refuses to kill Saul because Saul is the anointed king, even when ambition would have encouraged him and self-preservation would have justified it, Macbeth deliberately plots the murder of the king. Shakespeare accepts the scriptural principle that the king is God-ordained, to be honored even when, like Richard II, he is unworthy of that honor.

The turbulent period that followed the Elizabethan produced so many quarrels and wars, so much human drama, that authors were rarely inspired to portray their characters in heroic terms. Those who continued to support the king and his cause, even after the execution of Charles I became the last of the romantics, who dreamed of the restoration of their "rightful king."

The seventeenth-century writer Richard Lovelace captures the tone of these Cavalier warriors, with their plumed hats, ruffled shirts, and polished boots, elegant members of the forces of aristocracy. This "Renaissance Man" combines good looks, aristocratic heritage, learning, courteous behavior, and charm. In his poem bidding his beloved farewell, Lovelace writes: "I could not love thee, dear, so much,/Loved I not honor more.(Lovelace, "To Lucasta, on Going to the Wars," 479). In this poem, which has only three stanzas, Lovelace captures the artificial posture of the swashbuckling gentleman preparing for "glorious" warfare.

Lovelace himself, an educated young man, a defender of King Charles and a staunch Royalist, who went to prison for the King, became a kind of model for Sir Walter Scott (in *Here's a Health to King Charles*) and Robert Browning (*Cavalier Lyrics*). Scott's novels, especially those that capture something of the spirit of the followers of the royal Scots line, the "Jacobites," continue this romantic vision of the handsome, idealistic outlaw with hot aristocratic blood.

John Milton, by contrast, was a member of the opposition forces, the Puritans, who searched the scripture for their heroes. In his tragedy *Samson Agonistes: A Dramatic Poem* (1671), Milton portrays Samson, not as a young and glorious warrior, but as a dying and mutilated sinner. Attacking the narrative on the final day of Samson's life, when he is "eyeless in Gaza," Milton concentrates the action and turns the story into a powerfully philosophic meditation on power and predestination. Why would God have given such power and such temptation to so weak a man? Could this have been for the predestined purpose of destroying the Philistines and their "fish-god" Dagon?

Milton, whose own blindness must have made this figure a sympathetic subject, also shared with Samson an unhealthy desire for fame, which he considered "the last infirmity of the noble mind." For the Christian writer, this would be considered a sin—like the hubris of the hero.

Few others have followed Milton's example of honoring Samson as a hero. A curious exception to this is the twentieth-century American writer Vachel Lindsay. In "How Samson Bore Away the Gates of Gaza," Lindsay uses a galloping anapestic rhythm and heavy masculine rhymes to picture Samson's uprooting and destruction of Gaza's gates. Transforming the Old Testament judge into a pop hero like the heavyweight boxing champion Jack Johnson (a sports icon of the early twentieth century), Lindsay uncovers the standard temptations for the hero: women, drink, violence. Lindsay portrays a chastened Samson, not clearly revealed in the sparse biblical story, who repents, feels "honey in his soul," and laments his wicked ways, only to be awarded with "grace abounding." Lindsay envisions his death, like Elijah's, with a chariot carrying him off. Yet, in his circular, curiously inverted poetic structure, Lindsay begins the narrative with the triumph at Gaza and ends with the memory of Delilah's betrayal. He repeatedly invites the reader to meditate on Samson's sorrow: "Let Samson/Be coming/Into your mind." This refrain concludes the poem.

The refrain, a typical pattern in Lindsay's rollicking poetry, endows it with the quality of a song that might be used at a Salvation Army revival meeting. The writer, a twentieth-century American mystic from Illinois, was an enormously talented and deeply idiosyncratic wandering minstrel, whose religious fervor marks much of his poetry. He saw himself as a kind of modern-day troubadour who enthusiastically recited his own poetry to delighted crowds across the country. Samson was a clear choice of subject for him, and the refrain serves as a kind of evangelical altar call. He wanted to translate the wayward judge's experiences into the vernacular of modern Americans. In "How Samson Bore Away the Gates of Gaza," Lindsay takes considerable license with Samson's story, while remaining faithful to the biblical view of the man. As he says to God, "You made me Judge, and I am not wise" (in Ackerman, 156). His repeated return to his sinful path foreshadows the final cataclysmic scene in Gaza.

Although Milton's *Samson Agonistes* is a tragic masterpiece, *Paradise Lost* was far more influential. His characterization of Satan, a magnificent fallen angel, as majestic in his defiance of God, had a powerful impact on the concept of the hero for later English writers. This rebellious hero dominates much of nineteenth-century literature, from Byron to Wilde. Mario Praz tracks this "fallen beauty, of splendour shadowed by sadness and death ... majestic though in ruin" (Praz 56 ff.). Goethe revived the medieval fable of Faust; Byron enjoyed the perverse exploits of the legendary Don Juan; and others continued the tradition of the hero of sinister charm, sometimes a sublime criminal, sometimes an angel-outlaw. During the nineteenth century, even Russian and American literature reflected this Byronic hero the Romantics loved so dearly. The Brontë sisters both used the model—for Heathcliff in *Wuthering Heights* and for Mr. Rochester in *Jane Eyre*. Dostoyevsky follows the trend in *The Possessed*, with the twisted aristocratic hero Nicholas Stravrogin; and Poe loved the perverse hero, often doomed, vicious, and mysterious, who dominates most of his Gothic tales.

For most of these figures, the combination of great gifts and twisted values provide a grotesque thrill for the reader, who both admires and dreads the figure at the center of the story. He is different from the later anti-hero, who has none of this grandeur or deliberate preference for contamination. Lord Byron's influence on moderns is obvious: the Byronic hero has no respect for women, no love of country, no moral values. Often a handsome man of great talents, he wastes his life, destroys those who love him, and leaves behind nothing but disaster. The women in the stories usually hope to redeem him by their love. Sometimes they succeed.

On a much less majestic and toxic level, American writers have sought to turn middle-class men into heroes. The great example of this is Arthur Miller, who insists that Willie Loman, whose very name argues against his heroism, is nonetheless an Aristotelian hero in his love for his family. *Death of a Salesman* (1949) is surely a fine and representative American play, but hardly a tragic one. The old salesman is so stuffed full of shoddy values and silly goals that he is impossible to admire. His betrayal of his wife, his misleading of his sons, and his continual lying to himself force the audience to respond with sympathy, or pity, or sadness, but not admiration of his "heroism."

A far better example of the father as hero is to be found in David James Duncan's *The Brothers K* (1992). In contrast with the athlete of Housman's poem, this old pitcher for a minor league baseball team is crippled and worn out. He has dedicated his life to caring for his wife and children rather than his own career. His gentle spirit, strong sense of responsibility, tolerance and acceptance of the crazy family he adores make him a powerful model of the nurturing father. His discipline and sense of calling as an athlete also teach his boys something about the right way to live their lives.

An earlier example of the sports hero is Clifford Odets' famous play *Golden Boy* (1939), which traces the rise of a talented fighter who is also a talented musician. Coming from a family that honors the music more than the battle, he is conflicted in his rise in the ring. He knows that dedicating himself to winning will result in the mutilation of his hands, rendering his violin-playing impossible. This tension between two cultural ideals makes this play much more powerful than later films such as *Rocky*, which deal in far simpler terms with the rise to fame as the champ.

The more common moral question for the hero of the boxing story is whether he should show any mercy for his opponent. The battle is not for country or culture, but for personal glory—much like the old Greek ideal in the Olympic Games. In the games, howerever, the athlete traditionally also ran or boxed for his city state's glory.

A more recent trend in American literature has been the veneration of the gentle, sensitive man, like Atticus Finch in Harper Lee's *To Kill a Mockingbird* (1960). The thinking hero, the lawyer-father seeks to save the weak and helpless. His faith is in mercy and justice, not in violence and power. He is one of many secular saints who have replaced the Old Testament prophets in modern literature. They take the central role in their stories by their wisdom and kindness. Their strength is within, and their heroism merits no great monuments or heroic war songs. Like "gentle Jesus, meek and mild," they become the loving transformers of their world, kind to animals, children, and women. Lost in this figure is the blunt and sometimes angry Son of God, who confronted the money-changers in the Temple and called the scribes and the Pharisees a "brood of vipers."

The modern novelist or dramatist tends to prefer realism to idealism. The tradition of realism tends to flatten characters into recognizable figures with all the flaws we see in one another, all of the failures of faith and courage, and with few grandiose gestures. The inclination is to construct characters like J. Alfred Prufrock, the title character of T. S. Eliot's poem "The Love Song of J. Alfred Prufrock." As Prufrock himself says:

> No! I am not Prince Hamlet, nor was meant to be;
> Am an attendant lord, one that will do
> To swell a progress, start a scene or two,
> Advise the prince, no doubt, an easy tool,
> Deferential, glad to be of use,
> Politic, cautious, and meticulous;
> Full of high sentence, but a bit obtuse;
> At times, indeed, almost ridiculous—
> Almost, at times, the Fool.

(Eliot, "The Love Song of J. Alfred Prufrock," 7)

In the twentieth century, T. S. Eliot led a resurgence of Christian authors, who returned to many of the themes of the past. In his poetry and his essays, Eliot traces his own spiritual transformation. And in his plays, he seeks to revive the type of Christian hero. *Murder in the Cathedral* is a drama designed to be played in Canterbury Cathedral, where the original historical action transpired.

Thomas à Becket, the Renaissance politician who became the Archbishop of Canterbury, was forced to decide between his king and his faith. To personify Thomas's temptation to follow the king's will , Eliot chooses three tempters. Each echoes one of the three temptations of Christ in the wilderness, echoing Milton's *Paradise Regained*. Each comes as a courtier who has known Thomas since he was Henry's Chancellor: the first offers a return to the festive times of youth, when they enjoyed women, drink, and song—the delights of the flesh. The second offers a return to the king's court, as his Chancellor with all of the powers of the political sphere. The third proposes a more dubious dream of leading the landed gentry, who would usurp the king's power. Then comes a fourth, one who was not expected like the others. He offers the temptation of martyrdom, or as Thomas notes, doing the "right thing for the wrong reason."

Thomas rejects each in turn, facing his own death with resignation, knowing he is doing God's will. His final sermon (like Socrates's apologia) is an explanation of his motives in choosing martyrdom. We see the violation of the cathedral as the assassins storm in and kill him in full view of the priests, during vespers. The scene echoes the sacrifice of Christ. Performed during worship in the house of God, it mirrors the mass. The chorus of women, representing the common folk, and the priests listen as the murderers justify their heinous deed in words of low comedy, stripping the tragic majesty from the play, and perhaps suggesting that as moderns, we "understand" even the most blatant evil actions. The play ends with the chorus praising God for giving Canterbury another martyr and the Church another blessing.

Eliot was a Christ-haunted writer. He wrote often of the absence of faith, and of the "Fisher-King." He traced his own religious pilgrimage through a series of his poems. He used the saint-as-hero again in *The Cocktail Party,* a more modern play. Yet there is something tentative about his proclamations of faith. Just as *Murder in the Cathedral* ends with an embarrassed withdrawal of the claim to heroism, so Eliot seems to be afraid that he sounds unscholarly, naive, and grossly mid-American in his avowals of his own faith.

Conclusion

Many modern writers, like Eliot, find it difficult to write about heroes. A deep cynicism infects our culture, leading us to doubt the whole concept of the Great Man. The results in much of our literature is the destruction of credibility of the central figure, an explanation of sinister motivations, and a depiction of the twisting of relationships. Finally, the result is the preference for the anti-hero, the character who makes no pretence to idealism or perfection.

Tom Wolfe, who has chronicled modern American life for several decade in a series of novels and essays, demonstrates this change. The "hero" of *The Bonfire of Vanities* (1987) is one of the "masters of the universe," those young, rich, aggressive stock traders, who became so idolized at the end of the twentieth century. They enjoyed their conspicuous consumption, spending extravagantly, until their world came tumbling down. *A Man in Full* (1998) describes another hero, a former athlete, who is now a real estate developer in Atlanta, sliding toward bankruptcy. Each of these men is briefly at the top of his game, proud of himself for the moment, only to find Lady Luck does not smile on her favorites for more than a moment. The characters are affluent rather than virtuous. Rather than cherish their well-dressed wives, they proudly parade them as evidence of their success. They represent the shallow values of a post-Christian world. Wolfe chronicles their lives in powerful dramatic style.

Scripture is full of flawed people. The men and women who populate the Old and New Testaments have their failings, which they indulge and repent. The only sinless hero in all of scripture is Christ. Perhaps the mistake of many modern secular writers has been to try to construct flawless Romantic heroes, who resist credibility. The opposite temptation for writers is to reach for the other extreme, the complete cad, the anti-hero, who would have been the villain in earlier times. The hero at the center of Leif Enger's *Peace Like a River* (2001) is more like the biblical models. The self-sacrificial father in this wonderful story cares about his family, seeks to guide his children, and finally gives his life for them. He is an unlikely hero, the custodian in an elementary school who is fired for his defense of a child. But he is a modern day saint, a rare example in modern literature.

The public's hunger for heroes remains strong. Tales of heroism in war, courage in the face of natural disasters, financial ruin, or physical peril remain popular. When these stories have the foundations of altruism and faith, their power increases.

See also: **Predestination and Free Will; War; Women as Heroes.**

Bibliography

Ackerman, James S., and Thayer S. Warshaw. *The Bible as/in Literature*. Clearview, IL: Scott, Foresman and Company, 1971.

Aristotle. *The Rhetoric and the Poetics*. Trans., Ingram Bywater. New York: The Modern Library, 1954

Campbell, Joseph. *The Hero with a Thousand Faces*. New York: World Publishing Company, 1956.

Chayefsky. *Gideon*. In *Best American Plays, Fifth Series 1958–1963*, ed. John Gassner. New York: Crown Publishers, 1963.

Eliot, T. S. "The Love Song of J. Alfred Prufrock" and *Murder in the Cathedral*. In *The Complete Poems and Plays: 1909–1950*. New York: Harcourt, Brace & World, 1952.

Enger, Leif. *Peace Like a River*. New York: Atlantic Monthly Press, 2001.

Homer. *The Iliad.* Trans., Robert Fagles. New York: Penguin Books, 1998.

———. *The Odyssey.* Trans., Robert Fagles. London: Penguin Books, 1996.

Housman, A. E. *A Shropshire Lad.* In *Victorian and Later English Poets,* ed. James Stephens, Edwin L. Beck, and Royall H. Snow. New York: American Book Company, 1949.

Lee, Harper. *To Kill a Mockingbird.* New York: HarperPerennial, 2002.

Lindsay, Vachel. "How Samson Bore Away the Gates of Gaza." In *The Bible as/in Literature,* ed. James S. Ackerman. Glenview, IL: Scott, Foresman and Company, 1971.

Lovelace, Richard. "To Lucasta, on Going to the Wars." In *British Poetry and Prose,* vol. I, ed. Paul Lieder, Robert Morss Lovett, and Robert Kilburn Root. Boston: Houghton Mifflin, 1950.

Miller, Arthur. *Arthur Miller's Collected Plays.* New York: The Viking Press, 1957.

Milton, John. *Samson Agonistes.* In *The Student's Milton,* ed. Frank Allen Patterson. New York: Appleton-Century-Crofts, 1930.

Odets, Clifford. *Golden Boy.* In *Six Plays of Clifford Odets.* New York Grove Press, 1979.

Praz, Mario. *The Romantic Agony.* New York: The World Publishing Company, 1933.

Shakespeare, William. *Macbeth.* In *Shakespeare: Major Plays and the Sonnets,* ed. G. B. Harrison. New York: Harcourt, Brace and Company, 1948.

Wolfe, Tom. *The Bonfire of Vanities.* New York: Bantam, 1990.

———. *A Man in Full.* New York: Farrar, Straus and Giroux, 1998.

Women as Heroes

Readings

Genesis
Ruth
Judges
Susanna and the Elders (in the Apocrypha)
Esther
Sophocles, *Antigone* (442 B.C.)
Euripides, *The Trojan Women* (415 B.C.)
Geoffrey Chaucer, *The Canterbury Tales* (c. 1400)
Harriet Beecher Stowe, *Uncle Tom's Cabin* (1852)
C. S. Lewis, *Till We Have Faces* (1956)
Eudora Welty, *Losing Battles* (1971)
Louise Bogan, "Women" (1923)
Muriel Spark, "Sisera" (1968), *The Prime of Miss Jean Brody* (1961)
Maxine Hong Kingston, *The Woman Warrior: Memoirs of a Girlhood Among Ghosts* (1976)
Alice Walker, *The Color Purple* (1982)
Toni Morrison, *Beloved* (1987)

Introduction

> Whither thou goest, I will go; and where thou lodgest, I will lodge; thy
> people shall be my people, and thy God my God. (Ruth 1:16)

The term *hero* usually refers to men, usually warriors: slashing and smashing the enemy in bloodthirsty displays of wrath, bellowing our fierce war cries, daring great dangers, and escaping using breathtaking devices or supernatural physical strength. The real hero of the popular imagination is aggressive, strong, smart, and triumphant. For women, who are usually smaller, weaker, and more vulnerable, such grand adventures and colorful victories are usually impossible. Women have rarely been recruited to suit up and fight wars. The female strategy in conflict tends to be more subtle, indirect, and subversive. The attractive woman may use her sexual appeal to turn the adversary's appetites against him to win the day. More likely still, her conflict will be psychological and moral rather than a test of brute strength. Her enemies are more often sickness, poverty, hunger, and death. Few outside her own family are likely to understand that she has displayed courage and overcome incredible odds.

Heroism, for women, therefore requires a different definition. It may still involve risk, courage, daring, and shrewd planning, but it is less likely to include battles, quests, or triumphant celebrations. Especially in a world like that of the ancient Hebrews, where a woman's life was limited to serving as her father's obedient daughter or as her husband's loving wife, or her son's grateful mother, she spent her whole life in the care of one man or another. She may even have been taken as one of the spoils of war or imprisoned in a harem. Women, at least in the Old Testament, are rarely seen alone.

This fact makes the story of Ruth and her mother-in-law, Naomi, unusual and particularly heroic. These women are without male custodians; they have lost their husbands and sons. Ruth could return to her father's home in Moab, as Orpah does, but chooses instead to cast her lot with her old mother-in-law. On this heroic decision depends much of the history of Israel and of Christendom. This forlorn woman becomes the wife of Boaz, the ancestor of David, and of Jesus.

"Unimportant" women, with the courage to stand on their own, are heroic figures in a different sense from either traditional heroes or heroines. They are not classic "heroines," women saved from a fate worse than death by brave men. They are instead strong in their own right, willing to step out in faith. In a few cases, they do employ manly tools of weapons and warfare: such is the story of Deborah and Judith. More often, they are gentle folk who have moments of splendid strength, like Hagar, protecting her child in the wilderness; or Esther, facing her king with a challenge that will save her people; or Mary, bowing to the will of God, at the moment of the Annunciation. and accepting the burden of becoming the mother of God's Son.

Literature has often taken note of such understated heroism. Although women heroes have appeared in violent stories from classical Greek drama to modern feminist novels, more frequently the strong woman is nothing more impressive than a good mother or a committed schoolmarm. The authors help us to see that strength and grace can appear in any person of uncommon courage facing adversity.

Scripture

Women rarely take center stage in Bible stories. Eve does have an unfortunately prominent role in the narrative of the Fall, dooming not only herself and her husband, but all humankind. The wives of the patriarchs, carefully chosen, and sometimes colorful characters in their own right, are important primarily for their roles in the continuation of the race. Sarah is amazing, even in her old age, for her beauty, and eagerness to partner with Abraham in heading out for the Promised Land and to begin a family. She is also individualized in her very realistic laughter at the angels' promises of a child long after she has passed the time for childbearing. This laughter is echoed in her delight nine months later when she discovers she can breastfeed the infant Isaac.

Rebekkah is portrayed as a woman who makes up her mind quickly and has a strong will. Her readiness to travel with Isaac's servant from her own country in order to marry a man she has never met signals her spirit of adventure. Her preference for her younger son leads her to betray her husband and her elder son, while bringing the blessing on Jacob. Her headstrong action sets Jacob on a new path, but costs her his companionship in her old age, when she is forced to live with the husband and son she has cheated for Jacob's sake. Scripture does not recount the rest of her story, but she must have paid a high price for her decisive actions.

For the most part, the women are targets of love, lust, manipulation, and violence. They have little "heroic" potential. Their most important choices and intense actions tend to be private, unseen and unknown to the world. It is the man's career that forms the central narrative. The women are forced by the customs of their day to act through the men in their lives.

This is not true of Ruth, whose story of loyalty, self-control, and blessedness is carefully told. She is brave, willing to strike out with her mother-in-law when both of them are widowed. Rather than taking the safe course, she chooses to go with this woman she has come to love, journeying to a strange country, a new life, and a different god. She further proves her physical courage by gleaning in Boaz's field among rowdy workers who might well molest her. She charms Boaz at first sight; this old bachelor (or perhaps widower) offers her special considerations, even before recognizing her to be his kinswoman. Her adventuresome streak is further evidenced in her willingness to dress herself up and go to sleep "at his feet" after an evening of celebration at the barley harvest. Surely, going to this place alone when he might be drunk and lecherous, she must realize she might be raped and dishonored by this gesture. Yet she is encouraged by Naomi, her scheming mother-in-law, who devises the strategy to win this young woman a good husband. Blessed in finding a redeemer in this kinsman, Ruth wins the day by his generous offer of marriage. She is further blessed in the negotiations preceding this ceremony, and the child born to the union afterwards.

In all of this, Ruth plays the role of the submissive woman, taking chances, but always using her charm, beauty, and wits to achieve her goals. She never demands what is rightly hers (the redemption by a kinsman), nor does she seek to defend herself. She relies on the kindness of men to win her victory. The traditional victory for a woman, after all, is security and happiness of marriage and children.

In both scriptural and apocryphal stories, we see other women using their feminine wiles to achieve their purposes: Esther charms her way to success with her king-husband, thereby saving her people. Judith (in the famous apocryphal book of Judith) relies on her considerable beauty to gain access to her enemy and her charm to win his trust. She then slaughters the brutal Holofernes. This assassination of an enemy of Israel, often portrayed in art, is a rare example of a woman using violence: After she lulls the old warrior to sleep with sweet talk and drink, Judith cuts off his head.

There is one example of the warrior woman in scripture. Deborah, in the book of Judges, is unique. She is a judge, a wife, a poet, and a warrior. As a judge in Israel, she becomes aware of the threat from Sisera, the leader of the Philistines. She warns Barak (who may be her husband) that he must attack this gathering threat, but he refuses to go without her. She agrees, warning him that a woman will win the fame and glory from the victory. Her strategy is to use the geographical situation of the Kishon Valley to her advantage. Her soldiers are on foot, less heavily armed than the giant Philistines in their iron chariots. By choosing to fight when the Kishon is flooding and the ground is muddy, she enmeshes their chariots in mire, rendering them useless. When Sisera flees the battlefield, pausing at the tent of a "friend," he is warmly welcomed by Jael, his friend's wife. She offers him warm milk and a bed to rest, and then drives a tent peg through his temple as he sleeps. Like Judith, she cannot confront the enemy in physical combat, but she can use her feminine wiles to destroy him as he sleeps.

This deceptive role is celebrated here in the Song of Deborah. Even the betrayal of the ceremony of hospitality is forgiven in this case, because Sisera is the enemy of Israel. Yet, when the Philistine temptress Delilah betrays Samson as he sleeps, she is seen as a guilty harlot. Context is everything: Is the man a friend or an enemy of Israel? If a friend, then this is an act of betrayal. If an enemy, then it is a clever device, blessed by God.

Dame Muriel Spark, a modern Scots novelist, poet, and literary critic with a sharp tongue and quick wit, has written a poem called "Sisera," which takes issue with the usual interpretation of Deborah's victory. Rather than celebrating the "kite" or hawk, as she describes Deborah, who sings her song of victory, she takes the part of the Philistine warrior Sisera. As she notes, the "hostess" in this case betrayed her guest— hardly a heroic act. Nor is Spark enthusiastic about Deborah's pleasure in the fate of Sisera's women, who "waits for the loot." In the scripture records, these women find no sympathy in the harsh words of Deborah, who knows that the Israelite women would be the apprehensive mourners should the tables have been turned.

Spark, like many others, finds the celebratory tone of victors offensive. Rather than taking victory graciously with self-effacing understatement, Deborah shows her delight in the Philistines' misery. Songs such as Deborah's, like the imprecatory Psalms, which gloat over the misery and ruin of Israel's enemies, are predicated on the belief that Israel's enemies are God's enemies, that their downfall proves God's power. Such triumphalism strikes many modern writers as improper and boastful. The eleventh-century B.C. Judges would have seen this differently from a twentieth-century A.D. British lady. For the Israelites, it was not a matter of polemic style or pleasure in slaughter, it was a matter of life and death. Had the Israelites not defeated the Philistines, they would have surely been slaughtered themselves. Nor were the Philistines modest in their claims of superiority. The critique, which does indeed echo much of modern disgust with warfare, fails to capture the culture that shaped the Song of Deborah.

Many moderns would be inclined to agree with Spark, who touches on the possibility that Fate determines the outcome of battles, not human wit or spring rains. Although Spark refused to accept the ethical views implied in these chapters of scripture, she did her religion seriously. She was a thoughtful and sharply critical Christian writer in the Catholic tradition. She was also a gifted and astringent writer. In the poem "Sisera," her irregular lines and occasional rhymes make the three stanzas of the concise argument effective and efficient. Her tone and point of view are consistent from beginning to end. Like the irony in many of her novels, the implied prayer, "may God perfectly defend" is a sharp commentary on the kind of prayers that Deborah would have uttered.

The Old Testament view of heroism does change from Deborah's chest-thumping to the prophets' view of the suffering servant. The warrior hero, not a comfortable fit for a woman, is gradually modified to the gentle saint, more willing to die for her faith than to kill for it. This becomes more explicit in the New Testament, where it is personified in Christ and those men and women who gather around him.

The New Testament has only one hero—Jesus Christ. Even such remarkable women as Mary, his mother, and Mary Magdalene are diminished in comparison with him. Women in the Christian era do often assume a new role. Rather than victims or heroes, they become fellow pilgrims. They appear all through the Gospels, asking questions, offering food or water, seeking healing, praying, helping, following—much like the men. Certainly, the Virgin Mary, with her courageous acceptance of her role as mother and disciple, stands tall as an example of grace and strength. All the women, including Mary Magdalene, who had the fortitude to leave their homes, follow their lord, and invest their modest fortunes in supporting him and his ministry, are heroic figures.

Still, other than Christ himself, the New Testament is not a place for heroes. The Disciples and apostles are saints, who accept the limits and challenges of that role. They do not fight for the faith or kill for it, they prefer to serve as Christians or die as martyrs. The Christian women follow the same path, encouraging Paul and his friends as they strive to make disciples of all people, taking the Gospel to the ends of the earth.

Literature

Classical Greek literature is full of strong women who behave much like the goddesses who were thought to control their lives: Clytemnestra, wronged by her husband, awaits his return from the Trojan War, welcomes, and then murders him and his captive, Cassandra. Even more striking is the witch-mother Medea, who murders her husband's lover, as well as her own children in savage acts of vengeance.

Sometimes the Greek women play the traditional feminine role. Helen of Troy, noted for her great beauty, is a passive victim in the whole Trojan war. She is stolen from her husband (though this may actually be a deliberate act of adultery on her part), and then is fought over for 10 years. At the end of that time, she is returned to her husband and her home. No one seems to blame her for the unpleasantness in between these domestic scenes. Women are seen as pawns in battle, not as actors, even though some of the Greek goddesses are warrior maidens, and part of Greek mythology includes the stories of the Amazons. Like the Hebrews and most other ancient peoples, the Greeks generally saw women as property, to be stolen, enslaved, used, enjoyed, and discarded. They also knew them as people, to be loved, hated, and mourned. Both cultures saw individual women as distinct from the general class. The literature most often focuses on strong individuals.

A pair of Greek plays about remarkable women reveals the admiration that the writers felt for women's courage and endurance. In *Antigone*, Sophocles portrays a strong woman, motivated by her love of her brothers and her respect for her faith. She knows she must bury her dead brother Polynices, even though he is labeled a traitor and his burial is forbidden by the king. In order for him to find peace in the afterlife and for the city of Thebes to escape pollution, he must have a ceremonial burial. When ordered to leave Polynices's body dishonored and rotting in the dust, Antigone chooses to disobey her king. She comes by night to pray over the dead and to sprinkle dust on his body. She knows that her action will result in her own death for defying the state. Her position is strengthened by the words of the wise man, Tireseas, and by the loving advocacy by her beloved, Haemon. Creon, the king, nevertheless, is adamant, demanding that she be buried alive. By the time he reconsiders his cruel judgment, she has hanged herself.

This firm resolution in the face of power is the mark of the tragic hero. Antigone is not swayed by consideration of her own youth, her hope for love and marriage, or her recognition that she is breaking the law. For her, only this moment and this decision matter. She reveals herself to be a true daughter of Oedipus, hard-headed, self-sacrificial, and doomed. The play is full of beautiful philosophic speeches on the nature of justice, the limits to human knowledge, and the role of fate. Antigone herself, in her single-minded drive to do what she thinks the gods demand, is often portrayed as the embodiment of faith in the never-ending conflict between church and state.

Another Greek tragedy, by a later and more complex playwright, Euripides, is a more realistic and sympathetic portrayal of the roles that women are forced to play in a man's world. *The Trojan Women,* a rare study of the way that women fare in the epic battles, shows the aftermath of the Trojan war and the fate of the women of Troy. These women demonstrate their heroism by dealing with the fate handed them. If "grace under pressure" is the ultimate test for humans, these playthings in the hands of vengeful gods are great examples. After the war, the women of Troy are all taken captive by the Greeks.

Cassandra, the princess cursed with the gift of foresight, foretells the whole fate of each of the women. She knows that she will be taken home with Agamemnon and share in his bloody death at the hands of his queen. Helen, the cause and victim of the war, is taken home by her husband, who cannot bring himself to kill this great beauty. But it is Hecuba who takes the central role as the strongest of the women. A queen of Troy one day, she becomes a widow and a slave the next. She is allowed to bury her child on his father's shield. After she performs the funeral rites, she tries to explain to the women the grandeur of this hideous moment in their lives: "If God had not overturned us, throwing that which was exalted beneath the earth, we should have vanished, never hymned by the Muses, never giving songs to those of men who come later" (Euripides, 283). Out of their suffering will come eternal glory. At this point, the boy's body is carried off, Troy is burned, and Hecuba has to be restrained from hurling herself into the fire. The play ends with Troy ablaze, the women singing a dirge as they embark on Greek ships to begin their lives as slaves in a foreign land.

This theme of the ennobling effect of suffering is much like the Hebrew view. The older concept of the man or woman of war, who kills his "tens of thousands," is replaced by the gentle victim, who faces defeat with dignity. Like Isaiah's Suffering Servant, this new kind of hero mirrors the actual role imposed on women in war. The test of the hero is how that person will maintain her moral character in the face of disaster.

Western literature did not abandon the warrior-hero image just because Christ was a man of peace who refused to defend even himself. The Crusades, in fact, introduced the Christian Warrior, whose task is to fight for his King and his Savior. The Arthurian romances are also filled with heroes equipped mentally and physically to fight for their beliefs. The women in these romances take the elevated role of "ladies," but remain free from the bloody actions.

At such a time, only a heroic woman like Joan of Arc could hope to compete with their derring do. The story of Joan of Arc is one of the real life stories of the Middle Ages that had profound impact on literature. This warrior woman, much in the mode of Deborah, has encouraged writers to consider the fierce nature of women that can be ignited by spiritual fires.

George Bernard Shaw in *Saint Joan* (first published in 1924), uses this authentic fifteenth-century French hero, Joan of Arc, a simple teenager from a farming village, and places her at the center of the religious and political debates of the era. Listening to her voices rather than to her father (who thinks she should be drowned), or to her church (which considers her a sorceress and a heretic), or to her dauphin (who is too frightened to fight the English invaders), this young woman changes her world.

She confronts the cowardly dauphin, offering to lead his armies against the English, to drive them out of Orleans, and to crown him king in the cathedral at

Rheims—"where all the true kings of France are crowned." The Dauphin balks at paying for her horse or her armor; the Archbishop worries about her not being a respectable woman: "She does not wear women's clothes. She is dressed like a soldier, and rides round the country with soldiers." By sheer force of will, she convinces them of her God-sent mission. Miracles follow in her wake, the peasants believe in her vision, and the English are indeed defeated.

At this point, having accomplished as much as the church and the state considers desirable, they try to send her back home to her father's home, where she will return to petticoats and to a healthy life, "but a dull one." As it turns out, she has fallen in love with fighting and wants to continue even after all the men around her are ready to sign treaties. Her firm insistence on her vision over their wisdom puts her at odds with all of the authorities, who disown her, and finally hand her over to the English and the Inquisition. She dies at the stake, burned as a martyr, and is so beloved in her death that she finally is canonized as a saint.

Shaw clearly admires her as an example of "will to power," ignoring the established powers in the face of the need to communicate her vision of the world as sent by God. Like many of his other heroines, Joan of Arc is strong, smart, down-to-earth, and interesting. For Shaw, her religion, her piety, and her innocence are more reliable testimonies to the true faith and the tradition of scripture than all the established structure of the Church that she confronts. He treats the Archbishop and even the Inquisitor with respect, allowing them to explain their rationale for ridding themselves of this troublesome and independent voice of simple faith in God's will.

In the play, the Inquisition attacks Joan's insistence that her "voices" give her direct access to God's will, sometimes in direct opposition to the will of the Roman Catholic Church. Though the court acknowledges her piety, her fervent prayers, her strength, and the miracles that appear in her wake, they can not accept her claims to authority. She seems to have behave as both a Protestant and a Nationalist long before either concept is popular. To maintain order in the kingdom and in the Church, the Inquisition accuses her of sorcery and heresy and finally burns her at the stake. In this sacrificial death, she achieves sainthood, making her fame outshine all of those who have stood against her. Like the classic tragic hero, she wins by losing.

In medieval Romances, most women have roles very different from Joan's. They are usually pictured as idealized ladies, delicate and endangered. The role of the masculine hero is to save the helpless maiden in the tower. In these Romances, short stories that became popular in southern France and England, the knights pay homage to their beloved ladies, whom they adore from afar. In this veneration of women, the Virgin Mary blended with the "lady" the knight served as an earthly exemplar of the Madonna. The woman's role in romances is largely passive. An impressive exception is "Aucassin and Nicollette," a French tale in which the pretty young maiden is obliged to do all the work to defend herself and her helpless lover. The ideas and actions are all hers.

Geoffrey Chaucer, who often included romance narratives in his tales, is remarkable for his exceedingly realistic portrayal of the Wife of Bath, one of the few examples of a believable woman character during this period. This lively pilgrim, who is introduced in the Prologue to *The Canterbury Tales*, has had several husbands. Her gap teeth signal that she is lusty, as does her sanguine coloring and hearty manner. She is a vigorous pilgrim who goes often on pilgrimages to shrines of saints, and clearly lives a full, sexual, and religious life. The ballads of the period are also full of strong women, often temptresses or devouring mothers who destroy everything in their paths. These folk poems probably recount real stories much embellished.

The Germanic literature of the Medieval period also has stories of strong women, such as Brunhilde, the warrior woman of the *Nibelungenlied*. Nonetheless, this tradition was not evident in most of English literature, where, women characters may be most notable largely for her position. By the Elizabethan era, when the British had known the strong leadership of both Queen Mary and Queen Elizabeth, authors were inspired to think of women in a more active role.

Shakespeare draws his women with considerable realism. In *Antony and Cleopatra* (1607–08), he pictures the beautiful queen of Egypt as a cynical manipulator. She has the shrewdness to use her lover to her advantage, tragically bringing about his defeat and death as well as her own. She tempts Antony into lascivious living, interferes with his official duties, tricks him into losing a sea battle, costs him most of his friends and followers, and disgraces him. When he reaches such a pitch of anger that he contemplates killing her, she pretends that she has committed suicide because she has lost his love. Poor Antony ends up killing himself. Rather than be taken prisoner by her great enemy, Octavius Caesar, she dresses regally, applies an asp (a small snake) to her breast, and dies splendidly.

Cleopatra has the qualities of the old Greek heroine: she is not concerned with anything outside of her own desires; she is not willing to share power even with the man she loves. She is as merciless as Medea or Clytemnestra. In her destruction of a great man, this famous temptress is like Delilah. Although a queen, she sacrifices her people for herself—the very antithesis of Esther.

The growth of the novel marked the greatest change in the characterization of women in Western literature. The novel became the first popular literary form to attract women as both writers and readers. The eighteenth century marked the rapid development of the English novel, along with the increased education of middle-class women, and the interest in women as the subject of literature. Until the eighteenth century, most women were silent members of the society. Neither public persons nor highly educated, women traditionally focused their attention on domestic matters. Suddenly, writers found that their audience wanted to hear more about women's lives. Virginia Woolf, in *A Room of One's Own*, discusses this new freedom to read, to write, and to perceive in commonplace activities great depth of meaning. Even if a woman spends her entire day preparing for a dinner party (as in *Mrs. Dalloway*), the series of inconsequential acts, such as buying the flowers, preparing the food, inviting the guests, dressing for the event, become important. Each moment lived has a kind of shimmering delight that makes life worth living.

This audience of women readers brought the domestic novel to its fruition, allowing writers like Jane Austen, the Brontë sisters, Harriet Beecher Stowe, Edith Wharton, Virginia Woolf, Willa Cather, Eudora Welty, Flannery O'Connor and many others to provide insights into women's lives and dreams. With these writers has come a new sensitivity to the inner strength of many women who may seem gentle or nondescript to an outsider. Male writers have joined the ranks of novelists and playwrights now exploring women's day-to-day heroism. At the same time, a small group of writers have continued to seek example of the old masculine standard of the hero for women, finding extraordinary mythic figures to present as models.

Maxine Hong Kingston, the author of the novel *The Woman Warrior* (1976), draws inspiration from a Chinese myth of a great warrior woman. The novel is a dazzling example of imagery and imagination told in a manner quite alien to the usual western narrative style. Like Joan of Arc, the protagonist of the novel sallies out to battle dressed as a man. When she falls in love and marries her lover, she continues to fight, even after bearing a baby. Her village needs her help.

Such novels as *Till We Have Faces* or *The Woman Warrior* are the exception to the rule. Most women's lives are not entangled with wars and grand adventures. The woman cannot usually go on the quest for the Holy Grail, fight the great battle, or win the great victory. She may appear as a nurse in a war novel or as a fellow freedom fighters (in Hemingway's *A Farewell to Arms* and *For Whom the Bell Tolls*), but the man tends to be front and center for the action.

As Eudora Welty reveals in her novels about women in the American South, women fight and often lose battles daily, but through continuing effort may win the great war of life. Her *Losing Battles* is the story of a school teacher in Mississippi who sees one after another of her talented students settle for less than their potential. They drop out of school or move away from the community. The poor, frustrated teacher feels she is always losing her battles to make these children achieve their full potential. But she continues her determined fight to make her bright young students better than the world around them, to rise to the challenge of their talents and gifts. Sometimes they end up in prison, sometimes they become judges. When she dies, her remains are buried under the schoolhouse steps, where she can continue to hear the school bells ring each morning summoning another crop of young children to education.

This serio-comic tale of the "battles" of life captures much of the role of women. Working with the materials at hand, most women lead lives of modest successes and quiet failures. Like their ancestors whose stories are only partially told in both the Old Testament and the New, these women live courageous lives, filled with deep emotions, but not wide experience. They live close to their families and close to the soil, finding their victories in the marriage of a daughter or the success of a son. Without great fortune, they offer the gift of a beautifully baked cake and prove their talents by playing a song perfectly on the piano. Like Jane Austen's tiny square of ivory, the world of Eudora Welty is full of small blessings, fearful challenges, and quiet victories.

For many middle-class women in both the nineteenth and the twentieth centuries, teaching was the only profession possible. In fact, Jane Austen points out in her novel *Emma* that the role of the governess is almost the only one that a single, educated young lady of the nineteenth century could comfortably take. She might be treated like a servant, but the job was considered respectable. The unmarried woman, largely unknown in the ancient world where men had multiple wives, was a new character in literature. After the Protestant Reformation, there were fewer convents she could join, even if she were so inclined. With houses shrinking in size and supernumerary persons considered a burden, she might be shuttled from one relative to another. Alone and seeking to make her own way through life, teaching other people's children, she tried to make sense of life. Charlotte Brontë's *Jane Eyre* romanticizes the governess-as-hero. Jane dreams of becoming a missionary, but settles for teaching. The greatest hope for such a character is that some wonderful man will discover her in her isolated existence and marry her. In this story, she retains her idealism, saves her lover, and ends in a sad kind of triumph.

Most of these realistic and romantic novelists describe the tightly circumscribed world of the woman, realizing that characters must find their drama in depth of feeling rather than in breadth of experience. This was the very reason that Jane Austen, when asked to consider writing a novel on the Napoleonic Wars, demurred, preferring to restrict herself to her tiny bit of English countryside and the narrow world she really knew. She saw herself as a miniaturist, not a mural painter. In such writing, the term *hero* can hardly apply.

Most of the nineteenth-century women writers draw on scripture for their imagery without being particularly religious. An exceptions to this pattern is Harriet Beecher Stowe, who wrote *Uncle Tom's Cabin* as her powerful attack on the cruelty of slavery. Rather than behaving like a man and writing tracts or going to war over slavery, she tried to change the hearts of her fellow countrymen.

By picturing dozens of families touched by slavery, Southern and Northern, black and white, Stowe reveals how the practice hurts men, women, and children. She portrays slave mothers stripped of their children, forced into prostitution, and driven mad by their lives. The novel is full of sentimental scenes, heart-wrenching stories, and heroic figures acting out biblical roles. She names her characters after Bible women, relying heavily on the human heart to understand the cruelties of a system that should not be tolerated in a "Christian" country.

One of the dominant lines of narrative in the story involves a beautiful quadroon, the descendant of white "aristocrats" and black slave women. Both Eliza and her son, Harry, have been encouraged to behave as white middle-class citizens: they learn to read and write, to behave in cultured and religious ways, and to cherish their family ties. Eliza has married another quadroon from a neighboring estate, whom she sees only occasionally. George Harris, her husband, has a much more tyrannical master, who finally forces George to run away to preserve his manhood. Eliza follows him, knowing that she cannot bear to relinquish her child her son as well as her husband. Although a gentle, domestic sort of woman, she finds within her enough courage to gather up a bundle of belongings and run off into the night, carrying little Harry.

Eliza heads north, chased by slave traders, racing over the broken hunks of ice in the Ohio River, clutching her toddler. The novel traces her passage along the Underground Railroad, shows her staying with farmers, legislators, Quakers, and others. Along the way, she and George are united, and they find their way eventually to the Promised Land—in this case Canada, a place of freedom. Their escape and happy reunion they attribute largely to the kindness of people along the way, their own individual effort, and to the grace of God.

While Uncle Tom provides the Christ-figure in the story, the victorious saint who dies for others, Eliza acts out the role of the loving Madonna, fleeing to protect her child from the slaughter of the innocents. The ideal mother, she defends her child, finding a strength that would otherwise appear unfeminine.

Stowe was hardly the first to use words as a weapon, but she was certainly one of the best. She was audacious enough to use the cult of domesticity, so strong in the nineteenth century, to plead her case against slavery, presenting her hero as the ideal woman and as a black Madonna.

The change in the twentieth century presentation of women in literature is quite remarkable. For a black writer like Toni Morrison, who has less faith than Stowe in the benevolence of white sympathizers or God Himself, the slave mother must risk even more than Eliza did. In the case of the mother in *Beloved* (1987), she must have the courage to escape, and when trapped and pressed back into slavery, she must also have the courage to kill her own child rather than allow her to return to bondage.

In this deeply disturbing novel, which is based on a real life incident, the mother, Sethe, tries to kill all of her children, but is able to murder only the baby. This infant haunts her, like the mark of Cain, frightening those around her and clouding her life. Years after the infanticide, a young woman about the age her child would have been, enters Sethe's home and wins her love. Named "Beloved," this young woman is the ghost of her remorse that lingers on, draining all her strength until exorcised by Sethe's youngest daughter and a group of women from the community.

The story is more Gothic than Christian, but does contain reminders of the long and impressive heritage of Christian practice and thought in the black community from early days in slavery. Zora Neale Hurston also drew on this tradition and used it in her numerous novels, often based on biblical themes adapted to black folk culture. Alice Walker followed in Hurston's steps, also chronicling the roles of black women in rural communities of the South. Walker reveals the tough life that a poor black girl is forced to live, long after the abolition of slavery. In *The Color Purple* (1982), Celie is raped by her own father, sees her child sold, and is then sold herself to an old man who brutalizes her. Silent, invisible, and passive in order to survive, she writes letters to God. Drawing on the style of the old slave narratives, Walker turns this modern tale into a feminist protest as well as a racial one. Celie finds comfort in the love of another woman, who teaches her that she must take charge of her own body; she must write her own narrative and construct her own life. Up until this point, Celie has envisioned God as an old white man. Shug, her mentor and friend, teaches her to believe that God is neither male nor female, black nor white, simply an "it." In Shug's "Womanist" religion, this It delights in creation and wants humans to love what It has created.

Thus freed from a patriarchal God, she becomes a strong woman, cursing her husband, who becomes a Christian convert. She finds her closest relationships with other women, and sets up her own business. Eventually, she has control of her own body and her own economic life. In her final letter, she writes: "Dear God. Dear stars, dear trees, dear sky, dear peoples. Dear Everything. Dear God." By reimagining God to reflect Shug's advice, Celie demonstrates that she is no longer just a silent object of someone else's care and brutality, but an independent woman. She is now ready to create her own narrative.

With the rise of feminism, a new kind of heroism became apparent in novels by women—often mimicking masculine definitions of the term. The white farm women like those Jane Smiley describes in her novels (e.g., *A Thousand Acres*, 1992) have education, freedom, money, choices that they can make. Although they are forced to resist the corrupt patriarchal society and fight for their values, such as preserving the environment, they are not victims like Celie or Sethe. Feminist novels like those of Margaret Atwood (e.g., *A Handmaid's Tale*, 1986) show the modern woman deciding whom she will marry, the career she will follow, and so forth. When these freedoms are taken away by a new, patriarchal government and she is reduced to the role of the handmaiden (as in ancient Israel), she feels like a prisoner. Her unwilling service as the surrogate wife by one of the elders (as in the case of Hagar and Abraham) horrifies both her and the reader. Atwood shows that the modern woman is determined to fight for her independence, while recognizing that this was not an option for Sarah or Hagar.

Atwood's novel is certainly an attack on Old Testament ideals of masculine dominance. Placing a thoroughly modern woman in such a context shocks the sensibilities. The story bears of the markings of a feminist mentality, fearful of allowing unlimited power to males. The feelings of the woman at the center of this story are natural enough for a twentieth-century career woman. They would make no sense to a woman in Abraham's day. Nor would they resonate with many women in other parts of the world today. If anything, the novel reminds us of the incredible progress women have made in the past centuries, especially in the west. For the first time in history, women really have the opportunity to behave as heroes, to take up arms, to travel all over the world, to seek political office, or to become professors or writers or senators. Novels yet to be written will celebrate this new woman who is learning to use these new opportunities for larger purposes than simple success or creature comfort.

From the beginning of the American experiment, both girls and boys learned to read. They studied the words of scripture and were encouraged to apply those words to their own lives. They wrote their diaries, in which they examined their own souls for possible contamination. The young girls were taught that Eve was the main actor in the Garden of Eden, the prime cause of Adam's fall into sin. From that time of Eden, woman was expected to be subservient to man.

The life of the pioneer and the mid-western farmer tended to require that women take on the same work as men, to have the same kind of courage in the face of peril, to raise their children, and tend their work even when men were hurt in accidents or killed in war. Sturdy frontier folk could hardly wait to be saved by heroes. Willa Cather's novels, such as *My Antonia* or *O Pioneers* are full of strong farm women who know how to run the farms, cook the meals, make financial decisions, and stand tall in times of tragedy. These American women share with the Old Testament matriarchs the kind of strength that characterize the woman as hero.

Conclusion

Louise Bogan, a twentieth-century American poet, describes the role of women (at least the role of white, middle-class, Western women) in a manner that might summarize the modern critique. She constructs her argument in a series of stanzas, with regular rhyme and meter, perhaps because she is making a fairly traditional argument. She hypothesizes that women are no adventurers. They fail to look at the "big picture," spending their time on small tasks, content "to eat dusty bread." Expecting little, preferring safety to wilderness, they miss much of life, including the beauty of nature: the "cattle cropping red winter grass" or "Snow water going down under culverts/ Shallow and clear." Fearful, they wait and "stiffen," afraid to journey or to bend, hurting only themselves. Even their love has an "eager meaninglessness." Women, she insists, listen for every small hint of trouble, taking "life over their door-sills" when they should "let it go by" (Bogan, 165).

This may describe many women that Louise Bogan knows, focused on petty things and missing the great moments of life, but it is hardly true of such remarkable heroic figures as Ruth. This woman does take the grand journey; she risks the new love, and grabs life by the throat. Instead, Bogan is describing Orpah, the sister-in-law who remains in Moab with her folks rather than taking a chance on a new life. It may even describe Naomi when she first sulks in her bitterness and sends Ruth off to glean in a relative's fields. Yet even Naomi has a larger vision than this poem suggests. It is certainly not the way Deborah sees life, nor Jael, both of whom prove themselves to be great risk-takers.

On the other hand, many of the incidental and unnamed women in scripture may match Bogan's pitiful description of the cramped life of woman. Samson's first wife, a woman who was used by him, her family, and others, simply follows the orders given by the men of her household. She has no say over her life, and offers no complaint or rebuke. She is simply a possession, first of her family, and then of her husband. That may actually be the role played by the harlot in Gaza and by Delilah in Samson's story. Both of these women are used as pawns by their countrymen. Delilah does seem to gain something from her seductive tricks, suggesting that she is less a plaything than a villain in the story.

With more opportunity, especially in the past two centuries, women have flourished, coming out of their restricted worlds to be all they can be. Mirroring this cultural change, women's literature in the past two centuries has flourished, presenting women more often as *heroes* rather than *heroines*.

In some sense, women have always been heroes in special circumstances. While the *heroine* is usually a passive character in a story, loved, married, pampered, entrapped, saved, wronged, or forgiven, the *heroic* woman becomes an active force. She makes the decisions, takes the actions, saves the child, runs the race, and achieves the victory. As we see in the ancient story of Hagar in the wilderness with her child Ishmael, any woman may become strong when her child is threatened. In this dark moment, cast out by Abraham and Sarah, this woman carries the boy to a shady spot, finds him water, and is granted a theophany, a moment when God speaks to her directly about her son's future. Toni Morrison's more troubling vision of heroism shows the woman willing to kill her children rather than let them become slaves. Somehow, this seems as brutal as the old Greeks. The Hebrew tradition always saved the children, the precious heritage of the people.

To see the woman as *heroic*, the reader must redefine the term. Most of these people are not aristocrats, they do not range far from home, they have few grand adventures. But they do make daring choices, live and die for others, and seek to live lives of moral integrity.

See also: **The Hero; Love and Marriage; War.**

Bibliography

Ackerman, James S., and Thayer S. Warshaw. *The Bible as/in Literature.* Glenview, IL: Scott, Foresman and Company, 1971.

Arlandson, James Malcolm. *Women, Class, and Society in Early Christianity: Models from Luke–Acts.* Peabody, MA: Hendrickson Publishers, 1997.

Atwood, Margaret. *A Handmaid's Tale.* New York: Everyman's Library, 2006.

Bogan, Louise. "Women." In *The Bible as/in Literature,* ed. James S. Ackerman and Thayer S. Warshaw. Glenview, IL: Scott, Foresman and Company, 1971.

Brontë, Charlotte. *Jane Eyre.* New York: Signet Classic, Penguin, 1988.

Chaucer, Geoffrey. *The Canterbury Tales.* New York: Modern Library, 1994.

DeBeauvoir, Simone. *The Second Sex.* Trans., H. M. Parshley. New York: Alfred A. Knopf, 1993.

DeJong, Peter, and Donald R. Wilson. *Husband and Wife: The Sexes in Scripture and Society.* Grand Rapids: Zondervan, 1979.

Euripides. *The Trojan Women.* In *The Complete Greek Tragedies,* ed. David Grene and Richmond Lattimore. Chicago: University of Chicago Press, 1959.

Gilbert, Sandra M., and Susan Gubar. *The Madwoman in the Attic: A Study of Women and the Literary Imagination in the Nineteenth Century.* New Haven, CT: Yale University Press, 1979.

———, eds. *The Norton Anthology of Literature by Women: The Tradition in English.* New York: W. W. Norton, 1985.

Kingston, Maxine Hong. *The Woman Warrior: Memoirs of a Girlhood among Ghosts.* New York: Knopf, 1976.

Lewis, C. S. *Till We Have Faces.* New York: Harcourt Brace Jovanovich, 1980.

Morrison, Toni. *Beloved.* New York: Alfred A. Knopf, 2006.

The Nibelungenlied. New Haven: Yale University Press, 2006.

Shaw, George Bernard. *St. Joan: A Chronicle Play in Six Scenes and an Epilogue*. New York: Penguin Books, 2001.

Sophocles. *Antigone*. In *The Theban Plays*. Trans., E. F. Watling. Baltimore, MD: Penguin Books, 1946.

Spark, Muriel. *The Prime of Miss Jean Brody*. New York: Dell, 1974.

———. "Sisera." In *The Bible as/in Literature*, ed. James S. Ackerman and Thayer S. Warshaw. Glenview, IL: Scott, Foresman and Company, 1971.

Stowe, Harriet Beecher. *Uncle Tom's Cabin*. New York: Barnes & Noble Classics, 2004.

"Susanna." In *The HarperCollins Study Bible: New Revised Standard Version*, ed. Wayne A. Meeks. New York: HarperCollins, 1989.

Tischler, Nancy M. *Legacy of Eve: Images of Women in Scripture*. Atlanta: John Knox Press, 1977.

———. *A Voice of Her Own: Women, Literature, and Transformation*. Grand Rapids, MI: Zondervan Publishing House, 1987.

Walker, Alice. *The Color Purple*. New York: Harcourt Brace Jovanovich, 1992.

Welty, Eudora. *Losing Battles*. New York: Vintage Books, 1990.

Woolf, Virginia. *Mrs. Dalloway*. San Diego: Harcourt Brace, 1997.

———. *A Room of One's Own*. New York: HBJ, 1989.

The Journey of Life

Readings

Dante Alighieri, *The Divine Comedy* (1321)
Geoffrey Chaucer, *Canterbury Tales* (The Prologue) (1387–1400)
"Sir Gawain and the Green Knight" (c. 1375)
John Bunyan, *The Pilgrim's Progress* (1675)
Tennyson, "Ulysses" (1842)
Eudora Welty, "A Worn Path" (1941)
Robert Frost, "The Road Not Taken" (1920)
John Steinbeck, *The Grapes of Wrath* (1939)
Ernest Hemingway, *The Old Man and the Sea* (1952)

Introduction

> Though I walk through the valley of the shadow of death, I shall fear no evil:
> for thou art with me, thy rod and thy staff they comfort me. (Psalm 23:4)

The ancient Hebrews were sturdy walkers. For most of their history, they were herdsmen, tending their flocks of sheep and goats, often taking a solitary path away from the camp to find strays or to search for green pastures and still waters. For shepherds, the darkness of the walk on a moonless night felt like "the Valley of the Shadow of death." The dangers along the way—the lion lying in wait to kill the lambs or the men—became images of Satan and his malevolent plans. The welcome waters for which the dusty wanderer longed became symbolic of God's comforting nourishment of the soul. The rocks that littered the hilly paths all over Israel forced the weary traveler to follow a crooked road, unless industrious workers "made [it] straight" for the Lord, just as they cleared it for visiting dignitaries.

Neither the Hebrews nor the early Christians were as idealistic or interested in abstractions as the contemporary Greek philosophers. Their faith, rooted in reality, dealt with the physical world in very tangible ways. The psalmist frequently uses images of walking, standing, or sitting as portrayals of attitudes and choices in life. Jesus speaks of himself as "the Way, the Truth, the Life." As he says, "There is no way unto the Father but by me." The terminology of the Way in the New Testament characterizes the Christian life, not so much as a series of rules to obey, but a path of life to walk. Followers of Jesus were at first called followers of "the Way."

The devout Catholic novelist Flannery O'Connor, in *The Habit of Being* (1988), captures something of this concept, that the manner in which a person lives her life determines who she is and where she will live eternally. This particular book is a collection of her letters, chronicling her journey to death, and demonstrating both heroism and wit in her courageous struggle with lupus, the disease that finally killed her.

In choosing the imagery of the path of life, the "habit of being," O'Connor followed a tradition that can be traced back as far as the earliest scripture.

Scripture

Walks, journeys, paths, pilgrimages, and quests permeate scripture. The Bible is full of movement: Adam leaves the Garden of Eden for life, "east of Eden." The murderous Cain is driven forth, bearing a mark to preserve him, dooming him to live as an endless wanderer. Abraham leaves Ur for the Promised Land, following the caravan route of the Fertile Crescent, settles for a while in the Promised Land, then wanders into Egypt, and returns to the Promised Land. Jacob leaves Canaan for Padan-Aran and then brings back his vast family and flocks. Joseph, when sold into slavery, is carried captive into Egypt, where his whole family later migrates to escape the famine in Canaan.

Moses, with God showing him the path, leads his people out of Egypt, through the waters of the Red (Reed) Sea, with a pillar of fire guiding them by night and a pillar of smoke protecting them by day. They wander for 40 years in the wilderness, sometimes within sight of the Promised Land. At God's signal, Joshua leads the Hebrews back into Canaan, again crossing through the waters which are providentially stopped during their passage. For some centuries, the Israelites settle in this land, building their homes and their cities, making their pilgrimages to Jerusalem for ceremonial occasions. To go from place to place, they still need their donkeys and their own sturdy legs.

Eventually, after repeated warnings from the prophets, the Babylonians and Assyrians march the Jews, bound as captives, out of their land, into foreign cities, where they live for centuries. In the course of time, Ezra and Nehemiah lead a remnant of delighted pilgrims back to Jerusalem. Finally, the Romans destroy Jerusalem, killing multitudes and driving many of the inhabitants into the countryside, where they hide from the victors. The Romans march others to Greece or Rome as slaves and emblems of conquest.

In this catalogue of travels, scripture has multiple references to the significance of the walk with God. As God tells Joshua: "Only be thou strong and very courageous, that thou mayest observe to do according to all the law, which Moses my servant commanded thee: turn not from it to the right hand or to the left, that thou mayest prosper whithersoever thou goest" (Joshua 1:7). Psalm 1, like many of the other psalms sung during long walks to Jerusalem for festivals, points out the importance of the company a person keeps on the journey of life: "Blessed is the man that walketh not in the counsel of the ungodly, nor standeth in the way of sinners, nor sitteth in the seat of the scornful." The godly man follows the straight and narrow.

The Proverbs use the path of life in a parallel manner, advising, "Better is the poor that walketh in his integrity, than he that is perverse in his lips, and is a fool"

(Prov. 19:1). Because morality is a matter of action, the *path* is ideal for portraying daily decisions made in accordance with the law of Moses. Jews saw morality as a way of habitual behaving as well as way of thinking.

The New Testament continues the journeys: Jesus and his disciples walk constantly, from Galilee to Jerusalem to Caesarea and back again. Even the resurrected Christ greets his friends walking along the road to Emmaus. Along the way, the people, the landscape, the events, the encounters lead to discussions of morality and faith. When he calls his disciples, Jesus commands them to "follow me." Much of the teaching of Jesus comes as he strolls along the countryside or pauses for a drink, responding to questions posed by a woman at a well or a man at the side of the Sea of Galilee. After he begins his ministry, Jesus has no home on earth. He is a perennial pilgrim, a sojourner on the road during the final three years of his life.

One of Jesus's most famous parables tells the story of a traveler on the road from Jerusalem to Jericho (Luke 10:30–36). Along the way, he "fell among thieves, which stripped him of his raiment, and wounded him, and departed, leaving him half dead." The perils of the road are accepted as a part of life, as is the subsequent behavior of other travelers, a priest and a Levite, who cross to the other side of the road rather than touching this poor man. It is the Samaritan who "went to him, and bound up his wounds, pouring in oil and wine, and set him on his own beast, and brought him to an inn, and took care of him." This good Samaritan is apparently fully equipped, on a long journey, with a beast of burden, and knowledge of the inns along the way.

Jesus uses this famous story to set up his final question to the lawyers who are challenging his interpretation of the law and the definition of *neighbors:* "Which now of these three, thinkest thou, was neighbor unto him that fell among the thieves?" He interweaves the message of morality with life experience, and fills it with movement and experiences from actual lives his audience will understand and remember. They all know this particular road to Jericho and the perils along the way.

When Jesus sends the twelve disciples out to carry his message, he instructs them to preach as they go, healing the sick, cleansing the lepers, raising the dead, and casting out devils. He also directs them to go without food or money: "Provide neither gold, nor silver, nor brass in your purses, Nor script for your journey, neither two coats, neither shoes, not yet staves: for the workman is worthy of his meat" (Matt. 10:5–15). He wants them to stay with worthy people, and when they are not received properly or listened to, they are to "shake off the dust of your feet." This became the pattern for the itinerant preachers who followed in the way of their Savior.

The book of Acts expands this pattern of voyaging forth. Paul is converted on the Road to Damascus in a startling experience that leaves him temporarily blind (Acts 9). From this point, he is taken to a "street which is called Straight," where he inquires for a certain house. Notice how specific the places and paths are in scripture. This continues as Paul begins his ministry, sailing or walking throughout the known world of the Roman Empire, taking the Gospel to Asia Minor, Greece, and finally to Rome. Along the way, he is arrested, beaten, shipwrecked, and stoned. Yet he continues his predestined path with a cheerful outlook. He encourages others by describing his adventures and telling them to "walk so as ye have us for an example" (Phil. 3:17).

If all the paths, roads, byways, and highways of scripture were tallied up, we would be dazzled by the sheer activity of these people. Although many of the paths were physical, the symbolism was often clear to the participant and to the reader. Unlike the Greeks, who had a grand sense of adventure, a hunger to slay the dragon or sail into the unknown, the Jews, and later the Christians, traveled for a purpose: because they needed to escape hunger, to worship, return home, or spread the good news of the Gospel. They had to protect their families, assure survival of their flocks, or celebrate a holy day at the Temple. A journey was not a romantic opportunity for new experiences; it was an obligation to God or to the clan. Jesus's father, Joseph, did not take the infant Jesus and Mary to Egypt for sightseeing. He was escaping the slaughter of the innocents, preserving the precious child.

Some of the journeys were religious. The annual pilgrimage to Jerusalem was for many a long walk and a tough climb through the hill country to the heights of the Holy City. The Psalms that they sang along the way gave meaning to the journey, preparing hearts for the celebration of the Passover, that great moment in Jewish history when God saved his people and set them on the path to the Promised Land. It also gave special meaning to the message of Jesus, who explained that the path to hell is wide and easy, but the path to salvation is narrow and difficult. His audience would have pictured the narrow passages on the rugged climb that brought them to the Temple.

More specifically for women, the book of Ruth portrays the sad and lonely path that the widow traditionally takes back to her father's home and hints at the great courage involved in any other choice of a path. It would have been dangerous and unusual for women to travel alone, but the deaths of the husbands of the three women leaves them without protection, forcing them to take the journey without masculine protection. The frightened Orpah takes the safe way, returning over familiar territory to her own family in Moab. The braver Ruth, though protected only by her mother-in-law, Naomi, chooses the dangerous path to a strange land and a people who despise Moabites. Her declaration reflects remarkable courage: "Entreat me not to leave thee, or to return from following after thee: for whither thou goest, I will go; and where thou lodgest, I will lodge; thy people shall be my people, and thy God my God: Where thou diest, will I die, and there will I be buried: the Lord do so to me, and more also, if aught but death part thee and me" (Ruth 1:16–17).

The path she chooses takes her and Naomi to Bethlehem, to labor in the fields of Boaz, to marry Boaz, and to bear Obed, the ancestor of David. Her choice at this fork in the road determined much of Israel's history. So also did each recorded path matter—Abraham's, Joseph's, Moses's, and Joshua's. Certainly, the path Jesus chose from the Garden of Gethsamane to Golgotha made all the difference for humankind. The path is clearly a metaphor for life's choices.

Literature

For the Greeks, the journey was often a sign of Fate. The gods chose, according to their own whims, to cause a collision at the intersection of three roads (for Oedipus and his father), or a storm that sent a sailor into troubled waters (for Odysseus and his crew). For the most part, the Greeks were sailors rather than walkers, so their imagery followed their customary activity. A hero would sail to the ends of the earth to seek adventure, to perform a task, to win a war, to prove his heroism, to fight monsters, and return to his home.

The adventures of the hero are carefully documented in Joseph Campbell's *The Hero with a Thousand Faces.* He notes the departure as generally involving: the call to adventure, the refusal of the call, supernatural aid, the first threshold, and "the Belly of the Whale." These are universal categories, referring not only to the Greek adventurers, but also to Moses, Joseph, and Jonah, not to mention Sir Gawain, Ahab, and Tom Sawyer. The adventure itself usually involves challenges from nature; temptations from seductresses, and finally the confrontation with the object of the quest. (Tolkien makes remarkable use of the classic mythic structure in his *Lord of the Rings.*) In most of these adventures, it is hard to discern a moral quality to the journey. Rather, the hero is intent on proving his courage, winning fame.

The "voyage out" is the archetypal journey of the young man—Achilles or Jason. The "return," or journey back, is the path of the old man—Odysseus after the Trojan War or Oedipus after he blinds himself and achieves inner vision. Contrast this with the biblical use of journey imagery. For both Abraham and Moses, the journey into the wilderness, which each takes as an old man, is to a new home, the Promised Land. Joshua is also an old man when he sets out to win Canaan and settle it for his people. These Hebrew "heroes" undertake these travels, accompanied by multitudes of their people, because God commands them. Along the way, they meet enemies and hardships, but not great monsters nor seductive women. Only Joseph is tempted by a seductress, Potiphar's wife, whom he rejects at his peril.

Alfred Lord Tennyson, a Victorian poet of great renown, wrote a famous poem about the aged Ulysses (the alternate name for Odysseus). In "Ulysses" (1842), Tennyson pictures the return of the old hero to his wife and family, only to discover that he is bored with the settled life of Ithaca. After a brief stay with his wife, he bequeaths his homeland to his son and those who eat and sleep and "know not me." He then gathers his faithful shipmates together and sets sail for the ends of the earth. This romanticized version of a medieval legend that takes Odysseus beyond the story in the *Odyssey* ends with his continued craving: "To strive, to seek, to find / And not to yield." Rather than rest, the romantic hero believes that his salvation lies in continual struggle.

By contrast, the Hebrew leader longs for his own vineyard and his own home in which the children grow up around him like sprouts of an olive tree. As the psalmist explains the ideal path:

> Blessed is every one that feareth the Lord; that walketh in his ways.
>   For thou shalt eat the labor of thine hands: happy shalt thou be, and it shall be well with thee.
>   Thy wife shall be as a fruitful vine by the sides of thine house: thy children like olive plants round about thy table.
>   Behold, that thus shall the man be blessed that feareth the Lord. (Ps. 128:1–4)

The Jew, long deprived of a settled life, dreams of home, not of adventure.

Drawing on both the classical and the biblical sources of journey imagery, the great medieval Italian poet Dante undertook an imaginary journey through the afterlife. In *The Divine Comedy* (1321), he pictures his own trip through hell, purgatory, and heaven, led for a part of the way by the Roman poet Virgil. Using the classical epic design along with a rhyme scheme *(terzarima)*, a tribute to the Trinity, he describes a journey into the imagination. At times, he and Virgil stroll along easily, chatting about the folks they see; sometimes they have to climb over rocks and broken bridges; sometimes they find themselves on a mountain side with one foot always above the other. Finally, with Virgil unable to continue the trip, Dante feels himself being lifted up, free of gravity, into heaven. Using the idea that sin is the force that draws man toward hell, the writer makes his travels seem easier as he climbs higher and escapes the pull of evil. This great epic of the afterlife ends with a glorious vision of God surrounded by all of the saints.

The Middle Ages were full of stories of travels, pilgrimages, and quests. The Arthurian legends, which deal with the search for the Holy Grail, are all adventure tales in the style of the Greeks and Romans, with a focus on the events along the way. "Sir Gawain and the Green Knight"(c. 1375), which deals with Sir Gawain's obligation to find the Green Knight who challenges Arthur's court, speaks less of the path itself than of the places the knight stayed, the people who threatens him along the way, and the temptations he faces. It is full of mystery and magic, designed to show that even the Christ-like Gawain can be tempted.

Another, far more earth-bound and realistic Medieval example, is Chaucer's *Canterbury Tales* (1387–1400). Geoffrey Chaucer's pilgrims, who come from all walks of life, are on their way to Canterbury Cathedral to see the tomb of Thomas à Becket. The Inn Keeper welcomes the Wife of Bath, the Knight, the Priest, the Prioress, and Chaucer himself, as well as such simple folk such as the Plowman and the Parson. Each promises to tell a story to make the journey more lively as they ride from Southwerk to Canterbury. Ironically, this agreement produces only a few religious tales and numerous bawdy ones—reflecting the nature of the individual narrators, their tastes, and moral and spiritual habits. For some of these pilgrims, this is a welcome vacation rather than a pious pilgrimage.

Given the universality of this popular "way" imagery, it is hardly surprising that one of the great masterpieces of English fiction is based on the image of the Christian life as a journey. *The Pilgrim's Progress* (1675), by John Bunyan, is an allegory of the spiritual life, from the City of Destruction to the Celestial City. Bunyan uses the materials of the medieval Romances, with their adventure-packed narratives, their giants, dragons and assorted monsters, their castles and secret gardens to build a fast-moving story. This book, like its companion that tracks the journey of Christian's wife Christiana, has proven a delight to each generation since the seventeenth century, when it first appeared. Bunyan uses the design of the Arthurian legends with the quest for the Holy Grail, but makes his hero a common fellow, with a wife and family. His wife and children later take their trip along the same route but with slightly different adventures in the second volume.

Considered one of the first novels in English, this imaginative travel story is surprisingly realistic, containing natural conversations and close observation of details. For example, in one scene in the sequel, Christiana and her children come to a great mist and darkness. They cannot find their way: "so that they could scarce, for a great while, see the one the other; wherefore they were forced, for some time, to feel for one another by words; for they walked not by sight." In this tiny detail where the pilgrims encourage one another in the darkness, Bunyan makes an important point of the need to walk by faith. On occasion, the weary Christians are tempted to sit down and fall asleep, forgetting the path they must walk. "The way also was here very wearisome, through dirt and slabbiness. Nor was there on all this ground so much as one inn or victualling-house, therein to refresh the feebler sort. Here therefore was grunting, and puffing, and sighing. While one tumbleth over a bush, another sticks fast in the dirt; and the children, some of them lost their shoes in the mire." Such a detail about the children's shoes is exactly what anchors this highly imaginative book in reality, making the allegory all the more lively.

Some of the characters are quite comic, with Bunyan quickly capturing a tone of voice that portrays them. Note of the efficiency, for instance, in Ignorant's assertion: "I take my pleasure in walking alone." Recognizing that he did not want the company of fellow Christians, the group leaves him to go his erroneous path. He tries to come to the Celestial City through the wrong route, and finally is denied entrance. The book is full of such quick studies of different folk in the typical English community. Their names characterize them, as do their words and actions.

The great English tradition of the novel started with this love of journeys and a taste for realism. In the Renaissance stories of travels to unknown places by courageous heroes and heroines provided vicarious adventure for those stuck at home. Tales of the Orient, of America, of exotic places and interesting people delighted and entertained the increasingly literate middle class as well as the upper class. The reading public also loved the more realistic stories of the *picaro*—the colorful young mischief-maker who took to the road. Sometimes this rogue was a highwayman (robber), sometimes a reckless young fellow from a good family who followed the path of the Prodigal Son (Luke 55:11–32).

Moll Flanders (1722), Daniel Defoe's supposedly penitent heroine, finds her way from prostitute and felon in England to wealthy landowner in America, protesting that she is airing her dirty linen in order to preserve others from following her wicked path. An unusual heroine, Moll is part of a group of highway robbers for a time; she is a talented thief, marries several times, once to her own son, and is ever eager for a new adventure. Each time, she tallies up her money and makes some pat moral comment about how much she has learned from her iniquities.

Tom Jones, by Henry Fielding, is one of the best written of these stories. Unlike DeFoe, Fielding makes no pretence that he offers any moral uplift. Even *Gulliver's Travels*, by Jonathan Swift, follows the episodic novel form, this time turning a shallow adventure story into a fascinating moral, political, and religious allegory.

American readers and writers have also adopted the travel tale, including the picaresque novel (in which the picaro, or rogue, has a series of adventures). Most readers are familiar with Mark Twain's adventure tales, both his own autobiographical tales and the ones he tells of Tom Sawyer and Huckleberry Finn. Tom is content to run away from home briefly, to get lost in caves, to float down river, but Huck has greater hungers and greater reasons. At the end of the story, he determines to "light out for the West." Both lads learn a great deal about themselves in these adventures, their weaknesses, their prejudices, and their core values.

Much of American history has been a record of travels: first to this country from various regions of the world, then to build a "home." Sometimes the immigrants have followed Huck's leading and gone West. The many American stories of families seeking a home to raise their young sound much like the ancient Hebrew scriptures and the dream of the Promised Land. The travels of many of the first frontiersmen, the hunters and traders, echo the adventures of the Greeks, with their joy in discovery. The later pioneers, who followed in the ruts made along the trails where the wagon trains had cut deep into the ground, were much more like the Hebrews on their trek across the Wilderness of Zin. The enormously popular series by Laura Ingalls Wilder, *The Little House on the Prairie, The Little House in the Big Woods*, and so forth, develop this perennial American dream. The craving for a home, for land that they might settle, has driven many to the journey.

Interestingly, the women who became part of the wagon trains west often brought culture, education, and faith as well as the promise of a home in which the family could settle. Some of these "Madonnas of the Prairies," with the circular opening of the covered wagon forming a kind of halo, do function as strong models of the righteous path. More often, however, these Western narratives are stories of men who were seeing treasure and adventure. The Jack London stories celebrate courage and strength, bur rarely mention faith. Mark Twain's Western stories, and those of Bret Hart are also chronicles of the rough and tumble masculine life of the region before women came to civilize and domesticate it—bringing religion and education with them.

The remarkable diaries of the Western women are evidence that they had much the same courage and sense of adventure as the men, though not always the same wanderlust. Willa Cather's novels, which chronicle the hard life for both men and women on the Western Plains, reveal the strength of many of the immigrant women. Such tales as *O Pioneers!* (1913) tell of women willing to work in the home and in the fields, resisting further travel, clinging to the land and the shelter—no matter how humble. Alexandra Bergson is a splendid example of the woman who ventures forth to discover whether other sites would be more favorable for her family. When she sees the problems of life elsewhere, she returns to improve her own farm and turn the prairie into a productive business. Only at the end of her life is she satisfied that she can travel again, this time for the sheer delight of seeing other places such as Alaska with the man she loves. Up to this point, her path in life has been restricted to the fields that she cultivated, leading her stubborn brothers to the good life. Her motives are not religious; she has promised her father to save the farm and is being faithful to that death-bed pledge she made to him.

For the migrants in Steinbeck's *The Grapes of Wrath* (1939), the drought and the struggle for survival are the keys to their travels. These are not religious quests, and the way that they take is important only as the easiest way to arrive at a destination. Even so, Steinbeck's narrative, *The Grapes of Wrath* (a title taken from Revelation), is a return to the theme of the biblical journey. Like the family of Jacob, leaving Canaan for Egypt, they are setting forth because of the family's need for work and food.

The wrath of God seems to have descended on this poor, illiterate farm family, the Joads. They hope to escape the drought in the Southwest and find a New Eden in California. But this ironic paradise does not welcome outsiders. It is guarded not by cherubim, but by landowners and lawmen. Worn out by their struggle, these courageous survivors find their strength in the community of shared suffering. The story concludes without any discovery of a home, with no real hope for prosperity. For these poor Oakies, sheer survival will be enough. Their story echoes the times. The novel grew out of the Great Depression, the terrible times of the Dust Bowl in Oklahoma, and the hopeless condition of many of the hoboes and landless people who wandered the countryside.

For other writers, the path continues to have the strong biblical symbolism that Jesus repeatedly used. In Southern literature, where a sense of place is powerful, each road has meaning. Faulkner often describes the dusty road along which a mule drags the farm wagon, the vine-covered trails that hunters trek through as they follow the hounds, or the paved streets of the small town that was central to his imaginary world of Yoknapawpha County.

One modern Southern writer, Eudora Welty, in her short story "A Worn Path" (1941), tells a simple tale of an old black woman who has made a path from her home in the country to town through her repeated ritual of duty. Her painfully disabled grandson needs his daily medicine, and she walks to town to fetch it for him each day. This act of love has dominated her life and defined her being, just as the path has become worn by her weary old feet. This beautiful short story, published in *A Curtain of Green* when Welty was only 32 years old, helped establish her as a major writer of fiction. Her close observation of the poor, African American woman and her sickly grandson is typical of her gentle and loving style, set firmly in the Mississippi countryside. In everyday life, Welty could discover universal truths.

In another of her works, a novel called *Losing Battles* (1971), Eudora Welty's school teacher notes the changes that have come with time. When she first began teaching, she walked to school and home each day. The slow pace allowed her to admire every flower garden and know every child and dog in the neighborhood. Later, more rushed, she rode a bike, becoming more focused on hazards, such as fallen tree limbs and perilous ditches, seeing less of the individual lives around her. When she is finally able to afford a car, she loses touch with most of her neighbors. Rather than relishing the "way," she has become fixated on the destination.

Most American stories reflect the tradition of Hebrew narrative. As a people who spent years in the constant struggle to settle the land, moving from the East coast to the West, Americans have resonated to the land-locked tales of the Bible. Only a few American authors have undertaken the Greek pattern of sea stories. Even in *Moby-Dick* (1851), the most famous of the novels dealing with voyages, Melville draws more on Jonah than on Odysseus.

Ernest Hemingway, always the lover of adventure, always frenetically in search of it, describes an old man on a last great voyage. In *The Old Man and the Sea*, the ancient mariner fights his last great battle. Unlike Tennyson's Ulysses, the old man gratefully returns home and is content with the prospect of a placid life. For his final years, he limits his voyages and relies on companionship of his young friend. Not a religious man, he uses remembered bits of prayer to change his "luck," relying on his experience, strength, and courage to survive. Hemingway, as usual, rejects the biblical possibilities—the transforming experience of Jonah or the purpose-driven voyages of Paul. His old man simply does that which he has been doing all his life, fighting for his life here and now.

Conclusion

Robert Frost, a twentieth-century American poet who loved to write about his New England countryside and his own experiences in it, catches something of the modern experience of choosing paths through life. In "The Road Not Taken," he describes life as a set of choices on the road he takes:

> Two roads diverged in a yellow wood,
> And sorry I could not travel both
> And be one traveler, long I stood
> And looked down one as far as I could see
> To where it bent in the undergrowth.

He decides to take the other road—the one that "wanted wear." Realizing that he will never return to this fork in the road, he continues his path, always wondering what life might have been like had he made the other choice:

> I shall be telling this with a sign
> Somewhere ages and ages hence:
> Two roads diverged in a wood, and I—
> I took the one less traveled by
> And that has made all the difference.

(Frost, "The Road Not Taken," 202)

Without relying on religious referents, Frost nonetheless takes the linear concept of Judeo-Christian scripture as his basic assumption: Life is lived as a pattern of steps we take, choices we make, destinations we seek.

Time proceeds from one moment to the next, one event to the next, one choice to the next. Our chosen path determines the nature of the life we live. All things progress this same way, with one person after another walking along until his or her life ends, and finally Time itself will end. In many other religions, experience is circular. A person, in perhaps another life, will have a chance to take the second path, know another kind of experience. But for the Jew and the Christian, the limits are clear and the selection of the wrong fork in the road may prove catastrophic. Although Frost sees his choices as equally desirable, such life-changing decisions are never trivial.

Another modern poet, T. S. Eliot, who traces his spiritual pilgrimage in a series of poems, describes life in terms that echo the Eastern religions. He sees human experience as a series of explorations, ending where it began. In his long poem *The Four Quartets*, the final section of "Little Gidding" concludes with these provocative words about the spiritual pilgrimage, using the symbols of fire and roses and journeys:

> What we call the beginning is often the end
> And to make an end is to make a beginning,
> The end is where we start from....
>   We shall not cease from exploration
> And the end of all our exploring
> Will be to arrive where we started
> And know the place for the first time....
> And all shall be well and
> All manner of thing shall be well
> When the tongues of flame are in-folded
> Into the crowned knot of fire
> And the fire and the rose are one.

(Eliot, "Little Gidding," 144–145)

Eudora Welty's stories point to the changes in life and literature since biblical times. The loving attention to details that we see in scripture, the awareness of a fig tree failing to bear fruit in season, or a deer panting for water is lost on most city-dwelling moderns. Fewer people walk to work or school as the worn path has become the highway or the skyway. Images such as a "stumbling block" have lost their poignancy as we no longer have to "make straight the way." Roads are already level and straight in much of our world of superhighways. We can fly from New York to California without noticing the so-called "flyover country" in between.

As our feet have lost their contact with the ground, so have our hearts lost a love of tiny, closely observed details. Without the ancient need for laborious walking, the exhaustion from the journey, the thrill of the quest, the weariness at the end of the day when we sit down, take off our sandals and rub our feet, it is hard to understand how refreshing it must be to have a hostess greet us at the door with a basin to wash our dirty feet. We can hardly recapture the delight of walking in green pastures or lingering beside still waters. Only those who walk or run, take off their earphones and listen to the sounds along the road can recapture something of the biblical sense of the path.

See also: **The Hero; Women as Heroes.**

Bibliography

Alighieri, Dante. *The Divine Comedy.* Trans., Dorothy L. Sayers. New York: Basic Books, 1973.

Bunyan, John. *The Pilgrim's Progress.* New York: Pocket Books, 1957.

Campbell, Joseph. *The Hero with a Thousand Faces*. New York: The World Publishing Company, 1956.

Cather, Willa. *O Pioneers!* New York: Vintage Books, 1992.

Chaucer, Geoffrey. *The Canterbury Tales*. New York: Modern Library, 1994.

Defoe, Daniel. *The Fortunes and Misfortunes of the Famous Moll Flanders*. New York: The Heritage Press, 1942.

Eliot, T. S. *The Four Quartets*. In *The Complete Poems and Plays, 1909–1950*. New York: Harcourt, Brace and World, 1952.

Frost, Robert. "The Road Not Taken." In *Modern American Poetry*, ed. Louis Untermeyer. New York: Harcourt, Brace and Company, 1950.

Hemingway, Ernest. *The Old Man and the Sea*. New York: Charles Scribner's Sons, 1952.

Matarasso, P. M., trans. *The Quest for the Holy Grail*. Baltimore, MD: Penguin Books, 1969.

O'Connor, Flannery, and Sally Fitzgerald. *The Habit of Being*. New York: Farrar, Straus, and Giroux, 1988.

"Sir Gawain and the Green Knight." In *British Poetry and Prose*, vol. I, ed. Paul Lieder, Robert Morss Lovett, and Robert Kilburn Root. Boston: Houghton Mifflin, 1950.

Steinbeck, John. *The Grapes of Wrath*. New York: Penguin Books, 2002.

Tennyson, Alfred Lord. "Ulysses." In *British Poetry and Prose*, Vol. II, ed. Paul Lieder, Robert Morss Lovett, and Robert Kilburn Root. Boston: Houghton Mifflin, 1950.

Welty, Eudora. *Losing Battles*. New York: Vintage Books, 1990.

———. "A Worn Path." In *Stories, Essays & Memoir*. New York: Library of America: Distributed by Penguin Books, 1998.

Slavery and Freedom

Readings

Exodus
Hebrews
Philemon
John Milton, "Aeropagitica" (1643)
John Stuart Mill, *On Liberty* (1869)
Harriet Beecher Stowe, *Uncle Tom's Cabin* (1852)
Fyodor Dostoyevsky, *The Brothers Karamazov* (1880)
Aleksandr Solzhenitsyn, *One Day in the Life of Ivan Denisovich* (1996)
Toni Morrison, *Beloved* (1987)

Introduction

> And ye shall know the truth and the truth shall make you free. (John 8:33)

The old, blind, imprisoned Samson, betrayed by his Philistine lover Delilah, stands chained to the pillars of the temple of Dagon in Gaza, the laughing stock of his enemies. Yet, with God's help, he regains his power and his freedom. In one final effort, he "bow[s] himself with all his might," and pulls down the temple pillars, burying himself and his captors in one tragic action (Judges 16:30–31). The tough lesson Samson teaches the world is that no man or woman can ever be kept in bondage if that person has the absolute will to be free and no fear of death. For most of us, such heroic resistance is unrealistic; we learn to live with some degree of submission.

Slavery and freedom are like fraternal twins in human history. Adam is told, at the time of the Creation, that he might "freely eat" of the fruits of the gardens, but is also warned of the limits of that freedom: he might not eat of the Tree of the Knowledge of Good and Evil. Free will implies that we are free to make choices, but must also live with the consequences of our choices.

Throughout scripture, this linked pair of opposites weave in and out of Hebrew history. In the New Testament, Christ speaks frequently of the freedom he brings to his followers. The Apostles write of the nature of Christian liberty, even as they are in prison.

So also throughout the literature and history of the Western world. The rhythm of bondage and liberty mark human experience and underlie much of human aspiration. Martin Luther considered liberty the essential characteristic of the Christian faith. American Revolutionary writers thought it a "God-given" right, along with life and the "pursuit of happiness"; French Revolutionaries proclaimed their dream of "Liberty, Fraternity, and Equality."

The aftermath of each of the great upheavals in history has repeated this tragic pairing. Abuses of liberty, violations of the rights of others generally follow the great revolutions fought for freedom. The human inclination to lawlessness, to taste of the fruit of the knowledge of evil, to claim power over others, invariably undermines ideal liberation, transforming the golden moment into lead.

Great philosophers, theologians, and poets have explored servitude to other humans and to God; they have explored the nature of true liberty, its sources and boundaries. Philosophers tell us that any discussion of liberty tends to be quite particular: freedom *from* hunger, theft, or terror; freedom *to* speak freely, vote, hold property, or worship. Absolute and ideal freedom does not exist on earth.

Luther, in his famous letter to Pope Leo X (1520) expresses the essence of the great paradox of Christian freedom: "A Christian man is the most free lord of all, and subject to none; A Christian man is the dutiful servant of all, and subject to every one."

Scripture

In ancient times, slavery was an almost universal practice. If a family were poor, they might sell their children into slavery; or if they fell into debt, the whole family might all become slaves. If a tribe were victors in war, they took the vanquished as slaves. Slavery has no racial overtones in most of scripture: anyone (even captive royalty) might find himself or herself a slave at some time in life. In many cases, their term of indenture is limited to seven years, but it might also continue for a lifetime. Women in bondage often find themselves sexually abused. They might also become mistresses or wives of members of the owner's family, depending on the circumstances. Some slaves are so beloved that they were considered members of the family and even become heirs. Some, on the other hand, are so brutally treated that they choose to run away and face death rather than continue under their bondage.

All through the Old Testament, slavery plays a significant role. The actual words used for slavery vary—sometimes *maidservant* or *manservant*, sometimes just *servant*, and sometimes *slave*. These nouns and their related verb—*to serve*—are occasionally used metaphorically rather than as actual descriptors of social roles. In fact, as a matter of courtesy, a host might refer to himself as "your most humble servant," not meaning that he is a literal slave to his guest. It takes on more significance in religious speech: David, for example, is called a "servant of the Lord" (Ps. 18:1); and the Israelites are admonished to "serve Jehovah" (Deut 11:12). Other times the words refer to actual servitude, as in the enslavement to the Egyptians or to the kings of Israel. The prophets, for example, criticize King Ahaz for taking captives from Judah (2 Chron. 28:8–15); and Isaiah calls on Israel to let the captives go free (Isa. 58:6).

Abraham's family undoubtedly are slave holders in Haran, and some of these slaves are part of his caravan as he leaves for the Promised Land. He apparently has sufficient "servants" to man his army when he needs to fight and to tend to his host of animals along the way. One of his long-time servants, his steward Eliezer, is so close that he is considered as a possible heir when Abraham remains childless. The custom of enslavement was also practiced in Egypt, which is the source of the maidservant, Hagar, whom the Pharaoh gives to Sarah. Hagar, at Sarah's bidding, subsequently serves as a surrogate mother for Abraham's first son, Ishmael.

Abraham's grandson Jacob, fleeing his homeland and his angry brother, has no bride price to pay for his beloved Rachel. He indentures himself to Laban, his wily relative, who tricks him into working seven years for each of his two wives. Each of these women brings (as part of her dowry) her own slaves or bondswomen, who subsequently serves as concubines for Jacob, contributing to the large family of twelve sons and probably numerous daughters who eventually return with him to Canaan. The children of slaves were designated slaves at birth, known as "house born slaves." In Jacob's family, however these children are apparently treated as legitimate sons, inheriting equally with their brothers at the time of Jacob's death.

Jacob's son Joseph is kidnapped and sold into slavery by his brothers, beginning the great drama of the Exodus. The descendants of Jacob, who are at first welcomed as honored guests in Egypt, are eventually reduced to slaves, building Ramses's great monuments. Forced to work under the cruel lashes of the Egyptian overseers, these Israelites are further tormented by the slaughter of their children birth to keep down their numbers.

Even so, when they have escaped by the grace of God and under the guidance of his chosen leader, Moses, they lament the loss of the good food and good living conditions they enjoyed in Egypt. Freedom to eat unleavened bread after enjoying "the fleshpots of Egypt" does not seem an unmixed blessing. The taste for liberty often turns sour in the face of the obligations of the freedmen to fend for themselves. Nonetheless, the Psalms are full of grateful praise for God's great act of bringing his people out of slavery.

The law given to Moses by God reminds the Israelites that they were once slaves and foreigners themselves and that they should be gracious to others who have fallen on such hard times. The law provides for the fair treatment of slaves, including the terms of their bondage and the arrangements for their release. Husbands are forbidden to sell their wives into slavery, and slaves are protected from harm. Considered property, slaves are covered in much the same way that other "animal" property under the law. Nevertheless, in most Hebrew households, the maidservant or manservant is treated as much a member of the family. The men are circumcised and become a part of the local congregation of worshippers. Servants of the priests are allowed to share in the sacrificial meat. Although the Hebrews accepted the institution of slavery, like most of the ancient world, they tended to be benign in their interpretation of it and protective of their slaves.

Even so, abuses invariably occur where one group of people have absolute power over another. Some believe that slaves were marked. Scripture notes that a slave who chose the security of perpetual enslavement rather than manumission at the end of his six years, was to have his ears pierced (Exod. 21:6; Deut. 15:17). They may also have been tattooed or branded, like cattle. This may explain the reference in Isaiah to having the name of Yahweh written on the hands of the faithful (Isa. 44:5), a sign that they belong to God. It may also explain the "mark of the Beast" in Revelation (13:16–17), which echoed the tattoo marks of Hellenistic cults.

When Joshua fought the various indigenous peoples of Canaan for the Promised Land, he enslaved some of them, forcing them to agree to their perpetual bondage.

The Hebrews regularly took hostages in warfare, particularly women, who became slaves to their masters. In some ways, the captives probably thought such enslavement a kindness, since the laws of warfare often required the holocaust of whole cities, with every living creature massacred and burned; or sometimes the more moderate action of putting the men to death and reckoning the women and children as booty (de Vaux, 81–84).

When David became king, he entailed certain laborers to work on his projects. Solomon, finding this the easiest way to provide plentiful free labor for the mines and the great projects, followed the path of the Egyptian Pharaoh, enslaving those who were needed, whether foreign or native. Certain kinds of labor were thought to be too menial to be performed by free men. These would have included heavy construction work, and labor in the mines. The monarchy apparently saw large numbers of Israelites, as well as Canaanite, Midianite, and Moabite captives, reduced to the status of slaves, working on the many public and royal buildings of David and Solomon.

In later years, the various conquerors transported the captive Hebrews off to Babylon or Suza or other exotic places, where they frequently served as slaves for foreign peoples. Babylon came to represent the enslavement for the Israelites. In this splendid city, the subjected and displaced peoples wept for their homeland. Although many of them prospered in the period of deportation and dispersion, they nonetheless perceived themselves as humiliated, serving as slaves to a foreign power.

The books of Daniel or Esther, though heroic, nonetheless tell stories of a people in bondage. Some of the Jews were treated with respect and given positions of honor, but they were not free to go where they chose and live as they wished. This remained the situation later under the Hellenistic and Roman Empires. At various times, their conditions were more painful than others, but the occasional rebellions suggest that the sense of bondage grated on men and women who hungered for freedom.

During this period, the prophets dreamed of freedom. They envisioned the return to the Promised Land, the rebuilding of the Temple, and the reign of a benevolent Messiah-King. Even when Cyrus allowed the remnant of the Jews to return to Jerusalem, they found themselves permitted only limited and temporary freedom to rebuild and to worship.

Later, Herod enslaved Jews to work on his massive projects, and the Romans used many of the Jews—along with other laborers—in the building of roads, aqueducts, baths, amphitheatres, and temples. Jesus was born into this world full of various levels of human bondage: the overall rule of the Roman Empire, the local rule of the king and the officers of Rome, the financial control of tax collectors, the religious rule of the Sanhedrin, scribes, Pharisees, Sadducees, and lawyers. Within this general system of controls over the citizens of Palestine, the practice of slavery continued. Poor families still sold off their children, usually their daughters, rather than face the expense of raising them and providing them with dowries. A man in debt might even sell himself into slavery to satisfy that debt. It is interesting that Jesus includes the concept of debt in his model prayer: "Forgive us our debts as we forgive our debtors." Jesus tells numerous parables about good and bad servants working for stern masters and benevolent ones.

The "servant girls" who accost Peter during the hours of his denial are probably slaves in wealthy households. Undoubtedly there were slaves in the crowds that listened to Jesus's sermons and proclaimed his entry into Jerusalem. The dream of freedom, especially freedom from Roman control, is thought to be the motivating force in Judas's life and betrayal. If he was, as suspected by many scholars, a member of the Zealots, he was probably eager to see Jesus become an earthly king, challenging Rome's power over the Jews.

Jesus often speaks of offering "freedom" to his followers, but seems to have meant freedom from the law as interpreted by the Scribes and Pharisees. It also means freedom from Satan and the temptations that would lead to damnation (John 8:34–36, 41–44). His public ministry is focused on liberation, beginning with the announcement that he is the fulfillment of Isaiah 61:1: "he has anointed me...to proclaim release to the captives" (Luke 4:16ff). As Messiah, he comes to overthrow "the prince of this world," and to release his prisoners (John 12:3f; Mark 3:27; Luke 10:17f). He frees possessed people from their demons, crippled people from their diseases, and sightless people from their blindness. He promises his followers that they will be welcome in the kingdom of God, where forgiveness and salvation awaits them.

All through the New Testament, slaves are a regular part of the social fabric. They are not mentioned in the households of Jesus and his disciples, who are probably too poor to have slaves. There seem to have been some household slaves in homes where Jesus visited (Luke 7:1–10; 12:37–46; Matt 26:51; 2445–51; 25:14–30). In such cases, affection and a sense of mutual respect and responsibility appear to have prevailed, leading New Testament writers to speak of the "household of God" (Eph. 2:19) in a positive manner. Some of the households mentioned—like that of Lydia—may well have had paid servants rather than slaves. In fact, slaves themselves were allowed to have possessions, including their own slaves. They were often allowed to carry on their own businesses. The household slave was considered a domestic, joining in the family worship, resting on the Sabbath, celebrating at religious feasts, and even marrying into his or her master's family and becoming an adopted son and heir, wife, or daughter-in-law.

Paul himself is thought to have come from a family that had once been enslaved and were "freemen" by his day—giving his concern with the "yoke of slavery" and thrill of freedom an additional power and poignancy. A whole synagogue in Jerusalem was known as the "Synagogue of Freemen." When Paul sends the runaway slave Onisemus back to his owner, Philemon, he acknowledges the system of slavery, but implores mutual respect within it. Both master and slave are Christians, and therefore brothers "both in the flesh and in the Lord" (Philem. 16:17).

Under the Greeks and Romans, house slaves were sometimes educated men, serving as tutors to the children of the household. Some believe that many were authors as well. In fact, Roman comedy often portrays the slave as the witty rogue, the clever character who carries messages and plots the intrigue.

On several occasions, the early apostles meet slaves in their travels. Paul's encounter with fortune-telling slave girl, who annoys Paul and his companion, is apparently being exploited by owners who use her "gifts" for their own gain. They are furious when Paul exorcises the spirit and leaves her healed and worthless. Consequently, they drag the missionaries to the "marketplace to face authorities" (Acts 16:16–19). Because the Romans were less restricted by law or religion in their treatment of their slaves than were the Jews, they were more likely to abuse both children and adults. There are, for example, stories of sexual abuse of both male and female children and of mutilation or crippling of adults who sought to run away. Attractive young women were the subject of assault by the various men in the family, and the children that resulted became slaves for life. Tragic stories of botched abortions and brutalized women are only hinted at in the literature of the period.

The pervasiveness of slavery made it less of a matter of shame for the family than as a simple indication of status. It is used in scripture to describe the worshipper's relationship to God and the true believer's relationship to his fellow Christians. Christ takes the role of the slave in washing his disciples' feet, and speaks of making himself a "servant" to others. His death on the cross is the humiliating punishment usually reserved for slaves (Phil. 2:7).

It is clear from the message of the Gospels and many of the Epistles that true discipleship involves accepting the humble status of a slave to God and to his people. Paul, who characterizes himself as God's servant, also speaks of mutual service among believers (Rom. 1:1; Phil. 1:1). He uses the image of the heir-slave in his statement to the Galatians, "So you are no longer a slave, but a son; and since you are a son, God has made you also an heir" (Gal. 4:7). He contrasts Abraham's two sons, "one by the slave woman and the other by the free woman," using the law to explain that it is the free woman's child who is the legal heir (Gal. 4:23–31). And it is Paul who proclaims that in Christ Jesus, "there is neither Jew nor Greek, slave nor free, male nor female." Gal. 3:28). The concept of manumission, liberation from slavery, and adoption by the owner as a son and heir becomes a powerful image of the work of Christ and his followers (Rom. 8:15–17; Gal. 4:5–7).

Paul is also firm in the belief that true freedom does not lie in one's material circumstances, but in his or her spiritual condition. He tells the Galatians, "Stand fast therefore in the liberty wherewith Christ hath made us free" (Gal. 5:1). Christian liberty allows the imprisoned Paul to sing and preach, rejoicing in his service. His enemies can only hurt his body; they can not touch his soul. His spirit remains free to the end.

Literature

Slaves in ancient literature carry messages, comment on their masters' affairs, and generally act as a chorus. Tragedy focuses on the decline and death of "important" people, eliminating mere slaves from consideration. Cassandra, a princess who is taken captive by Agamemnon, is murdered along with him by his angry wife, Clytemnestra (Aeschylus's *Agamemnon*). Another member of the Trojan royal family, Hecuba, Hector's wife, is portrayed in Euripides's *The Trojan Women* as one of the real sufferers of warfare, the captive women. Classical comedies, dealing as they did with the lower classes, often used slaves as clever rogues.

This peripheral role of the slave character continues through much of later Western literature until late in the nineteenth century. In the writing of the American South, where slavery was practiced in a manner modeled, in part on the customs of the ancient world, the slave characters in antebellum literature generally serve as little more than local color in the background. In English literature, slave/servant characters, such as Robinson Crusoe's man Friday, are characterized as a kind of comic innocents or noble savages. Crusoe automatically assumes that Friday, because he is a black savage, will become his servant. By the end of the eighteenth century, this assumption was open to challenge. By that time, sympathy with slaves and consternation at the cruelty of slave traders and slaveholders precipitated the passing of laws forbidding the trade, eventually followed by laws forbidding the whole practice of slavery in most of European countries and their colonies.

The prevalence of black slavery, where families were enslaved in perpetuity, became an increasing shame to the Christian community. There had been no stigma associated with voluntary servitude. The white settlers in the New World frequently paid for their passage by becoming indentured servants for seven years or less. The first African servants who arrived in America were also considered indentured servants with fixed terms of service, but this changed to a system of permanent bondage based on race, with increasingly cruel restrictions.

The cruel irony of this heinous practice living side-by-side with robust discussions of the universal human right to liberty was not lost on the idealists among the Reformers and the revolutionaries in England, America, and France. Attacks on slavery blended naturally with the rhetoric of freedom. The pragmatic compromise hammered out by the authors of the Constitution did not satisfy the Abolitionists. (The founding fathers had decided that a slave was a fractional person for the purposes of the census, but was not allowed to vote.) Attacks on their treatment of their slaves and the dissonance between their Christian faith and their lives as slave owners led many Southerners to adopt a defensive tone.

In the writing of the period before the Civil War, slave owners defended their position on slavery by references to scripture, insisting that slaves were "sons of Ham" and that respect for authority was the clear lesson of Philemon. Although many slave owners were kind to their slaves, introduced them to their Christian faith, and taught them to read, the system became increasingly oppressive in the years leading up to the great conflict. Slave narratives, such as Linda Brent's (or Harriet Jacob's) journal, record some of the efforts to escape, but most of these were not published until late in the twentieth century.

One of the earliest white women to express her horror at the plight of the slaves (on her husband's plantations in South Carolina) was Frances Anne Kemble, an early nineteenth-century actress. She came to America to marry Pierce Butler, who owned large holdings on St. Simons and Butler Islands. "Fanny" Kemble was particularly offended by the treatment of the African-American women, who could not expect legal marriages, protection during pregnancy, nor control over their own children. She observes in her diary that the treatment of female slaves "becomes mere breeding, bearing, suckling, and there an end" as the slave woman "adds to the number of her master's livestock by bringing new slaves into the world" (Kemble, 95). The publication of these diaries, her return to England, and her divorce from her husband scandalized many genteel folks in the Victorian era.

It is clear from the observations of another nineteenth-century woman, Harriet Beecher Stowe, that this exposé of conditions on the great plantations did not change circumstances. Stowe, a devout Christian, felt a call to tell the stories of the many slaves she met in Cincinnati, where they stopped briefly on their way to freedom. In Uncle Tom's Cabin, she blends hundreds of slave narratives into an epic account of slavery in America. It has been widely reported that, come years later, when she visited a White House reception, President Lincoln greeted her with: "So this is the little lady who wrote the book that made this great war." Stowe's conscientious and sympathetic narration of the lives of men and women in slavery is a great masterpiece of polemic prose.

She sets her story in a variety of places, beginning with a border state, Kentucky. She chooses two major figures to trace on their travels, using a series of domestic scenes to plot both paths. Uncle Tom, a Christ-like old retainer, loyal to a fault, is sold south into deeper slave territory, where he is treated sometimes generously and sometimes cruelly. In the final scenes, he faces the brutal Simon Legree, who tries to break his faith through torture and threats. Uncle Tom resists the temptation to become brutal or faithless. His death is modeled on Christ's, with the forgiveness of his persecutors, the vision of the afterlife, and the sense of tragic drama. He provides an example of Christian liberty, based not on his physical conditions, but on the liberation of his immortal soul. For the black community, the Christian promise of freedom and the Hebrews' experience of liberation from bondage made the Christian faith enormously appealing.

In a parallel plot line, Eliza, a beautiful young mulatto woman who has been gently raised on the same plantation, serves as the typical romantic heroine. She is married to a handsome, brave, and courageous young man on a nearby plantation, and has a young son. Stowe models her heroine on the Virgin Mary, who sees the threat to her young child, chooses to escape across the water, this time the Ohio River rather than the Red Sea, to Ohio rather than Egypt. She follows the path of the Underground Railroad toward Canada, finally reuniting with her beloved husband and keeping her family intact as she arrives at freedom. For her, the liberty is physical, familial, and social. She and her husband plan to take their son back to Africa in their final expression of true freedom.

The adventures of Uncle Tom and Eliza chronicle much of the pattern of slavery in the states before the Civil War, with long discussions of the theological positions of slaveholders and abolitionists punctuating the domestic scenes. Stowe, who interviewed a large number of former slaves and also relied on accounts accumulated by other abolitionists, manages to personify the different ideological positions, providing dramatic incidents to explain the consequences of the various views on slavery. For example, a slave appropriately named "Hagar," who has been sexually abused, seeks to protect her child, the creature she loves most dearly. She finally accepts her helplessness and commits suicide. Stowe, the mother of a large family herself, was particularly sensitive to the problems of slave mothers. She found it shocking that a slave mother was not free to hold and protect her own children. Just as in ancient times, they did not belong to her.

A century later, another author picked up on this theme of the slave mother. Toni Morrison wrote *Beloved*, a novel of love and violence, chronicling a slave mother who escapes much as Eliza had done. In her case, however, the trackers discover where she has settled and are prepared to drag her back into slavery. Rather than submit, she murders her own child, thereby frightening the slave traders and restraining them from further efforts to reclaim her. The violent scene, which has precedent in actual history, becomes the center of the story's haunting exploration of the mother's subsequent life.

Other modern novels explore other elements in the American experience of slavery. One of the most controversial efforts is William Styron's novel *The Confession of Nat Turner*. Nat Turner, a historical figure, was a slave on a Tidewater plantation, a brilliant man, who resented his enslavement. He organized a bloody rebellion against the slave owners that involved a number of slaves from surrounding plantations. Although the rebellion was brief and the perpetrators quickly caught, imprisoned, tried, and executed in a particularly hideous manner, the action frightened the whole white slaveholding community. Having assumed that their slaves were submissive and content, they were startled at the level of brutality, the viciousness of the rebellion. This may have precipitated the withdrawal of many of the benefits that slaves had heretofore enjoyed—including the right to congregate for religious services, to preach to one another, to learn to read and write, to enjoy a fair amount of freedom to visit one another. The new slave codes made the plight of the slave increasingly brutish, leading to deeper resentments. Ironically, the slave owners found that even small glimpses of freedom only led to rising expectations and unrest, sowing the seeds of rebellion.

Styron writes with passion and drama. The hero is presented as a prophet in the Old Testament mode. His gathering of disciples and his sacrificial and heroic death mirror the narrative of Christ's life in death. This, however, is combined with considerable sexual activity, including rapes and homosexual encounters that enraged both ortho-dox Christian and African American readers. Vividly written about a landscape that Styron knew from childhood, the book was thoroughly researched. It nevertheless aroused great controversy that diminished its potential impact.

Other writers in the years since the end of slavery in America have meditated on details that interested them. Some were African-American writers, like Booker T. Washington, who wrote *Up From Slavery* (1901); W.E.B. DuBois, who wrote *The Souls of Black Folk* (1903); and James Weldon Johnson, who wrote *Autobiography of an Ex-Colored Man* (1912). The twentieth century was full of talented African-American writers who struggled to come to terms with the history of their people in America. Richard Wright's *Black Boy* (1945) is one of the most realistic depictions of the black child growing up in the twentieth-century South. James Baldwin, one of the most subtle of these group of writers, vividly depicts the emotional power of a service in a Harlem storefront church filled with passionate African-American worshippers in *Go Tell It on the Mountain* (1953).

Ralph Ellison draws on these earlier writers. *Invisible Man* (1952), Ellison's masterpiece, is one of the most thorough and fascinating studies of the nature of the American black man. Puzzled about his own identity as a black man in white America, where the whole culture was designed to pressure him to deny his own identity, the narrator of *Invisible Man* explores what it means to be a black man in white America. Echoing the God of Moses, he finally proclaims, while eating a yam without embarrassment, "I yam what I yam." He is also laughingly citing the famous comic strip of the time, Popeye, who would frequently exclaim, "I am what I am, Popeye the sailor man!"

While this path of exploration of slavery prompted a vast outpouring of litera-ture from writers of all races, authors also meditated on another path to freedom. Paul notes that freedom came with Christ, not with a political or material action. Many writers, especially those who lived through the controversies surrounding the Reformation and the political turmoil that followed, explored in their writing the real meaning of freedom in personal and theological terms.

John Donne, in his *Holy Sonnets* (XIV), invites God to "enthrall" him, acknowledg-ing that he will never otherwise be free. Another Metaphysical poet, George Herbert, who also struggled with the great theological problems of the age, portrays his strug-gles with God in gentle, but dramatic, dialogues. He tends to see God's constraints as a "collar" that holds him back from the pleasures that attract him; he rebels against this restraint, and finally, after raving at God, comes to a peaceful acknowledgement of God's lordship. Poems like "The Collar" or "The Pulley" are lyrical reminders of another kind of service, based on love rather than forced servitude.

Milton, for example, points out that freedom is not license, that the Christian assumes responsibilities along with freedom. Because of Milton's own involvement with the government of the Commonwealth in seventeenth-century England and his concern for the limits of freedom, both religious and political, he wrote exten-sively about the subject. His most famous treatise is *Aeropagitica*, a classical speech, in the form that would have been addressed to the Aeropagus in ancient Athens. It is a defense of freedom of the press. He makes the case for the knowledge of good *and* evil: "It was from out of the rind of one apple tasted, that the knowledge of good and evil, as two twins cleaving together, leaped forth into the world." Sometimes, paternalistic leaders seek to protect citizens of any potential knowledge of evil for fear they will be damaged by it. Milton, however, insists that Adam came to know good through his fresh understanding of evil. He also argues that we underestimate the power of truth when we discourage an open combat between truth and falsehood: "Let her and falsehood grapple; who ever knew truth put to the worse, in a free and open encounter?" The truly free Christian or the truly free British citizen is the man "that can apprehend and consider vice with all her baits and seeming pleasures, and yet abstain, and yet distinguish, and yet prefer that which is truly better, he is the true warfaring Christian." He goes on to insist, "I cannot praise a fugitive and cloistered virtue unexercised and unbreathed, that never sallies out and sees her adversary, but slinks out of the race, where the immortal garland is to be run for, not without dust and heat."

Some of the same arguments for freedom on speech and thought reappear in John Stuart Mill's book *On Liberty* (1859). He takes a wider view of the concern, and a less theological one, arguing for liberty in the face of a movement toward increasing authority by rulers. Within his discussion of liberty's role in governance, he explores liberty of thought and discussion. His justly famous essay defending freedom of the press includes this statement: "If all mankind minus one were of one opinion, and only one person were of the contrary opinion, mankind would be no more justified in silencing that one person, than he, if he had the power, would be justified in silencing mankind."

Fyodor Dostoyevsky, living at the same time, in Russia, having seen the consequences of political power in the Church and the terrors of the French Revolution, casts his comments on freedom in a much more cynical manner. In *The Brothers Karamazov*, his story of "The Grand Inquisitor" tells of human preference for comfortable slavery rather than anguished freedom. The aged Grand Inquisitor, a sixteenth-century Church leader, living in Seville, has just burned a host of heretics at the stake when he comes face-to-face with Christ. Seeing the threat to his own authority, the Inquisitor throws him into prison and threatens to execute him in the morning.

In the meantime, he explains to him why it was a mistake for him to return, and why he was in error for his choice during the scene of the temptations for rejecting the bread Satan offered. The Inquisitor notes that bread is the secret of human nature: "But Thou didst reject the one infallible banner which is offered Thee to make all men bow down to Thee alone—the banner of earthly bread. And Thou hast rejected it for the sake of freedom and the bread of Heaven." He goes on to explain that Christ overestimated the heroism of mankind: "Didst thou forget that man prefers peace, and even death, to the freedom of choice in the knowledge of good and evil?" The Grand Inquisitor argues that, because Christ sought the free love of mankind, not the "base raptures of a slave," he forced unwanted freedom on humans. He says, "Thou didst ask far too much from him."

Then the Inquisitor lays out the role of the Church, to "correct" the errors of Christ. Their objective is to "persuade them that they will only become free when they renounce their freedom to us and submit to us." The people will be happy, having recalled "the horrors of slavery and confusion to which Thy freedom brought them." They simply cannot bear "Freedom, free thought and science" and the "marvels and insoluble mysteries" to which these will bring them. Some will destroy themselves, others will rebel and destroy one another. By giving up such temptations and accepting slavery to the Church, they will have the peace and security that come with obedience.

This is a powerful condemnation of the Church, both the Roman Catholic and the Lutheran, which Dostoyevsky considered far too worldly, rational, and un-Christian. Yet he feared that a totally free man would be free of morality or social obligations. "Without God, anything is possible."

For the Soviet Union, much of the twentieth century presented a problem of a people in bondage, not burdened with a surfeit of freedom. Aleksandr Solzhenitsyn, a novelist who served eight years in prison for calling Stalin a silly name in a letter to a friend, explored the issue of penal servitude and faith. In his novel *One Day in the Life of Ivan Denisovich* (1962), he traces a day in the gulag system. The prisoners, underfed, bitterly cold, overworked, and cruelly treated, nonetheless find a way to discover happiness in their lives. For Shukhov, the hero, the day is a success because of several "strokes of luck." In the midst of his deprived and apparently desperate life, he discovers the joy of doing his work with professional attention to excellence. He is setting bricks in a wall, using the trowel he carefully hides each night so he can claim it again the next day. He not only does his work precisely, he stays after the others to finish off a bit of mortar. To do a solid job of building, even under these circumstances, has redeemed the day.

Another of the prisoners in the gulag, Alyosha, the Baptist, celebrates his imprisonment since it gives him time to read the Bible and meditate on his salvation. When the mind is liberated, the body's condition is less important. The apostle Paul, who discovered this truth when he was in prison, told the Philippians that he was a happy man, regardless of his material circumstances, even if they should include martyrdom: "Yes, and even if I be offered upon the sacrifice and service of your faith, I joy, and rejoice with you all" (Phil. 2:17).

Conclusion

Moderns are deeply engaged in discussions of bondage and freedom. Most often these debates focus on problems of political powers, brutal dictatorships, and the potential of uneducated peoples to govern themselves. This is quite different from the biblical concept of freedom. In scripture, freedom is deliverance from prior bondage, the release from servitude. In the Old Testament, this is the literal enslavement in Egypt or Babylon. In the New Testament, it is the release of captives from prison or the release of sinners from sin. Christ proclaims that he has come to free the prisoners of Satan (John 12:31ff; Mark 3:27; Luke 10:17f).

Other New Testament writers expand this metaphysical tone of Christian liberty to reveal that "all things are lawful" but all things are not useful for the Christian (1 Cor. 6:12, 10:23). With freedom come obligations and responsibilities. The true believer must understand the positive uses of freedom so as not to hurt others. Called to be citizens of another kingdom, the Kingdom of God, Christians can reject the powers and principalities of this world.

Yet this world continues to have challenges. We still argue about the proper limits of freedom, about our right to force others to accept our notions of freedom, and about the burdens that free people must bear.

See also: **Government and Politics; The Hero; The Journey of Life; Justice; Predestination and Free Will; Women as Heroes.**

Bibliography

Arlandson, James Malcolm. *Women, Class and Society in Early Christianity: Models from Luke–Acts*. Peabody, MA: Hendrickson Publishers, 1997.

Bieman, Elizabeth. "Freedom, Bondage." In *A Dictionary of Biblical Themes in English Literature*. Grand Rapids, MI: William B. Eerdmans Publishing Company, 1992.

deVaux, Roland. *Ancient Israel: Its Life and Institutions*. Trans., John McHugh. Grand Rapids, MI: William B. Eerdmans Publishing Company, 1961.

Donne, John. *Holy Sonnets*. In *British Poetry and Prose,* vol. I, ed. Paul Lieder, Robert Morss Lovett, and Robert Kilburn Root. Boston: Houghton Mifflin, 1950.

Dostoyovesky, Fyodor. *The Brothers Karamazov*. Trans., Constance Garnett. New York: Barnes & Noble, 1995.

Edersheim, Alfred. *The Life and Times of Jesus the Messiah*. Peabody, MA: Hendrickson Publishers, 2004.

Ellison, Ralph. *Invisible Man*. New York: Random House, 2002.

Hedrick, Joan D. *Harriet Beecher Stowe: A Life*. New York: Oxford University Press, 1994.

Herbert, George. "The Collar" and "The Pulley." In *British Poetry and Prose,* vol. I, ed. Paul Lieder, Robert Morss Lovett, and Robert Kilburn Root. Boston: Houghton Mifflin, 1950.

Jacobs, Harriet A. *Incidents in the Life of a Slave Girl (1818–1896)*. Cambridge, MA: Harvard University Press, 1987.

Kemble, Frances Anne. *Journal of a Residence on a Georgian Plantation in 1838–1839*. New York: New American Library, 1961.

Mill, John Stuart. *On Liberty*. New York: Liberal Arts Press, 1956.

Milton, John. "Aeropagitica." In *The Student's Milton*, ed. Frank Allen Patterson. New York: Appleton-Century-Crofts, 1930.

Morrison, Toni. *Beloved*. New York: Alfred A. Knopf, 2006.

Solzhenitsyn, Aleksandr Isaevich. *One Day in the Life of Ivan Denisovich*. Trans., Max Hayward and Ronald Hingley. New York: Praeger, 1963.

Stowe, Harriet Beecher. *Uncle Tom's Cabin*. New York: Barnes & Noble Classics, 2004.

Styron, William. *The Confessions of Nat Turner*. New York: Random House, 1967.

War

___

Readings

Joshua
Judges
I Samuel
Isaiah 2:4
Homer, *The Iliad* (c. 800 B.C.)
Aristophanes, *Lysistrata* (412 B.C.)
The Song of Roland (c. 1050)
The Nibelungenlied (c. 1200)
Stephen Crane, *The Red Badge of Courage* (1895)
Ernest Hemingway, *A Farewell to Arms* (1929)
Kurt Vonnegut, *Slaughterhouse-Five* (1969)
David James Duncan, *The Brothers K* (1992)

Introduction

> From whence come wars and fightings among you? come they not hence,
> even of your lusts that war in your members? (James 4:1)

War stories have always been the stuff of literature. Whether pitting cosmic or
human forces against one another, battles are thrilling. They offer a heady combination of violence, discovery, adventure, hurried love affairs, young people at the peak
of their vigor, and untimely death in far-away places. Sometimes they portray high
ideals and challenges to fixed views of life's ultimate meaning. Sometimes they are
grubby accounts of bloody details, brutal actions, and obscenities that erase any hint
of romance. Loosing the dogs of war is the decision that makes or breaks kings and
emperors.

In the Bible, especially the Old Testament, the Israelites fight wars to correct wrongs, to protect God's people, to take the Promised Land, or to defend the

Promised Land. When waged for Israel, warfare is usually portrayed as a good; when against her, it is evil. By the days of the prophets, when great empires had long held the Jews hostage or devastated their land, dreams of peace become more compelling than the excitement of war, with the hope of spears being beaten into pruning hooks (Isa. 2:4). This dream continues into the New Testament, with the coming of the Prince of Peace.

Nonetheless, neither Christian nor secular history has long remained free of the drums of war. Literature chronicles the changing attitudes toward battle, sometimes heroic, sometimes savage. The point of view moves from a concern with the victims to a delight in the heroes, and then returns to a horror at the devastation. The prophesy in Matthew seems to be proven true time after time: there will be wars and rumors of wars until the end of time (Matt. 24:6).

Scripture

Scripture begins and ends with hints of war. Even as God is creating the world, Satan rises up in rebellion against the Heavenly Host. The Battle of the Angels, an epic battle alluded to through numerous bits of scripture, begins with Satan's refusal to serve God, his challenge to His authority, and the recruitment of angels to fight on his side. By Milton's day, this sketchy story had become a full-blown myth, which *Paradise Lost* describes as a quick and decisive battle. *Paradise Lost* ends with God, the Commander of the Heavenly Hosts, casting Satan and his rebellious cohorts from heaven into their new God-less habitation, hell. Dante and others of his time believed that this new habitat of evil was in the center of the newly created earth.

The final battle on earth, referred to regularly through scripture as the *Day of the Lord*, is thought to be the coming Armageddon. This world-wide clash of nations during the Last Days, will bring time to an end. This oft-predicted human battle has also served as a source of inspiration for writers—especially moderns, who believe each new weapon or conflict can usher in this catastrophic conclusion to human history.

In their early history, the Hebrews were not a warfaring people; they were a nomadic people, who lived in tents, tending to their animals. Abraham was a reluctant warrior, willing to fight only to protect his family. As part of a clan, jealous of their integrity, Jacob's sons did attack Shechem when one of its princes seduced their sister Dinah (Gen. 34). But this was considered a serious error, for which Simeon and Levi were punished by their father in his dying prophesy (Gen. 49:5).

The Hebrews, held in captivity in Egypt for centuries, did not rise up as rebels against their Egyptian overlords. Rather, their leader, Moses, who, as a young man had killed an Egyptian, begged the Pharaoh to set his people free, calling on the Lord to reinforce his request. The Israelites left only when allowed by the Pharaoh. After their escape, they avoided fighting, even when hostile peoples of Moab and Edom forbade their travel along the easier path to the Promised Land, the King's Highway. Instead, they were forced to take the much more difficult way, along the cleft of land that leads to the Gulf of Aquaba, thus avoiding Moab and Edom. Moses did allow his people to fight the fierce Amalekites, and later the Amorites, but this was for survival and land. These were tribes who repeatedly attacked the Israelites, and Moses was responding to God's specific guidance.

The Israelites took the shedding of blood very seriously, believing that blood is life. Yet the victory songs of Moses and Miriam are evidence that they saw this kind of bloody power, given by God, to be a great blessing. Even with the commandment

"Thou shalt not kill" in hand, the Israelites never saw any barrier to warfare. In fact, they chose Joshua as their leader largely because of his loyalty and his success in battle.

The Hebrews of this period were clearly tough enough for battle. The life of the shepherd is not easy. He walks long distances, climbs up and down mountain slopes to keep his sheep safe. He sleeps out of doors much of the time, sometimes even serving as the "door" of the makeshift sheepfolds, where he shelters his sheep for the night. If wild animals come attacking the sheep, he has to fight them off. In the Bible, there are several references to fighting lions, chasing off foxes and, even battling bears. Joshua finds his men in good shape for battle, even though most have never been trained for warfare. David later notes, when Saul points out he is only a boy: "Sir, I am my father's shepherd; when a lion or bear comes and carries off a sheep from the flock, I go after it and attack it and rescue the victim from its jaws. Then if it turns on me, I seize it by the beard and battle it to death. Lions I have killed and bears, and this uncircumcised Philistine will fare no better than they; he has defied the army of the living God" (1 Sam. 17:34–36). We forget sometimes that this land was once full of forests and wild animals. Shepherds were not like modern nomads; they had to be more like cowboys, living in the open, fighting all sorts of predators—animal and human.

Nonetheless, the Israelites were poorly equipped for warfare. They had little military armor and had to fight with primitive weapons. The slingshot was a favorite weapon in a land full of rocks. A rock can be lethal, as Goliath discovered. (A common form of punishment was stoning, where every member of the community picked up a stone and threw it at the malefactor.) The rod which the shepherds used for the sheep, was like a club and could also do real damage to a skull. They had bows and arrows, but the tips of the arrows were usually made of stone. Even their knives were flint rather than metal. The few pieces of iron they had, which they used as goads and plows, had to be melted down to form spears and swords.

The Canaanites, by contrast, were a settled people who lived in fortified cities. They had iron-tipped spears and arrows, sophisticated siege weapons, battering rams, and metal swords. Even more impressive, they had horses and chariots "with iron wheels." While the Israelites fought on foot, without any armor other than round shields. their enemies had great shields and even shield-bearers, who held these enormous devices in front of the warriors.

So the Israelites learned to use what they had: speed, flexibility, surprise, wit, and the leadership of God. They could dash in on foot, infiltrate a town, surprise the citizens, and burn all the homes to the ground. Like our Special Forces, the Israelite warriors knew strategies for achieving their goals with minimum loss of life on their own side. Throughout the Bible, the Israelites learn the tricks of a small under-class: win by subterfuge when possible, and remember that you fight for your tribe, and for your God. Gideon is encouraged to battle with a chosen few rather than a vast army. There is no hope for them in direct frontal attack on a superior force. Deborah discovers that she can use her knowledge of the land to achieve victory over the Sea Peoples with their iron chariots. She waits to fight until the spring floods come and then tricks the enemy into a battle where their wheels become mired in the mud while the Israelites race about on foot about their adversaries. Jael, a friend to the Israelites, even uses the clever feminine strategy of pretending to offer hospitality, while planning to slaughter the leader of the opposition.

The Ark of the Covenant leads the Israelites in battle, reminding them that God is in their midst. Their leaders receive their marching orders from God. They believe that they are fighting a holy war, one that God orders them to fight. He tells them to "take the land." God himself is pictured as a warrior, surrounded by the Heavenly Host, his angelic troops. Thus, war itself, when commanded by God, is a religious act. Before Joshua leads his men against Jericho, he circumcises them and leads them in the celebration of the Passover. Only then does the heavenly "Commander of Hosts," come to him and give him instructions regarding the plan of battle.

The Israelites believed that God must be consulted before going into war, and the leader was then possessed of "the spirit of the Lord" (Judg. 6:34). Without this spirit, the leader was powerless before the enemy, as Samson discovered. War was "sanctified," and the camp was a holy place, where God himself was present (Deut. 20:4, 23:14), as is evidenced by the presence of the Ark of the Tabernacle. The camp must therefore be kept clean, without any sexual intercourse, human excrement, or other "unclean" things or activities. The priest was present to give counsel and encouragement, and those who were not able to devote themselves fully to the battle were sent home (Deut. 20:2; 5–8). Sacrifice was offered before the conflict began (1 Sam. 7:8–10).

God also decided the fate of the defeated enemy. Since a holy war was not for booty or for glory, but for God, the army was directed how to treat the enemy. At the end of the battle, terms of peace might be offered, but if rejected, the Israelite army was to carry out the Lord's judgment (Deut. 20:10–14). In the case of Joshua and the city of Jericho, God ordered the leader to destroy all of the people (except for Rahab and her family) and all their animals and possessions (except for precious metals, which were to be given to God's priests). This pronouncement of *harem* seems incredible to the modern mind, but in a land that believed fervently in vengeance, even the smallest child might grow up to seek revenge on those who had killed his family. The Greeks behaved the same way when they captured Troy. Later, the Romans (as well as most other invaders) found that the total destruction of the city was the best strategy to avoid future problems. They were known to sow salt on the land to render it barren. After the Jews rebelled against Rome (70 A.D.), the empire turned on them and leveled Jerusalem, including the Temple and all the great buildings on the Temple Mount. They killed thousands, drove others into the countryside, and took many others captive.

When the Jews acted this way, it was not simply a primitive impulse by barbarian invaders; their action was in response to the explicit command of God. This became a pattern that continued into the time of the judges, and on into the days of the kings. Saul and David were chosen to be kings because they first proved they were good warriors, able to slay their thousands and tens of thousands. Saul even commanded David to bring him the foreskins of the slaughtered Philistines, probably as evidence of his kills. The story of Judith, full of bloodthirsty glee, reflects this conviction that God's enemies deserve brutal treatment. When she cuts off Holofernes' head and carries it home in a bag, the people "bowed down and worshipped God" and then celebrate, crowning themselves with olive wreathes and joining in a dance (Ackerman 1971, 292–3).

The psalms—especially the "imprecatory" psalms—are full of bloodthirsty words.

As C. S. Lewis notes, the enemies of Israel were considered the enemies of God. It was fair game to curse them and their children. Psalm 46 is a good example of the Israelites' view of their God—a refuge and "a very present help in trouble." They can count on Him, though "the nations rage." The great hope of this "Song of Zion," is that the time will come when he will break the bow and shatter the spear.

These words are echoed in Isaiah's famous dream of the Day of the Lord, when the Peaceable Kingdom will see the nations "beat their swords into plowshares, and their spears into pruninghooks" (Isa. 2:4).

For the Jews, the great hope lay in the coming of the Messiah. As this people were overrun by one empire after another, enslaved, deported, abused, and finally scattered, they dreamed that a great warrior would finally prove their savior. Believing that their God would pull them out of the fire, preserving them as he did in Moses's day, they dreamed of the Day of the Lord, when justice would sweep down like a mighty river on the enemies of Israel.

Jesus's entrance into the world as a small child in an obscure village in the family of a carpenter, his message of the blessed peacemakers, and his Triumphal Entry into Jerusalem on a donkey, as the Prince of Peace, could hardly have measured up to the vision of the Messiah they had in mind. Yet Christ also had his fierce side: he said that he came, not to bring peace to earth, but a sword (Matt. 10:34). When his followers were about to face a hostile world, he advised them to sell their robes and buy a sword (Luke 22:35–36, 38). Yet, unlike the Emperor Constantine and the prophet Mohammed, Christ never commanded his followers to use warfare as a means of conquest or conversion.

He himself was a man of peace. When the soldiers came to take him prisoner, he stopped Peter from using his sword to protect him, admonishing him that those who live by the sword will die by the sword (Matt. 26:51–53). He told Pilate that his kingdom was not of this world (John 18:36). Insofar as war is often about power or property, he had little reason to fight. These were not his concerns. Instead, he accepted martyrdom and saw a kind of victory in suffering for righteousness sake.

Peter, the disciple who had resorted to the sword, eventually recommended that we accept suffering and adjust to our leaders rather than joining in rebellion. The message of the Beatitudes is clearly this, that the peacemakers, not the warriors are "blessed."

Paul tells the Ephesians that they should "be strong in the Lord, and in the power of his might. Put on the whole armor of God, that ye may be able to stand against the wiles of the devil. For we wrestle not against flesh and blood, but against principalities, against powers, against the rulers of the darkness of this world, against spiritual wickedness in high places" (Eph. 6:10–12).

Literature

The Greeks' view of war was even fiercer than the Hebrews'. War was accepted as a normal part of human life, essential to the survival of the state. The warrior was the hero, the healthy, strong, ferocious man who could outfight, outrun, and outshoot the enemy. Achilles fought for honor, though supposedly motivated by the gods. A demigod himself, the child of Aphrodite and a human, he was larger, stronger, handsomer, and prouder than those who surrounded him. The historian Thucydides wrote that men fight for honor, fear, and self-interest, clearly true of Homer's depiction of the battle of Troy in the *Iliad*. The battle, which kills the Hector, the decent man who has no help from the gods, preserves Helen, the guilty cause of the fight. It also results in the eventual doom of the magnificent hero Achilles and the fall of the beautiful city of Troy. Homer portrays heroism and passion and brutality, a final defeat through the trickery of the Trojan Horse that leaves the world with no real sense of a glorious victory.

This ancient epic reduces a barely remembered historic clash of cultures to a struggle between two men in the tenth year of the siege of Troy. The rationale for the war seems trivial to us, a matter of personal honor, not a national catastrophe: Paris, the princely son of the king of Troy, steals the wife of Menelaus, Helen of Troy. All of her suitors from her earlier days along with their followers are consequently obliged to sail to Troy and punish this gross violation of hospitality. Thousands of innocent people on both sides die because of the unbridled lust of two illicit lovers. Homer, ever the realist, pictures Helen as still beautiful, but ashamed of her role in this conflict. And Paris, the one who provoked the war, tends to run from battle, proving himself more a lover than a fighter. Others pay the price of this couple's infidelity.

It is hard to find a moral here. Unlike King David after his affair with Bathsheba and the death of their child, no one laments his "sin" or begs forgiveness of God. It would make no sense, since most of these gods have neither honor nor any sense of right and wrong. At the end, according to some myths, Helen goes home with Menelaus, who does not blame her for the adultery.

Later Greek literature, based on the same myths and the same characters, explore the Trojan War in somewhat less heroic ways. Euripides, for example, wrote *The Trojan Women*, showing the hideous aftermath of war. The men have proven their bravery and defended their honor, but the women are bereaved and enslaved. They are the final victims of battle. For Euripides, the price in human blood and sorrow magnifies the carelessness of the gods who play heedlessly with human lives.

Aristophanes' play *Lysistrata* presents a comic version of the females' antagonism to war. The central joke of the play is that women, who are sick of having their men going to war, decide to refuse sex until the men swear off warfare. This play, written in 412 B.C., the very darkest period of the Peloponesian War, is a semi-serious commentary on the very real threat facing Athens and her empire. The story takes place in Athens, where the Athenian and Spartan women join the Boethian and Corinthian women in this boycott of sex. The results are funny, grotesque, obscene, and successful. By this point in their history, the Athenians were convinced that war solves no problems. They had begun to see it as a kind of cosmic joke on human kind provoked by gods who cared nothing for justice or goodness or human happiness.

The literary influence of Greece eventually proved at least as strong as that of Christianity, which became the dominant religion of the Holy Roman Empire. For a time, the official status of the religion provided a kind of peace, a *Pax Romana*. But the continued attacks of barbarians and the rise of Islam reinvigorated the ancient spirit of Holy War. The Church came to believe in St. Augustine's concept of a "Just War": if a civilization is attacked, it is appropriate to defend itself against aggressors, especially those considered pagans.

A few vestiges of the barbarian culture that attacked Rome have survived. One of the most interesting is *The Nibelungenlied*, an epic that celebrates the achievements, adventures, and battles of several heroic figures, all of whom are larger than life. In keeping with the later conversion of the scribes who turned the oral tradition into written form, it includes courtly behavior and chivalry. Transcribed perhaps as early as 1200, this is the German version of the Volsung Saga, written in alliterative verse that also appears in *Beowulf*. *The Nibelungenlied* draws on history, mythology, and legend for its details.

It is a curious blend of fifth-century Germanic Nieblungs and contemporary knights, medieval magic and Christian worship. Brutal at times, it also has feudal and chivalric practices. The ancient virtues of honor and revenge, loyalty and heroism are paramount with Siegfried and his men. The women in the story, especially Brunhilde, are as powerful and savage as the men.

A somewhat more civilized, genteel song of war, or chanson de geste, was popular in the French courts. *The Song of Roland* was probably written down sometime in the middle of the eleventh century, taking the present form near the end of the twelfth century. The chanson recounts the heroic deeds of the Franks under the leadership of Charlemagne's nephew Roland. This extended poem is written in assonant verse (a form of vowel-rhyme) that was popular at the time. It celebrates the battle against the Saracens in the Pyrenees. After the death of Mohammed in 632, Moslems spread their faith through much of the known world, entering Spain in 711, and threatening the Franks in a series of murderous raids over the mountains.

Roland (called *Orlando* in Italian) and his friend Oliver are the targets of a complicated plot to ambush them and destroy the valley of Roncesvaux (or Roncevalles), a pass through the Pyrenees. Ganelon, Roland's step-father, proves the arch-villain in the story, tricking both Charlemagne and Marsilla, the leader of the Saracens. Roland finds himself at the rearguard of Charlemagne's retreating army. They are under attack, but Roland is too proud to blow his horn to signal the need for Charlemagne's help.

In keeping with the idea of the holy war, the Archbishop Turpin inspires the army, promising paradise to the warriors. They do fight magnificently, putting the Saracens to flight. With only 60 of the French left alive, they are overpowered by a new wave of invaders. In the meantime, the crafty Ganelon discourages Charlemagne from turning back to help Roland. Finally, Roland dies, praying. Charlemagne returns too late to save him, but learns the truth of the false promises and wreaks revenge on all the evil-doers. In a trial by combat, Ganelon is torn apart by horses. Marsilla dies in combat, in his final instructions directing that his widow be sent to France to be converted to Christianity. The remaining Saracens are all baptized and accept Charlemagne's rule over them. Christianity is clearly victorious.

The Crusades, those remarkable and often Quixotic efforts to take back the Holy Land from the Moslems, lasted from 1098 till 1291. They captured the imagination of rich and poor, young and old alike. The concept of the Christian warrior lived on in literature long after their historical memory had faded. King Arthur and the knights of the Round Table (as portrayed in Sir Thomas Malory's *Le Morte Darthur*) believed that they fought for God and country, in the tradition of Joshua or Gideon. The warriors in the Medieval Romances prove an interesting blend of Greek and Hebrew, with the armor, arms, and protocol of Greek warfare, and the piety and purpose of the Hebrew. Their additional commitment to the ladies of the court, their attention to personal honor, and their solitary quests for the Holy Grail seem more like Greek myth with Christian embellishments.

Even after the Crusades had come to an end and people grew increasingly cynical about the real purpose of battles, the heroic view of warfare continued, especially among the king's supporters in England. In the seventeenth century, when the king-to-be (Charles I), was in exile in France, these Cavaliers adopted the elegant clothing styles of the French court, with the high boots, lace sleeves, and plumed hats. They chose picturesque modes of battle. Sitting on their prancing horses, armed with spears and swords like gentlemen, they fought for king and country.

Their Puritan adversaries, the Roundheads, were less inclined to idealize the conflict. They tended to dress in the plain style of their fellow believers, fighting staunchly for their faith and for survival. They had few dreams of adventure or romance. Actually, both sides served their own theological purposes, one supporting the divine right of kings, the other proclaiming that only Christ is King. In the American Revolution, the colonial heroes were more like the Puritan Roundheads, simply dressed and battling for survival. The royalists, who lost the war, have never been lionized in American literature. Their red-coats and powdered wigs struck Americans as pretentious.

The heroic cavalier stance reappears in Civil War stories, especially those coming out of the South, when the swashbuckling cavalier tradition was cherished. *Gone with the Wind* (1939), the Southern epic of the war, shows the soldiers riding off to war, fully expecting to return triumphantly as heroes. Faulkner often mentions this image of the heroic warriors heading off to save their homeland and their way of life as a perennial myth of the South. The realistic final chapters of Margaret Mitchell's popular novel show the bedraggled soldiers returning after their defeat to the ruined land—with only the profiteers like Rhett Butler surviving. The horrors of the burned city of Atlanta and the scarred Southern landscape make this a more realistic novel than most. A modern novel by Charles Frazier, *Cold Mountain* (1997), captures some of this realistic detail. It tells of a Civil War deserter trying to return from the war to his beloved wife and home in the Smokies, the tale of a modern day Odysseus.

One of the first fully realistic writers to attack this persistent heroic vision of warfare was Stephen Crane. He wrote *The Red Badge of Courage* as if it were a first-hand account of warfare, told from the point-of-view of Henry Fleming, who is referred to throughout the story as "the youth." Even before he goes off to war, Henry acknowledges he is a romantic: "He had, of course, dreamed of battles all his life—of vague and bloody conflicts that had thrilled him with their sweep and fire." He realizes that these are a faded and anachronistic part of the world's history, and he "despaired of witnessing a Greeklike struggle."

His mother's placid acceptance of his misbegotten decision to enlist only reinforces his distress over the loss of splendor. She deflates his heroic gesture by her motherly and practical preparations: "Don't forgit about the socks and shirts, child; and I've put a cup of blackberry jam in your bundle.… Good-by, Henry. Watch out, and be a good boy." These are hardly appropriate words to leave ringing in the ears of a departing warrior. This untried Union soldier soon finds himself fighting Civil War skirmishes in Virginia. He is frightened and confused. At one point, he runs breathlessly from the battle, returning without admitting his panic. Later, he is caught up in the passion of the battle and proves to be a ferocious fighter. Even so, he is disappointed that he never achieves his "red badge of courage," a wound in battle.

In much of the novel, Crane echoes the lines from Matthew Arnold's famous poem "Dover Beach":

And we are here as on a darkling plain,
Swept with confused alarms of struggle and flight,
Where ignorant armies clash by night.

(Arnold, "Dover Beach," 580)

The "youth" in *The Red Badge of Courage* discovers that death is not pretty, that generals are not wise, and that service to the gods of war is a savage religion demanding mindless sacrifice. Rather than a series of heroic gestures, it is a business of long waits, self-doubts, sore feet, and short rations. By the end of the story, he has become a different person who has "rid himself of the red sickness of battle." He discovers he is insignificant in the large design of things, referred to as a "mule driver." Even the great scholar of warfare Karl von Clausewitz notes that it is difficult telling what is happening in the field when you are in the midst of battle. He calls this the "fog of war." This confusion in battle is part of the youth's discovery. He finds his real love is not the bloody ground of battle, but the soothing green "cathedral" of the forest, with cool brooks and fresh meadows—the dream of "an existence of soft and eternal peace." The youth walks down the "aisles" of the trees, finding peace not in traditional religion but in his communion with nature. Ironically, in other stories, Crane pictures nature as an impersonal and disinterested force, with no concern for human existence.

The nineteenth and early twentieth centuries saw so many revolutions and international conflicts that war became a favorite topic of world literature. The classic of its kind, an epic of the wars of Russia, is Leo Tolstoy's *War and Peace*, covering hundreds of characters and multiple battles. He describes Napoleon's invasion of Russia in 1812, while also tracing the lives of four aristocratic families who are caught up in world events. In this remarkable study of both ballrooms and battles, Tolstoy makes the point the there is a historical determinism over which humans have no control. Yet every human is sacred and can make moral choices in his or her personal life.

A later war novel that tells a more limited story of lovers during the Russian Revolution is *Dr. Zhivago* (1965), by Boris Pasternak. His is a love story told against the violent and chaotic days of the Revolution. His respect for the beauty of life stands above all dogmatism and logic. He criticizes both the Revolutionaries and the Christian idealists, who inspired them. For him, love and respect for life are more important than dogmas. Both of these great novels capture something of the confusion and violence of a war fought in one's own country, forcing thousands of innocent people to face sacrifice, brutality, and death.

The Russian experience of war was somewhat different from that of the rest of Europe and of America. These western peoples had forgotten the ugliness of war by 1914. Paul Fussell refers to the spirit of "innocence" among Americans and English citizens at the time that the "Great War" was threatening. A new generation had arisen who had no recollection of the horrors of war and were curiously eager to join in battle. World War I revived much of the spirit of heroism among both British and Americans, who soon found that the trenches of Europe were hellholes.

English writers, among the many soldiers who died in shockingly large numbers in the trenches of France, at first wrote brave poems, filled with patriotism, which made them popular at home. Rupert Brooke, for example, who died in 1915, even before he arrived at the battlefront, was such an idealist. In his poem "The Soldier," he wrote these frequently quoted words:

> If I should die, think only this of me:
>> That there's some corner of a foreign field
> That is for ever England. There shall be
>> In that rich earth a richer dust concealed,
> A dust whom England bore, shaped, made aware,
>> Gave, once, her flowers to love, her ways to roam,
> A body of England's, breathing English air,
>> Washed by the rivers, blest by the suns of home.

(Brooke, "The Soldier," 324)

The following lines of this two-stanza poem create a sense of peace and tranquility, the dream of "an English heaven." This handsome young poet, remembering the English countryside, exemplified the spirit of patriotism that inspired many youths at the outset of the war.

Siegfried Sassoon paints more cynical vision of warfare and the English response to the sacrifice of the young men. He fought in the war, was wounded, and returned to fight more. Sassoon was horrified by the nastiness of battle, of living conditions, and of bad leadership. He also found the home front disgusting. He sneered at the frivolous women who encouraged men to go off to battle and become "heroes." In his poem "Glory of Women," he says:

> You love us when we're heroes, home on leave,
> Or wounded in a mentionable place.
> You worship decorations; you believe
> That chivalry redeems the war's disgrace.
> You make us shells. You listen with delight,
> By tales of dirt and danger fondly thrilled.
> You crown our distant ardours while we fight,
> And mourn our laurelled memories when we're killed.
> You can't believe that British troops "retire"
> When hell's last horror breaks them, and they run,
> Rampling the terrible corpses—blind with blood.
> O German mother dreaming by the fire,
> While you are knitting socks to send your son
> His face is trodden deeper in the mud.

(Sassoon, "Glory of Women," 982)

This final twist, allying the women with the German enemy, while having insinuated all through the poem that they are English, is typical of Sassoon. He loved the English countryside, but hated the English government that led young men into war, eventually calling it a "war of aggression and conquest." For him, there was a moral equivalence between the British and the Germans. His memories of trench warfare are the most detailed and shocking of all those written by World War I poets.

The American novelist, Ernest Hemingway, who also saw World War I up close and personal as an ambulance driver in Italy, was appalled by the futility of most of the battles. His wounded hero in *A Farewell to Arms* tries to be loyal and brave, just like the youth in *The Red Badge of Courage*. Soon Lt. Henry finds that, if he pursues his romantic dream of honor and glory, he is a fool and will soon be a dead fool. He sees war as an ugly and meaningless struggle of mindless forces. Choosing love rather than battle, he declares a "separate peace."

He explains his disillusionment in his flat, matter of fact style:

> I was always embarrassed by the words sacred, glorious, and sacrifice and the expression in vain. We had heard them, sometimes standing in the rain out of earshot, so that only the shouted words came through, and had read them, on proclamations that were slapped up by the billposters over other proclamations, now for a long time, and I had seen nothing sacred, and the things that were glorious had no glory and the sacrifices were like the stockyards at Chicago if nothing was done with the meat except to bury it. There were many words that you could not stand to hear and finally only the names of places had dignity. (Hemingway, *A Farewell to Arms*, 137)

This "Lost Generation" denied not only the glorious aspect of warfare, but also the faith in country and in God. It became a challenge to find anything worth fighting for. Lt. Henry, the hero of *A Farewell to Arms*, acknowledges that he has no faith, nor does his lover, Catherine. They try to construct a kind of religion out of their love, but find that they cannot escape from the hideous reality of their god-free world. No one is allowed a "separate peace," because life is lived by rules as irrational as those of warfare, rules that sound a bit like the old Greek notion of *Necessity*. While meditating on his dead child, who was not baptized, Henry laments his "wife," who lies dying also without the blessings of faith or ritual: "That was what you did. You died. You did not know what it was about. You never had time to learn. They threw you in and told you the rules and the first time they caught you off base they killed you."

Hemingway did grow more enthusiastic about the glories of warfare some years later, when he was excited about the cause and courage of the Republicans in the Spanish Civil War. Franco's fascist regime seemed a solid enough enemy and the fledgling Republic of Spain a worthy enough cause to merit going to war. His novel about this war, *For Whom the Bell Tolls* (1940) makes no pretence that the warriors are beautifully dressed or fighting for honor or glory. The battles are simply for control of the government of Spain. Yet it is clear to the reader that Hemingway thinks the fight for the freedom of the Spanish peasants a worthy goal. On this occasion, he even allows his hero a final act of heroism.

In modern warfare, it is hard to see the heroism. Men and women dress in olive drab instead of wearing red coats with gold braids. They ride in jeeps or hummers instead of being mounted on prancing horses. The pilots drop bombs from high in the sky on people they never see. No brightly arrayed cavaliers engage in elegant swordplay. The sailors send missiles into countries they never visit. It is no wonder that Vietnam produced stories such as *Catch 22*, or that the Korean conflict resulted in the movie and television series *M*A*S*H*, or that World War II drove one author, Kurt Vonnegut, to write *Slaughterhouse-Five* (1969) about the blanket bombing of Dresden, a jewel of a town with no strategic value. The novel is yet another tribute to Crane's *Red Badge of Courage*, which is mentioned several times in the book. Vonnegut's anti-hero, Billy Pilgrim, is no warrior. Confused and taken prisoner by the Germans, after losing his shoes and his coat, he dresses in ridiculous clothing. Unlike the Christian in *The Pilgrim's Progress*, this comic Pilgrim has no real purpose in his struggle. He hides with his guards and fellow prisoners in a slaughterhouse during the bombing by the Americans, emerging later to see the city reduced to rubble:

> There was a fire-storm out there. Dresden was one big flame. The one flame ate everything organic, everything that would burn.
>
> It wasn't safe to come out of the shelter until noon the next day. When the Americans and their guards did come out, the sky was black with smoke. The sun was an angry little pinhead. Dresden was like the moon now, nothing but minerals. The stones were hot. Everybody else in the neighborhood was dead. (Vonnegut, *Slaughterhouse-Five*, 194)

Billy lives on, learning about the bomb at Hiroshima. This, an even greater horror, was applauded by most Americans. Billy is barely interested in President Truman's declaration regarding the atomic bomb (with the author omitting the explanation for its deployment from the text). Billy simply judges the act as immoral.

The plot in this peculiar novel. as the author himself has noted, is as "short and jumbled and jangled" as the war itself. It is a mirror of the reality Billy has witnessed:

> There is nothing intelligent to say about a massacre. Everybody is supposed to be dead, to never say anything or want anything ever again. Everything is supposed to be very quiet after a massacre, and it always is, except for the birds.
>
> And what do the birds say? All there is to say about a massacre, things like *"Poo-tee-weet?"* (Vonnegut, *Slaughterhouse-Five*, 205)

This is exactly how the novel ends, with the absurdity of the birds singing this silly, quizzical song to Billy Pilgrim. Nature survives, as in Crane's novel, but not as a "cathedral." The bird only emphasizes the absurdity of the bombing and reinforces the apocalyptic laughter of the tale.

One Christian position on war is vividly portrayed in David James Duncan's fine novel, *The Brothers K* (1992). The boys of the family in the story, who were raised as Seventh Day Adventists, come of age at the very moment that America enters the war in Vietnam. One is deferred because of his bad eye, one has an academic deferment, and one flees to Canada to avoid the draft. The one who is most religious, even saintly, and the most pacifistic, is the one who is drafted and forced to fight. Accepting his obligations after being denied conscientious objector status, he becomes outraged when a superior officers orders the killing of a suspected Vietnamese boy. Irwin attacks the officer with a tube of toothpaste, babbling a children's song, "Jesus Loves the Little Children." He is brutally beaten, taken to a mental hospital, and treated for delusions. His family insists that he is being punished for his Christian faith. The story deals with his suffering, his family's determination to save him, and the church at war with the government to save his soul.

This novel captures the many difficult choices young men were forced to make during the Vietnam War. It also captures the contemporary attitudes toward warfare.

Conclusion

The sense of collective guilt has lingered in the human imagination after the dropping of the atomic bomb on Hiroshima and Nagasaki. Since Vietnam, war has been viewed cynically by many as some kind of obscene game. Increasingly Americans want our wars to be antiseptic, with no one hurt, no damage. If we must fight, we want victory to come quickly. Actually, most Westerners prefer to avoid war altogether, relying on negotiations to make things right. This is a far cry from the old Israelite sense of God's blessings exhibited in the annihilation of their enemy. With a declining force of patriotism and a loss of the clear belief that God is on the side of the good, warfare is bereft of glory and honor.

Stories in the wake of 9/11 have revived the sense of heroism in our world. Once again we relish stories of individuals who save others' lives, protect their buddies, attack a terrorist, or throw their own bodies on a hand grenade. Young men and women are once again celebrated for their heroism. In the rhetoric of our time, the revival of the Holy War concept has returned. The clash of cultures, with Islamic militants on the move in much of the world, has resulted among many in a new sense of patriotism and respect for Judeo-Christian religions.

At the same time, a deeply sensed fear is arising in the West. For many years, wars have been fought between nations, with clear delineation of combatants and non-combatants. Suddenly, we begin to see that great masses of humankind see war as the first, not the last resort, with no limits as to the slaughter, and no plans for eventual peace. The rationality has disappeared, along with uniforms and codes of proper respect for hostages, for women and children, for proper behavior. A savage tribalism has replaced the apparently civilized conventions of modern warfare.

The landscape of nightmare which haunted much of the literature in the twentieth century has been replaced by a new fear of terrorism. This awareness that anyone, anywhere may turn out to be the enemy in this new "asymmetrical warfare" is perhaps best expressed in the poem by the twentieth-century Irish writer William Butler Yeats:

> Mere anarchy is loosed upon the world,
> The blood-dimmed tide is loosed, and everywhere
> The ceremony of innocence is drowned;
> The best lack all conviction, while the worst
> Are full of passionate intensity.

(Yeats, "The Second Coming," 184)

This seems very different from the ultimate battle of Armageddon that the Book of Revelation has led us to expect.

See also: **Good People; Government and Politics; The Hero; Justice; Slavery and Freedom; Temptation and Sin; Women as Heroes.**

Bibliography

Ackerman, James S., and Thayer S. Warshaw. *The Bible as/in Literature.* Glenview, IL: Scott, Foresman and Company, 1971.

Aristophanes. *Lysistrata.* In *Five Comedies of Aristophanes.* Trans., Benjamin Bickley Robers. Garden City, NY: Doubleday & Company, 1955.

Arnold, Matthew. "Dover Beach." In *British Poetry and Prose,* vol. II, ed. Paul Lieder, Robert Morss Lovett, and Robert Kilburn Root. Boston: Houghton Mifflin Company, 1950.

Brooke, Rupert. "The Soldier." In *Modern British Poetry,* ed. Louis Untermeyer. New York: Harcourt, Brace and Company, 1950.

Crane, Stephen. *The Red Badge of Courage.* New York: Puffin Books, 2005.

Duncan, David James. *The Brothers K.* New York: Bantam Books, 1996.

Euripides. *The Trojan Women.* In *The Complete Greek Tragedies,* ed. David Grene and Richmond Lattimore. Chicago: University of Chicago Press, 1959.

Fussell, Paul. *The Great War and Modern Memory.* New York: Oxford University Press, 2000.

Hemingway, Ernest. *A Farewell to Arms.* Thorndike, ME: G.K. Hall, 1995.

Homer. *The Iliad.* Trans., Robert Fagles. New York: Penguin Books, 1998.

Lewis, C. S. *Reflections on the Psalms.* New York: Harcourt Brace and Company, 1958.

The Nibelungenlied. New Haven: Yale University Press, 2006.

Pasternak, Boris. *Doctor Zhivago.* Trans., Manya Harari and Max Haywar. New York: Knopf, 1991.

Sassoon, Siegfried. "Glory of Women." In *British Poetry and Prose,* vol. II, ed. Paul Robert Lieder, Robert Morss Lovett, and Robert Kilburn Root. Boston: Houghton Mifflin, 1950.

The Song of Roland. Trans., Patricia Ann Terry. New York: Macmillan Publishing Company, 1992.

Spender, Stephen. *The Edge of Being.* New York: Random House, 1949.

Tolstoy, Leo. *War and Peace.* Trans., Anthony Briggs. New York: Viking, 2006.

Vonnegut, Kurt. *Slaughterhouse-Five: Or the Children's Crusade, a Duty-Dance with Death.* New York: Dell, 1999.

Yeats, W. B. "The Second Coming." In *The Collected Poems of W. B. Yeats.* New York: The Macmillan Company, 1959.

Good People

Readings

Genesis 1–3, 22
Job
Acts 5:1–11
Dante Alighieri, *Purgatorio* (1321)
William Shakespeare, *Hamlet* (1600)
John Milton, *Paradise Lost* (1667)
Samuel Richardson, *Clarissa* (1748)
Henry Fielding, *Joseph Andrews* (1742), *Tom Jones* (1749)
Nathaniel Hawthorne, *The Scarlet Letter* (1850)
Thomas Hardy, *Tess of the d'Ubervilles* (1891)
Flannery O'Connor, "Good Country People," "A Good Man Is Hard to Find" (1955)

Introduction

> He hath showed thee, O man, what is good; and what doth the Lord require
> of thee, but to do justly, and to love mercy, and to walk humbly with thy
> God? (Micah 6:8)

The prophet Micah sums up the path of the "good" person as one that includes justice, mercy, and obedience to God. This terse bit of scripture illuminates many of the stories in the Bible, spotlighting the central point of stories like that of Job or Joseph or David or Philemon or Ananias. Multitudes of significant choices scattered through the Bible reveal how a person can love justice, show mercy, and walk humbly with God. No one but Christ, the God-man, manages to do all three all the time.

Various philosophers have considered the nature of goodness, how we recognize it, and how it functions in human affairs. Some believe that morality is innate, a kind of universal intuition. Some think that some faint memories of the prelapsarian human condition is the source of this widely accepted understanding of decency—a kind of natural law. Some think that God spoke with Adam in the Garden during their walks, impressing him with the fundamental laws of nature and rules of conduct. Some believe that morality comes from rational deduction, the human use of the God-given capacity to think and to know the good and distinguish the good from the evil act or person. Some believe morality derives directly from God, that humans can discover the path to goodness only by following divine law that God gave to Moses on the mountain.

Socrates, the fifth-century B.C. Greek philosopher, who frequently used the term *good*, ended his famous dialogue on civics, *The Republic*, with this advice: "Seek and follow one thing only … to learn and discern between good and evil." Some philosophers, even before Socrates, believed that morality is simply following the conscience in human activity: as Protagoras said, "Man is the measure of all things." Some think this means that morality is purely subjective or relative, dependant entirely on the person and the moment. Reduced to its bluntest and least responsible summary by moderns, this is the philosophy that says, "If it feels good, do it." Others believe that morality is basically a community virtue, the key to civic behavior, the way in which family members and neighbors exist in harmony. An action is good or bad when judged by its effect on others: Does it hurt your neighbor? Does it help that person?

Certainly the great contest between good and evil is central to the narrative of the Bible. Many of the world's literary masterpieces also depend on an understanding of morality and the challenges faced by humans seeking the Good, the Just, and the True. The conflict is most often expressed in specific lives at precise times, when very real challenges face the hero or the villain. He or she must decide to choose the Lord's side, or fall in with the Enemy. The concept of the good person is not an abstraction for Jews or Christians.

Scripture

When God judged the earth, sky, sea, and all the animals and people he had created, he called them "good." In the Garden of Eden, prior to the first act of disobedience, Adam and Eve were good. They had never sinned nor separated themselves from the will of God. This brief state of innocence became the ideal for future generations. For Adam and Eve, the question was simply obeying God's instructions. Curiously, the tree from which they chose to eat the fruit was the Tree of the Knowledge of Good and Evil. Through the discovery of evil, they learn more fully the good that they had lost. In their exercise of free will, the ability to decide whether to choose the moral or immoral path, humans found their dignity and their downfall.

For the generations that have followed Adam and Eve, moral education has often proven a painful experience. Cain discovers the difference between good and evil when, feeling a surge of jealousy and hurt that the Lord prefers Abel's sacrifice to his, he strikes and kills his brother. He lashes out at Abel rather than correcting his own errors, choosing murder over reform. In this rash action, which is quickly followed by lying to God and denial of his guilt, he follows the path of his parents, setting in action a chain of actions and reactions that will resonate throughout history. The individual violence of brother against brother escalates to become skirmishes that pit kindred tribes against one another, and finally wars that neighboring nations wage in savage fury.

The ideal of the "good person" or the "righteous one" is a constant theme in scripture. The terms *good* and *righteous* appear hundreds of times, more frequently in the Old Testament than the New. The Psalms and Proverbs are especially rich with examples of good people and righteous behavior. In Romans 5:7, Paul distinguishes between the terms *good* and *righteous*, indicating perhaps that the *righteous* live according to the law, while the *good* have an eagerness to serve God. Except for Christ, he insists that no one can be really good. This is a result of Adam's original sin.

The Hebrew word that has been translated *righteous* means someone or something proven true, especially in a legal sense. The term is applied to a person who performs his role in life the right way. For a ruler, it means he is a good ruler, who governs with justice and mercy. For ordinary people, it means treating neighbors as partners of the covenant, neither oppressing them nor appeasing them.

For the early Hebrews, questions of morality and obedience to God were personal decisions and sometimes heart-rending ones. When God required Abraham to sacrifice his own son, Isaac, as an offering, Abraham must have been shocked (Gen. 22). Here was God, the author of morality, who had forbidden the spilling of human blood, requiring an act that contradicted his own unwritten laws. Abraham, acknowledging that God's word is supreme, over all other considerations, approaches the altar with fear and trembling. When, at the last minute, God stays his hand and substitutes the sacrifice of a ram, saying: "Do not lay your hand on the lad or do anything to him, for now I know that you fear God, seeing you have not withheld your son, your only son, from me" (Gen. 22:1–15). This drama presupposes that God's will is the ultimate guide for morality, sweeping aside all natural inclinations, rational decisions, and traditional understandings.

If God sets a test for the good man, as he does with Job, that person is not free to challenge God's judgment. Job is one of the few figures in scripture who is characterized as good, even by God in his discussion with Satan. His goodness does not protect him against disasters or give him any special insight into that suffering. During most of his trials, Job understands and faithfully acknowledges that the Lord gives and the Lord takes away. "Blessed be the name of the Lord." While his wife challenges him to curse God and die, Job remains faithful.

Finally, provoked beyond human capacity to accept his situation, he does cry out to God, demanding that he know why such evil would fall on a good man. God's thunderous response, leaves him gasping that he spoke that which he does not understand. He then returns, repenting, to the obedient role of the true believer. His blessedness comes when he finally accepts God's will without presumptuous questions. He proclaims (Job 25:4): "How can a man be righteous before God?" By recognizing the righteousness of God and the great gulf between His goodness and human efforts, he sheds a bright light on the unworthiness of even the "good man."

Job's case is extreme. Most people in scripture are characterized as seriously flawed. One unusual example from the Old Testament of the near-perfect man is Joseph, the beloved son of Jacob. Bright, handsome, gifted with visions and insights, this young man grows to adulthood as the apple of his father's eye. His blunt, and apparently self-serving interpretation of dreams, as well as his father's clear preference for him over his other 11 sons, turns most of his brothers against him. They sell him into slavery, pretend that he is dead, and go on with their lives.

Once he has been re-sold to Egyptians, he continues his moral path, serving faithfully even in prison, refusing the attentions of his master's wife, and showing affection for those around him regardless of their social standing. His wise counsel eventually leads to his elevation to an impressive role in the Pharaoh's kingdom. In this position, he proves a good manager and a good servant.

When his brothers are forced by drought to plead with this man that they do not recognize as their long-lost brother, he is generous to them. Although he does play some tricks to test them, largely to determine if they have matured and are now good sons and brothers, he forgives them and provides for their families. His clear-eyed understanding that this happy outcome is God's doing, not theirs, reveals that he understands their motives and yet holds no grudges.

In all of this story, the reader is hard-pressed to find any flaws in this man, whether as a son, a servant, or a vizier. If he has a flaw, it is his blindness to his brothers' feelings, an acceptance of special treatment from their father, signaled by the gift of the coat of many colors, and a foolish openness in his explanation of dreams that reveal his final leadership role. A normal brother would find Joseph hard to stomach, but their brutal behavior is in no way justified.

On a day-to-day basis, the Hebrews did try to settle disputes through justice rather than violence. They sometimes avenged wrongs, but were later sorry as they saw the painful results of their actions. During their best times, when not tempted by their pagan neighbors, they tried to manage their daily lives by basing their actions on the teachings of God. They did accept the current customs in many of their actions, even when these actions strike the modern as immoral. For example, Abraham apparently had no problems with lying about Sarah's relationship to him if this would save both of their lives. Later, after God had destroyed Sodom and Gomorrah, the "good man" Lot proved open to drunkenness and incest. Jacob cheated his own brother out of their father's blessing, and then tricked his father-in-law in the breeding of sheep.

The Hebrews were probably guided in their behavior by the laws of Hammurabi, the customs of the ancient world, and their own experience in their sometimes-faithful walk with God. It was centuries later that these rules of conduct were codified, along with commandments from God. When they became a people, not just a tribe, Moses brought them the Law. From this point forward, morality was far easier to measure.

Hebrew law is both universal and individual. It deals specifically with the faith and practice of the community to whom it was first delivered. Remarkably, it has also provided guidance for peoples all over the world in the centuries that followed. In Exodus and Leviticus, we find not only the regulations about stealing and killing, but also the moral issues of coveting and lying, and the religious concerns for worshipping the Lord. Unlike secular law, the Law of Moses covers many of the details of their daily life—the family, the animals, the proper selection and preparation of foods, and the worship festivals and practices of the people.

Following the law, however, was never enough to make a person good. For the Hebrews, morality, or "righteousness," was a positive quality, not just the absence of evil. The "good" person is the person close to God, who is the very essence of the Good. The Psalms talk about good people, who keep good company and walk the good path throughout their lives. They not only follow the law, they relish the study and practice of it (Pss. 1, 32, 47). They love the law. The Proverbs also give practical advice on the moral life—the avoidance of wicked women, the appropriate treatment of children, the problems of alcohol abuse, and the values of industriousness. For these people, the obedience to the law is only the beginning. The good person meditates on the law "day and night," tastes it and finds it as sweet as honey.

Both the psalmist and the prophets note that God is not interested in external rituals of obedience, but the "circumcision of the heart." The true sacrifice is not the burnt animal, but a "broken and a contrite heart." The tender conscience, the loving heart, the love of God—these are the bases of moral behavior. Nonetheless, during the period between the Testaments, the scribes and Pharisees thought it necessary to expand the law by including hundreds of new rules and regulations to encourage righteous behavior. Under their leadership, the law-abiding person was considered righteous or good, even if he or she had no interest in the spirit of the law. Propriety had replaced goodness or godliness as the goal for many.

This increasingly legalistic vision of morality led to a faith in good works—the idea that one could win God's favor by the punctilious adherence to every jot and title of the law. The prophets, and later Jesus argue against this rigid view of righteousness. No person can be fully "righteous"—no matter how careful he or she follows the straight and narrow—unless he is God Incarnate (Rom. 3:10): "There is no one righteous, no not even one." The good person is one who seeks to do God's will, not just follow His law. Paul, a Pharisee to his very core, has to see himself as a persecutor of a saint in Stephen's dying gaze and face the Savior on the road to Damascus before he can become a man worthy of God. For such a man to preach against the legalistic view of goodness is a real tribute to his conversion experience.

Jesus defines morality in positive terms, not just what we should avoid, but what we should do. The good life is one that involves loving God and one's fellow man. The Beatitudes succinctly define the blessed person. That person is "poor in spirit," and meek before God's majestic power and goodness. He mourns for his own iniquities and those of a troubled world (Matt. 5). Especially interesting is the story of the sinner, lamenting his sinful ways and the Pharisee, expressing delight that he is not like other men. Jesus sees the one who proclaims and weeps for his or her sinfulness as the truly good person.

Throughout most of this history, the good woman has been defined differently from the good man. Proverbs 31 describes the good wife as a person of industry and good sense. By contrast, Jesus tends to describe the saintly life in almost feminine terms—meekness, gentleness, and sympathy. In addition, he addresses women whom he meets or those who follow him in the same way he addresses men, challenging them to turn away from their sins and follow him.

This was a remarkable attitude toward women in a world which traditionally interpreted the Fall, so far as it related to women, sexually. In the eyes of most of society, the primary female sins were the loss of virginity or adultery. The "fallen women" who appear in the Gospels are treated as fully human by Jesus. He stops the stoning of the adulterous woman, calling on the one who is "without sin" to cast the first stone. And he notes the flawed morality of the Samaritan woman at the well, who has had numerous "husbands," but then he shares theological insights with her about the nature and place of worship. Accused of cavorting with publicans and sinners, Jesus acknowledges that he came into the world to save people such as these. "I have not come to call the righteous, but sinners" (Mark 2:17). He reserves his fierce judgments for the so-called "good" people, the scribes and the Pharisees, whom he calls "whitened sepulchres."

When the rich young ruler comes to ask what he must do to be saved, Jesus tells him to follow the law and the prophets. The man responds that he has been obedient from his earliest youth. Then Jesus adds that he must sell all he has and give it to the poor. At this point, the young man walks away. "And when he heard this, he was very sorrowful; for he was very rich" (Luke 18:23). This extreme act of mercy that Jesus demands proves a reach too far for the young ruler. Each person has his or her own secret sin, in this case, love of luxury, which stands in the way of perfect morality and blocks the entrance to the Kingdom of Heaven.

In the early Church, morality was a significant concern. Although the Christians believed that they were saved by faith, not works, they also acknowledged that faith without works is dead: "Pure religion and undefiled before God and the Father is this, To visit the fatherless and widows in their affliction, and to keep himself unspotted from the world" (James 1:27, 2:17).

Luke, in writing the book of Acts, juxtaposes two examples of behavior among the early believers. In the first case, Barnabas "having land, sold it, and brought the money, and laid it at the apostles' feet" (Acts 4:37). This act of generosity, which reminds the reader of the Rich Young Ruler's failure to follow this path of discipleship, foreshadows Barnabas's career as Paul's faithful co-worker and companion.

The second case described by Luke relates to the practice at the time of the Church community, which held all things in common. This was a voluntary agreement among the members. Ananias and his wife Sapphira sell some property, but keep back part of the price. On the surface, they act like Barnabas, bringing the money and laying it at the apostles' feet. But Peter recognizes their greed and guile. These hypocrites are pretending to be generous while actually being covetous, lying to the apostles and to God. Peter accuses Ananias abruptly: "Why hath Satan filled thine heart to lie to the Holy Ghost, and to keep back part of the price of the land?" After all, Ananias need not have given anything to the community. He has lied not only to men, but to God in this action. God's hand of judgment strikes this couple, killing them both. In both cases, the sin against the Holy Ghost as well as the sin against the community of believers makes their supposedly "generous" gift sinful and deserving of punishment.

Paul, who was also a strict moralist, looks with jaundiced eyes at the bad behavior of the early Corinthian church. They indulge in gluttony, lust, and other blatant violations of decent behavior. Even the heathen do not behave like this. In this case, he cites "the union of a man with his father's wife," (1 Cor. 5:1) and later notes that they "must have nothing to do with any so-called Christian who leads a loose life, or is grasping, or idolatrous, a slanderer, a drunkard, or a swindler" (1 Cor. 5:11). He tells them that they have brought shame on the Church.

Such harsh judgments for breaches of conduct seem strange to many moderns, given the ease with which Jesus had forgiven adulterers and others. This, however, is clearly a lesson to the entire community: the peace and purity of the church matter more than the life of any individuals within it. Jesus himself provides the model for rage at the contamination of the house of God in his overturning of the tables of the moneychangers in the temple.

The doctrine of the Fall and the universal need for redemption was central to the early Church. Paul advises each Christian to strive to be perfect for the greater glory of God. Morality in the Christian Church involved constant prayer and the study of scripture. Paul and other apostles apply moral principles to specific situations faced by either churches or individuals, teasing out the motives as well as the actions involved in each. In most cases, as with the Philippians, Paul gently encourages them to put their immoral actions aside and love one another.

Literature

Early Christian literature was deeply spiritual and moral. For believers, art was suspect unless it had a moral purpose, to glorify God rather than to celebrate humans. Some of the early masterpieces of the Middle Ages are spiritual autobiographies, and some are allegories of the moral life, providing a clear path to the Celestial City.

The great anatomy of biblical morality is Dante's *Purgatorio*. Actually, the entire *Divine Comedy*, starting with the *Inferno* and concluding with *Paradiso*, reveals that God's love and His goodness undergird all human goodness. We seek to do good because we love God and want to conform to his will. As Augustine says, "His will is our peace." Dante takes his pilgrim through the landscape of the afterlife, from the gates of hell to the glories of heaven. The middle section, the journey up Mt. Purgatory, is a careful study of the seven deadly sins, outlined by Gregory the Great (540–605 A.D.): pride, greed, lust, envy, gluttony, anger, and sloth. The soul of the believer gradually makes his or her way up the seven-story mountain along a rugged path, pausing at those levels of sin that mark their individual lives, to be instructed and cleansed. On each cornice is a penance, a meditation, a prayer, a guardian angel, and a benediction. On each is also a series of examples of the opposing virtue (the "whip") and deterrent examples (the "bridle"). Thus, the souls of the penitents are progressively cleansed, becoming lighter and happier until they arrive at the top of the mountain—the earthly paradise, a return to primal innocence.

Moral issues are central to most of Western literature. How the human must make choices, the courage involved in the right choice, the pain involved in the wrong one, what are the ramifications of those choices—these are constant concerns. Sometimes the morality is in conflict with the law or with faith, forcing the author to work through the issues. European literature is rich with these concerns.

The great Shakespearean play *Hamlet* is a powerful study of a complex moral dilemma. It begins with the revelation of a murder: the ghost of Hamlet's father tells Hamlet of "murder most foul." Notice that these supernatural scenes establish the basis for the subsequent actions. Hamlet is not free to ignore the crimes of people he loves, nor can he forgive them. The King, his father, was poisoned by his own brother, who then assumed the crown and married the queen. This dark knowledge and the ghost's fierce insistence force the hero to swear that he will avenge this atrocity.

The ghostly king does distinguish between the sins of the brother and the wife, telling Hamlet that he should "Leave her to heaven / And to those thorns that in her bosom lodge / To pick and sting her." Hamlet's taking of the un-biblical oath itself, however, proves an act that is both faithful to the memory of his father and fatal to his mother, whom he loves. He challenges the biblical admonition to honor his parents, which flies in the face of his need to restore the family honor by convincing her to reject her new husband and his heinous deeds. She does, in fact, repent when faced with the truth by her son, but is killed at the end of the play in the spectacular cascade of related deaths.

The villainous uncle, now the King, presents another dilemma. On the one hand, he is Hamlet's sovereign, to be respected as the Lord's anointed. On the other, he is the murderer of the previous king, Hamlet's father, and the seducer of his mother. The King acknowledges to friends that he is "proud, revengeful, ambitious ... we are arrant knaves all." He understands his crime and delights in the fruits of it. He admits he cannot seek pardon because he will not relinquish his ambition, his scepter, or his queen. Realizing Hamlet's menacing aspect, he plots the murder of this dangerous heir to the throne and sworn enemy. Hamlet, realizing all this, now believes that not only should his uncle die, but he wishes him to die unrepentant—thus damned for eternity. (His father died without the last rites and is spending time in purgatory as a result.)

In his lust for vengeance, Hamlet himself becomes cruel and destructive. His friends and family recall that he was once a brilliant and charming young man, witty, scholarly, and loveable. At first, he is cautious in checking the facts of the case, testing his uncle to see if he is indeed guilty. When convinced, he confronts his mother, accuses her in terms that suggest an obsession with the nastiness of her lust. He then strikes out blindly at the harmless old Polonius and turns cruelly against his beloved Ophelia, driving her to commit suicide. In this flurry of destructive action, he notes: "There is nothing either good or bad but thinking makes it so."

The final episode in this sad tale shows his good friend Laertes, son to Polonius, forced to duel with Hamlet for the family honor. "Honor," a much respected moral value in the Renaissance, is more Greek than Christian in its origin. It smacks of pride in family, requiring respect from others. It is a characteristic of the Homeric hero. In *Hamlet*, this hunger for pagan values, like vengeance and honor, results in an avalanche of deaths. The context, however, is thoroughly Christian, with the view of man echoing the psalms and the awareness of human capacity for beastliness quite clear. When Hamlet comments that "Use every man after his desert and who 'scape whipping?" he echoes the Apostle Paul, who said that all have sinned and fallen short of the glory of God (Rom. 3:23). Acknowledging human depravity, Shakespeare ends with a thorough cleansing of the state: Hamlet's entire family is destroyed, yet justice has prevailed. The truth has been revealed, the guilty punished, and the community is saved at the end of the play.

John Milton, the great Puritan poet of the seventeenth century, faced his own moral dilemmas in life, and projected these concerns onto his literary masterworks. He puzzled over the primal innocence of the first couple, picturing it as idyllic in *Paradise Lost*, but thinking too that the fall into sin is "fortunate" in that it provides for a richer form of blessing in the coming of Jesus Christ. In his thoughtful consideration of good and evil, *Areopagitica*, Milton laments that a "cloistered virtue" is not so strong as one that has been out into the "warfaring world." Like the Pilgrim in Bunyan's novel, the true seeker faces temptation and goes through suffering and yet remains true to his beliefs.

As literature has become increasingly secular, the temptation has been to write of the sinners rather than the saints. Even when people of faith are central to the narrative, they tend to be warped morally. They pretend to seek goodness, while in fact they are as selfish as the Pharisee in Jesus's parable. Hypocrisy, of course, is the superficial show of virtue, hiding a cruel or depraved reality. It can be either funny or nauseating, depending on the context in which it appears. For Jesus, the scribes and Pharisees, those "whitened sepulchres," were covering the deadly sickness of the organized religion. For Shakespeare, the Puritanical figure of Malvolio in *Twelfth Night* is comic, revealing his lechery and ambition as soon as a bit of flattery comes his way. So long as the character can do no serious harm, he or she is laughable.

The Victorian poet Robert Browning, who loved to let his characters reveal their own psychological disorders, found plenty of hypocrisy and pretence for portrayal. In his "Soliloquy of the Spanish Cloister," for example, Browning explores the potential for both malice and benevolence in the sequestered life of the medieval monastery. The speaker in the soliloquy is a nameless Spanish friar who is so jealous of Brother Lawrence, a gentle soul who is beloved by all, that he is gnawing away at his own daily potential for happiness and endangering his immortal soul. Under these circumstances, a superficially satiric soliloquy becomes a lacerating attack on human envy. The poem starts in these thoroughly unpoetic words:

> Gr-r-r—there go, my heart's abhorrence!
>   Water your damned flower-pots, do!

If hate killed men, Brother Lawrence,
   God's blood, would not mine kill you!

           (Browning, "Soliloquy of the Spanish Cloister," 258)

In this poem, Browning is pointing to the very issue raised by Jesus in his analysis of the Law of Moses. It is not enough to follow the law, which the unnamed speaker does (laying his knife and fork cross-wise in praise of Jesus, when he finishes his meal). Refraining from the actual murder of Brother Lawrence is not enough, he needs to be reconciled with him and learn to love him before he can worship God properly. The inner motivation is the key to morality, not simply the outward action. Like Cain in his jealousy of the gentle Abel, this brother is opening the door for Satan and damnation.

A famous nineteenth-century American novel by Hawthorne, *The Scarlet Letter* (1850), is one of the best examples of the complexities of morality. The central sin, in the view of the community of Puritan New England, is Hester's adultery. When her husband is away, she gives birth to an illegitimate child, and refuses to name the father. Her lover, the "virtuous" minister, Arthur Dimmesdale, allows her to bear the brunt of the social ostracism and vitriol, while she cherishes the product of their illicit affair, their little girl, and continues to love the child's father. Her self-sacrifice, her joy in the child, her acceptance of the verdict of the community all make her the very image of Christian love. The father, a prim and scholarly minister, on the other hand, by refusing to admit his sin and repent of it publicly, compounds his immorality and destroys his own life.

The moment of temptation for the doomed couple has strong echoes of the Garden of Eden. The beautiful young woman and the sensitive young man meet and love in the forest, following their natural inclinations rather than God-given law. The damage done to their lives causes ripples of harm through all those associated with them. Hawthorne treats the original immoral action as less serious than the consequent judgments and evasions. Like Jesus, who refuses to join in the stoning of the woman taken in adultery, Hawthorne appears to believe that Hester has paid the price for her lapse. The men involved, including the cold and negligent husband, have more complex moral problems and pay much greater prices.

Perhaps because women increasingly became the readers of novels, they also became the subject matter of them. From the earliest novels in English, women often had a central role. The moral issue most frequently addressed by the writers, and most often enjoyed by the readers, was the woman's sexuality. The beautiful young woman, innocent and untested in the ways of the world, must find the right mate, one that is worthy of her and one whom she can love. When marriages were simply arranged, these stories were not possible, but with the rising middle class and the isolation of families from their traditional homes, women were compelled to make their choices with only limited understanding of the masculine world and sexual perils.

Samuel Richardson, one of the first to exploit this new social issue, wrote *Pamela, or Virtue Rewarded* (1739), to demonstrate in practical terms the value of preserving one's chastity until marriage. Pamela, an innocent and pretty young servant girl, writes a series of letters that sound rather more advanced than her 15 years. When her mistress dies, she faces the lewd advances of her handsome young master, the son of the old lady. He finally relents and agrees to marry her in order to enjoy her favors. The mercenary and contrived aspects of this situation led other writers to laugh at the practicality of this "virtue" that Pamela protects.

Richardson's later novel on much the same subject, *Clarissa* (1748), is a far more compelling story. This time, the heroine refuses the arranged marriage that her parents seek to force on her; she runs away with her handsome lover, who tricks her into a fake marriage, and then ravishes her. When she discovers that she has been used by the man she loves, she decides to die. He repents, but cannot stop her descent into despair and death. In this melodramatic story, the psychology is far more penetrating and the moral dilemma more interesting. After all, Clarissa unwittingly allows herself to become tainted. Her love and her intentions are honest. The nobility displayed by this beautiful young woman is so saintly as to be unreal to most readers, but touching to the eighteenth-century women who wept as they followed her tragic decline.

Thomas Hardy also loved to write about "fallen women," often innocents who were tricked by unscrupulous men or betrayed by those who should have protected them. His powerful novel *Tess of the d'Urbervilles* (1891) describes Tess as a country lass, an innocent who is easily seduced by a wealthy suitor. She has her child, leaves her seducer, and wanders off to try to earn her own way. She loves the babe, but it does not live long. She goes from farm to farm, looking for work, hoping for a shelter from the weather and enough food to take her through the day. The farm scenes are realistically described, as is the life of the isolated woman.

The seducer, realizing that he loves Tess, regrets his cruel behavior, finds her, and tries to make amends. But poor Tess is doomed from the outset. She has fallen in love with a pure young man, interestingly named *Angel,* who abandons her when he discovers her sordid story. Only after she has married this man she despises, feeling obliged to make this acknowledgement of social norms, does she realize that her true love wants her back. She murders her seducer, is hunted down by the law, and is captured while she is sleeping on the altar rock at Stonehenge (a Celtic worship site in southern England). The book ends with her execution, even though Tess is presented as a good person, seeking always to do the right thing, a hapless victim of evil forces in humans and in the universe.

For Hardy, humans have few real moral choices to make. The more impressive people are marked for doom from the outset. This takes the responsibility away from the individual and puts it on the malevolent universe instead. Although the men and women in scripture face difficult circumstances, they are never seen so helpless as Tess. Ruth, for example, chooses to take the hard path with her mother-in-law, to work the fields, to take chances, and to put her faith in God. The marriage to Boaz, the redemption of the family, and the birth of the child are blessings that flow from obedience to God's will. Hardy does not believe that God is in charge, that scriptural laws of morality are appropriate for human existence, or that people can be judged for what they do, only for what they are in their hearts.

Much of the nineteenth-century literature focuses on the debate about morality: Is it natural and intuitive, born into humans as instincts are in animals? Or is it rational, a matter of intellect? Is scriptural authority essential as the basis for morality? Is morality nothing more than a societal construct? With these fundamental questions, the foundation was being laid for modern relativism, with situational ethics, where anything can be good or bad given the circumstances.

One of the most formidable influences on that century was Frederich Nietzsche, who transformed the whole discussion of morality. For Nietzsche, morality is a private choice. In *Beyond Good and Evil,* he notes that there are two types of morality, *master morality* and *slave morality.* Rejecting biblical teachings of law and examples of the blessedness of generosity, he considers such teachings slavish and low, typical of harmless, stupid people. The master, by contrast, chooses to set his own moral path regardless of its impact on others. The individual in his hunger for power is absolute. Measured by this standard, Satan, the angel who refuses to serve God slavishly, and Eve, who refuses to bow to God's simple rules, are both "masters" in their morality. By biblical standards, this rebellion, or insistence that they will not serve, renders them fallen creatures. They choose to set their own will above the will of God. By Nietzsche's standard, they are heroic.

The twentieth century, with its combined influences of Freud, Darwin, and Marx, as well as Nietzsche, produced a flurry of novels and poems that call traditional moral values into question. A number of the works written between the great wars of the twentieth century reflect the moral confusion of that period. Hemingway's *The Sun Also Rises* portrays a generation of people trying to have fun, unable to discover much depth in human relations and much hope in religion. Like the characters in *A Farewell to Arms,* they hesitate outside of churches, realizing that faith is an option for some people, but not for them. It is interesting that *The Sun Also Rises* is named for a section of the world-weary book of Ecclesiastes (1:5): There is nothing new under the sun. After a lifetime full of great works and great wealth, many women and many banquets, the old king laments: "Then I looked on all the works that my hands had wrought, and on the labor that I had labored to do; and behold, all was vanity and vexation of spirit, and there was no profit under the sun"(Ecc. 2:11). God lets his rain fall on both the just and unjust; some struggle for righteousness and others enjoy their wickedness, yet "All go unto one place; all are of the dust, and all turn to dust again" (Ecc. 3:20 see also Matt. 5:45).

This age-old cynicism permeates the whole period of post–World War I literature. As T. S. Eliot wrote:

We are the stuffed men

. . .

Headpiece filled with straw, Alas!

(Eliot, "The Hollow Men," 56)

C. S. Lewis, in *The Abolition of Man,* calls these new characters "men without chests." For both T. S. Eliot and C. S. Lewis, this meaningless life without moral sharpness reduces humans to scarecrows, filled with the straw of empty ideas, leaning together for fear of individual responsibility.

Conclusion

Neither the Bible nor secular literature has many really good people. Scoundrels and sinners are much more interesting to most readers. Many heroes are striving for goodness, but most are flawed, perversely determined to do the wrong thing or to do the right thing for the wrong reason. The few examples of unmitigated goodness that we do discover tend to be either simple and untested people, or tiresome ones who are proud of their own virtue.

C. S. Lewis speaks of this in his delightful *The Screwtape Letters,* when the minor devil who is assigned to torment the new Christian is encouraged to make him proud of his humility. It may be humanly impossible to be thoroughly good without developing some sneaking self-satisfaction. In most of literature, such people become the butt of comedy, not ideal examples. Shakespeare makes such folks into buffoons or secret villains. He does not trust people who pose as perfect. Henry Fielding laughs at the comic hero in his novel *The History of the Adventures of Joseph Andrews* (1741), in which the young innocent is modeled on Joseph in scripture.

In "A Good Man Is Hard to Find," Flannery O'Connor reveals that the "good man" of the title is, in fact, a murderer. Building on this trite saying that "a good man is hard to find," she turns it into a theological statement. As Paul had pointed to our original sin, derived from the first couple's fall, we are all of us totally depraved. Only God's grace, the faith in Christ's saving power, can redeem us. In O'Connor's story, the grandmother, so pleased with her goodness, emphasized by her proper manners and dress, proves herself completely ignorant of the true nature of humans. The Misfit, the escaped prisoner, tries to explain to her that Christ himself was a "Misfit," who turned the world upside down. But this silly woman with her shallow faith insists on keeping her world right side up, ignoring the tough lessons of scripture.

The author's philosophy becomes apparent from the shape of the story, the view of the characters, and the treatment of the events. The pattern of virtue and of villainy tells the reader about the values of the writer and of his or her audience. What constitutes the good person in stories or plays by this author? Must she be sexually pure? honest? brave? loyal? The reader may also determine what the author considers evil. Is it sexual sin? Is it the failure to be a success? Or is it violence against others? Or despoiling the environment?

The motives for virtuous behavior are also apparent. Does the character act out of concern for himself and his own well-being? Is he more intent on saving his family or his society? Or is she dedicated to perfecting herself in order to please her God and bring him glory?

As God has disappeared as the primary motive for morality, the moral codes themselves have become increasingly individualized, socialized, and fuzzy. The kind, generous, loving, and honest person is still considered moral. If that person also commits adultery, lies out of sympathy for another, or evades responsibility, he or she is easily forgiven. No modern author would allow Clarissa to sink into illness and death because of her betrayal. Authors today are hard-pressed to find an action that is not forgivable. The desire to do good, even when not followed by any positive action, is credited. Thus, even criminals can be sympathetic characters; we can understand why a father might abandon his wife and children, or why a wife might be forced to kill her husband. A therapeutic culture has replaced a theological one.

It would be interesting to analyze our own world by reading its literature. The good people tend to live in the country, love nature, reject limitations on their lives, enjoy their healthy sexuality, and defend their friends and family. Not guided by a set of rigid rules, they determine for themselves how to live the virtuous life day by day and avoid judging others. Some are religious, but few determine their actions by asking God for guidance. Characters rely on their feelings to determine what they should do. Their moral compass seems to be within each individual, who strives to be at peace with his or her conscience. This is the world of the autonomous self. It has echoes of scriptural ethics, but is largely a construct of evolving social and moral values.

Morality is clearly far more than simple obedience to a set of rules. It involves what O'Connor calls "a habit of being." It is the journey of life, with all the forks in the road and all the decisions that make people what they finally become. The moral person looks closely at each situation, each choice, and determines how this confirms to the laws of God and man. Jesus sums up the scriptural response for the Pharisees: "Thou shalt love the Lord thy God with all thy heart, mind, and spirit. And the second is like unto it. Thou shalt love thy neighbor as thyself."

See also: **Creation; The Hero; Predestination and Free Will; The Journey of Life; Justice; Temptation and Sin; Women as Heroes.**

Bibliography

Adler, Mortimer *The Great Ideas: A Lexicon of Western Thought.* New York: Macmillan Publishing Company, 1992.

Alighieri, Dante. *The Comedy of Dante Alighieri,* Cantica II, "Purgatory." Trans., Dorothy L. Sayers. New York: Basic Books, 1973.

Browning, Robert. "Soliloquy of the Spanish Cloister." In *Victorian and Later English Poets,* ed. James Stephens, Edwin L. Beck, and Royall H. Snow. New York: American Book Company, 1949.

Eliot, T. S. "The Hollow Men." In *The Complete Poems and Plays (1909–1950).* New York: Harcourt Brace and World, 1952.

Fielding, Henry. *The History of the Adventures of Joseph Andrews and his Friend Mr. Abraham Adams.* New York: Norton, 1958.

———. *Tom Jones.* New York: Modern Library, 1985.

Hardy, Thomas. *Tess of the d'Urbervilles.* New York: Barnes & Noble, 1993.

Hawthorne, Nathaniel. *The Scarlet Letter.* Belmont, CA: Fearon Education, 1991.

Miller, Arthur. *Arthur Miller's Collected Plays.* New York: The Viking Press, 1961.

Milton, John. *Paradise Lost.* In *The Student's Milton,* ed. Frank Allen Patterson. New York: Appleton-Century-Crofts, 1930.

Nietzsche, Friederich. *Beyond Good and Evil.* In *Basic Writings of Nietzsche.* Trans. and ed. Walter Kaufmann. New York: Modern Library, 2000.

O'Connor, Flannery. "Good Country People" and "A Good Man Is Hard to Find." In *Collected Works.* New York: Literary Classics of United States, 1988.

Richardson, Samuel. *Clarissa.* New York: Penguin Books, 1980

Shakespeare, William. *Hamlet.* In *Shakespeare: Major Plays and the Sonnets,* ed. G. B. Harrison. New York: Harcourt, Brace and Company, 1948.

Ziesler, John. "Righteousness." In *The Oxford Companion to the Bible,* ed. Bruce M. Metzger and Michael D. Coogan. New York: Oxford University Press, 1993.

Justice

Readings

Exodus 20
Leviticus
Job
Aristotle, *The Nicomachean Ethics* (c. 340 B.C.)
Aeschylus, *Orestia* (458 B.C.)
William Shakespeare, *The Merchant of Venice* (1594)
Fyodor Dostoyevsky, *Crime and Punishment* (1866)
Herman Melville, *Billy Budd* (1924 published, written c. 1891)
Shirley Jackson, "The Lottery" (1949)
Franz Kafka, *The Trial* (1914)
Harper Lee, *To Kill a Mockingbird* (1960)

Introduction

> Let the floods clap their hands; let the hills be joyful together
> Before the Lord; for he cometh to judge the earth; with righteousness shall
> he judge the world, and the people with equity. (Ps. 99:8–9)

The abstract concept of *Justice* is more Greek than Hebrew. The Hebrews were more likely to use the concept not as a noun, but as an adjective or an adverb—*just,* or *justly.* The *just* person was the righteous man or woman who walked the straight path, conforming humbly to the will of God. For the Greeks, the more idealistic image of *Justice* as the perfect balancing of competing claims was foundational in their philosophy and drama.

The issues of justice in both scripture and literature have divided into two major categories—human justice and divine justice. Many of the quarrels that become trials or battles begin in conflicting claims regarding, property, behavior, or beliefs. Even such a primitive community as the one William Golding portrays in *Lord of the Flies* reveals the children crying out for "fair play." Certainly older and stronger brutes can triumph over the young and the weak, but society can hardly see this as just. The many stories that deal with human justice tend to focus on its failures, the innocent who are punished, the guilty who are rewarded, the need for some reconciliation to make the community whole again after some gross violation of standards.

Divine justice is a far more puzzling concern, beginning with the concept of a just and awesome God, who knows and wills beyond any ability of humans to conceive. Thus, seeing the good person facing one catastrophe after another or the evil person triumphing over weaker and more moral opponents, tempts the observer to challenge God's justice. At the very least, the complainant hopes to discover the reasons for such incomprehensible behavior on God's part. Very often, the reconciliation comes only in the hope that a final judgment, outside of time, will bring some kind of justice to bear.

Scripture

The God of the Old Testament is himself a just god, who has stamped a concern for just behavior on his final, and most complex creation. Within biblical texts, humans can never quite measure up to God's perfect standards of justice. Even before God hands the law to Moses, there is divine guidance. Adam and Eve have a clear covenant with God: they are to live their blessed life in the Garden so long as they refrain from eating the fruit of the Tree of the Knowledge of Good and Evil. Once they transgress, they suffer the consequences. Their awareness of their own guilt is evident in their response to God's summons to answer for their transgression. They have no adequate means of returning to Eden and the earlier relationship with God, which they have lost for themselves and their posterity.

Subsequently, their son Cain replicates their violation, guilt, and shame. He knows that he is not permitted to kill his brother. Long before God gives the tablets of the Law to Moses, he sets in human hearts a sense of fair play, an awareness of limits to behavior. This is, perhaps, something of the "image" of God that is stamped on the First Couple. God again reveals his justice by sending Cain away from the family, marked for life, thereby punishing him fully for his sin. The purpose of punishment in scripture is to readjust the community that has been thrown off kilter by the unfair or unlawful action of one of its members. That person must be judged and punished before the community can return to equilibrium. In this case, Cain is cast out of the family, but not killed.

God himself, the creator of all things, can never be controlled by laws outside of himself. Unlike the Greek gods, who are themselves under the authority of Necessity (or Fate), the Hebrew God, though just by nature, might not choose to act according to human understanding of justice. Whether or not humans understand the justice of his actions or directions, they cannot judge them or him. Thus, when Abraham is faced with the direct order to sacrifice his son Isaac, he must feel that God is contravening his own rules against killing, which Abraham probably understands from the experience of Cain and Abel. Yet Abraham also realizes that God, the author of law and the very essence of the concept of "justice," can never be unjust in his commands.

Much of the narrative of Genesis reveals an evolving sense of justice, with a series of covenants made and broken. When the behavior grows too outrageous for God to countenance, he interferes, using earthquake or flood, punishing great groups of people for their egregious ways. It is only in Exodus that God finally provides a clear set of laws that he requires his people to follow in order to maintain a harmonious relationship with him and with one another. Jesus summarizes these many rules and regulations, which appear through much of Exodus and Leviticus, in these simple sentences: "Thou shalt love the lord thy God, and with all thy heart, and with all thy soul, and with all thy mind. This is the first and great commandment. And the second is like unto it, Thou shalt love thy brother as thyself. On these two commandments hang all the law and the prophets" (Matt. 22:37–40). In the incomparable example of Jesus, who forgives his persecutors even as he hangs on the cross, we see the total rejection of the old system of vengeance.

The basic book of justice for the Hebrews is the Law of Moses, where we see the manner in which many arguments between individuals or families or tribes may be settled in an equitable manner. Rather than the more primitive *Lex Talonis*, or the Law of Retaliation, a life for a life, an eye for an eye and a tooth for a tooth, which was the most prevalent system in much of the Fertile Crescent, the Hebrew law is a more rational and humane system. Vengeance is replaced by negotiated exchange, allowing the society to return to a normal, peaceful condition.

Some of the leaders whom God chooses for Israel exemplify this system of justice. Moses himself serves as the chief judge for many years, later appointing minor judges to settle small disputes, reserving the ultimate authority for himself. Still later, the Judges of Israel, a series of charismatic leaders, hand out judgments in their tribes and seek to right wrongs. The litany that runs through the book of Judges ("every man did that which was right in his own eyes") suggests that the system proved to be chaotic. Eventually, when the Israelites insist on a king, the anointed of God serves as the chief judge of the country, though most local disputes are still settled by local elders, who sit in judgment at the gates of the city. They are all expected to make their findings on the basis of the Law of Moses.

It is rare that an argument over parentage, such as the one presented to King Solomon, would rise to the king's level. Surely Solomon's famous solution, to divide the disputed child in half, is an ironic device for encouraging the real mother to express her sympathy with her baby. Solomon's "justice" in this case seems brutal, but reveals his wisdom: he assumes that the real mother's love would overcome her demand for justice, allowing a "just" outcome for the baby. Here we see how cruel justice can be if strictly enforced. The psalmist knows this, pleading for mercy rather than justice. The prophets also seek to mitigate God's mighty justice by begging that he show mercy on his people.

Increasingly, the kings themselves require judgment: David, in his adulterous relationship with Bathsheba and the contrived murder of her husband, has no one over him to bring judgment. For this purpose, the prophet Nathan's intervention is needed, forcing David to judge himself by the clever use of a parable. The prophetic and the wisdom literature (Proverbs and Job) often portray law in action, posing profound questions, such as: Who will judge the judge? The issue in the book of Judges is that, without a king, the uneven application of law verges on anarchy. The issue in the books of Samuel and Kings is the opposite: when there is an ultimate authority, there is no guarantee that the king himself will be fair in his judgments.

The great scriptural exploration of justice is found in the Book of Job, a story that begins with God's whimsical decision to allow the tormenting of his faithful servant. The good man does not deserve to suffer, yet troubles come upon him in an avalanche. Job seeks to challenge God, but discovers that he has no standing in God's court and no knowledge worthy of God's power and glory. He assumes that, because he is a "good man," he will receive God's blessings for the whole time he is on earth.

The withdrawal of those blessings—his animals, his possessions, his children, and even his health—leads him to question God's justice. Certainly his "friends" are no help as they also assume a neat cause-and-effect relationship between morality and rewards. But God has made no such promise to humankind.

In *A Masque of Reason,* the twentieth-century American poet Robert Frost makes a similar point: "There's no connection man can reason out/ Between his just deserts and what he gets." Of course, the preacher in Ecclesiastes has also said this, noting that the rain falls on the just and the unjust, that the race does not always go to the swift. Archibald MacLeish in *J. B.,* another modern poetic drama based on the story of Job, makes an even more subtle point. Humans frequently think they can "justify" God's behavior, as if they are able to comprehend what God thinks and plans.

Job soon learns that God owes humans nothing. We bring nothing to God that is not already his. He gives humans life, food, family, prosperity. Job does bow his head and acknowledge, "The Lord gives and the Lord takes away," following this with "blessed be the name of the Lord." In Job, we see that we humans have no standing in any celestial court that would allow us to challenge the justice of God's ways. The best that Job (or any person) can hope for is the intercession of a Redeemer. "I know that my Redeemer liveth and that he shall stand at the latter day upon the earth" (Job 19:23). In Christian thought, this voice that makes the case for humans is Christ's. Only he has standing in Heaven as God and on earth as man. Jesus also enlarges the concept of the afterlife as the time of judgment, when the punishments and rewards will be handed down by the ultimate Judge, God himself. Without a concept of an afterlife with rewards and punishments, Job is left seeking earthly rewards, and he actually receives them at the end of the story. For him, the ultimate punishment is human suffering.

With the increased interest in the coming Day of the Lord and the hope for an afterlife with a time of judgment, the prophets expect less and less of justice on earth. They look forward to a final reckoning. Jesus and his followers expand this vision, with the clear promise of a time when God will separate the sheep from the goats, punishing the evildoers and showering his people with blessings. The Pharisees often ask Jesus questions about the law, usually in hopes of tricking him into a blasphemous response. In some of his answers, Jesus explains that he has not come to abolish the law, but to fulfill it. He explores the deeper meaning of the laws, showing that they are not meaningless rules, but based on the desires of the human heart. It is not just a matter of avoiding murder, a person should also avoid the anger that leads to killing. His lessons encouraging his followers to go the extra mile, turn the other cheek, and avoid casting the first stone put a more positive face on the law.

Jesus often tells parables that reveal some of the more complex issues of judgment, such as the parable of the Prodigal Son. In this story (Luke 145:23 ff.), the one son takes his inheritance and wastes it, while the other preserves his and remains home. Many listeners must feel that the stay-at-home son is correct in complaining about the justice of rewarding the prodigal with a great feast on his return. Simple justice would demand that he be treated according to his actions, just as the prodigal himself expects. But Jesus makes a point that God is a generous and gracious father, welcoming back the one who has wandered. Further, the son who stays at home has had the blessedness of living happily with his father rather than suffering the privations his brother undergoes. Nor is the "good" son in a position to judge his father's actions. Any inheritance is a gift, not an obligation of the father. He is free to bestow his own wealth and love as he chooses. As the son may not control the father, so humans have no right to question God.

In a parallel story about workers in a vineyard (Matt. 20), Jesus tells of a man who employs workers early in the morning at an agreed-upon rate. Late in the day, he hires other workers, whom he pays the same amount, though they have worked a much shorter time. The first workers complain about the justice of this action. The employer's reaction is to assure them that they had been paid what they have agreed to, that it is his right to reward this "last" at the same rate if he so chooses. This "unjust" employer, like God, is distributing his own goods and has every right to reward any people in any way he chooses. God has offered salvation to those who repent on their deathbeds, rewarding them with the same blessedness as those who repent in their youth. It is not for humans to complain about the nature of God's gifts. Only God is just, and only he can fully define the just act, knowing as he does the whole sweep of history and the hidden depths of human depravity. If God chose to treat humans "justly," we would all hang. We rely instead on God's mercy for our very existence. In some ways, this is much the same lesson Job learned centuries earlier.

The most impressive working out of cosmic justice, which proves ultimately unjust on the human level, is the Crucifixion. In this case, perjured witnesses come before an illegally convened court to judge a God-man of blasphemy. The reluctance of the different judges, the Sanhedrin, Pontius Pilate, and Herod, to declare the verdict is evidence of the weakness of the trumped-up charges and shaky grounds for the conviction. Jesus's silence in the face of this travesty of justice is a tacit commentary on its farcical nature.

Yet, in the great unfolding drama of man's relationship with God, the action is just: the Crucifixion demonstrates God's justice in a remarkable manner. The transgression of Adam and Eve in the Garden of Eden demands a response from God, who predicts their tormented future and that of their descendants. The life for the first family east of Eden, cursed with the original evils of the Fall, leaves humans forever separated from fellowship with God. In his pure justice, God is obliged to leave mankind in their fallen condition. Yet, in his mercy, God finds a means for his only begotten Son to pay the price for their sin and restore them to his presence. In the sacrifice of his own innocent son on the cross, he satisfies his self-imposed justice and reveals his mercy. Foreshadowed for thousands of years by the sacrifice of flawless animals on altars, this incredible sacrifice of the Crucifixion has formed a central theme for writers throughout the ages.

Literature

The classical Roman image of Justice is a blindfolded goddess holding a scale. The impartial measurement of two conflicting claims is the ideal portrayed here, but not quite applicable to the richer, more internalized Hebrew concept of virtue as a way of life. The blindfold implies that the judge shows no favoritism. For most people in a society, the idea that all people are equal before the law means that they have equal access and equal claims. Yet even the ancient Greeks, in spite of this symbol of ideal justice, knew that more often than not, might makes right. The stronger force, usually the conqueror, generally determines the laws that the weaker have to obey. Kings and people of wealth are often above the law, even in control of it, using it to punish those who cause them trouble.

Nonetheless, the ancient philosophers discuss ideal justice and the just person in their writings. Aristotle, for example, in *The Nicomachean Ethics*, explains the concept as the mean between inequalities. He tells us:

> A man is unjust if he breaks the law of the land; he is unjust if he takes more than his fair share of anything. Clearly then the just man will be (1) one who keeps the law, (2) one who is fair. What is just is (1) what is lawful, (2) what is fair; what is unjust is (1) what is unlawful, (2) what is unfair.

In this prosaic definition, Aristotle assumes a common understanding of both law and fairness. For him and for many Greeks, justice was the basic principle of order, the bond that allows people to dwell in peace with one another.

Plato includes Justice along with Truth and Beauty among his Ideas—those eternal and changeless essences that mankind senses without fully achieving or understanding. In his Republic, the imaginary just state, he assumes that every man would do the work for which he is best fitted, under the direction of the wisest men. For him, as for the ancient Jews, the just person is one who possesses integrity, lives according to consistent principles, "and is not diverted from them by consideration of gain, desire, or passion" (Benn, 301).

In Greek literature, the *Orestia* trilogy is one of the clearest statements of the evolving view of justice. Orestes, whose mother murders his father because of his own slaughter of their daughter, feels compelled to kill both her and her lover in order to exact vengeance for her deeds. This is the proper action under the ancient *lex talonis*, a life for a life. It is clear that, when he completes the murder, his sister or a relative of her lover will be obligated to kill him. There is no end to the relentless chain of vengeance. In the third play of this trilogy, the Furies are prepared to pursue Orestes forever. Apollo, however, graciously intervenes. Insisting that enough is enough, he transforms the Furies into Eumenides, who recall the actions without perpetually tormenting mankind for them or requiring further bloodshed. This allows the rule of law to succeed the old rule of blood-vengeance.

The Greeks were primarily concerned with justice among humans, expecting no justice from their petulant and irresponsible deities. Their gods tended to behave worse than humans. Even the "good" god Apollo might appear suddenly on stage to award those he loves—the people of Athens—a generous verdict. No one anticipated that he would be impartial or fair. None of the gods in the *Iliad* or the *Odyssey* ever considered what would be the fair treatment of the warriors or their families. Their whole concern was their own petty quarrels.

For the medieval poets of Europe, however, God's justice was a very significant concern. Dante, in his magnificent epic of the afterlife, presents the world with a vision of Hell, Purgatory, and Heaven, shaped by a just God. The rich irony of the *Inferno* is that the inhabitants receive the very things they sought on earth: the Trimmers, who could not make up their minds about their faith on earth, remain forever in an anteroom to Hell, neither punished by intense pain nor rewarded by God's blessedness. Those who lusted after one another on earth now are eternally yoked together in the circle of the lustful, whirling in the winds that mirror that passion, forever sad and forever together, doomed to playing out endlessly their sexual sin.

The Great Judge places each person where he or she chooses to be, either with God or apart from him, in darkness or in light. At the center of Hell is Satan, the "ruler" of this kingdom of darkness, himself doomed to spend eternity apart from God in this world of damnation. When the poet begins to show sympathy for the anguish of the tormented souls, his guide sternly admonishes him that he is witnessing God's justice. Any sympathy is an impious comment on God's perfect judgment.

By the Renaissance, literature was more commonly focused on human problems of justice rather than on divine judgment in the afterlife. One of the most famous meditations on justice and mercy is Shakespeare's play *The Merchant of Venice*. This is a cruel story of a vicious Jew, exacting vengeance on his tormentors, only to have his own "justice" turned back on him. Shylock lends a young Christian money in return for the promise that, if the loan is not paid back on time, he is due a pound of flesh. After the deadline passes, the borrower returns to Shylock, offering to pay more than the original loan to settle the account, but Shylock is adamant. He demands his pound of flesh. The wily judge agrees that his is the winning argument, but when Shylock moves to cut his adversary, the judge admonishes him that he may not shed any blood, nor may he take more nor less than the precise pound of flesh. Relenting in the face of this impossible task of cutting flesh without causing bleeding, Shylock offers to settle for the earlier offer. This option, however, has now been withdrawn. Thus, the trickster is tricked, and the cruel lender is left without his loan or his sick hope of judicial murder.

Interestingly, the most famous lines are Portia's speech about mercy, not justice: "The quality of mercy is not 'strained. It falleth as the gentle rain from heaven." The outlandish demand for a pound of flesh, though legal, is not just. Yet, it is the Jew rather than the Christian who points out the need for human sympathy, insisting that Jews are humans too. The ending of the story seems nonetheless vicious to modern minds: the Jew is forced to convert to Christianity and his fortune is forfeited to his enemies. Both sides fall short of their own concept of both justice and mercy.

Another Shakespeare play, *Measure for Measure*, is also based on a judicial quandary. In this case, a law is used by the ruler of Vienna to enforce virtue: any man caught in sexual "incontinence" is to be put to death; any woman guilty of such a sin is to be exposed to perpetual shame. In the story, classed with Shakespeare's so-called "unpleasant plays," Claudio proves to be an offender of the law. His sister seeks to save him from death, only to be propositioned by the formerly upright deputy, Angelo. In order to save her brother Claudio, she must sacrifice her own honor. Furthermore, her selfish brother is willing to allow her to make this sacrifice. Through a series of complex maneuvers, everyone is saved, all honor is preserved, and the virtuous people marry each other. But in the meantime, the concept of real justice is trashed. Some believe that Shakespeare's real point was to reinforce Christ's admonition: "Judge not that ye be not judged." None of these people really deserve the mercy they are granted.

As the British legal system developed and litigation became more of a problem for most simple people, courts and trials assumed a larger role in plays and novels. One of Charles Dickens' characters, Mr. Bumble in *Oliver Twist*, expresses his view of confusing and unjust laws of England in the nineteenth century quite bluntly: "The law is a ass, a idiot." No author attacks the law more frequently or with more fervor than this novelist. His characters are frequently in trouble with the law, whether for crimes or for debt (e.g., in *Oliver Twist, Great Expectations*, and *David Copperfield*), probably because of his own family's checkered background. Rarely is the law a friend to the innocent or poor, and often it is so complex that cases take decades to work their way through the courts. *Bleak House* tells this particular story in great detail. As legal scholars insist, justice delayed is justice denied. When lawyers are able to stretch trials out over generations, the original litigants go to their graves with their cases still undecided. In such a system, only the lawyers prosper. As Dickens saw it, the law itself could be "unjust" and the punishment far out of proportion to the crime.

One turn of the century British writer, A. E. Housman, took an ironic view of the laws of God and man, believing them both irrelevant to his life. After all, he never made them, yet was expected to follow them:

> The laws of God, the laws of man,
> He may keep that will and can;
> Not I: let God and man decree
> Laws for themselves and not for me.

This neo-pagan view ends with a wistful note of submission, recognizing the threats of hell or the gallows:

> I, a stranger and afraid
> In a world I never made.
> They will be master, right or wrong;
> Though both are foolish, both are strong
> And since, my soul, we cannot fly
> To Saturn nor to Mercury,
> Keep we must, if keep we can,
> These foreign laws of God and man.

(Housman, "The Laws of God, the Laws of Man," 890)

This particular view of laws tends to nullify the very laws by which the culture is governed. Much of modern thought is based on an expansion of this concept.

Another nineteenth-century British poet, Gerard Manley Hopkins, in a very personal way, addresses God's injustice to him. In the sonnet "Thou Art Indeed Just, Lord," he asks some of the same questions Job posed. The poet in this case sees God as both friend and as his Lord (Hopkins took orders to become a Jesuit priest), yet laments the injustice he sees in his own life: "Why do sinners' ways prosper? and why must/ Disappointment all I endeavor end?" The man who seeks to be good and obedient notices that others of apparently lesser morality seem to prosper while he fails to thrive. He begins the poem with a proclamation that God is just. Then he goes on to question this divine justice. Like the Old Testament prophets who lament that God allows the pagan nations to triumph over their own people, so Hopkins wonders that God chooses to "thwart" him while others build and enjoy their lives. Hopkins imagines his life to be like a stream that is confined by high banks and blocked by weedy growth. Continuing the nature imagery, he looks at the birds' nests and laments his own Christlike path, with no place to lay his head.

> Thou art indeed just, Lord, if I contend
> With thee, but, sir, so what I plead is just.
> Why do sinners' ways prosper? and why must
> Disappointment all I endeavor end?
> Wert thou my enemy, O thou my friend,
> How wouldst thou worse, I wonder, than thou dost
> Defeat, thwart me? Oh, the sots and thralls of lust
> Do in spare hours more thrive than I that spend,
> Sir, life upon thy cause. See, banks and brakes
> Now, leavèd how thick! lacèd they are again
> With fretty chervil, look, and fresh wind shakes
> Them, birds build—but not I build; no, but strain,
> Time's eunuch, and not breed one work that wakes,
> Mine, O thou lord of life, send my roots rain.

(Hopkins, "Thou Art Indeed Just," 39)

The ending of the poem is a prayer for revival and fruitfulness, a new sense of the value of his life's labor. In the poem, he echoes Paul, who recommends that some make themselves "eunuchs for Christ." This is to make them more productive in their labors for God, not to keep them from bearing spiritual fruit. Like Job, Hopkins is begging God for justice, or at least for mercy.

Taking a somber tone regarding divine and human justice, the American novelist Herman Melville wrote a short novel, *Billy Budd* that quarrels with both human and divine justice, incorporating the classic trial scene to underscore the theme. The author assumed of his audience an understanding of biblical stories as well as much of English history. Shrinking the world of the drama to a single warship and narrowing humankind to the crew of this ship, he tries to capture the inexplicable need for law and the horror of enforcing it when the "criminals'" motives are benign. It is not just another run-of-the-mill courtroom drama, but a deeply philosophic study of unjust justice. In this case, the sacrificial victim, who is designated to satisfy the British Navy's concept of justice, is a young seaman named Billy Budd.

The story is introduced against a background that proves crucial in the shape of the story; it is set at a time in history when other mutinies have rocked the British Navy and officers are on the alert for signals of trouble. Billy appears on board a man-of-war, delighting most of the crew and the captain with his sunny manner. A handsome and innocent fellow, Billy has the appearance of an angel (as did the martyr Stephen, when he was stoned to death for preaching his faith). For various reasons, the master-at-arms, a man named Claggart, becomes passionately antagonistic to the handsome sailor: "To be nothing more than innocent!" is his private meditation. Melville notes that Claggart has an "elemental evil" in him, "for which the Creator alone is responsible." His role is simply to act out this evil.

Claggart acts in a friendly manner toward Billy while he secretly plots his destruction. He finally charges Billy with being the "one dangerous man aboard," insisting that Billy is planning an insurrection. Captain Vere cannot believe this, though other ships have quite recently faced mutinies. He confronts the young foretopman, who appears before him like "a statue of young Adam before the Fall." There is no clear evidence of Billy's religion; he is simply a natural innocent. Yet he has his flaws, a quick temper and a mighty fist. Though usually placid and loving, he cannot abide liars and lying. He also has a speech impediment that keeps him from explaining his innocence when false charges are brought against him. Thus, he suddenly strikes out at Claggart when he speaks his lies, killing him. Ironically, the false charges precipitate the violence—the murder of a superior officer—and insure that all the witnesses against Billy are credible. The Captain, himself a witness to the incident, serves as both the prosecutor and the judge, forced to find against Billy even though he sympathizes with his action. Billy is not a man of faith or a willing sacrifice. Nor is he innocent of the formal charge brought against him. Yet the acting out of this just-yet-unjust judgment has eerie parallels to the events leading up to the Crucifixion.

Here again the "system" destroys the innocent man. The Captain must punish such violence in order to maintain order, especially at this particular time in naval history. Both he and the officers who sit in judgment with him are afraid that forgiving such a clear breach of the code of military justice will incite mutiny among the rest of the crew.

Melville fills the story with echoes of Hebrew sacrificial imagery (altars, priests, Abraham and Isaac, etc.) as well as the narratives of the Crucifixion (Billy's silence in the face of the accusation, his calm approach to death, his forgiving last words, even the hints that nature itself responds to the death). Yet the author, an interesting philosophical writer of the American Romantic period, who used his own sea-going experience in his longer study of life aboard a ship—*Moby-Dick*—is hardly an orthodox Christian in his interpretation. He appears to reject the idea of original sin, replacing it with psychological quirks and individual twists. The chaplain is rendered mute in the face of this natural (and secular) saint. The only religion that enters the story is as a means to keep the crew in order. In fact, at the end of the story, Billy Budd himself has become the object of veneration and the subject of myth-making. Bits of the spar on which he was hanged become relics for the crew, like pieces of the true Cross. The crew finally contribute to the ballad that sailors sing about "Billy's last day."

The story challenges many ideas and images in scripture, conflating Adam and Christ in this simple figure of the Handsome Sailor. It points to the inherent evil of social mechanisms, which cannot take into account individual differences or consider the innocent heart of the guilty man. The hero is a victim of justice, not a willing challenger of it. His inability to articulate his arguments, his silence in the face of lies make him a symbol of the period, a tragic "allegory of nineteenth century American society"—a piece of ironic social criticism (Zink, 131–139).

The modern tendency to question divine justice and to argue with the basis of society's rules appears in a dark parable told by Shirley Jackson, a twentieth-century New England short-story writer. Her narrative in "The Lottery," a story of "divine" justice, exaggerates the senseless perpetuation of outdated practices we venerate as "law." The human sacrifice at the center of her story perhaps derives from the primitive practices of Canaanites and others whose gods demanded human sacrifice to bring fertility to the land. The Israelites were themselves often tempted by Baal worship to pursue these ancient rites. Jackson, however, removes the sensuality and splendor from the practice, reducing it to a flat Midwestern practice, like American Gothic figures voting for mayor. She employs practices of ancient Israel as well, including the practice of stoning to death those who have brought evil into the community—adulterers, disobedient sons, and so forth.

The author chooses to set her tale in a modern setting, mundane and lackluster. It has the tone of a farm community in twentieth-century America, with the families gathering for a lottery. The ominous hints of fear that begin early in the narrative contrast with the usual hope for the winning a lottery. Even as the boys gather their piles of stones, the reader does not expect death by stoning in this so-called normal American small town, where the farmers depend on good weather for their subsistence.

Their loyalty to the very old custom—the lottery—at first sounds like any ritual of a village, no more significant than dressing up for a square dance or Hallow-een. However, with subtle foreshadowing, the ceremonial aspect becomes clear: the careful attention to the attendance of everyone in town, the reluctant gathering by families, the concern with the actual date of the event, the memories of the old chant, "Lottery in June, corn be heavy soon," the insistence on the tradition even after the box has been lost, the words forgotten. Only at the end do we discover that the winner is "honored" to be selected as the human sacrifice to an unnamed fertility god. The village turns and stones the "winner" to death. It is a chilling horror story, told without emotion. The final turn of the screw is the identity of the victim, a middle-aged wife and mother. Her son, little Davey, even contributes a few pebbles to her suffering. Her final words are, "It isn't fair, it isn't right."

The concept of selection by lottery is itself very ancient. The Jews and many other peoples believed that God was the one who made the choice in a toss of the dice (or the Urim and Thumin). When Joshua realizes that one person is responsible for the failure of the Israelites in battle, he has the priest cast lots to determine that the sinner is Achan. Because of his sin and the problems that sin brought on the community, he and all his family, his oxen and asses and sheep, are taken to the Valley of Achor, "And all Israel stoned him with stones, and burned them with fire, after they had stoned them with stones" (Joshua 7:25). Even in Christian times, the choice of the disciple to replace Judas is done by lottery. This process leaves the decision to God, relieving the villagers of any guilt. These villagers, unlike Captain Vere, show no remorse in acting out their ritual of a "just" killing.

In twentieth-century literature, and in modern drama, courtroom stories continue to appeal to the public. Focusing on law, writers like John Grisham can allow characters to act in antisocial ways, to investigate transgressions, to confront one another, and to render judgment, measuring actions against a yardstick of the law. They often take measure of the law as well, calling into question the whole issue of honest judgment.

The popular novel, also made into a popular film, *To Kill a Mockingbird*, makes an interesting point about human justice. Several times, Harper Lee has her lawyer-hero, Atticus Finch, speak of certain things as "sins." For instance, his father tells him it was a sin to kill a mockingbird, which causes no harm and only provides pleasure. He tells the jury that is intent on finding an obviously innocent black defendant guilty that it would be a sin to vote against the solution they consider "just." But for the jury, the black man, who has the temerity to feel pity for a poor white girl and to turn away from her advances, has to be found guilty. His guilt lies in his violation of community values, though these are obviously warped values. Later, the death of the accuser is overlooked, as a means of balancing the unjust death of the innocent man, providing a just solution outside of the formal system of justice. Harper Lee leaves it to the reader's imagination as to what power inspires the sheriff to make things right, forgiving the likely suspect, avoiding a trial, and letting the death become simply an accident—an act of God.

Franz Kafka, a German writer of the twentieth century, had a troubling vision of the whole concept of justice. Like many moderns, the hero of *The Trial* is unable to determine the nature of his errors. He knows only that he is charged with some crime and that he is considered guilty until he can prove himself innocent. Since he is puzzled about the nature of his crime, the time and place of his trial, and the system of justice involved, he stumbles from one clue to the next, wandering up one path after another, hoping for clarity and understanding. In all the dark rooms, among all the frightened people he meets, he finds nothing more than hints at his situation. He is not allowed to see the law book on which his trial is based, nor does he meet his judge.

At one point, he discovers an artist who is painting a judge's portrait, with the image of Justice in the background. Ironically, this portrayal of Justice is a blend of the classic study of blindfolded Justice with the wings of Victory attached: "There's the bandage over the eyes, and here are the scales. But aren't there wings on the figure's heels, and isn't it flying?" asks Joseph K. of the artist. When the artist explains the combination of the two figures, K. responds, "Justice must stand quite still, or else the scales will waver and a just verdict will become impossible." That, of course, is the very outcome that Joseph K. is denied.

In a late scene, Joseph K. finds himself in a dark cathedral, empty of all worshippers, with nothing to guide him except a sightseeing manual. The priest takes time to explain some of the law to the poor suffering sinner, but with such ambiguity that the "scripture" is useless as a guide for his actions. The priest describes the Law as a "doorkeeper" and then tells a parable of a man seeking to go through a door, but he is denied entrance by a doorkeeper. After spending a lifetime trying to understand what he must do to enter, the man finally is told that this door is indeed "his," but he may never enter it.

In the distance, he glimpses "a radiance that streams inextinguishably from the door of the Law." Yet he dies without ever going through it to experience that radiance.

The story, which ends with K's sacrificial death on an altar, is a reminder of many points in scripture and in literature. Like the Pilgrim in Bunyan's famous novel, K. finds that the law stands between him and the Celestial City. Paul speaks of the law as a "schoolmaster" for humanity, but notes that no one can be perfect. Rather, the believer must trust in mercy rather than justice. When Jesus says that the faithful must knock on the door, and it will be opened, he goes beyond the ancient idea of the law as the path to salvation. Rather, it is the faith of the believer and the atoning death of Christ, which allows the faithful to avoid the full power of the law. Poor Joseph K. never finds this key to the door that blocks him from the solution to his deep sense of guilt.

For those of us who live in a nation that has laws, a clear system of justice, and a belief that we are innocent until proven guilty, this novel is particularly horrifying. The arbitrary and murky system of so-called justice we see here mirrors that which exists in much of the world under tyrants, who become the law through their sheer power. The nightmare world that results is beautifully mirrored in Kafka's prescient novel.

Conclusion

Over time, justice has wandered far afield from the concept of righteousness and the rule of law. The just God, who can promise rewards and punishments in the afterlife has been challenged for his management of this world and doubted for his promise of a life to come. Few modern European or American writers would agree with Dante's vision of a tri-partite afterlife. Increasingly, writers attack the very law itself as unjust, antiquated, and arbitrary.

Literature, like scripture, is full of stories of cheats and villains, and of those who seek in their own clumsy way to bring them to justice. Readers find the solution to the crime or the verdict in favor of the innocent party a relief, nicely closing a story. But more and more often, stories end with wrongful verdicts and quarrels with the law itself. Like Housman, many moderns believe they are subject to laws of man and laws of God that they never made and do not accept. The temptation is often that of the Israelites during the days of the Judges, when there "was no king in Israel, but every man did that which was right in his own eyes" (Judg. 17:6).

Poetry and philosophy often echo Job's complaints about the perceived injustices of God himself. Revelation proclaims (15:3) that God is "just and true" in his ways. This is not always easy for humans to see in their own lives or in the world around them.

See also: **Death and the Afterlife; Good People; Government and Politics; The Hero; Last Days.**

Bibliography

Aeschylus. *Orestia*. Trans., Ted Hughes. New York: Farrar, Straus and Giroux, 1999.

Aristotle. *The Nichomachean Ethics*. In *The Works of Aristotle*. Trans., W. D. Ross. Chicago: Encyclopædia Britannica, 1952

Benn, Stanley I. "Justice," In *The Encyclopedia of Philosophy*, vol. 4 (298–302). New York: Collier Macmillan Publishers, 1967.

Dickens, Charles. *Bleak House*. New York: Penguin, 1996.

———. *Oliver Twist*. New York: Dodd, Mead, 1984.

Dostoyevsky, Fyodor. *Crime and Punishment.* Trans., Constance Ganett. New York: Modern Library, 1994.

Hopkins, Gerard Manley. "Thou Art Indeed Just." In *Modern British Poetry,* ed. Louis Untermeyer. New York: Harcourt, Brace and Company, 1950.

Housman, A. E. "The Laws of God, the Laws of Man." In *British Poetry and Prose,* vol. II, ed. Paul Lieder, Robert Morss Lovett, and Robert Kilburn Root. Boston: Houghton Mifflin Company, 1950.

Jackson, Shirley. *The Lottery.* Mankato, MN: Creative Education, 1983.

Kafka, Franz. *The Trial.* Trans., Breon Mitchell. New York: Schocken Books, 1998.

Lee, Harper. *To Kill a Mockingbird.* New York: HarperPerennial, 2002.

Melville, Herman. *Billy Budd, Sailor and other Stories.* New York: Penguin Books, 1986.

Shakespeare, William. *Measure for Measure* and *The Merchant of Venice.* In *Shakespeare: Major Plays and the Sonnets,* ed. G. B. Harrison. New York: Harcourt, Brace and Company, 1948.

Shields, Charles J. *Mockingbird.* New York: Henry Holt and Company, 2006.

Untermeyer, Louis, ed. *Modern British Poetry.* New York: Harcourt, Brace and Company, 1950.

Zink, Karl E. "Herman Melville and the Forms—Irony and Social Criticism in *Billy Budd.*" *Accent: A Quarterly of New Literature, 12* (Summer 1952), 131–139.

Government and Politics

Readings

I and 2 Samuel

Plato's *Republic* (c. 390 B.C.)

Thomas More, *Utopia* (1515)

Niccolò Machiavelli, *The Prince* (c. 1505)

William Shakespeare, *Richard II* (1594), *Henry IV*, Parts 1, 2 (1597);
   Macbeth (1605)

Jonathan Swift, *Gulliver's Travels* (1726)

Charles Dickens, *A Tale of Two Cities* (1859)

Fyodor Dostoyevsky, *The Possessed* (1872), *The Brothers Karamazov* (1879)

Joseph Conrad, *The Secret Agent* (1907)

William Butler Yeats, "The Second Coming" (1921)

George Orwell, *Nineteen Eighty-Four: A Novel* (1949)

Franz Kafka, *The Castle* (1926)

Introduction

> Put not your trust in princes, nor in the son of man, in whom there is no
> help. (Ps. 146:3)

A perennial question in literature and in society is, *How shall a society be governed?* Even in as small and primitive a society as that in William Golding's *Lord of the Flies*, one of the first questions the stranded boys ask of one another is, "Who will be the leader?" Coming from a British background, the children accept the rule of the majority, voting for a charismatic teenager who is attractive and self-assured, ignoring the wiser boy, who is near-sighted and asthmatic. When a struggle for the leadership position arises, with a debate between the hunters and the keepers of the flame, the mindless youngsters quickly abandon the elected leader for the one who offers bread and circuses (or roast pig and nightly dances around the fire).

Among the standard issues addressed in both scripture and literature are: the nature of leaders and of leadership, the rules of governance, the proper means of establishing authority, the proper limits of governmental power, the rights reserved for the individual, and the appropriate manner for changing leaders or overthrowing unjust government. These are real-life issues that the Israelites struggled to resolve in their own tumultuous history. They are also the issues that philosophers and creative writers have addressed in their essays, poetry, novels, and plays in many other cultures.

Scripture

The old prophet Samuel knew that humans should not be trusted with inordinate power. He believed that only God should be the ruler of Israel, but the Israelites wanted to be like their neighbors and demanded that they be granted a king. Samuel warned them that they would indeed be like their neighbors: the king would become a despot, demanding taxes of them, and taking their sons as warriors, their women as slaves, their land for their own.

Although some of Israel's kings proved to be good rulers, concerned primarily with their people's well-being, only too often they were dazzled by their own affluence and authority. Saul, the first king in Israel, moved quickly from being a simple, good-hearted leader of the tribes of Israel to an arrogant ruler who disobeyed God, ending as a mad tyrant. Even David, often cited as one of the best of the kings of Israel, did not pause before stealing another man's wife; Solomon, for all of his wisdom, enslaved his own people as if he were the Pharaoh, took an inordinate number of wives and mistresses, and worshipped strange gods.

Probably no king was so beloved in Israel's history as David, who united the tribes and expanded the kingdom. It was he who brought the Ark of the Covenant to Jerusalem, "David's City." With him began the sense of the king's household and his palace as the center of governance. With him, the old image of the city as an evil place was transformed into the "shining city on the hill." Although he was a man after God's own heart, he was also a man who made many mistakes. On the one hand, he sang and danced as he brought the Ark of the Covenant into Jerusalem, thrilled at the fulfillment of a long dream of finding a home for this relic from the days in the wilderness. He delighted in the building of his holy city and accepted God's judgment that, as a man of war, he should not be the one to build the Temple. Yet, fully human, he used his power as king to begin the taxation and recruitment that would burgeon under his son Solomon. He refused to put down the rebellions of his sons and have them executed, causing others to die for his selfish indulgence. He took more wives and concubines than other men of the kingdom, and set up a pattern that was carried to an extreme by Solomon.

The prime example of evil in later years is Queen Jezebel, a foreign-born queen who dominates her weak husband, demanding her neighbor's vineyard, bringing in her priests and pagan worship, and generally inciting the citizens against her high-handed ways. When she falls from the latticed window to the courtyard below to her death and is eaten by dogs (except for her hands and feet), her fate strikes the prophets and the people as divine justice.

The fall of kings, always dramatic because of their exalted rank, is a recurrent part of scripture. From the defeat of the Pharaoh in the waters of the Red Sea, to the five kings that Joshua hanged on the trees in Canaan, to the death of Saul and Jonathan, lamented by David, all point to the transience of earthly power. "How the mighty have fallen," sang David, lamenting the old king and his son.

The period of the Exile and the experience in foreign courts with foreign monarchs taught the Jews that they should not put their faith in princes. They might love a David or respect a Solomon, but only God is king. This great power over human life should not be entrusted to any human. The prophets of the Exile begin to lay out the ideas of the Kingdom of God, the Day of the Lord, and the perfect Ruler—a redeemer, shepherd, and suffering servant, willing to die for his people. Isaiah anticipates the Messiah, the King of Kings. Ezekiel envisions a New Jerusalem with a glorious Temple in its midst, in a city not built by men.

The Return from Exile of the remnant only reinforced the need for a transformation of earthly power. Although Cyrus proved benevolent to these people, the years that followed saw one tyrant after another take control of the Promised Land and the people of Judah. Whether the Hellenistic rulers or the Roman ones, they failed to understand the culture and faith of this special people. Antiochus Epiphanes horrified the Jews with his "abomination of abominations." He erected a statue of Zeus in the Temple and sacrificed swine on the altar. In the rebellions that followed, one leader after another promised the restoration to the true faith, but none could deliver on this promise.

The Romans offered little relief, bringing their own brand of "tolerance," and enthroning the despised Herod the Great, an Ideomaen as King of the Jews. The history of this period makes clear the hunger of the Jews for a Messiah who would bring God's authority back to earth. The Zealots were among many groups determined to see revolution against both the power of Rome and the corruption of Palestine's leaders. Usually, Judas is considered to have been one of this group, and perhaps Barabbas, the prisoner whom Pilate freed in the place of Jesus, was also a Zealot.

When Jesus is tempted by the Devil in the wilderness, he is offered all the kingdoms of the world: "All this power will I give thee, and the glory of them: for that is delivered unto me; and to whomever I will give it." Christ responds by refusing to turn his worship from God to the would-be benefactor standing before him. One commentator notes: "How interesting, though that power should be at the Devil's disposal, and only attainable through an understanding with him! Many have thought otherwise, and sought power in the belief that by its exercise they could lead men to brotherhood and happiness and peace, invariably with disastrous consequences" (Muggeridge, 26).

Certainly, the disciples consider the possibility of an earthly kingdom when they gather around Christ. The mother of the Zebedees is clearly relying on the assumption that Jesus will establish such a kingdom when she requests that her boys be given high positions in it, and is undoubtedly surprised, and probably disappointed, when he responds that his kingdom is not of this world. In the Kingdom of God, Jesus explains, the first will be last and the last first. The true nobility will be those who suffer for the faith.

Nor is Christ willing to advocate the overthrow of Caesar, counseling his followers and those who are quizzing him on the subject, "Render unto Caesar the things that are Caesar's" (Mark 12:7). Showing them a Roman coin, he points out the image of the emperor engraved on it, revealing that mere money belongs to Caesar. God demands more than this; he requires hearts filled with love for him, followers who are citizens of a better world. For the time being, his followers are to continue paying taxes, obeying the law, respecting the government that God allows to remain in power.

When Peter tries to stop the arrest of Jesus by drawing his sword, Jesus reprimands him, telling him that those who live by the sword will die by the sword. He himself dies according to Roman (and Jewish) legal patterns, which are corrupt and unjust. He obeys the authorities, even when they try, condemn, and execute him unjustly.

The Roman Empire was to prove jealous of its power and unwilling to allow the Christians to pledge their fealty to King Jesus rather than Caesar. John's great Revelation is full of horror at the violent actions and abuses of the Great Satan, the Roman emperors, and Rome herself—the "Whore of Babylon." The monsters that populate this apocalyptic vision are largely secular powers that continue to oppose the will of God on earth. Like the book of Daniel, this vision of a succession of brutal empires points to the travails of humankind for centuries to come. The prophesies of persecution were soon fulfilled, as Christians suffered and died for their allegiance to the Kingdom of God. For centuries, Rome was the great enemy of the Christian Church. In the fourth century, the Emperor Constantine made the Christian Church the official church of Rome, thereby uniting church and state once again as in the days of Israel, and creating a new series of power struggles.

For many Christians throughout the ages, the only real king was and continues to be Christ. Any earthly power corrupts the humans who seek to wield it. Nonetheless, kings and queens are anointed by clergy and permitted to remain on their thrones by God. The usurper of such "divine right" is himself considered a great sinner.

The lessons of scripture seem clear (if unpalatable): the ideal government for God's people is theocracy. Unfortunately, most rulers and most citizens are not worshippers of God, making any blending of religion and government potentially dangerous for those who do hold fast to the faith of their ruler. Nevertheless, if God places a king on the throne, Christians have traditionally believed that they should respect his authority and obey him. Rebellion against unjust rulers has no support in scripture. The believer must wait on God's Day of Judgment for justice. For Christians, the only utopian dream is in the anticipated Kingdom of God. For the time being, all people live under the authority of earthly rulers.

Literature

Playwrights and novelists love to write about power and politics. These themes can be based on real life, with stories full of high drama, that involve vigorous conflict, life-and-death struggles among significant and sometimes heroic people. They often end in tragedy. Such topics are clearly the stuff of theater, like the tales of Oedipus or Antigone. The Greeks knew that their kings were all too often *tyrants* (the Greeks' term for rulers), concerned primarily with their own power and not with justice. Antigone, honoring her religious obligation to bury her brother, challenges the authoritarian state that refuses to allow her to fulfill this obligation. For this heroine, the personal and religious take precedence over the social or legal. Rather than allow Creon to desecrate her brother's memory and his body, she is willing to die.

Although their plays were written and produced as part of civic religious festivals, the Greeks had few limitations on their religious or political speculations. Especially in Athens, the home of the golden age of classical literature, the playwrights and philosophers felt free to debate different forms of governance and to laugh at their rulers.

In Plato's *Republic,* the rulers of his utopian city, designed partially along the model of Sparta, are to be wise men, philosophers, who provide justice and order for their followers. Plato spends much of this dialogue in discussing how these philosopher kings will be educated for their roles as governors of the people. In his supremely rational contemplation of an ideal society, he does not consider the issue of original sin, which corrupts even the most decent of humans and perverts the best-laid plans for a social system. He might have been less sanguine if he had known the example of Solomon, an anointed king noted for his wisdom, concerned with the arts and the building of the Temple, who enslaved many of his own people, taxed them mercilessly, indulged in excesses of sexuality and left his kingdom hopelessly divided. The Israelites remembered Adam and Cain and Solomon—and did not share Plato's faith in human reason.

On the other hand, Plato believed that his ideal republic could rid itself of the undesirables, control the sexual habits of the people so as to encourage selective breeding, manage the education of the young, and ensure that the rulers would be the perfect people for their assigned tasks. Plato was convinced that a kind of communist government, with central controls and cradle-to-grave planning would produce ideal people. He was too early in history to be disturbed by the brief experiment of the later Christians with communism, which taught them that even the people of God could not be trusted to ignore self interest.

The Renaissance English writer Thomas More draws heavily on Plato's *Republic* in his book *Utopia* (1518), an attack on the England of Henry VIII. Although the book begins with a polite tribute to the king, the author launches quickly into a criticism of kings, whose role is largely fighting wars. He explains, "the moste parte of all princes have more delyte in warlike matters and feates of chivalrie…than in the good feates of peace; and employe much more study, how by right or by wrong to enlarge their dominions, than howe wel and peaceablie to rule and governe that they have alredie." He doubts that kings would become philosophers, and thinks them unlikely to seek the advice of philosophers. Without any limits to their power, they tend to become increasingly greedy, arrogant, and self-indulgent. As he notes, "no abundance of gold can be sufficient for a prince, which muste kepe and maynteyne an armie." In addition, because the king has no limits to his power, "all that all men have, yea also the men them selves be all his."

In the place of this unlimited monarchy, he describes a mythic republic that his friend supposedly has visited, governed primarily at the local level. Rather than a king at the center of the country, local magistrates manage a system that is controlled by checks and balances. Each cluster of 30 families selects a chief or philarche. These in turn gather and, by secret election, choose a prince, who then serves for life "onles he be deposed or put downe for susption of tirannie." These magistrates and princes rule with consultation "amongst themselves" in a thoroughly reasonable manner. Note that, unlike traditional monarchies, the children of the monarch do not necessarily succeed to the throne.

More's imagined system is a form of communism, but with the stipulation that every person has a share of the wealth only by working for it. With the general distribution of wealth and power, he anticipates little crime, no need for theft or for lawyers. When wars must be fought, the prince and his people enter into conflict reluctantly, with no love of glory or chivalry. In fact, they are "ashamed to atchieve the victorie with bloudshed." Rather, "they rejoyse and avaunt themselves if they vanquishe and oppresse their enemies by craft and deceite." When it proves necessary to raise an army, they prefer volunteers, often drawn from neighboring cities. Religious wars are eliminated by the system of complete freedom of religion in the Utopia, a land of good government, decent folk, and general harmony.

Certainly, these are not the characteristics of the world in which Machiavelli found in his society a century earlier. An Italian author and statesman of the Renaissance, Machiavelli was far more cynical about human nature than Plato. He knew that, in the real world, we cannot clear the society of misfits and malcontents and start afresh. Rather than assume a world full of decent people and enlightened rulers, we must work with what we have, including flawed and greedy people. As he comments, "It had seemed wiser to me to follow the real truth of the matter than what we imagine it to be." He also knows Italian history, having witnessed the great cruelty of powerful families at war with one another in his own country. He comes to realize the values of power, noting that "it is better to have an evil prince than no prince at all." When Machiavelli wrote his classic study of the pragmatic ruler, *The Prince* (1513), he was providing practical advice for Lorenzo de' Medici. He hoped that this prince would prove himself as cold and ruthless as his heroes, princes like Cesare Borgia and Ferdinand of Aragon. For Machiavelli, strength and success are the most cherished characteristics of the ideal prince.

Among the bits of practical advice he offers the reader are such cynical thoughts as: "men must either be dallied and flattered withall, or else be quite crusht; for they revenge themselves of small dammages; but of great ones they are not able; so that when wrong is done to any man, it ought to be done that it need feare no returne of revenge again." When a prince usurps power and gains control of a state, "the usurper thereof ought to runne over and execute all his cruelties at once; that hee bee not forced often to returne to them, and that hee may be able, by not renewing of them, to give men some security, and gaine their affections by doing them some courtesies." The prince should make the people his friend for his own benefit, not for theirs. He needs to profess honesty, but he must "be able to make use of that honestie, and to lay it aside againe, as ned shall require."

Perhaps his most famous tidbit of advice is, "it is much safer to be feard, than be lov'd" (Machiavelli, 62).

Realizing that reason and craft are not always enough to control a people, Machiavelli admits that Fortune often intervenes, giving one man a kingdom, taking it from another. The cold-blooded tone of the whole book is quite remarkable. While Machiavelli, like most people, may have preferred benevolent and generous rulers guarding a loving and appreciative citizenry, his own experience led him to believe that the prince could preserve his authority only through judicious use of power.

During the seventeenth century, the British system of governance was undergoing radical reconsideration, as was church governance. Having broken from the Church of Rome, the Church of England soon splintered.

The turmoil of the Renaissance provoked a host of literary masterpieces that dealt with politics. Among them, Shakespeare's history plays and his tragedies rank high. This master craftsman used historical records and contemporary events to reveal the rise to power of such kings as Richard II or Henry V in a manner that also sheds light on the controversies surrounding Henry VIII and Elizabeth. He also ranged further afield to find the paradigm of ill-gotten power in the rise and fall of the Scottish monarch Macbeth. In his studies of the ancient Romans, he explored Mark Antony's pride and passion. In his plays, he revealed the universal hunger for high position, portrayed the corruption of decent men who find themselves faced with cruel circumstances, and tracked the loss of prestige, of integrity, and finally of life.

The faith in the divine right of kings, the sense that their anointing is a sign that God's authority lies on the head that wears the crown, makes many kings ruthless.

They forget their covenant with the people, their obligations as God's regents on earth. Shakespeare confronts the reality of the evil monarch, with no concern for God or his subjects. Scripture provides no basis for deposing God's anointed, but Shakespeare shows that history is full of human "solutions"—imprisonments, rebellions, and murders.

Richard II is one of Shakespeare's most colorful heroes, an anointed king who tragically combines charisma and intelligence with incompetence. He makes rash decisions, ruining his own reputation, and then blames forces outside himself for making him "woe's slave." Eventually, Henry (his successor who usurps the throne) puts him in prison. Richard is later murdered at the king's clear hint: "Have I no friend will rid me of this living fear?" Henry laments his own role in the death of this king, promising to do penance by making a pilgrimage to the "Holy Land, to wash this blood off" his guilty hands. Henry does not, however, relinquish the crown.

In Shakespeare's play, *Richard II* (1594), the king eloquently laments his own impending death: "Let's talk of graves, of worms, and epitaphs." He invites his audience to tell

Sad stories of the death of kings:
How some have been depos'd, some slain in war;
Some haunted by the ghosts they have depos'd;
Some poisoned by their wives, some sleeping kill'd;
All murdered.

(Shakespeare, *Richard II*, 210)

This famous speech, ends with the commentary on the "hollow crown" making clear the transience of royal power and glory. At the end, "a little pin/Bores through his castle wall, and farewell king." Part of Richard's tragedy lies in his failure to use his brilliance for ruling his kingdom.

The subsequent plays in the series (*Henry IV*, Parts 1 and 2, 1597; and *Henry V*, 1605) are also thoughtful studies of the nature of the king's power, the potential the good leader has for greatness, the constant and omnipresent threats to his reign. The cynical advice of his dying father, to engage in foreign wars as a distraction from unrest at home introduces Prince Hal to the grim realities of governing. (The advice sounds as if it came from Machiavelli.) This youthful Henry V, who appears in his father's stories as well as in the play that bears his name, realizes at the very moment he gains the throne that he must relinquish his old friends and his old follies. He proves himself to be a real hero, a great leader in battle, and a strong patriot. His speech at the battle of Agincourt is justly famous for the sense of pride he inspires in preparation for the battle.

Shakespeare's anatomies of authority chronicle the ways in which rulers gain power, their temptations, the distortions that come with the threats, the increase in cruelty as they struggle to maintain control, their ever-present fear of displacement and death, as well as the inevitable loss of the throne and of life.

The eighteenth century continued this debate on the shape and limits of political power. This was a time of violent arguments, political intrigue, and bloody revolutions. Some of the more entertaining critiques of eighteenth-century British politics are found scattered through *Gulliver's Travels*. Jonathan Swift, a minister of the Church of England, with parishes in Ireland, grew weary of the petty religious and political quarrels of his day. In Gulliver's travels to the land of the Lilliputians, Swift satirizes these contemporary quarrels by reducing them to diminutive debates. Candidates for positions at the Lilliputian court must dance on ropes, and then creep and leap over and under a stick. Political parties divide over whether to wear high heels and low heels. Religious factions argue over which end of the egg is preferable for breaking, dividing into the "Big Endians" and the "Little Endians."

In Gulliver's second voyage, to the land of the Brobdingnags, Gulliver himself seems Lilliputian in comparison with the giants in the land. These giants' view of the world proves as grand as their physical presence. When the king of Brobdingnag asks Gulliver to describe England, Gulliver complies. The king, in turn is

> perfectly astonished with the historical account I gave him of our affairs during the last century, protesting it was only an heap of conspiracies, rebellions, murders, massacres, revolutions, banishments, the very worst effects that avarice, faction, hypocrisy, perfidiousness, cruelty, rage, madness, hatred, envy, lust, malice, and ambition could produce. (Swift, 107)

The king then summarizes his understanding of the British: "I cannot but conclude the bulk of your natives to be the most pernicious race of little odious vermin that nature ever suffered to crawl upon the surface of the earth."

The following voyage is to islands full of intellectuals incapable of managing even their own lives, much less deriving any logical system of government. But then, Gulliver concludes the record of his travels with an account of his idyllic voyage to the land of the Houhynms. Here he portrays a folk (actually horses), who are so decent that they need no governance. Reasonable and totally honest, they have no interest in property, wealth, or power. The less aristocratic varieties of horses perform the heavy labor, as suits them, just as in Aristotle's world of a God-given class structure. In addition, the nearly-human creatures called the Yahoos are a particularly nasty breed of beast, who love to fight, lust after glittering rocks, and are grossly sexual and obscene in their behavior. Wisely, they are reduced to serfdom by the governors of this utopia and kept under tight control.

The land of the Houhynms is a comic inversion of Rousseau's ideal world of good people who need no government, have no private property, and are guided by reason. Rousseau and his followers believed in the essential goodness of people, forgetting the clear lessons of Eden, including human depravity. Their social designs were doomed because they were built on human nobility, forgetting the recurrent Yahoo patterns in human conduct. The utopian dreams of the early nineteenth century were soon balanced by Darwin's cruel animalistic doctrine of the survival of the fittest. The century was filled with skirmishes over philosophies of government, each based on a competing vision of human nature. Socialism, communism, and anarchism were particularly popular ideas.

The fresh theories of *anarchism*, the absence of any government, were beginning to attract many intellectuals during the late years of the eighteenth century and have continued on to the present day. Some, like Rousseau, believed that if government were destroyed and people were free to govern themselves as they chose, they would cluster into voluntary associations. Among the Romantics, a hunger for liberty and a new faith in the common person encouraged this vision of libertarianism.

Some anarchists were less benign, feeling that first the old system must be swept away before the new cooperative society could emerge. The American Revolution replaced its distant despotic British king with a constitutional republic based on the consent of the governed. On the other hand, the French Revolution, motivated more by anarchistic thinking, proved much more violent. The most radical anarchists were communists who believed in God-given goodness and the rational nature of humans. For them, the best outcomes would come without force and would result in the abolition of property and the withering away of government.

A number of the English Romantics were initially thrilled at the French Revolution, which they thought was based on rational views of human virtue. William Wordsworth, for example, who was in France in the early days of the Revolution, was at first caught up in the excitement and then frightened at the bloodbath and at the possibility that the spirit of revolution would migrate to England. He wrote, remembering the events of another time, "Milton, thou shouldst be living at the hour" (Wordsworth, 45). Milton had, of course, been present during the fearful days of the Commonwealth that beheaded Charles I, and the Glorious Revolution that unseated James II.

Charles Dickens wrote one of the most powerful descriptions of the French Revolution. His *Tale of Two Cities* captures much of the violence and the chaos of the time. He includes the abuses of the aristocrats, the storming of the Bastille, the extravagant use of the guillotine against all suspected enemies in this stormy, bloody, and complicated drama. The details of his history are drawn largely from Thomas Carlyle's account of the French Revolution. Although Dickens's sympathies are typically with the common folk, in this novel he shows his disgust with figures like Madame Defarge (descended from aristocratic ancestors). On the eve of the Revolution, she sits carefully knitting her planned execution list. Dickens tends to believe that some poor people are born good and some are born evil—much like the rich. Both rich and poor are capable of heroic actions and brutal behavior. Some are even able to learn from experience and change their ways. He rarely searches for any over-arching theological or philosophic theme in his stories. Rather, he tends to be content with encouraging sympathy with those who deserve our charity. He also delights in those rare examples of heroism, as in the concluding scene of this novel and Carton's famous line: "It is a far, far better thing that I do, than I have ever done; it is a far, far better rest that I go to than I have ever known." In this act, reflected in this line that sounds like a prayer, Carton achieves through death a fulfillment he never knew in life. This generous act does give the individual sacrifice a Christian tone and a sense of redemption.

This faith in the common man and woman became so pervasive that even the great Russian Christian writer Tolstoy was convinced of the possibilities of building a system of society based on this notion. Fyodor Dostoyevsky, his fellow countryman, however was not convinced. His novel *The Devils* or *The Possessed* (1870–72) portrays the dangerous and self-destructive nature of the anarchists. In this remarkable story, Dostoyevsky seems to blame the chaotic thinking of the terrorists on the liberal intelligentsia of the previous generation, who rejected religion and authority, leaving their children without any foundation for their morality.

Among some secret revolutionary groups in southern Russia, the name *terrorist* was considered a badge of honor. The terrorists were primarily a group of idealists, not an oppressed segment of the lower classes. The characteristics of terrorism that are depicted in the novel are familiar to moderns: it unleashes people from their natural restraint against killing and suicide; it is usually a form of targeted political violence which is then dramatized through journalism. This terrorism of the anarchists involves daring crimes, attacks on the courts and the government by those who are brought to justice, and a sensationalized assault on the existing order.

The three characters central to Dostoyevsky's novel include Stepan Verkhovensky, an idealistic aristocrat; his son Peter, a nihilistic extremist; and Nicholas Stavrogin, a demon-possessed intellectual aristocrat. Nicholas is Stepan's former protégé whom Peter is seeking to recruit for his secret organization. He makes a mess of his own life, never settling on a reason for existence, not even in the terrorists' rebellion. Stepan is simply a limp "thinker," who achieves nothing in his life. His son is a diabolic personality, abandoned by his father as an infant, believing in nothing, with no commitment to people, truth, or faith and no vision of what he might accomplish in his creative destruction. As a result, his destruction appears to be meaningless criminality and petty vengeance, not the prologue to a new world.

The title of the book may also be translated *The Possessed*, a direct reference to demon possession, which is portrayed frequently in the New Testament. Dostoyevsky's cure for terrorism is religious, a revival of Russian Orthodox Christianity. He believed that these demons must be exorcised before the nation can be cured. His novel does not end happily. The most radical of the characters, Peter, is still alive. Looking forward to the utopian horrors of the Soviet Union under communism, he says, "Starting out from limitless freedom, I end up with limitless despotism." The radicals soon find that their freedom from social restraints make anything possible, including their own enslavement.

Another European author who was concerned with the rise of anarchism was Joseph Conrad. His novel *The Secret Agent*, which was written early in the twentieth century, points to the seemingly meaningless terrorism of this group. Symbolic acts of violence have proven a horrifying strategy in the subsequent years, killing the innocent who happen to be in the vicinity, whether in Algeria or Palestine or New York City. The anarchist character in *The Secret Agent* is not heroic, nor is he the one who actually does the killing. He is a dreamer who hopes for a world without rules. The anarchist in the story hopes to upset all the government authorities and to overturn the will of the majority simply by acts of carefully planned terrorism. Like the terrorists in the modern world, the agent uses a small number of people and modest means to destroy symbolic targets, sending shivers down the spines of all who watch. They tend to have no definite program for reform in mind at the time they undertake their creative destruction. They simply seek to annihilate the status quo.

It was this frightening image of twentieth-century political and social chaos that haunted William Butler Yeats when he wrote his famous poem "The Second Coming," shortly after World War II and the Russian Revolution. It reads in part:

> Things fall apart; the centre cannot hold;
> Mere anarchy is loosed upon the world,
> The blood-dimmed tide is loosed, and everywhere
> The ceremony of innocence is drowned;
> The best lack all conviction, while the worst
> Are full of passionate intensity.

(Yeats, "The Second Coming," 184)

Using a cyclical vision of human history, he contemplates the coming of a new Messiah, some "rough beast" which is even now slouching "towards Bethlehem to be born." The image of the beast, of course, sounds more like John's Apocalypse than like the Gospels. These lines do capture the fear-inspiring quality of the terrorists. Like the old Zealots of the New Testament, these violent idealists are willing to loose a "blood-dimmed tide" on the world.

A fascinating poem by a modern British writer, Kingsley Amis, celebrates the glory of creative destruction and the transfer of power, the moment of exhilaration that is followed by the recognition that power requires responsibility. Amis, in his brief poem "After Goliath," considers the moment of David's triumph over Goliath. With the cheers ringing in his ears, the young king-in-waiting senses that this victory, which is a prelude to his ascending the throne, is not altogether his work. It is "too good to be true." He knows that the hand of God lies on him as the "first shot out of the sling" finishes off the champion of the Pharisees. He also feels suspicious that the applause sounds "shrill and excessive" as he looks at the pack of followers and sycophants who will become his followers. The example of the fallen giant, Goliath, with his broken sword, reminds him that such adulation is temporary, and that he has battles yet to fight. By making the poem's point-of-attack the moment after the battle instead of the dramatic build-up to it, Amis reminds us of the fleeting nature of glory and power. It also captures the sour taste of success, the disillusionment that creeps into the mind of the victor as he views with increasing cynicism the turncoat cliques now cheering him instead of the vanquished hero.

Among the saddest and most profound of the modern commentaries on power is Franz Kafka's novel *The Castle*. This bizarre story tells of a puzzled hero who tries to understand the country that he is visiting, where characters pop out of windows and streets lead nowhere. Telephone calls end with curious buzzing sounds or children's voices, never with useful information. The ruler and the nature of his rule remain a mystery. In a land of bureaucrats, where the complex lines of authority make every action an ordeal, and with laws so numerous and complex that no one is every quite within the law, Kafka's nightmare scenarios ring true. A haunting sense of guilt hangs like a cloud over the confused and lonely visitor. All he really wants is to understand the system, follow the proper path, and do his job.

Equally sinister and frightening are the dystopias produced by twentieth-century writers. Aldous Huxley presents a benign set of rulers in *Brave New World*, but his people are all programmed to accept their leadership and to follow their guidance without question. Free will is taken out of this neatly manicured world. Only among the "savages" is there any real freedom. More realistic and more brutal is George Orwell's view of what the world is becoming. First in *Animal Farm*, he points to the ironies of the Communist take-over of Russia, beginning with an idealistic vision of shared property and benevolent behavior, the animals on this farm (all of whom represent various parties in the Revolution), gradually fall under the brutal tyranny of the pigs. While the original motto was "All animals are equal," the edited version adds, "but some animals are more equal than others."

In *Nineteen Eighty-Four*, Orwell projects a world where Big Brother has surveillance cameras in all homes and offices, utilizing the increasingly sophisticated technological and psychological devices available to governments. Stripped of privacy, the citizens are assigned tasks that give them no joy in their labor. Even their "love life" is programmed to rob them of romance. The rulers use perpetual warfare to justify this totalitarian control over its citizens, fermenting hate at regular, carefully orchestrated hate-rallies. In the debased language of this state, the wars are managed by the "Ministry of Love."

A prescient writer and shrewd judge of human malevolence, George Orwell paints a picture of a world we still see emerging, well beyond the date he set for its accomplishment. His world is stripped of history, transcendence, love, and worship. Its citizens know only the present moment. The people have no choices; they are pawns in the hands of the rulers, who are mostly faceless bureaucrats. Like the children in *Lord of the Flies*, William Golding's chilling myth of a society regressing into savagery, the characters in *Nineteen Eighty-Four* become limited, selfish, and only marginally human. In this case, they are dehumanized by the very state that should have been their servant. Instead, they are nothing more than slaves to the system they have created, serving at the pleasure of the government.

Conclusion

So many different kinds of government have emerged in the modern era that the average person is befuddled at their purposes and structure. The old days when God anointed a king to rule his people have long since disappeared. The British see their queen and her dysfunctional family as silly puppets in a soap opera, preserved for their appeal to American visitors. Many of the countries across the world have some form of democratic governance and have limited the power of leaders. Yet, even the democracies all too frequently have only one election ever; they place a "democratically elected" despot in power for life. Many others have military leaders who use revolutions to grab the reins of government, powerful despots who control with or without reference to any God-given authority., Some believe that the god who gave them the authority is named *Allah*, and the law under which they should live is *sharia*.

Since the nineteenth century, numerous utopian dreams have flourished briefly and crashed. Experiments in socialism and communism have come and gone without destroying the eternal hope that such systems might somehow work. Kings have been overthrown, revolutions have replaced one form of tyranny with another. Even the constitutional democracies seem confused and without direction, subject to the same perversions of power that turned the Promised Land into a site of turmoil and corruption.

The rise of Nazi Germany, in the midst of a cultured and sophisticated people frightened many modern writers, calling into doubt the survival of Western civilization. Nor have those in the Eastern nations fared any better. If the Chinese, with their ancient culture, can submit to the brutal stifling of human liberty; or if the Russians, with their long tradition of Orthodox Christianity, could allow the slaughter of millions of their own citizens, how can we proclaim that humans are basically good or that power need not corrupt rulers? All over the world, totalitarian states have risen, subordinating and dehumanizing suffering people.

The old prophet Samuel, in his sage advice to the people of Israel, demonstrated the perils of naming a king and endowing him with the power to enslave his own people. He understood the doctrine of total depravity. He knew that Israel wanted a king, largely because their neighbors had kings, but he also knew that only God deserved to be king of his people.

The arguments about power on earth continue from biblical times: What form of government, if any, does God bless? Is the covenant formed between the ruler and the people binding? What is the obligation of the citizen to obey an unjust government that rules without his or her consent? What is the proper way to rid a country of a corrupt or unjust ruler? Should the religious person respect a secular government? Should government be controlled by a single religious group? Are humans able to live in a society without some controlling authority?

A few rulers in scripture and in history since biblical times have accepted leadership as a form of stewardship, considering their temporary guardianship a covenant between the leader and the consenting citizens. Some have been able to maintain a decent respect for the law and remember that they are only humans, that they will be in power only for the moment. Such humility among the great is rare in this fallen world.

See also: **Good People; The Hero; Justice; War.**

Bibliography

Bowen, Catherine Drinker. *Miracle at Philadelphia: The Story of the Constitutional Convention, May to September, 1787.* Boston: Little, Brown, 1986.

Burke, Edmund. *Reflections on the Revolution in France.* New Haven: Yale University Press, 2003.

Conrad, Joseph. *The Secret Agent.* New York: Modern Library, 1998.

De Toqueville, Alex. *Democracy in America.* Chicago: University of Chicago Press, 2000.

Dickens, Charles. *A Tale of Two Cities.* New York: Barnes and Noble Classics, 2003.

Dostoyevsky, Fyodor. *The Brothers Karamazov.* Trans., Constance Garnett. New York: Barnes & Noble, 1995.

———. *The Possessed.* Trans., Andrew R. MacAndrew. New York: New American Library, 1980.

Godwin, William. *The Anarchist Writings of William Godwin.* London: Freedom Press, 1986.

Heilbroner, Robert L. *The Worldly Philosophers: The Lives, Times, and Ideas of the Great Economic Thinkers.* New York: Simon and Schuster, 1999.

Hobbes, Thomas. *Leviathan.* London and New York: Dutton, 1973.

Kafka, Franz. *The Castle.* New York: Knopf, 1964.

Locke, John. *Two Treatises on Government.* London: Cambridge University Press, 1970.

Machiavelli. *The Prince.* In *Three Renaissance Classics.* New York: Charles Scribner's Sons, 1953.

Mill, John Stuart. *The Basic Writings of John Stuart Mill: On Liberty, The Subjection of Women, and Utilitarianism.* New York: Modern Library, 2002.

More, Thomas. *Utopia.* In *Three Renaissance Classics.* New York: Charles Scribner's Sons, 1953.

Muggeridge, Malcolm. *Jesus Rediscovered.* Garden City, NY: Doubleday and Company, 1969.

Orwell, George. *Nineteen Eighty-Four: A Novel.* New York: Plume, 2003.

Plato. *The Republic and Other Works.* Trans., B. Jowett. New York: Anchor Books, 1989.

Rousseau, Jean Jacques. *The Social Contract.* Baltimore, MD: Penguin Classics, 1978.

Shakespeare, William. *Henry IV, Macbeth,* and *Richard II.* In *Shakespeare: Major Plays and the Sonnets,* ed. G. B. Harrison. New York: Harcourt, Brace and Company, 1948.

Smith, Adam. *An Inquiry into the Nature and Causes of the Wealth of Nations.* Chicago: Encyclopaedia Britannica, 1952.

Swift, Jonathan. *Gulliver's Travels.* New York: Barnes & Noble, 2003.

Wordsworth, William. "London, 1802." In *British Poetry and Prose,* vol. II, ed. Paul Lieder, Robert Morss Lovett, and Robert Kilburn Root, eds Boston: Houghton Mifflin, 1950.

Yeats, W. B. "The Second Coming." In *The Collected Poems of W. B. Yeats.* New York: The Macmillan Company, 1959.

Predestination and Free Will

Readings

Genesis
Jonah
Acts
Aeschylus, *Prometheus Bound* (c. 479–478 B.C.)
Sophocles, *Oedipus Rex* (420 B.C.)
William Shakespeare, *Macbeth* (1606)
Christopher Marlowe, *The Tragical History of Dr. Faustus* (1592)
Daniel Defoe, *Robinson Crusoe* (1719)
Fyodor Dostoyevsky, *The Possessed* (1872)
Edward Fitzgerald "The Rubáiyát of Omar Khayyám" (1859)
Francis Thompson, "The Hound of Heaven" (1893)
William Ernest Henley, "Invictus" (1875)
Thomas Hardy, *Tess of the d'Urbervilles* (1895)
Enrique Lihn, "Jonah" (1969)
Wolf Mankowitz, "It Should Happen to a Dog" (1961)

Introduction

> Let us run with patience the race that is set before us, looking unto Jesus the
> author and finisher of our faith. (Hebrews 12:1–2)

We run a race for the prize of immortal life, on a course set out before us, choosing
to be patient to the end or to quit and take another, easier path. Such is the imagery in
this passage of Hebrews, which captures the dual nature of life: plotted by God from
eternity, yet chosen by each person one moment at a time. We have plenty of choices
to make along the way, but God has the master plan. This is the dichotomy of free
will and predestination.

Fate, luck, fortune, necessity, predestination, foreknowledge, providence—our language is full of words that point to a grand design in human life over which the individual has little or no control. Whether random chance, Lady Luck, a mechanical wheel of fortune, a blind force leading even the gods, or a wise deity ordaining human activity, humans have sensed from early in history that their free will is sorely limited. We are dealt a hand at birth: born in a certain year in a certain country to a certain family; healthy or challenged, talented or limited; each of us will have so many years on earth to go from birth to death. The task is to determine how we will play the hand we are dealt.

Many poets and playwrights have sensed the approaching footsteps of doom and have provided strong foreshadowing in their stories to warn us that we should not celebrate the hero's triumph too enthusiastically on the eve of his greatest triumph. All glory may turn to dust the next day. As the Scots poet Robert Burns expresses it, when he turns up a mouse's nest with his plow and sees the "wee-bit housie" that should have sheltered the rodent family for the winter reduced to rubble: "The best-laid schemes o' mice an' men / Gang aft agley" (Burns, "To a Mouse," 1006).

Scripture

Isaiah uses the image of the pot and the potter for the relationship of humans to God: "But now, O Lord, thou art our father; we are the clay, and thou our potter; and we are all the work of thy hand" (Isa. 64:8). It is a standard symbol in scripture, which plays with the words of Genesis 2:7: "And the Lord God formed man of the dust of the ground, and breathed into his nostrils the breath of life; and man became a living soul." The difference between the potter-pottery imagery and the Genesis quotation is striking: for the Creator in Genesis, the human is not an inanimate pot, but a living soul, with the freedom to obey or disobey his Creator's commands. The pot is a passive creation, with flaws that are the fault of the Creator himself. Adam and Eve are hardly passive creations.

The following verses in Genesis make clear that this living soul has the freedom to choose: "Of every tree of the garden thou mayest freely eat; But of the tree of the knowledge of good and evil, thou shalt not eat of it" (Gen. 2:17). The man and woman are free to eat, but will suffer the consequences. This is the first example of free will.

The questions that arise from this scene are multiple: Did God create Adam flawed so that he would disobey? Since he must have known that Adam would choose unwisely, why did he give his creature such a choice? Why did God allow the snake to live in the Garden of Eden with his precious humans? Shortly after the Temptation and Fall, God foretells the history of the human race; did God himself plan for humans to fall? Was it predestined?

Many theologians have speculated over such questions through the centuries, sometimes concluding that, because the God of the scripture is all-knowing, he naturally knows the future, foreseeing all events even to the end of time. Because he is all-powerful, he also controls these events, allowing floods and droughts, playing a role in the birth of children and the death of heroes, choosing whom he will bless and whom he will curse. And yet, because he is a God of love who seeks the free response of his creatures to come to him in love, he has given humans the gift of free will. Even in the moment of the Fall, God certainly knew the plan of redemption and the design that would place his only begotten son on a cross to suffer for the sins of humanity. From the beginning of time, he knew how this created world would end.

God's power and foresight are clear in the Creation story. Nothing about Creation suggests chance. God is portrayed as the author, creator, sustainer, and judge of humankind, who planned the whole universe from before time. The very frequency of dreams, visions, signs, omens, and prophesies all through scripture indicates that God sometimes allows humans a glimpse of his great plan. Jacob, for example, on his deathbed, predicts with great precision the destiny of each of his sons and their tribes (Gen. 49).

The grand design is only occasionally visible to the actors in the Bible's drama. Joseph's brothers, for instance, when they sell him into slavery, set in action a series of events that ends with the whole family migrating to Egypt, where they beg Joseph (now vizier of the Pharaoh) for food and protection. When he reveals his identity to them, they try to excuse their own iniquity, pretending they meant only the best. Joseph, however, sets the record straight by explaining that they meant it for evil, but God has used it for good: "You intended to harm me, but God intended it for good to accomplish what is now being done, the saving of many lives"(Gen. 50:21, NIV). God, having the foreknowledge of degenerate human choices and actions, can use even human transgressions to work his larger purposes. He can interfere by means of Providence, bringing to fruition those things he has planned.

The whole epic of Israel is based on the concept of predestination: God chooses Abraham and his seed to be his chosen people. This blessing also proves a burden for these children of the covenant, who see their faith as central to their lives. Chaim Potock captures this anguish of unique fate in his fine novel *The Chosen* (1967), a twentieth-century story about a Hasidic boy obsessed by his sense of being chosen, having a path predetermined for him. It is clear that God chooses leaders out of each generation out of his own inscrutable will. He does not follow any logical pattern of the first-born, but sometimes selects the younger twin or the dreamer to be the special bearer of his blessing. Jacob and Joseph find their lives dominated by their awareness of God's role in their lives. So do Moses and Joshua and any number of the judges and kings.

The survival of the Jews is one of the most amazing stories in all of history. Hundreds of peoples and empires have come and gone, most of them larger and more impressive than Israel, yet (as Walker Percy has noted) there are no Hittites in New York City. This people, blessed, tutored, and preserved by God, are testimony to God's hand in history.

Certainly the prophets built their prophesies on the understanding of God's foreknowledge of events, and their hope on the expectation of God's judgment on their enemies. The Psalms constantly note the strong hand of God in determining the victories that the Israelites have won and the defeats they have suffered. The psalmist also notes that God knows each human being, even from his life in the womb. Before his birth, each human exists in the mind of God, his life known in full (Ps. 39).

Behind such statements is the faith in a benevolent and thoughtful deity, designing each human from the very moment of creation, planning all our lives to the very end of time. Not every prophet in scripture portrays God's plan in quite so benign a manner. Many of the Old Testament prophets see the judgment of God rolling down like mighty waters on the wicked of the earth. In some cases, they are gratified to contemplate such a turn of events and in no hurry to encourage their enemies to repent. Jonah, for example, is told to go and prophesy to Nineveh, a city he despises. God tells him that the citizens of that wicked city will face God's wrath unless they repent. This reluctant prophet is not particularly eager that these pagan Ninevites should avoid God's just wrath.

Poor old Jonah finds that he can not escape God's will, even by sailing in the wrong direction. The comic treatment of this tale in Wolf Mankowitz's "It Should

Happen to a Dog"(1961) is fairly close to the biblical narrative. God's display of mercy contradicts Jonah's own preferred outcome for this despicable folk. Mankowitz characterizes Jonah as a traveling salesman, who represents "Top Hat; Braces For The Trousers" and other "good brands," samples of which he carries in his briefcase. In this modern version of the Jonas parable, the anti-hero realizes that God "knew right from the start exactly what He is going to do about everything," evidence once again of God's clear foreknowledge of human activity—including their choices.

Jonah's smug tone is echoed by a modern bureaucrat in Enrique Lihn's poem, which uses the form of a dramatic monologue to speak the despair of a modern "clown of heaven." Bearing kinship to Jonah in his old age, he mentions his "incendiary briefcase under the sweaty armpit," seeing himself, like the prophet, as "an old tool of uncertain usefulness/ fallen at last into perfect disuse." He identifies with this prophet in his willingness to "damn all things equally." By the end of the poem, he both wonders about "the hand of the lord whose name I don't remember" and prays for his grace.

Jonah is finally forced to understand God's grace, provided to him as well as to the dwellers in the despised city. This mercy is symbolized by Jonah's gourd vine, which shades him one day and then shrivels and dies the next. The prophet mourns the vine as he is unable to mourn the people. God shows the prophet that He is not subject to human whims and preferences. God's will is absolute—and more gracious than sinful humans have any right to expect.

The New Testament is even clearer on God's hand in human history. The Gospel of John begins with a re-phrasing of Genesis, placing Christ at the Creation, and showing that the whole of the vast sweep of events has been planned by God, who chooses to make the Word flesh. Jesus foretells the events of his own life and death, propheses about the fall of Jerusalem, and the destruction of the Temple. He knows how his followers will be persecuted. He even foresees the end of the world, the Last Judgment.

The last days of his life provide interesting evidence of his understanding of his role in the drama of redemption. For example, in the Gospel account of Judas's treachery, we see that Jesus knows what the disciple is planning (Matt. 26:2). It is even possible that he knew this would be the outcome at the moment he called him to be a disciple. At the Last Supper, the dialogue is clear: Jesus expects the betrayal. He then cites the prophetic words of Isaiah (53) and Daniel (9:26): "The Son of man goeth as it is written of him; but woe unto that man by whom the Son of man is betrayed! it had been good for that man if he had not been born" (Matt. 26:24). Although the action was planned from the beginning of time and is necessary for the great act of God to be completed, Judas's free choice is nonetheless damnable.

In the prayer Jesus prays in the Garden of Gethsemane, he notes that he has lost only one of his disciples, "the son of perdition; that the scripture might be fulfilled" (John 17:12). Curiously, in the recently rediscovered Gnostic *Gospel of Judas*, the story is turned upside down. In this spurious account, Judas is reluctant to become the betrayer but is encouraged by Jesus, who conspires in his own death. Judas, in this case, becomes the hero rather than the villain!

Actually, the prayer scene in the Garden of Gethsemane, which comes between the Last Supper and the kiss of betrayal, is a good example of the double nature of determinism. Jesus knows God's plans for his death, but hesitates, asking that "this cup be taken from me." Finally, accepting that his sacrifice is essential, he bows to God's will, with the telling words, "Nevertheless, not as I will, but as thou wilt" (Matt. 26:39). It is clear in numerous foreshadowings throughout the Gospels that Jesus knows he is God's Son, predestined to die as a sacrificial offering for the sins of the world, and to be raised again. In the end, he bows his head, as Isaiah prophesied, and goes like a lamb to the slaughter. In this free acceptance of God's plan, he models for humankind the joyful marriage of predestination and free will.

Christ's enthusiastic convert, the apostle Paul, becomes the preacher of predestination and the defender of the doctrine. In his epistle to the Romans, he explains:

> And we know that all things work together for good to them that love God, to them who are the called according to his purpose.
>
> For whom he did foreknow, he also did predestinate to be conformed to the image of his Son, that he might be the first-born among many brethren.
>
> Moreover whom he did predestinate, them he also called: and whom he called, them he also justified: and whom he justified, them he also glorified.
>
> What shall we then say to these things? If God be for us, who can be against us?
>
> He that spareth not his own Son, but delivered him up for us all, how shall he not with him also freely give us all things?...
>
> Who shall separate us from the love of Christ? shall tribulation, or distress, or persecution, or famine, or nakedness, or peril, or sword?...
>
> Nay, in all these things we are more than conquerors through him that loved us.
>
> For I am persuaded, that neither death, nor life, nor angels, nor principalities, nor powers, nor things present, nor things to come,
>
> Nor height, nor depth, nor any other creature, shall be able to separate us from the love of God, which is in Christ Jesus our Lord. (Rom. 8:28–38)

A parallel message opens his letter to the Ephesians, where he notes that these are people whom God has chosen "before the foundation of the world, that we should be holy and without blame before him in love: Having predestinated us unto the adoption of children by Jesus Christ to himself, according to the good pleasure of his will" (Eph. 1:4–5). Paul's strong sense of God's hand in history and in the individual lives of his chosen people led him to use such phrasing repeatedly in his letters. He believes that the Elect are empowered to know and do the will of God, and in this find their blessedness.

In Christian thought, this concept of "election" of those predestined from the beginning of the world, continued among the Christian believers. St. Augustine had much the same experience as St. Paul, struggling against God until he was converted, when he finally acknowledged that "His will is our peace." In *The Confessions of St. Augustine*, the erstwhile pagan comes to a saving experience of God's grace in spite of himself.

Augustine, a North African scholar, tried the path of the intellect, relished the indulgence of the flesh, and lived a free-wheeling pagan life until God forced him to his knees. In this powerful autobiography of one of Christendom's earliest and greatest saints, we see that it was all God's doing, using Augustine's loving mother as His intercessor and the means to bring about his conversion experience.

Among the Reformers, both Calvin and Luther emphasize the doctrine of predestination, believing it to be essential to the understanding of the awesome power of God. In doing so, both minimize the element of free will, which the Armenians thought to be equally important.

In Literature

Even the Greek gods were subject to "Necessity." In Aeschylus's powerful play about the punishment of the Fire-Bringer, *Prometheus Bound*, Zeus is trying to discover his own fate. He is a powerful god, but not an omniscient one. It is Prometheus, whose name means "forethought," who has the knowledge of his destiny. Just as

Zeus has cast his own father into Tartarus, so he also expects to lose his power over time. Only Zeus, of all the Olympian gods, has some freedom, but only for the time being. The three fates, usually presented as women, were thought to spin out human destiny, weave out the pattern of life, and cut the tread at death. The *Moirae*, the three sister goddesses, were thought to be daughters of the Night: Clotho was the Spinner, Lachesis the Allotter, and Atropos the one who cut the thread, the symbol of Death. The *Theogony* (Hesiod's narrative of the generations of the gods) shows gods, like men and women, being born, attaining maturity and authority, being overtaken and destroyed by younger, stronger gods. Necessity, who is stronger than any of the gods, will eventually set Prometheus free and curse Zeus.

The humans obviously have almost no control over their own lives, though they might have the choice of Achilles—a short, glorious life, or a long dreary one. Oedipus, who seeks to escape his own fate, ends by fulfilling it. He nonetheless accepts the guilt for killing his father and marrying his mother, with whom he had children. Oedipus's desire to avoid this hideous prediction seems to the modern a thoroughly honorable choice. It is hard to see why he would be held responsible for his own ignorance of his parentage. In Sophocles's *Oedipus Rex*, the fearful recognition scene and the subsequent horrifying act of self-mutilation are among the most moving in any drama. The message of the drama appears to be that no human can escape his fate. Apparently, it is an act of *hubris* (pride) to challenge destiny.

Greek philosophers found some small comfort in materialistic determinism. By the fifth century B.C., atomists, Epicureans and others saw the universe as nothing more than atoms and space. The poetic interpretation of this dry philosophy in Lucretius's *On the Nature of Things* (175 B.C.) strips all nobility from life or death. The Roman writer Lucretius, having described the whole system of the universe as nothing but matter and space, with some movement, elects the Stoic solution to view the drama of life from a distance and cultivate equanimity in the face of determinism. For him, fate is not a god but an inevitable process.

Ironically, Lucretius uses elevated language and epic form to produce his materialistic poem. He tracks the evolution of all living creatures, describes landscapes with all the flora in lavish details, and comes finally to the question of the nature of the human being. He denies the spirit in people, insisting that even the mind is nothing more than atoms. Nothing but the atoms are immortal. This he finds comforting:

> If the future holds travail and anguish in store, the self must be in existence, when the time comes, in order to experience it. But from this fate we are redeemed by death, which denies existence to the self that might have suffered these tribulations. Rest assured, therefore, that we have nothing to fear in death. One who no longer is cannot suffer, or differ any way from one who has never been born, when once this mortal life has been usurped by death the immortal. (Lucretius, "Life and Mind," Book III)

By the Middle Ages, the Wheel of Fortune had become a powerful symbol of Fate. Lady Luck or Dame Fortune turned her wheel so that the great men rose and fell, regardless of their merit. Chaucer's "Monk's Tale," for example, is a catalogue of examples of men who have "fallen out of high degree." There are tragedies from Boccaccio, Greek, Roman, and Spanish history, and mythology here—a lengthy and boring list of lost causes.

Shakespeare uses this popular concept in his history plays and some of his tragedies, which are based on the idea that the man who rises to earthly glory is doomed to a tragic fall. One of the most fate-obsessed of Shakespeare's tragedies is *Macbeth*. The play opens with three witches gathered around a pot of magic brew on the barren heath of Scotland. Macbeth addresses these "weird sisters," in an echo of the Anglo-Saxon word *wyrd* for Fate. They flatter him with the promise that he will be thane of Glamis, thane of Cawdor, and "king hereafter." In the rapid, but partial fulfillment of this prophesy, Macbeth is lured into making sure the rest of it comes true. In doing so, he sells his soul to the devil, bringing death to those around him, and finally to himself.

Unlike Oedipus, Macbeth embraces this prophesy and plans to nudge fate along. The rise to power is followed quickly by his fall into suspicion, increased cruelty, and violence. In the early part of this rising wheel of Fortune, his wife is a willing partner. Hectate, the Queen of Evil joins with the three witches, who again use Macbeth's limited understanding to trick him into making the wrong choices. They show him three apparitions, each of which becomes a reality in an unexpected way. As the wheel turns, Macbeth faces the personal tragedies of his beloved wife's madness and death, the invasion by his enemies' forces, and finally his own death at the hands of an avenger's sword.

None of this is particularly religious. It tends to rely on a belief in the reality of fate, of witchcraft, and of ghosts and apparitions. The demonic world is fully in charge during much of the drama. The haunting force of the sins that Macbeth and his wife commit does speak of a faith orientation. The events are all foreknown to the witches, who use this understanding to trap Macbeth into a tragic misuse of his free will. His unrepentant death, after having killed (among others) an anointed king who is a guest in his home, points to his eternal damnation. Shakespeare, however, leaves the story to the readers' imagination to determine the theology, giving only glancing references to his hero's damnation. Macduff makes this explicit in these words to the would-be king, when describing Macbeth:

> Not in all the legions
> Of horrid Hell can come a devil more damned
> In evils to top Macbeth.

> (Shakespeare, *Macbeth*, IV, iii)

Viewing Malcolm as God's chosen king, Macduff finally offers to him the "usurper's cursèd head," noting that the threat is over from this "dead butcher and his fiendlike Queen." The final scene ends with a invitation to the coronation by the "grace of Grace." In Shakespeare's world, God, not Fate, Fortune, or Wyrd is still in control.

In the famous drama of damnation, Christopher Marlowe's *The Tragical History of Dr. Faustus*, the doctor chooses to trade his soul for indulgence and knowledge, assuring that Faustus will be taken off to Hell. This is clearly an act of free will, sealed by a pact signed in his blood. The debates between his good and evil angels are useless: he has said, "This night I'll conjure though I die therefore" (Act I, i). With Mephistophiles catering to his every whim, he lives out his promised 24 years, making his own appetites his god. Although he remembers the thief on the cross who repents in his last moments on earth, Faustus himself never truly repents. As he acknowledges, "My heart's so hard'ned I cannot repent" (III, ii). For this reason, with his own complicity, he dies with the full knowledge of his own iniquities. At the very end, he offers to burn his books, but it is too late. The Chorus enters to proclaim:

> Faustus is gone; regard his hellish fall,
> Whose fiendful fortune may exhort the wise

Only to wonder at unlawful things,
Whose deepness doth entice such forward wits
To practice more than heavenly power permits.

(Marlowe, *Doctor Faustus*, III, v)

He has chosen what God has foreordained.

The Protestant Reformation, especially in England, provided authors with abundant theological materials for their writing. Among the poets and playwrights of the period, the interplay of predestination and free will figured large. John Donne, one of the most brilliant of the seventeenth-century British Metaphysical poets, struggled with his conversion from Catholicism to the Anglican Church. He also struggled privately with his love of pleasure and his sense of guilt. He eventually found that he was free only when he surrendered to God. This colorful young man, a robust lover and a man-about-town, found his world turned upside down by his great love of the woman he married and his conversion to a deep and personal faith in Christ. As a clergyman, he became a popular preacher, while continuing writing his startling lyrics and meditations. His *Holy Sonnets* are powerful and beautifully crafted expressions of his surrender to a God he could no longer resist.

In the poem "Batter my heart, three-personed God," he compares himself to a tower being held by the Enemy. He also describes his reason as a captive maiden betrothed to this same Enemy. He cannot win freedom by himself, but needs God's providential intervention to take him to his bosom:

Divorce me, untie or break that know again;
Take me to you, imprison me, for I
Except you enthrall me, never shall be free,
Nor ever chaste, except you ravish me.

(Donne, *Holy Sonnets*, XIV)

The paradoxes he employs in these lines, as well as his intense, even sexual response to the god he loves and yet betrays are typical of Metaphysical poetry. They are also excellent poetic expressions of the tug-of-war in human souls as they seek God's will, yet prefer their own.

Another seventeenth-century Metaphysical poet, the gentle Anglican pastor named George Herbert, expresses his rebellion in less intense dialogues with God. For example, in "The Collar" (1633), we find the clerical collar has become a kind of dog collar, forcing the clergyman to obey God rather than enjoy his freedom. It is an implied story of rebellion and return, told in three simple stanzas. The angry opening: "I struck the board, and cried, 'No more.'" has some of the flavor of St. Augustine's rebellion, but without the ferocity of this passionate saint. Herbert simply argues against God's control until a loving Father admonishes, "My child," and the repentant rebel responds, "My Lord."

More like average people who wonder why they have been chosen to serve God, Herbert captures the age-old quarrel of the reluctant saint: "Why me?" God's determination to choose, to love, and to persevere in His choice becomes clear in this brief poem. For Herbert, as for Augustine, God's demands are softened by His grace. The sinner's response and submission to God's will is a gesture of free will after all.

The novel, which became increasingly popular in the seventeenth and eighteenth centuries, proved a perfect vehicle for describing this eternal struggle between God's providence and human will. The early novels were largely episodic, a series of adventures of one hero or heroine, woven loosely together to form a longer narrative. Providence proved a useful device for unifying the plot and providing it a coherent theme. Even wild coincidences could be easily explained if the plot is shaped, not by the author, but by God or some other extra-terrestrial force. Audiences who read for pleasure as well as for uplift came to expect happy and just endings, with the good folks rewarded and the evil ones punished. They also liked to see the conversion of the loveable rogue in the course of the narrative so that he or she could also enjoy the general happiness of the final pages.

Daniel Defoe, one of the earliest novelists, a talented if unschooled eighteenth-century middle-class tradesman, understood his audience. Coming from a religious background of the evangelical Dissenters, who rejected both Roman Catholicism and the Church of England, he suffused his stories with religious meaning. Although some critics have sneered at his easy blend of piety and middle-class materialism, he does seem sincere in his commitment to his faith. In his preface to *Robinson Crusoe*, he explains his motives in writing the narrative of the shipwreck: "The story is told with modesty, with seriousness, and with a religious application of events to the uses to which wise men always apply them (viz.) to the instruction of others by this example, and to justify and honor the wisdom of Providence in all the variety of our circumstances, let them happen how they will."

Although Robin begins as a rebellious son, intent on sea adventures, he soon finds himself in the midst of adventures that change him into a sober and reflective man of God. When he is first shipwrecked, he quarrels with God about this special determinism in his own life. After regular reading of scripture and meditating on his circumstances, he comes to accept God's providence and thanks him for each day's blessings. He is such a changed character by the end of the book that he is able to school his man Friday in theology. He explains to this savage the difference between his God and Friday's gods, and turns him into a true believer.

Most readers found the story exciting for the adventures and for Robin's creative and industrious means of survival for over two decades on a desert island, but underlying the plot is the constant awareness of God's providence, sustaining this poor abandoned sinner until he is totally transformed. Compared to other shipwreck stories, like *Swiss Family Robinson* or *Lord of the Flies*, where the characters either remain at the same level or deteriorate, *Robinson Crusoe* emerges as a serious consideration of God at work in one rebellious soul.

The Victorian era, a time of considerable religious turmoil, when the nature and power of God were under radical reconsideration, produced a number of thoughtful novels and poems about fate. The adaptation of classical Greek thinking appears to be at the heart of Thomas Hardy's novels, where the tragedy of the central figure produces a dark sense of fatalism. This is clear in most of his novels, particularly in *The Mayor of Casterbridge*, *Jude the Obscure*, and *Tess of the d'Urbervilles*.

Hardy, a popular turn of the century English writer of poetry and novels, frequently makes his helpless creatures innocent sufferers in the hands of malevolent gods. Hardy sees a mindless force in charge of the world similar in form to the old Greek concept of Fate, which selected for no apparent reason an unknowing man like Oedipus or Agamemnon to play (as Shakespeare said in *King Lear*) with as cruel children toy with flies, for their sport. Fate seems intent on destroying the nonconformist hero, one who appears to be a challenge to the gods. Hardy was quite explicit in his preference of "Hellenic Paganism" over Christianity. At the end of Tess's life, he even includes the altar stone at Stonehenge to give the ritual sacrifice of this beautiful "innocent," an archaic beauty. The final lines of the story, which follow the arrest and execution of

Tess for the murder of her tormentor, are rich with fatalism: "'Justice' was done, and the President of the Immortals, in Aeschylean phrase, had ended his sport with Tess."

Robert Burns, a free spirit usually at odds with the orthodox Presbyterian community in his native Scotland, found a way to laugh at the stern elders and their interpretation of the doctrine of predestination. His "Holy Willie's Prayer" (1799) is a comic monologue, a mock prayer by a hypocritical member of the "elect." Delighted that God has foreordained him for salvation, Willie is even more gratified that God has damned others. In his prayer, he takes it upon himself to suggest to God that he add a few people to his enemies list.

The poem is written in Burns' Scots dialect, with the quick lines and heavy rhyme suitable for comic stanzas:

> O Thou that in the Heavens does dwell,
> Wha, as it pleases best Thysel,
> Sends ane to Haven an' ten to Hell
>   A' for Thy glory
> And no for onie guid or ill
>   They've done before Thee!
> I bless and praise Thy matchless might,
> When thousands Thou hast left in night,
> That I am here before Thy sight,
>   For gifts an' grace
> A burning and a shining light
>   To a' this place.

The poem continues for 16 stanzas of blessing and cursing, making a mockery of the concept of the elect and of the notion that faith alone justifies the Christian. He cries for vengeance on one member of the congregation after another, including Burns' friend Hamilton:

> Lord, mind Gau'n Hamilton's deserts:
> He drinks, an' swears, an' plays at cartes,
> Yet has sae monie takin arts
>   Wi' great and sma',
> For God's ain priest the people's hearts he steal awa.

In fact, Willie calls down damnation against the entire Presbytery of Ayre, ending with his gratitude that he can look forward to the final day of vengeance, then humbly concluding:

> But, Lord, remember me and mine
> Wi' mercies temporal and divine,
> That I for grace an' fear may shine
>   Excell'd by nane;
> And a' the glory shall be Thine—
>   Amen, Amen!

(Burns, "Holy Willie's Prayer," 1006)

This new skepticism was not limited to rebels in Scotland. It permeated Victorian England. Edward Fitzgerald, for example, fell in love with Persian poetry, especially the work of the twelfth-century iconoclastic poet Omar Khayyám, who seemed to be a kindred spirit. He translated the elegant verses that reflect a love of earthly delights, an awareness of mortality, and a disdain for any god that would presume to judge humans. Set in the Middle East, "The Rubáiyát [or quatrains] of Omar Khayyám" has an exotic quality, with references to the Muslim faith and worship.

The poet asks of God why he put the temptation in the Garden of Eden, blaming God for man's sin:

> O Thou, who Man of baser Earth didst make,
> And ev'n with Paradise devise the Snake:
>   For all the Sin wherewith the Face of Man
> Is blacken'd—Man's forgiveness give—and take!

The light tone of the verses belies the fact that he is charging God with causing the Fall of man. In another verse, he employs the biblical image of the potter and the clay for the Creator and the created. A fellow "pot" speaks out, noting that the pot is not at fault if the potter has failed to make it properly. The hand of the Great Potter is the key to man's sinful nature. One of the loquacious pots insists that it has no fear of the afterlife or eternal damnation, concluding that God will not finally toss all his "luckless Pots he marr'd in making" into Hell. "Pish!" he proclaims, "He's a Good Fellow, and 'twill all be well." As for the poet, he seems to think the answer is to settle for the delights of the present moment:

> A Book of Verses underneath the Bough,
> A Jug of Wine, a Loaf of Bread—and Thou
>   Beside me singing in the Wilderness—
>
> (Khayyàm, "The Rubáiyát of Omar
> Khayyám," 903)

Earthly paradise, symbolized by wine, food, and love, here and now, is all he can count on having. Like a good Epicurean, he should enjoy every moment while he can.

Another Victorian went even further in the pursuit of free will and the rejection of either providence or judgment. In the famous poem "Invictus," William Ernest Henley, wrote one of the most famous and startling proclamations of human pride in British literature. Ironically, this poem is often treated as a courageous statement of heroism, with no thought of its challenge to God's power in human life:

> Out of the night that covers me,
> Black as the Pit from pole to pole,
> I thank whatever gods may be
> For my unconquerable soul.
>
> In the fell clutch of circumstance
> I have not winced nor cried aloud.
> Under the bludgeonings of chance
> My head is bloody, but unbowed.
>
> Beyond this place of wrath and tears
> Looms but the horror of the shade,
> And yet the menace of the years
> Finds, and shall find me, unafraid.

It matters not how strait the gate,
How charged with punishments the scroll,
I am the master of my fate:
I am the captain of my soul.

(Henley, "Invictus," 925)

In these four couplets, the author has reverted to the pantheon of Greek gods, the "shades" that the Greeks perceived in the afterlife, and has rejected both Jewish and Christian views of human history in the hands of a loving God. If he echoes any part of Judeo-Christian thought, it would be Satan's magnificent defiance of God as he proclaims, "I will not serve." It would seem that Milton's Satan, ruling in Hell, has become the modern folk hero, a kind of self-sufficient Ayn Rand figure (like the artist in *The Fountainhead*).

This is not to say that every Victorian and modern has rejected the concept of predestination. In at least one case, the poet felt that he could not deny the clear command of God to love him. Francis Thompson finally chooses to follow God's path, and relinquish his freedom. In his long poem, "The Hound of Heaven," he tells the world about his own spiritual experience as he fled God to no avail:

I fled Him, down the nights and down the days;
    I fled Him down the arches of the years;
I fled Him, down the labyrinthine ways
    Of my own mind; and in the midst of tears
I hid from Him, and under running laughter.

Finally, God speaks to him and shows him that he is seeking the very God that has been hounding him:

"Ah, fondest, blindest, weakest,
I am He Whom thou seekest!
Thou dravest love from thee, who dravest Me."

(Thompson, "The Hound of Heaven," 1073)

This poem presses the idea that God chooses those he predestines for salvation. Whether the chosen wishes to come to him or not, God will pursue and transform him or her. Many religious people believe that the human chooses to seek God, who welcomes the sinner. Just as God chose his people, the Israelites in the Old Testament and the Christians in the New Testament, so God continues to choose those whom he predestined from the beginning of time to be his own. Thompson sounds a lot like the apostle Paul. The God-haunted man, whether on the Road to Damascus or the path of life in nineteenth-century England, is a compelling topic for literature.

Conclusion

Moderns divide among these different points of view: some agree with Thompson and believe that God chases them down like the "Hound of Heaven." Others agree with Burns and laugh at the idea that God predestines anyone. Others agree with Fitzgerald and turn cynically to blame God for human problems, preferring to enjoy each day as it comes. Others take Henley's view of the autonomous self: humankind must make the most of life, take charge of their own lives, determine their own fate.

In Western civilization, where we have more freedom for more people than ever before in history, where class structure no longer serves as a permanent barrier to rising in the world, where kings and queens are considered quaint anachronisms, we are inclined to believe that we are self-made men and women, capable of leaping high buildings in a single bound. We are shocked to discover sometimes that we are limited by events out of our control—floods, earthquakes, tsunamis, hurricanes, droughts, wars, rebellions, atrocities, disease, and death.

See also: **The Hero; The Journey of Life; Justice; Slavery and Freedom; Women as Heroes.**

Bibliography

Aeschylus. *Prometheus Bound.* In *The Complete Greek Tragedies,* ed. David Grene and Richmond Lattimore. University of Chicago Press, 1959.

Augustine, St. *The Confessions.* Grand Rapids, MI: Baker Books, 2005.

Basinger, David, and Randal Basinger. *Predestination and Free Will: Four Views of Divine Sovereignty and Human Freedom.* Westmont, IL: InterVarsity Press, 1985.

Burns, Robert. "To a Mouse" and "Holy Willie's Prayer." In *British Poetry and Prose,* vol. I, ed. Paul Lieder, Robert Morss Lovett, and Robert Kilburn Root. Boston: Houghton Mifflin, 1950.

Calvin, John. *The Institutes of the Christian Religion.* Trans., Henry Beveridge. Grand Rapids, MI: William B. Eerdmans, 1990.

Creswell, Denis R. *St. Augustine's Dilemma: Grace and Eternal Law in the Major Works of Augustine of Hippo.* New York: Peter Lang, 1997.

Defoe, Daniel. *Robinson Crusoe.* New York: Aerie Books, 1988.

Donne, John. *Holy Sonnets.* In *British Poetry and Prose,* vol. I, ed. Paul Lieder, Robert Morss Lovett, and Robert Kilburn Root. Boston: Houghton Mifflin, 1950.

Dostoyevsky, Fyodor. *The Possessed.* Trans., Andrew R. MacAndrew. New York: New American Library, 1980.

Hardy, Thomas. *Tess of the d'Urbervilles.* New York: Barnes & Noble, 1993.

Henley, William Ernest. "Invictus." In *Victorian and Later English Poets,* ed. James Stephens, Edwin L. Beck, and Royall H. Snow. New York: American Book Company, 1949.

Herbert, George. "The Collar." In *British Poetry and Prose,* vol. I, ed. Paul Lieder, Robert Morss Lovett, and Robert Kilburn Root. Boston: Houghton Mifflin, 1950.

Kendal, James. "Fate," http.www.newadvent.org/cath/05793a.htm (accessed September 10, 2006).

Khayyám, Omar. "The Rubáiyát of Omar Khayyám." Trans., Edward FitzGerald. In *Victorian and Later English Poets,* ed. James Stephens, Edwin L. Beck, and Royall H. Snow. New York: American Book Company, 1949.

Lihn, Enrique. "Jonah." In *The Bible as/in Literature,* ed. James S. Ackerman and Thayer S. Warshaw. Glenview, IL: Scott, Foresman and Company, 1971.

Lucretius, *The Nature of the Universe.* Trans., R. E. Latham. London: Penguin Books, 1953.

Mankowitz, Wolf. "It Should Happen to a Dog." In *The Bible as/in Literature,* ed. James S. Ackerman and Thayer S. Warshaw. Glenview, IL: Scott, Foresman and Company, 1971.

Marlowe, Christopher. *The Tragical History of Doctor Faustus.* In *Typical Elizabethan Plays.* New York: Harper and Brothers Publishers, 1949.

Penny, D. Andrew. *Freewill or Predestination: The Battle over Saving Grace in Mid-Tudor England.* London: Royal Historical Society, 1990.

Potok, Chaim. *The Chosen: A Novel.* New York: Fawcett Columbine, 1996.

Shakespeare, William. *Macbeth.* In *Shakespeare: Major Plays and the Sonnets,* ed. G. B. Harrison. New York: Harcourt, Brace and Company, 1948.

Sophocles. *Oedipus Rex*. In *The Theban Plays*. Trans., E. F. Watling. Baltimore, MD: Penguin Books, 1946.

Thompson, Francis. "The Hound of Heaven." In *Victorian and Later English Poets*, ed. James Stephens, Edwin L. Beck, and Royall H. Snow. New York: American Book Company, 1949.

Zanchius, Jerome. *The Doctrine of Absolute Predestination*. Chateau, MT: Old Paths Gospel Press, n.d.

Truth

Readings

Introduction

> "To this end was I born, and for this cause came I into the world, that I should bear witness unto the truth. Every one that is of the truth heareth my voice."

> Pilate saith unto him, "What is truth?" (John 18:37–38)

Pilate did not bother to listen for an answer. His flippant response to Christ's great affirmation sounds like a postmodern question, as if no there is no such thing as the truth. For the Roman, there is one truth, for the Greek another, and for the Jew yet another. To claim a single truth seems ridiculous to this cynical bureaucrat.

Yet the question of truth is one of the oldest questions known to humankind. What is truth? How does one discover it? How can it be tested?

Lies, the opposite of truth, are as old as humankind. Sometimes the lie is a misunderstanding. Sometimes it is deliberate. Often it is inconsequential. On occasion, it is essential and fundamental to the choices we make and the way we travel.

Literature is usually based on colorful lies, pretty fictions that amuse but do not deceive. Coleridge said that the reader of books enters into a negotiation with the writer, in which he willingly suspends his disbelief (*Biographia Literaria,* 1817). Thoughtful people have acknowledged this harmless use of the human imagination, believing that fantasy is charming and may even contain a grain of truth deep inside. Even so-called realistic literature is not the same as reality. A reporting of an incident usually distorts the original incident, the motives of the people, and the causes. Anyone who has been the victim of news reports knows how quickly distortion enters the simplest story. The point of view is invariably different, the emphasis altered, details omitted. We all understand that even the most carefully written report is not the same as the event itself.

This entanglement of words and truth, with all the problems of exaggeration, twisting of meaning, and flat-out error, has led many in our era to deny the possibility of any reliable truth What was for the heroes of the Old Testament unchanging, rock-solid truth about the nature of God, humans, and history has become for postmoderns as wispy as the vapor trails left by airplanes in a blue sky on a windy day. Truth seems to exist only in the eye of the beholder, only for the moment. Today, it seems relative and evanescent.

Scripture

Jesus calls Satan the "Father of lies." In the guise of a serpent, the Devil certainly lies to Eve in the Garden of Eden. When Eve explains to him the rule forbidding her and Adam from eating of the tree in the midst of the garden, lest they should die, the serpent responds: "Ye shall not surely die. For God doth know that in the day ye eat thereof, then your eyes shall be opened, and ye shall be as gods, knowing good and evil" (Gen. 3:4–5).

In her paraphrase of God's law, Eve both subtracts from the truth (not mentioning that they might freely eat of all the other trees) and adds to it (saying they are not allowed to touch it). These misstatements make the serpent's statement partially true, for they will not die from touching the tree, only from eating the fruit. Rather than telling the truth, the whole truth and nothing but the truth, both actors in this drama are playing with words.

The serpent's promises regarding the consequences of eating the forbidden fruit are also duplicitous: the First Couple will know more, but the knowledge will come from their pain; their eyes will be opened to all of the world's evils, from which God has heretofore protected them. Telling a half-truth, emphasizing the forbidden knowledge, Satan's spokesman leads Adam and Eve into temptation and sin.

Lies in scripture are almost invariably evil: Judas gives Jesus a deceitful kiss; Cain pretends he is not the murderer of his brother; Potiphar's wife plans to lie about Joseph. Laban veils Leah when he tricks Jacob into taking her for his wife instead of the promised Rachael. Jacob distrusts his father-in-law and cheats him. Lies breed lies.

In the Old Testament, the concept of truth is not debatable. God speaks the truth, whether he speaks in a still, small voice or thunders out of a whirlwind. His Word is the ultimate truth, full of majesty and power. Rather than the petty little facts of everyday life, God tells humans the deep meaning of existence or forecasts the vast sweep of hisotry that lies ahead. God is to be trusted as is the Word of God. The experiences of Abraham, Isaac, Jacob, Joseph, and Moses, repeated to one generation after another, were believed to be true. It is true that God chose the children of Abraham, that he protected them and guided their lives.

Even though his chosen people were themselves not invariably committed to truth, God forgave them. When Abraham asks his beloved Sarah to lie about their relationship, he brings trouble on both of them and on their unwitting hosts. Attracted by Sarah's beauty and assuming that she is Abraham's sister, rulers on two occasions take her into their harems, only to be cursed for their actions. Only the truth clears the air and allows all involved to continue their lives in peace.

The revelation of Truth in the New Testament is quite direct. Jesus Christ comes into the world, lives out a life that fulfills God's enduring promise, and dies a death to confirm God's justice. He prophesies that he will rise from the grave on the third day and proves the truth of that prophesy. Rather than simply talking about Truth, he is the embodiment of the Truth and lives a life of truth.

He also says things about the nature of truth, and of falsehood, which leave vivid memories in the minds of his followers. In speaking to the Jews who turn against God's prophets and his Son, yet still claim to be Abraham's seed, he argues that their real father is the devil, not God: "Ye are of your father, the devil, and the lusts of your father ye will do. He was a murderer from the beginning, and bode not in the truth, because there is no truth in him. When he speaketh a lie, he speaketh of his own; for he is a liar, and the father of it. And because I tell you the truth, ye believe me not. Which of you convinceth me of sin? And if I saw the truth, why do ye not believe me?" He tells them that he is "the way, the truth, the life" (John 14:6) and speaks frequently of being or telling the truth. Notice, for example, how many of his statements open with "Verily, verily," a promise that the words to follow are true.

He encourages his followers to tell the truth. Going still further than the commandments, which forbids a person from swearing falsely against his neighbor or breaking oaths, he insists that all speech must be true: "Swear not at all, neither by heaven, for it is God's throne: Nor by the earth, for it is his footstool; neither by Jerusalem, for it is the city of the great King. Neither shalt thou swear by thy head, because thou canst not make one hair white or black. But let your communication be, Yea, yea; Nay, nay: for whatsoever is more than these cometh of evil" (Matt. 5:34–37). Swearing involves an oath that promises that the words to follow are truthful, and calls a curse down on the speaker if he or she lies. But the constant truth-teller has no need of such oaths, telling the plain truth without embellishment.

Such a stern admonition has left Christians with a severe aesthetic dilemma: How can the Christian justify eloquent teaching or embroidered language? How can the Christian traffic in lies by writing fiction? The Puritans of the sixteenth and seventeenth centuries were to return to this issue, sometimes stripping their speech and writing to its simplest forms. John Bunyan had particular problems in writing *Pilgrim's Progress*, which not only elaborates on the stories in scripture, but inserts mythical creatures to illustrate them. In his "Author's Apology for his Book," he points to the Bible's use of allegory and Jesus's love of parables. As he expresses it:

Solidity, indeed, becomes the pen
Of him that writeth things divine to men;
But must I needs want solidness because
By metaphors I speak? Were not God's laws,

His gospel laws, in olden times held forth
By types, shadows, and metaphors? …
My dark and cloudy words, they do but hold
The truth, as cabinets enclose the gold,
The prophets used much by metaphors
To set forth truth; yea, who considers
Christ, his apostles too, shall plainly see,
 That truths to this day in such mantles be.

(Bunyan, *The Pilgrim's Progress*, 1)

In the New Testament, with the Greeks debating the nature of Truth, philosophers analyzing the concept, and Romans content to accept all truths as equally valid, so long as they cause no civil discord, Pilate's frivolous question is right in style. Paul notes that the Greeks have "itching ears," seeking novelty rather than truth.

Doubting Thomas, apparently a materialist, has to establish truth of the Crucifixion by touching the wounds of his Lord. For Christianity, as for Judaism, the historical truth mattered in biblical times and continues to matter today. The historical reality of the ancestors, the detailed descriptions in prophesies of the Promised Land, the actual events in their lives are claims that demand belief.

Beyond this physical level of truth, the meaning behind these events also demand belief if the Jewish people are to base their lives on these words. They can not afford to doubt that God actually exists from eternity, that he has a plan for his people, whom he loves in spite of their constant backsliding, that he is in control of the universe he created. So also for the Christians, the claims of Jesus, the reality of his life, death, and resurrection from the dead are the rock on which their faith is built. If there is no truth in these events, there is no basis for belief. If God is not truth, then the rest of these faiths is but a tissue of lies.

Literature

Much of secular literature connects the make believe with the real world. In an attempt to discover the underlying truth behind superficial facts, data, and sense perceptions, writers rely on symbols, exaggeration, distortions, and fictions. As Bunyan acknowledged, the words are but a container for the truth, which must rely on the insightful reader to discern.

The Greeks puzzled about the nature of Truth more than did either the Jews or Christians. Their pantheon of gods with their conflicting claims and dubious morality laid open the charge that none of them were to be believed. Who would seek Truth from self-indulgent Zeus or petulant Hera? The Delphic Oracle, with her enigmatic sayings, might offer prophesies that would haunt the imagination. But she was hardly helpful in the daily search for a basis for belief.

It was the philosophers who explored the nature of reality, and of Truth in a deeper way, relying on human experience as much as on mystical insight. Some believed that only the material world and the testimony of the senses were to be trusted. Others insisted that man was the measure of all things. Plato sought to understand a level of reality that lies beyond our senses, that points to a truth that lies outside normal human experience.

Plato's Allegory of the Cave, which is part of his long dialogue known as *The Republic*, is a classic presentation of the nature of Truth. The speaker, as usual, is Socrates, who explains to his disciples that mankind is, for the most part, "unenlightened." Imagine, he proposes, that men live in a cavernous chamber, an underground cave. The entrance to the cave has light, but they have been chained with their backs to the light for all of their lives, with a fire behind them, casting up shadows on the wall in front of them. They are able to see only these shadows, not the fire or the sun. For such prisoners, the shadows become their reality. If one of them should be set free, stand up, turn around, and see the sources of the light and the meaning of the shadows, he would be dazzled. In this illumination, he would find it almost impossible to explain the reality he has now discovered to the poor benighted prisoners still chained to the wall, living in a world of shadows. If he should return to the dark cave, he would find himself temporarily blinded, stumbling about, unable to make out the familiar furniture of the cave. He would become the object of ridicule of his fellows. And if anyone should then propose to free the other prisoners and to allow them to see the light, they would see him as an enemy and would kill him.

In Plato's thought, this describes the difference between the simple people who live comfortably with shadows and the philosopher who dares to gaze on the light of knowledge. In the shadows, one may distinguish the approximate shape of things, but only in full light of understanding can one find the Truth—the ideal forms of Truth, Beauty, Justice.

Plato also disapproved of art, though he himself was a consummate literary artist. He considered stories or statues copies of the physical world, which was itself a copy of the ideal world. As a copy of a copy, a story is only superficially real, fixating human attention on the surface of things, distracting them from Ideal Truth.

This objection to art was to prove powerful for hundreds of years in the Christian Church. Although religious art was condoned by some factions of the Church, the writing of fiction was considered lying. Only reports of saints' lives and "history" was considered worthy of the Christian's attention. Nonetheless, folk tales abounded and the love of a good story never diminished, as we can see in the numerous ballads and romances.

Plato's view of the ideal world lying beyond the real one was to encourage medieval thinkers to believe that the world of physical things was only a shadow of reality. They thought that truth lay in the realm of the universal, the Ideal. This concept is more Greek than Hebrew or Christian. Both Christians and Jews have a solid faith in this world and its value as well as the immortal God and his legions.

Don Quixote (1616), a remarkable and very funny novel, satirizes the medieval world view as it is measured against Renaissance realism. In it Cervantes pits two concepts of reality against one another. For the hero, Don Quixote, only his idealistic visionary world is true. He has no faith in the evidence of his senses. An old, impoverished, gaunt idealist, he fixes on the idea that romantic adventures are still possible and necessary for faithful Christians. Since he *believes* himself to be a knight, he *is* one regardless of his ragtag appearance. His sad, swayback nag becomes his steed. He finds his so-called armor among the pots and pans of the household, claiming that these are proper accoutrements of the knight—because he would have them so.

By contrast, his sidekick Sancho Panza, lives fully in the physical world. His only brush with idealism is his foolish love of Don Quixote, whom he follows at his own peril. Like Doubting Thomas in the scripture, Sancho Panza is a materialist, who needs to test things by his senses. He learns from his own experience and determines what is true through this practical kind of realism. When the other guests at an inn where they are staying take the opportunity to play a trick with him and toss him in a blanket, he knows what they did. Don Quixote may speculate that demons were involved in the dastardly deed, but Sancho knows that he has been hurt. Physical reality is not enough for Don Quixote. Monsters and fair ladies make up his truth. A windmill becomes a giant, and a local farm girl becomes the princess of his dreams. To the workaday world, Don Quixote is a mad man. Yet Cervantes clearly loves and admires his hero, suggesting that all the so-called realists who snigger at him are blind to his truth—a love of ideals, of adventure, and of duty to his Lord.

The Renaissance revival of interest in scientific knowledge called all this old "Truth" into doubt. For centuries, the philosophers and churchmen thought they had understood the universe, with the earth at the center of it. They thought that they had found the truth of human governance in the Holy Roman Empire and truth of religious governance in the Roman Catholic Church, but Rome was dead and the Catholic Church was under attack by those who claimed it was teaching error.

John Donne, who converted from Catholicism to the Church of England, and who knew a number of the new scientists, lamented that the new science calls all in doubt. Another poet of the time, Thomas Nashe, is frequently quoted for another famous line that seems to sum up the loss of magic and mystery from the whole world of nature with the new focus on dreary facts: "Brightness falls from the air." Many, including T. S. Eliot, have quoted this line as a summary of the pall that fell over the world when idealism disappeared from so the prevailing worldview. Later, it was the Romantics who sought to dig behind the phenomenal (surface) world and find the meaning, the beauty, the spirit that dwelt within. In his poetry, Wordsworth sought to search for the "very heart of things," to bring a sense of inner truth back to poetry.

Considering this great transformation in the concept of *Truth*, or *truth*, in the seventeenth century, it is not surprising that Milton, in his essay on the need for freedom of expression, *Areopagitica* (1644), describes the body of Truth as fragmented. He pictures it as butchered and scattered, like the body of the Egyptian god Osiris. The truth seeker must gather up the pieces and fit them together to reform the mutilated remains. As Milton describes the birth and death of Truth:

> Truth indeed came once into the world with her divine Master, and was a perfect shape most glorious to look on; but when he ascended, and his apostles after him were laid asleep, then straight arose a wicked race of deceivers, who, as that story goes of the Egyptian Typhon [the god of Evil] with his conspirators, how they dealt with the good Osiris [the god of Good], took the virgin Truth, hewed her lovely form into a thousand pieces, and scattered them to the four winds. From that time ever since, the sad friends of Truth, such as durst appear, imitating the careful search that Isis made for the mangled body of Osiris, went up and down gathering up limb by limb still as they could find them. We have not yet found them all, Lords and Commons, nor ever shall do, till her Master's second coming; he shall bring together every joint and member, and shall mould them into an immortal feature of loveliness and perfection. (Milton, *Areopagitica*, 731)

It is therefore essential, according to Milton, that we be free to hear all possible ideas without censorship so that we can fit together this grand puzzle for ourselves. He bases his argument on Paul's advice to the Thessalonians, "Prove all things, hold fast that which is good" (1 Thess. 5:21).

Literature depends on the audience believing that some kind of truth exists, even if it is only one particular truth essential to this story. The discovery of the truth is the key to the unraveling of the story, known as the denouement. This structure for storytelling is as old as stories, typical of stories in both sacred and the secular classics.

Certainly in a mystery story, this is the case. Any of the stories of Edgar Allan Poe. Arthur Conan Doyle, Dorothy L. Sayers, or Agatha Christie depend on the revelation of the truth of the central event—usually the discovery of who committed the crime. But this moment of discovery is also central to such stories as ancient as *Oedipus Rex,* where the hero discovers that he has killed his own father and married his own mother, that his life has been built on a series of hideous actions.

A parallel discovery in *Macbeth* reveals to the hero that the witches are devious in their prophesies. They convince him that he is to be king and that he cannot be "vanquished" until "Great Birnam Wood to high Dunsinane Hill/ Shall come against him." What he later discovers to be truth, is that the woods can indeed move when used for camouflage, and that there is a man of his acquaintance who was "wrenched untimely from his mother's womb," therefore not *"born* of woman." By believing a cloudy "truth," he rushes toward his own tragic fall. Hamlet's fall is also based on the pursuit of truth, but in his case, the truth forces him to destroy all those about him.

These are factual kinds of truth, less important than the deeper Truth that both Plato and Milton discuss. The richer sense of an immortal Truth was also important to the Romantics, who felt that such a discovery would bring a new richness to human experience. John Keats was fascinated by the classics, believing that in the Greeks he had discovered a kind of immortal Truth. His poem "Ode on a Grecian Urn" famously concludes with these lines:

Beauty is truth, truth beauty—that is all
Ye know on earth, and all ye need to know.

(Keats, "Ode on a Grecian Urn," 820)

These puzzling words, supposedly the message of the urn, speak to the ageless power of a work of art. The poet has asked a number of questions regarding the figures painted on the urn, wondering: Who are those people coming to the sacrifice? Are they men or gods? What is the legend behind the image? Why are they running? What are they trying to escape? What is the town? Why it is emptied "of this folk, this pious morn"? The silent form of the urn, this "sylvan historian," teases him into such inquiries, but the urn responds only with its own quiet existence. This speaks of a power of beauty and truth that endure beyond the events they chronicle. While human life moves on, people grow old, love grows cold, this urn has a kind of immortality denied to fleshly creatures. This is the reason that Aristotle considered poetry more "true" than history.

Some of the Romantics, half in love with Plato's Ideas, ignored the obvious realities of the world. Keats knew as well as anyone living in London in the early nineteenth century that all truth is not beautiful and all beautiful things are not true. Often the truth proves quite ugly. And often very beautiful people turn out to be thoroughly nasty. Even beautiful words may cover a deep corruption of the soul.

For most of the nineteenth-century artists, Keats's aesthetic response to truth was not sufficient for the practical world. Henrik Ibsen was one of several European writers who tackled the problems of determining how to identify truth in a changing world of social and economic needs. His play *An Enemy of the People* (1882) sets the questions before the reader in strong terms. Dr. Stockmann, a man of high moral character, returns to his hometown in Norway, where he encourages the development of the local baths, making the town a popular resort. He is briefly hailed as a hero for the project and for his writings about the therapeutic value of the waters.

Later, when he undertakes a careful study of the reasons that some of the people who bathe in the waters and drink them have become sick, he discovers that the local tanning plant, owned by his father-in-law, is polluting the waters at their source. It would require enormous expense and a long-term shutdown of the resort to rectify the problem. At this point, the town turns against Dr. Stockmann. He loses his job, finds his friends at the newspaper will not print his articles, and is labeled an "enemy of the people." He even finds that his father-in-law has invested in the baths, so that he is risking his family's future by insisting on making public the facts regarding the pollution.

At first, he considers leaving the town and starting again in the new world, but finally determines to stay and fight, asserting, "This is what I have discovered: the strongest man in the world is the man who stands alone." For Ibsen, like Socrates, the key to progress is the individual with integrity, who is willing to ask questions and face the truth. The common person in a democracy can be an impediment to truth. Most folks will choose selfish desires over unpleasant truth that might profit the larger society in the long run. As Stockmann asserts: "I only want to drive it into the heads of these mongrels that these so-called liberals are the enemies of freedom; that party programs wring the necks of all young and living truths; that policies of expediency turn justice and morality upside down, until life here becomes not worth living" (Ibsen, 245).

This is parallel to the message Robert Penn Warren preached in his powerful political novel *All the King's Men*. Warren, who lived and taught in Louisiana for a time, watched with horror the increasing popularity of the cornpone populist Huey Long. This brilliant country lawyer dazzled Louisiana for years while he played fast and loose with the truth. He soon came to understand the value of the convincing lie, a regular device in literature and in life. In politics, the politician-as-liar has become a commonplace. Everyone now expects public figures to "spin" the facts.

In *All the King's Men*, Warren tells the story of Willie Stark's rise to power. He begins as a truth-telling small-town lawyer, who is "lucky" enough to insist on revealing the truth about a corrupt contract that leads to the death of young students at the local grade school. He knows the contract for the fire escape was fixed and has warned the officials, but is sneered at as a "hick" for his naïveté. Because of his reputation for honest dealings, he is invited to run for public office, only to discover that he has been set up to lose to a handpicked opponent. This defeat provides his moment of truth: he cannot win an election by simply standing in the hot sun explaining the facts to rednecks in overalls. And he cannot do any good without being elected. Telling the truth does not attract the crowds.

So he begins his political career of energizing crowds by shouting slogans at them, indulging in the usual, bloated promises, and working deals with corrupt moneymen. When he finally becomes governor, he is able to do some of the good things for his state and its people that he has promised, but loses his soul in the bargain. He ruins his own family and fritters away his own integrity. His ironic discovery of the so-called truth about a good judge, who has long hidden some shady dealings from early in his life, brings an unexpected series of events, including a suicide. The story ends with Willie's assassination.

The plot of *All the King's Men*, with all of its twists and turns, is too elaborate to summarize, but the novel is a classic of political fiction. It is full of comedy and tragedy, as well as philosophy solidly grounded on the doctrine of Original Sin. "Adam" is a major figure. Willie's name derives from the concept of Free Will, which goes awry in his case. Unlike Christ, he chooses to accept the Satanic promise of power and glory in this world. Warren seems to be showing that no man or woman is strong enough to play with lies without losing sight of the Truth. Like the path of the first couple in the Garden of Eden, Willie discovers that one little mistake entangles him in a web of lies, shifting blame, and shame. Compromise with evil is not an option.

Other writers have taken this troubled vision further, usually without the theological underpinning that distinguishes Robert Penn Warren's work. George Orwell, in his famous novel *Nineteen Eighty-Four* (1942), looks into the future and contemplates a world in which lies will become the only "truth" available to civilized people. His hero, Winston Smith, a historian working for the government, has forgotten most of the details of life before the Revolution that put the current government in place. He works at the Ministry of Truth, where his job is forging documents. He alters the past, makes up "facts," drops people down the "memory hole" when they have been "vaporized," and gradually reduces the vocabulary to exclude words like *God*. Those words he cannot eliminate, he drains of all meaning through "doublespeak," a process connected with "doublethink," changing a word so that it comes to mean its opposite.

By the time the Party finishes its task of manipulating the past and controlling the present, its members have developed "the ability to *believe* that black is white, and more, to *know* that black is white, and to forget that one has ever believed the contrary." Cut off from the past, just as they are cut off from other countries, the citizens lose any basis of comparison or judgment. They are reduced to believing anything the Party says is true. Through a vast system of "mental cheating," the Party leads people to accept the innate contradictions of doublethink, where "the Ministry of Peace concerns itself with war, the Ministry of Truth with lies, the Ministry of Love with torture, and the Ministry of Plenty with starvation" (Orwell, 164).

Orwell's frightening dystopia is a logical progression from modern totalitarian societies. Orwell was particularly horrified with the Communists and the Nazis, who perverted language with their "big lies," which rested on simple repetition of false statements in an authoritative manner. He saw textbooks being rewritten to alter the past, shouted slogans replacing reasoned debate, and war used to justify atrocities and centralize power. As a man who loved the subtleties of language and was fascinated by its power to communicate great truths, Orwell was frightened at the modern abuse of language and the reduction of thought to endless recitation of bromides.

Modern literature is often labeled post-Christian. Without the foundational belief in the truth of scripture, the poet and the novelist have to seek out their own individual truths. For the modern and the postmodern, this frequently involves the awareness that others have their individual truths that deserve equal respect and attention. With no means for judging which of these visions of reality has more value, the writer is left to juggle multiple truths, some of which have passionate advocates and most of which contradict one another.

A story like Henry James's *The Turn of the Screw*, for example, leaves unresolved the reality in the story. In such a tale, we cannot trust even the narrator, nor be sure that we understand the facts. James enjoyed playing with the notion of reality, considering art more real than actual life. A more extreme artist who focused much of his attention on the difference between truth and illusion was Luigi Pirandello, a twentieth-century Italian playwright. His famous play *Six Characters in Search of an Author* (1950) turns the tables upside down. The characters become so real that they take control of the play and try to force the writer to tell their stories.

An even more interesting example of this proclivity for confusing illusion with reality, especially in the deranged mind, is *It Is So! (If You Think So)* (1922). In some translations, it is called *Right You Are, If You Think You Are*. This very talky play, with almost no action, involves the search for the so-called truth about three people who have recently come to town. One is the husband and son-in-law of the two women. The question that is central to the mystery is the identity of the wife, whether she is the husband's first or second wife. The characters take turns telling perfectly plausible stories regarding this woman, and lamenting that the other characters are mad. After a series of contradictory interviews by a nosy and gossipy community, the townspeople decide that the only way they can determine who is mad, who is only pretending to be mad, who is dead, and who is the first wife, is to look at the documents. But this evidence has been destroyed by a catastrophe, leaving the community with the sad conclusion that they must ask the wife who she is. Without documents or credible witnesses to help them, they are forced to settle for individual truths. The wife's final comment is, "I am she whom you believe me to be."

One character in the play becomes the spokesman for the author, proclaiming a refrain about truth at the end of each act. He keeps asserting that truth cannot be known, even about ourselves. We change minute by minute and are different to each person who meets us. It is fitting that Laudisi has the final line, "And there, my friends you have the truth. Are you satisfied?"

A number of modern American playwrights have drawn on Pirandello's agnosticism to develop their own views of truths that are individual and valid. A writer like Eugene O'Neill, for example, believed that every person has a series of "life lies" that are essential to make life livable. The outsider may know that these stories are not true, but the believer needs to have them in order to survive. The cruelest possible action, as he shows at the conclusion of *The Iceman Cometh*, is to force objective truth on a person who is happy with his own pleasing and essential lie. Larry, who is characterized as having the "quality of a pitying but weary old priest's" face, explains this to the denizens of the saloon. When Rocky, another patron of the bar, laughs at the false hopes that his ship will come in tomorrow and everyone will have promises fulfilled and regrets cancelled, Larry responds:

> Don't mock the faith! Have you no respect for religion…. What's it matter if the truth
> is that their favoring breeze has the stink of nickel whiskey on its breath, and their sea
> is a growler of lager and ale, and their ships are long since looted and scuttled and sunk
> on the bottom? To hell with the truth! As the history of the world proves, the truth has
> no bearing on anything. It's irrelevant and immaterial, as the lawyers say. The lie of a
> pipe dream is what gives life to the whole misbegotten mad lot of us, drunk or sober.
> (O'Neill, 997)

Some modern writers still believe that Truth does exist, that humans can discover it, and that it is an essential quest in life. "Reality," too often, means facts and figures, documents and evidence. This is not the richest kind of truth, which lies behind the surface.

C. S. Lewis made great claims to the kind of truth revealed in the imagination, through fantasy. In *Narnia*, for example, his professor laughs at the young people's faith in logic. They go into the world on the other side of the wardrobe to discover a deeper truth than they can find in their textbooks. Lewis himself had such a discovery, as he tells it in his autobiography, *Surprised by Joy*. Early in his life, he found a delight in the ancient myths, and later in the Romantics, with all their faith in the imagination. He came to understand that the joy he occasionally had experienced came to him not through philosophy or reason, but through something much more mystical.

> We yearn, rightly for that unity which we can never reach except by ceasing to be the separate phenomenal beings called "we." Joy was not a deception. Its visitations were rather the moments of clearest consciousness we had, when we became aware of our fragmentary and phantasmal nature and ached for that impossible reunion which would annihilate us or that self-contradictory waking which would reveal, not that we had had, but that we *were*, a dream. (Lewis, *Surprised by Joy*, "Checkmate," 117)

It was only after this awakening to the truth that Lewis felt "like when a man, after a long sleep, still lying motionless in bed, becomes aware that he is now awake." Not that the joy he cherished was itself the truth, but that it was a "pointer to something outer and other," which could not be arrived at through logic. Joy set him on the road to Jerusalem, which he believed the true goal of human life.

Conclusion

In this return to Romanticism, C. S. Lewis was rejecting much of the underpinning of modern realism. His long study of myths, sagas, epics, and folk literature. encouraged him to return to the medieval concept that the visible and temporal are not the True. Truth is to be discovered through faith, through imagination, through insight. The realist sees truth as residing in the experience of the senses. Like Plato's cave dwellers, he believes that the shadows he can perceive with his eyes are the actual truth. In art, the realist seeks to replicate these images as precisely as possible, through the process known as *mimesis*. The Romantic, believing that an inner, more universal truth is the actual reality, seeks to go beyond the coats in the wardrobe, out the back, into the imaginary world of myth and mystery, dreams, and visions.

This ancient quarrel between those who believe in an objectively discovered truth and a deeply sensed Truth goes back to the Greeks and beyond. The philosophers have debated the nature of reality over many millennia, and the artists have followed their ideas. As C. S. Lewis portrayed it in his mythic story *Till We Have Faces*, based on Apulelius's account of Psyche, humans have two choices, parallel to those of the two sisters in the tale. We may choose the philosophy of Lysias the Fox, a wise Greek mentor, who believes that reason and the laws of nature will explain life and death and most things in our world. Or, on the other hand, we may prefer the way of Ungit, a fertility goddess the people of Glome worship. They make sacrifices of pigeons and even humans to her, believing that their prayers will be answered by this primitive blood goddess. The one view is clear and rational, but thin, the other difficult, bloody, and deep. Lewis believed that the "polluted streams of paganism flowed in the direction of the pure river of the blood of Jesus Christ" and that "Myth becomes fact" (Kilby, 134). For Fox, man is the measure of all things. For Glome's god Ungit, there is no chance of human measurement. There are no words adequate to express the deep mystery of the larger world, which we will never know in full—until death. Lewis believed that myth contains truth about the world that neither science nor philosophy can explain. Stories, not essays, are better paths to understanding the "deep magic." Religion differs from philosophy in that it has direct access to Truth through revelation, not through reason. The way of the Fox is not, ultimately, the way to Truth. In trying to discover Truth, the student of literature soon becomes a student of philosophy and of religion, searching for the definition of *reality* and of *Truth* that underlies the poem, the novel, or the play in hand.

Many moderns, confused by the constant attacks on the truth of religions and puzzled by the avalanche of lies descending daily, accept the painful worldview of Matthew Arnold. At the end of the Victorian age, this poet sensed the withdrawal of the "Sea of Faith" and chose to replace this old certitude with individual values—such as love:

> The Sea of Faith
> Was once, too, at the full, and round earth's shore
> Lay like the folds of a bright girdle furled
> But now I only hear
> Its melancholy, long, withdrawing roar,
> Retreating, to the breath
> Of the night wind, down the vast edges drear
> And naked shingles of the world.
> Ah, love, let us be true
> To one another! for the world, which seems
> To lie before us like a land of dreams,
> So various, so beautiful, so new,
> Hath really neither joy, nor love, nor light,
> Nor certitude, nor peace, nor help for pain,
> And we are here as on a darkling plain
> Swept with confused alarms of struggle and flight,
> Where ignorant armies clash by night.

(Arnold, 580)

See also: **Good People; The Journey of Life.**

Bibliography

Arnold, Matthew. "Dover Beach." In *British Poetry and Prose*, vol. II, ed. Paul Lieder, Robert Morss Lovett, and Robert Kilburn Root. Boston: Houghton Mifflin, 1950.

Auerbach, Eric. *Mimesis: The Representation of Reality in Western Literature*. Trans., Willard R. Trask. New York: Jovanovich, 1982.

Bunyan, John. *The Pilgrim's Progress*. New York: Pocket Books, 1957.

Cervantes Saavedra, Miguel de. *Don Quixote*. Trans., P. A. Motteaux. New York: Knopf, 1991.

Coleridge, Samuel Taylor. *Biographia Literaria*. Online at http://www.gutenberg.org/etext/6081 (accessed September 12, 2006).

Ibsen, Henrik. *An Enemy of the People*. In *A Doll's House, Ghosts, An Enemy of the People, The Master Builder*. New York: The Modern Library, 1950.

Jacobs, Alan. *The Narnian: The Life and Imagination of C.S. Lewis*. San Francisco, CA: Harper, 2006.

James, Henry. *The Turn of the Screw*. New York: W.W. Norton, 1966.

———. "The Real Thing." Online at http://www.cs.cmu.edu/ People/spok/metabook/realthing.html (accessed September 12, 2006).

Keats, John. "Ode on a Grecian Urn." In *Anthology of Romanticism*, ed. Ernest Bernbaum. New York: The Roland Press Company, 1948.

Kilby, Clyde S. *Images of Salvation in the Fiction of C.S. Lewis.* Wheaton, IL: Harold Shaw Publishers, 1978.

Lewis, C. S. *The Lion, the Witch and the Wardrobe.* New York: HarperEntertainment, 2005.

———. *Surprised by Joy.* New York: Inspirational Press, 1987.

———. *Till We Have Faces.* New York: Harcourt Brace Jovanovich, 1980.

O'Neill, Eugene. *The Iceman Cometh.* In *Best American Plays: Third Series 1945–1951,* ed. John Gassner. New York: Crown Publishers, 1952.

Orwell, George. *Nineteen Eighty-Four: A Novel.* New York: Plume, 2003.

Pirandello, Luigi. *Naked Masks: Five Plays by Luigi Pirandello,* ed. Eric Bentley. New York: E.P. Dutton and Company, 1957.

Plato. *The Republic and Other Works.* Trans., B. Jowett. New York: Anchor Books, 1989.

Warren, Robert Penn. *All the King's Men.* San Diego, CA: Harcourt Brace Jovanovich, 1990.

Death and the Afterlife

Readings

Introduction

> In the day when the keepers of the house shall tremble, and the strong men
> shall bow themselves, and the grinders cease because they are few, and those
> that look out of the windows be darkened....
>
> Also when they shall be afraid of that which is high, and fears shall be in
> the way, and the almond tree shall flourish, and the grasshopper shall be a
> burden, and desire shall fail: because man goeth to his long home, and the
> mourners go about the streets.
>
> Or ever the silver cord be loosed, or the golden bowl be broken, or the
> pitcher be broken at the fountain, or the wheel broken at the cistern.
>
> Then shall the dust return to the earth as it was: and the spirit shall return
> unto God who gave it. (Eccles. 12:3–7)

The manner in which we view death mirrors our concept of life itself and of any
hope for a life to come. Is it all vanity, as the cynical old preacher of Ecclesiastes

seemed to believe? Is death the end? Is it but a sleep and a forgetting? Is there a good way to die? one that is heroic? tragic? Are some forms of death forbidden? Are some required by justice? Are some a result of our values, such as love of family, of country, of honor? Is there an afterlife? If so, what is it like?

These are some of the many questions that have haunted humans from the beginning of time. They remain constant themes in literature and in life. Various cultures at various times have found different solutions to these perennial concerns.

Scripture

In her catastrophic conversation with the serpent in the Garden of Eden, Eve misquotes God as saying, "Ye shall not eat of it [the tree which is in the midst of the garden], neither shall ye touch it, lest ye die."

The wily serpent responded, "Ye shall not surely die" (Gen 3:3–4).

He lied. By eating of the fruit, Eve and Adam brought their expulsion from the garden, and therefore were denied the fruit of the tree of Life (Gen. 3:24). Thus did death come into the world.

Much of the Old Testament is a listing of the patriarchs who lived and died and were buried. There is little speculation in this section of the Bible regarding what death means or whether there is life after death. Death appears to be simply the natural end of life, when dust returns to dust. According to the Old Testament, when a person reaches a ripe old age, death itself is regarded as a sleep, a rest, and a blessing. By contrast, early death is seen as a dreadful misfortune. One critic summarizes this worldview this way: "Death is both natural and intrusive; it occasions no undue anxiety except in unusual circumstances such as premature departure, violence, or childless demise, and it is the greatest enemy facing humankind" (Crenshaw, 160). Without any sense of a beatific notion of the afterlife, the Hebrews thought of death as a "huge silence." The dead could "neither help nor be helped" (Segal, 121–123, 129).

Because they believed the living to be the "seed" sown by the dead, they conceived of death as the end of the individual but not of the family. They honored their ancestors and their ancestral faith, but they always looked to the future, when their progeny would be like the sands in the desert or the stars in the heavens.

This is not to say that they did not mourn the death of the individual. David's lament over Saul and Jonathan reveals the depth of his feelings for this loss. Later, in the New Testament, Mary and Martha weep over the death of Lazarus, and the whole family of believers mourn the death of Jesus. Many of the miracles deal with efforts to avoid death, especially the death of the very young. Rarely does anyone in the Old Testament face death with equanimity, though the great saints like Moses and Joshua face their deaths with dignity and courage.

The Hebrews believed that God alone has the authority to terminate life, even if the sufferer has no longer any desire to live. The world-weariness of the speaker in Ecclesiastes cannot be relieved by suicide, nor does Job feel he is free to kill himself, even when his wife suggests that he "curse God and die." It is for God alone to choose when the golden bowl will be broken and the dust return to the earth.

To have one's bones "gathered with his forefathers" is the literal description of the disposal of the physical remains. Among ancient forms of burial, a typical one was to have the body placed on a shelf in a cave, where it would remain until the flesh had decayed. At that point, the bones would be placed in the depository along with the person's ancestors' bones. The best hope for the dead was that their bones might be gathered properly. Jacob and Joseph, for example, asked that their bones be returned to the Promised Land rather than being left in Egypt. The burial place itself was respected, often sealed with a stone or marked in some way. One site often served for the burial of several generations' dead. The burial service itself and the rituals of mourning were important, but few cherished any hope for continuation of life beyond the grave. Only occasional hints in Job and Ezekiel suggest that there might be a time when the dry bones will rise again.

Nevertheless, the newly dead were thought to be able to communicate with the living, at least for a time. The Witch of Endor's ability to raise Samuel's spirit to speak to Saul suggests that people continue to exist in some kind of half-life well after their physical death—at least until the body is entirely disintegrated in the grave. In Jewish lore, many allegorical tales relate to the communication of the dead with the living, but the more common view is the one in Ecclesiastes (9:5): "The dead know not anything." Nonetheless, the practice of praying for the intercession of the dead reaches back as far as stories of Caleb, who was thought to have visited the cave of Machpelah, where he prayed to Abraham to save him from Moses's scouts.

Job is one of the earliest examples of the longing for resurrection (Job 19:25–26), for an existence that goes beyond life on earth. Later, perhaps under the influence of Greek thought, especially Plato, the Pharisees and Essenes came to believe in the resurrection of the dead, at least the resurrection of the soul if not the body. Eventually, resurrection became a dogma of Judaism, fixed in the Mishnah and the liturgy. It was firmly established as a part of the Messianic hope, largely tied to the resurrection of the righteous, as spirits only.

This tradition was the theological heritage of the early Christians, who were accustomed to hearing about the "dark land of death" (Matt. 4:16). They believed that the Creator had power over both life and death (Mark 5:38–42), as was demonstrated in various miracles. John's gospel has numerous references to death and resurrection, including the miracle of Lazarus's being called back from the dead (John 11:17). At that point, Jesus tells Martha, "I am the resurrection, and the life: he that believeth in me, though he were dead, yet shall he live" (John 11:25). Finally Christ appears in his resurrected body to his disciples and others. As a result, the concept of the bodily resurrection has became an essential of Christian thought. As the Apostles' Creed expresses the doctrine: "I believe in ... the resurrection of the dead, and the life everlasting."

Paul explains the theology of death in his letter to the Corinthians: "For since by man came death, by man came also the resurrection of the dead. For as in Adam all die, even so in Christ shall all be made alive." He ends this passage by proclaiming, "Death is swallowed up in victory. O Death, where is thy sting? O grave, where is thy victory?" (1 Cor. 15:22, 54–55). He writes to his beloved Timothy, "Christ ... hath abolished death, and hath brought life and immortality to light through the gospel" (2 Tim. 1:10). With the hope of eternal life with God, Paul could face death fearlessly, proclaiming that "For me to live is Christ, and to die is gain" (Phil. 1:21).

It was with this hope firmly imbedded in their thought that the early Christians were able to face martyrdom with a sense of joy, assured that they would be victors in their deaths, that they were going to a better world in which they would see God face to face, a place with "many mansions," as Jesus had promised. This is certainly clear in the Book of Acts, when Stephen forgives those who stone him, or when Paul and Silas sing and pray when imprisoned and threatened with death. Paul tells the Philippians that he can face his persecutors with equanimity, "For our conversation is in heaven, from whence also we look for the Savior, the Lord Jesus Christ: Who shall change our vile body, that it may be fashioned like unto his glorious body, according to the working whereby he is able even to subdue all things unto himself" (Phil. 3:20–21). The Apostle can therefore encourage them to "stand fast in the Lord." The assurance of a just and glorious life to come became the great consolations for generations to follow.

Literature

The Greeks were far more interested in the way a person dies and the possibility of life after death than the Jews. Their earliest literature includes speculation on the existence of an afterlife, the hope that some few of earth's heroes would continue to inhabit Elysium or the Happy Isles. When Odysseus sails to the end of the world and descends into this underworld, however, he discovers a number of the secrets of the hereafter. Seeking to embrace a friend in Hades, he finds, despite three frustrated efforts, that the dead have no material presence. He also discovers that the dead are worried about proper burial of their bodies and about affairs on earth. They continue to hold their old grudges, refusing to talk with those they despised on earth. When Odysseus meets Achilles, the young hero sourly informs the wily adventurer that he would rather be a "yeoman farmer on a small holding than lord paramount in the kingdom of the dead."

The manner in which the hero meets death is central to the Greek idea of tragedy. Aristotle, in his *Poetics* (c. 350 B.C.), outlines the ideals of the tragic hero as he understands them from contemporary dramas. To be truly heroic, the man or woman must be pre-eminently good, a person of stature, with a flaw which justifies the tragic pattern of their death. Usually, this flaw is pride or hubris, the decision to challenge the will of the gods. This noble hero, having fought against impossible odds, must choose a courageous death over a dishonorable life on earth. In this sense, the death is a spiritual victory. Suicides, self-mutilation, murder of the next generation by such famous folk as Achilles, Oedipus, and Medea, are all presented as powerful examples of the heroic life and death.

One of the Greeks' most powerful studies of the hero facing death is the fifth-century-B.C. philosopher Socrates. Plato, his disciple and chronicler, reported his words (probably altered to include his own thoughts) in dramatic and thoughtful dialogues: The "Apology" is the old man's defense of his life and thought before the Athenian court, the Aeropagus. In it, he explains his role as "gadfly" to Athens, which he compares to a horse. For him, the "unexamined life is not worth living." When offered a choice between exile from Athens and death by poison, he chooses to drink the hemlock. He explains this decision in more detail in the "Crito," a dialogue in which one of his followers tries to convince him to save himself by going to Thessaly. In the final dialogue, the "Phaedo," we have the moving account of the final hours of Socrates's life on earth. The old philosopher is joined by a few of his beloved disciples, who gather around him for a final discussion of death. He argues that there is no reason to fear death. After all, death is the release of the soul from the prison of the body:

> Those also who are remarkable for having led holy lives are released from this earthly prison, and go to their pure home which is above, and dwell in the purer earth; and those who have duly purified themselves with philosophy, live henceforth altogether without the body, in mansions fairer far than these, which may not be described, and of which the time would fail me to tell. (Plato, 487)

Having uttered these words, he tells his young students calmly that he is ready to drink the cup of poison. and go "to the joys of the blessed." He then bathes himself to relieve those who would otherwise be obliged to bathe his body after death, robes himself in his funeral clothing, and drinks the hemlock, dying quietly with a final reference to a debt he has left unpaid.

Plato sums up the final scene, in touching words: "Such was the end ... of our friend, whom I may truly call the wisest, the justest, and best of all men whom I have ever known."

This scene is often compared and contrasted with the final days of Christ five centuries later: the Last Supper, which Jesus shares with his disciples; the acceptance of the necessity of his death in the painful moments in the Garden of Gethsemane, and the unrelenting role of both the Jews and the Romans, who cannot tolerate his dissenting voice. There are also the parallel references to the "many mansions" that await the dead, the sense of peace and blessedness in the approach of death, and the assurance of a life to come.

Socrates's experience was, of course, quite different from Jesus's. In contrast with Christ, Socrates was an ugly older man, who lived a normal life with a wife and children. He was a teacher and philosopher, who was not seeking to establish a new religion. Nor was he the Messiah. Socrates's placid death was quite a contrast to the anguish of Christ's final days, the brutality of the trial, his silence in the face of his accusers, and the crucifixion itself. In every way, Christ's sacrificial death was a more violent and dramatic event, including the rending of the Temple veil and the darkness at noon. This was the death of God's son, not just of a good man. No one was redeemed by Socrates's death.

The bodily resurrection of Christ is the most striking difference between the two presentations. The Easter experience, the risen Christ's very physical meeting with the women at the tomb and with the disciples on the road and beside the Sea of Galilee provide the evidence on which Paul bases his strong insistence on Christ's victory over Death.

Furthermore the promise of bodily resurrection of believers in the Last Days is quite different from Platonism. In the death and resurrection of Christ, the whole concept of tragedy is transformed. Death is a very real victory for everyone who believes in the redeeming work of the Savior. For the Christian believer, in contrast to the Platonist, the hope is that the spirit and the body will finally be reunited in the Day of the Resurrection. The doctrine of the bodily resurrection stands in stark contrast to Platonic dualism, the clear division between the body and the soul. Plato, in fact, proposes the transmigration of souls, with the rebirth of souls in new bodies until the final purification is complete. For the Christian, there is but one life to live on earth, one chance to choose the right way, and one act of redemption that leads to eternal bliss. Death is the beginning of a time of joy for God's chosen, a time of torment for the damned. Thus, for the Christian, death is not a tragedy but a comedy, as Dante suggests in naming his grand epic of the life hereafter *The Divine Comedy*.

In spite of these clear differences between Platonism and Christianity, Plato's thought was to have enormous impact on the development of Christian theology. Neo-Platonism is particularly obvious in Dante's *Divine Comedy* (1321), the fullest expression of the medieval view of death and the life thereafter. In his journey through hell, purgatory, and heaven, the poet finds that he must portray his vision in graphic, physical terms. Although the spirits he meets along the way are not yet joined with their bodies, the story demands they have a physical presence so they can appear to the poet, suffer torments of hell, and experience the increasing pleasures and sense of lightness as they ascend to purgatory. The body becomes a metaphor for the spirit as the men and women live in darkness (absence of God's light), in bitter cold (absence of God's love), and are gnawed, disemboweled, split, or otherwise tortured. This willingness of Dante to present spiritual anguish in physical terms makes hell particularly vivid. The ascent up Mount Purgatory becomes increasingly abstract, as the spirits escape gravity (explained as Satan's pull on mankind) and fly toward heaven, which is their eventual home.

The abstractions of heaven, with God himself presented as three interlocking circles in the midst of blinding light, make this part of the trilogy the hardest to visualize. It is also the most Platonic. Abandoning Jesus's words regarding "many mansions," Dante pictures his heaven as a place of music, joy, and vision. The saints fly in and out of the Rose of the Blessed like bumble bees. In these strange images, Dante seeks to portray the eternal bliss promised for believers as ideal Love, Joy, and Peace.

Dante's afterlife is a mirror of earth itself. Men and women struggle with the same issues they did on earth. Hell is a continuation of their lusts, violations, hatreds, and cruelties. They embrace the sin they chose on earth and sink deeper into it, with no hope of redemption or love or light. Purgatory is a place of correction, where they are purged of their flaws, reformed, so that their will conforms to God's. Heaven is the reward, the bliss of the presence of God and the fellowship of the saints that they hungered for on earth. Those who rejected God on earth are now free of his presence; those who sought to follow his will are finally blessed to find their home in his undying love.

One of the most straightforward presentations of the medieval Christian beliefs regarding the moment of death can be found in the fifteenth-century English morality play *Everyman* (c. 1529). Using a series of personifications of human qualities, the play centers around a nondescript human—Everyman. Death summons him to take his final journey, much to his dismay, allowing him only his final hour to prepare for departure from this world. In a series of frustrating dialogues, he seeks the fellowship of all his trusted friends, including Fellowship, Kindred, Cousin, and Worldly Goods, but finds he must rely on Good Deeds, who is very weak at this point. Knowledge offers to go along with him, encouraging him to see a priest. In a fit of contrition, Everyman goes for his last confession, admits all his errors, and promises to do penance. He scourges himself briefly before he receives Extreme Unction, allowing him to face Death with Good Deeds, now revived, as well as Strength, Beauty, Discretion, and his Five Wits. As he stands on the brink of his grave, all but Good Deeds desert him, leaving him weak but full of confidence that he is saved. The play ends with angels' descending to welcome him to "the heavenly sphere." In an epilogue, continuing in the pattern of rhymed couplets, a Doctor enters to reinforce the moral of the play:

> This moral men may have in mind,
> Ye hearers, take it of worth, old and young,
> And forsake Pride, for he deceiveth you in the end;
> And remember Beauty, Five Wits, Strength, and Discretion,
> They all at the last do every man forsake,
> Save his Good Deeds there doth he take,
> But beware, for and they be small
> Before God, he hath no help at all;
> None excuse may be there for every man,
> Alas, how shall he do then?

For after death amends may no man make,
For then mercy and pity doth him forsake.

(Everyman, 304)

The Doctor ends with a benediction.

The play is quick paced and well told. Each of the personifications promises to go along with Everyman before discovering the grim nature of this journey. After a bit, the satiric quality of these extravagant promises becomes part of our pleasure in watching the deflated friends depart in shame. There is even a limited characterization of Fellowship as a drinking buddy full of bluster and affection, and of Family, filled with concern for their member.

The idea of the play, that good deeds are the key to salvation, is typical of popular medieval theology rather than scripture. The reliance on salvation through good works, and through the intercession of the Church marks this as a play that precedes the Reformation in England. Another medieval characteristic is the depiction of Death on stage as a character. In medieval paintings and plays, Death is often portrayed in grotesque ways, even as a partner in the Dance of Death. or the Dance Macabre.

Chaucer's pilgrims would have seen popular plays like this during their religious holidays, when the pageants, the wagons drawing the different scenes of biblical drama, carried local craftsmen enacting miracle, mystery (scriptural drama), and morality plays, provided entertainment and religious education for the common folk. The characters in *Everyman,* including the Seven Deadly Sins and the other personifications of people and qualities in life, were a standard part of the morality plays, which were mini-sermons, lively to watch and easy to remember. They often utilized the techniques of allegory, just as Chaucer did in some of his tales.

For example, the "Pardoner's Tale" is a moral fable about a man who proposes to cheat Death. A young ne'er-do-well, who has spent an evening drinking with a couple of friends, boasts that not even Death will take his life. The three young men then go in search of Death, but find a stash of gold instead. In their clever plotting among themselves to gain the whole treasure and cheat their friends, all of them end up dead, one by stabbing, two by poison.

Chaucer puts this fable about the perils of greed and pride in the mouth of the Pardoner, the character who most clearly exemplifies these very traits. The author enhances this well-known folk tale with a background of the Plague and a sinister old man whom the three drunken friends meet, not recognizing he is pointing the way to Death. Centuries later, the nineteenth-century American gothic short-story writer Edgar Allan Poe would use much the same theme and strategies in his "The Masque of the Red Death," another tale in which the very strategies to evade death lead directly to it.

With the Renaissance came the real flowering of the drama and the revival of the classical Aristotelian concept of the tragic hero. At the same time, the characterization in the plays was usually based on the notion of the humors, the classical idea of the four elements that supposedly shape human nature. Of these, the melancholy humor was the most popular in tragic drama, the gloomy intellectual hero, suffering from the sorrows of the world, preparing himself for his inevitable death. Wearing dark colors, this dramatic figure meditated on graveyard scenes, soliloquized on the nature of death, and lamented the evils of his world. Meditations on death became the vogue for centuries to follow, with a number of the finest poets writing odes on Melancholy. The graveyard scene in *Hamlet,* where the hero considers the skull of "poor Yorick," the late king's jester, is a famous example of this fad.

Another melancholy ode appears in *Richard II,* when Richard is facing disaster and death and feeling particularly sorry for himself. This soliloquy opens with the gentle words, "Let's talk of graves, of worms and epitaphs." His approaching death in this case provides the opportunity for a contemplation of the futility of life. Even the crown appears hollow to the once-ambitious king, now that even a "little pin" has bored "through his castle wall, and farewell king!" Realizing that he is doomed, that his followers are defeated and that Bolingbroke waits to fight and kill him, the king is forced to gather up all his strength and die like a man.

One of his lords, Carlisle, rebukes him for his cowardly acceptance of melancholy defeatism with strong words. He thinks he has nothing to lose and everything to gain by fighting to the very end:

> And fight and die is death destroying death,
> Where fearing dying as death servile breath.

Rather than a Christian solution to facing death as a willing martyr in anticipation of a better life to come, this heroic defiance is the classical stance. The real king should die like a king, not like a worm. As Dylan Thomas, a twentieth-century Welsh poet, cries to his father, do not accept death so easily. "Rage, rage against the dying of the light."

Richard chooses no such heroism. This corrupt king has looted the estates of dead noblemen, banished Henry Bolingbroke, the heir to the throne, and generally proven a lord of misrule, bringing misery on his unhappy kingdom. He has little hope of life eternal. He has dedicated himself to the lust after power on earth. Rather than fighting to the end, he is taken prisoner, tried and found guilty of high crimes against the state, and forced to abdicate. Later, he is murdered ignobly by a henchman of the new king. Shakespeare's tragedies invariably end with multiple deaths, and frequently with eloquent lamentations.

The seventeenth-century metaphysical writers also loved to meditate on death. For some of them, the physical death was but a superficial symbol of far more complex experiences that involve love and religion. For some, death represented the obliteration of self, the experience of ecstasy that one achieves in sex or in mysticism. John Donne often used the term *death* with double or triple meanings, making his love poems religious and his religious poems sexual.

In one of his *Holy Sonnets* (X), Donne sounds much like Paul. The sonnet addresses the personification of Death in a caustic tone:

> Death, be not proud, though some have callèd thee
> Mighty and dreadful, for thou art not so; …
> Thou art slave to fate, chance, kings, and desperate men,
> And dost with poison, war, and sickness dwell;….
> One short sleep past, we wake eternally,
> And Death shall be no more: Death, thou shalt die!

> (Donne, *Holy Sonnets,* X, 487)

Donne, who characteristically dramatizes his situation, lavishes scorn on the haughty figure of Death, making him a weak victim who has to wait on circumstances to claim his target. The clear hope of eternal life, noted in the penultimate line, makes the final proclamation clear and strong. Killing Death is a delightful paradox to put the finish on the sonnet.

Donne's justly famous sermon on death speaks of death as a "translation" into a "better language." He notes that all of mankind is "of one author," God, who is in control of "our scattered leaves" and of the whole library. He then goes on to speak of the bell that tolls for the dead and the proper response to that melancholy sound:

> Who bends not his ear to any bell which upon any occasion rings? but who can remove it from that bell which is passing a piece of himself out of this world? No man is an island, entire of itself; every man is a piece of the continent, a part of the main. If a clod be washed away by the sea, Europe is the less, as well as if a promontory were, as well as if a manor of thy friend's or of thine own were. Any man's death diminishes me, because I am involved in mankind, and therefore never send to know for whom the bell tolls; it tolls for thee. (John Donne, *Devotions Upon Emergent Occasions*, XVII, 488)

Most of the major writers of the seventeenth century wrote something about the nature of death, often mourning the death of a friend in meditative and beautiful prose or poetry. Sir Francis Bacon wrote one of his short essays on the subject. Milton wrote "Lycidas," a pastoral elegy for a friend who died at a comparatively young age.

One of the finest of these meditations is Sir Thomas Browne's *Hydriotaphia* or *Urn Burial*. In 1658, some buried urns were discovered in a field in England. Like most seventeenth-century writers, fascinated with death, Browne felt compelled to write an account of these urns and of the burial customs of antiquity. He then mused that "Time which antiquates antiquities, and hath an art to make a dust of all things, hath spared these minor monuments." He is alluding to Genesis here, with the famous lines often recited at the grave side: "for dust thou art, and unto dust shalt thou return"(Gen. 3:17). He considers briefly that we live only so long as we are remembered by those who are living: "There is no antidote against the opium of time, which temporally considereth all things; our fathers find their graves in our short memories, and sadly tell us how we may be buried in our survivors'. Gravestones tell truth scarce forty years. Generations pass while some trees stand, and old families last not three oaks." He concludes by discussing Christian views of death and the afterlife, which he purports not to understand, though he is touched by the "metaphysics of true belief" in which "to live indeed is to be again ourselves."

The seventeenth century was not the only period when poets were fixated on death. The eighteenth century also is full of odes to melancholy and pastoral laments for the death of young shepherds. Graveyard poets and Gothic writers were delighted to dwell on dark themes, set in gloomy settings, filled with hemlocks and ravens. Novelists even had characters bring their own coffins into the house so they could meditate on death during their lifetime. Richardson's Clarissa is famous for this preparation for her prolonged death scene.

The Romantics were inclined to make death a thing of sublime beauty. In "Adonais," his pastoral tribute to Keats, Shelley describes the young Keats as "half in love with vengeful death." These writers romanticized death and dying, especially when the deceased was young and attractive. Keats' own "Ode on Melancholy" seeks to extract beauty out of the dark, sad qualities of existence.

As Mario Praz noted in his famous study of this era, *The Romantic Agony*, "In fact, to such an extent were Beauty and Death looked upon as sisters by the Romantics that they became fused into a sort of two-faced herm, filled with corruption and melancholy and fatal in its beauty—a beauty of which the more bitter the taste, the more abundant the enjoyment" (Praz, 31). Even so charming a writer as Charles Dickens had his melancholy scenes, often long sentimental death scenes with much weeping and wailing. The American writer Edgar Allan Poe, who had his own tragic life and his grotesque death, was one of the most extreme writers in this tradition, loving to tell his dark stories in macabre ways.

At least one Romantic, Samuel Taylor Coleridge, introduced a different concept of death, parallel in some ways to scripture and to the theology of the medieval Church. In Coleridge's famous poem "The Rime of the Ancient Mariner," the old sailor who narrates the story has killed an albatross, a bird of good omen that had been following the becalmed ship. In this thoughtless act, he brings a curse on his whole ship and causes the deaths of all his shipmates.

Assuming he too will die on the doomed vessel along with all his fellow crew members, he suddenly spots a spectral ship approaching. The curse takes on new meaning when he sees "the nightmare Life-in-Death, / Who thicks man's blood with cold." This hideous creature grants him immortality at a terrible price. She makes him into a kind of Wandering Jew, cursed with eternal life, forced to roam endlessly telling his sad tale in a ritual manner, repeatedly feeling contrition, confessing his sins, asking for forgiveness, and seeking absolution. Real forgiveness never comes; he is doomed to repeat the ritual, wandering to the ends of the earth.

Later authors picked up on the idea of the living dead, a kind of half-life that is worse than death. Such gothic characters, like the Greek legendary character Tireseas, are shadowy figures in modern literature, appearing in such poetry as "The Wasteland." In Eliot's poem, this classical figure serves as the spectator, or chorus, who surveys the wasteland of modern society, remembering the many cultures that came before. Dorothy L. Sayers, in her radio drama on the life of Christ, *The Man Born to Be King* (1943), reverses this idea. Her dramatization of the raising of Lazarus suggests that his friend lived, truly lived, only after Jesus touched his life. He was a dead man walking until he found this new life in Christ.

The nineteenth century was a difficult time for people of faith. The attacks on the reliability of scripture, the rise of Darwinism, and the influence of Eastern religions called all claims to the Judeo-Christian faith into doubt. Alfred, Lord Tennyson was very much a man of his times, worried about all of these things. When faced with the death of Arthur Henry Hallam, his friend from school days at Cambridge, Tennyson struggled with his own feelings and challenged his own beliefs about the afterlife.

In Memoriam, a long sequence of rhymed iambic pentameter quatrains documents this struggle. It is constructed around three Christmases, each with a somewhat modified response to death. At the beginning, echoing the Victorian faith in progress, even after life, the poet asserts "That men may rise on stepping stones / Of their dead selves to higher things." This is clearly no orthodox Christian faith in the afterlife as a great divide between heaven and hell. It is more like Plato's transmigration of souls or the Hindu concept of the Oversoul.

Like the graveyard poets with whom he was so familiar, Tennyson dwells on his own moods regarding the death of his friend, contrasting the old yew tree with his own deep emotion. He toys with a sense of meaninglessness, with Sorrow whispering to him (with lying lips) that the stars "blindly run" across the sky and Nature is but a hollow echo, with little comfort. He even worries that trying to put grief in words is a desecration of his deep feelings, half revealing, half concealing "the Soul within." He does find, however, that writing furnishes a "dull narcotic" to dull the pain of loss.

This extended meditation on the mood of the mourner finally shifts to an affirmation of the value in suffering, a Romantic concept emphasizing the value of strong feeling.

I hold it true, what'er befall;
   I feel it, when I sorrow most;
   'Tis better to have loved and lost
Than never to have loved at all.

Like many believers over the years, he finds that the hope of heaven for oneself or one's beloved provides some comfort for the mourner. Yet the poet is tortured with problems with his faith, a virtual catalogue of the doubts that plagued his century. Like the writer of Ecclesiastes, he comes to the position that "life is futile" and frail.

The final section expresses the mourner's acceptance of death. He refuses to believe his doubts were "Devil-born" or that he was wrong to struggle with his and Hallam's subtle questions, summing up their shared theological agony this way:

Perplext in faith, but pure in deeds,
   At last he beat his music out.
   There lives more faith in honest doubt,
Believe me, than in half the creeds.

(Tennyson, "In Memoriam A.H.H.," 51)

From these "honest doubts" have come a stronger faith for both men. The following stanzas are full of joy, with the refrain of the Christmas bells: "Ring out, wild bells." In the last words of this long poem, the evil forces of the world, those who stand in the way of justice and truth will be toppled, and thrown into the fires of hell, while Hallum will become a "happy star," watching all from afar, smiling, "knowing all is well."

This poem is a powerful expression of many of the questions facing the modern believer, including whether the dead continue their concern with affairs on earth, whether there is a hell as well as a heaven, whether the dead are transformed in spirit. C. S. Lewis attacked a number of these concerns in different ways. In *A Grief Observed* (1961), he describes his own moods as he mourns the untimely death of his beloved wife, Joy. He too faces a number of the perennial questions about the meaning of death and the possibilities of an afterlife.

In an earlier work, *The Great Divorce* (1946), he takes a different, more objective, approach, describing the moment of death and the clear separation of the saved and the damned to their ultimate destinations of heaven and hell. He notes in his subtitle that the book is in the mode of Dante's *Divine Comedy*. A good Anglican, Lewis omits purgatory from his travels. He also hints that the damned may leave hell and stay in heaven if they prefer, realizing that they are in hell because they choose to be there. Critics note that he has no biblical foundation for a number of his basic ideas in this imaginative study of life after death.

A curious modern play, written in the last days of World War II by the existentialist philosopher Jean Paul Sartre, brings a different modern sensibility to the question of the afterlife. Sartre portrays his people entering hell at the moment of their deaths. Hell turns out to be a drawing room, without an executioner or fires or devils or pitchforks. A polite valet ushers the characters on stage, telling them that they can use the bell to call for whatever they need, though the bell does not always work. Soon we see why the play is called *No Exit*. The characters are doomed to live through eternity with one another, going over and over their corrupt lives and the manner of their deaths, trying to justify themselves to one another. Garcin, the central character, discovers "Hell, it is other people."

For existentialists, man or woman is an absolutely autonomous individual. The consequence of this philosophy is that each individual must accept the consequences of each action and choice and live with loneliness. As a matter of fact, Sartre had no reason to believe in hell at all since, in his philosophy, humans are defined entirely by this world and the life they live in it. For him, the afterlife is only a convenient fiction for the purposes of his drama.

The most popular and impressive of modern American plays that deal with the death (or death-in-life) of the hero are curiously quiet about the possibility of an afterlife. Arthur Miller, in *Death of a Salesman* (1949) makes Willy Loman a thoroughly secular man. He is judged in the final scene by those who were closest to him in life, his wife, his children, and his best friend. His goals prove to be foolish and his life a failure; even his funeral is poorly attended. All his wife can do is demand that attention be paid, but she can offer no comfort for her boys and no defense of her husband.

Tennessee Williams, in his play *Cat on a Hot Tin Roof* (1955), pictures the dying giant, Big Daddy, as an Old Testament patriarch, putting all his faith in future generations. His whole life has been about the accumulation of power and wealth, neither of which will serve him on his way to the grave.

In the saddest of the three, Eugene O'Neill, in his long autobiographical drama *A Long Day's Journey into Night* (1940), chronicles the decline of his beloved mother. She simply fades away into her fog of morphine, losing any sense of the intense feelings she leaves behind. The whole tormented family tries to reach out to her, but she retreats from them and their mutual recriminations like a ghost, drifting off into the night.

One of these writers came from a background that was Catholic, one Protestant, and one Jewish. Yet none projects any firm faith in the biblical meaning of death and of the afterlife. They are fair representatives of modern American culture. Like Tennyson, many moderns wrestle with their own anticipation of death, or the death of a loved one. The writers chronicle the suffering, the sense of loss. But rarely does an author reveal any clear conviction of life beyond the grave.

Marilynne Robinson's *Gilead* (2004) is a rare exception to this generalization. Her novel is an epistle, written by an ageing minister to his young son, trying to explain life and death to the child. He notes that he has often counseled others who faced death, and he would say, "it was like going home. We have no home in this world." For the rest of the book, he wrestles with this very issue. He and another preacher, his best friend, consider what heaven will be like, whether they will see their loved ones there. They have both known such joy in marriage and in their children that they dream that they will be able to embrace one another. The novel is liberally sprinkled with scripture passages. The dying pastor notes that he will leave this earth in the "twinkling of an eye," and that his soul after death will be "imperishable, somehow more alive than I have ever been, in the strength of my youth, with dear ones beside me…. I live in a light better than any dream of mine." He sees himself as a befuddled old man in this poor perishable world, but ends the section with, "Then I'll know." Echoes of the Gospels, the prophets, Psalms, and Paul resonate all through his meditations.

A more difficult challenge for the reverend lies in dealing with damnation. His namesake, a sadly lost young man, asks him about those predestined to damnation. He admits his failure to believe the doctrines of his own church, acknowledges his iniquities, and pleads for comfort, a release from God's pronouncements of hellfire to come. At first, the pastor is sympathetic, deeply touched, but finally he cannot retreat from the clear lessons of scripture. Eventually, seeing that John, his godson, has created for himself a kind of hell on earth, he forgives and blesses him. We sense that if this spokesman for God can forgive and bless this troubled soul, surely God, in all his mercy, will find the means to bless and forgive him as well.

Conclusion

Many moderns are inclined to turn both heaven and hell into abstractions. It is common to hear comforters indicate that the deceased person is now "at peace in Heaven," regardless of that person's path in life. Occasionally we even hear the comment, at the death of a particularly nefarious villain, that he or she now faces hellfire, but most modern and postmodern writers have deep reservations regarding the ancient doctrine of hell. If they think about life after death at all, they prefer to believe in universal salvation by a sweet old benevolent God. The assurance that the dead rest "in Abraham's Bosom" is a great comfort to the bereaved. Few modern ministers would dare to preach "Sinners in the Hands of an Angry God," that fearful sermon that made Jonathan Edwards famous. The eighteenth-century congregation listened to these dreaded words with fear and trembling. A twenty-first-century congregation would probably be outraged, leaving the church in a huff or expelling the minister for being so judgmental.

As Alan Segal notes, cultural pluralism has opened up vast doubts about life after death. The suicide bombers of the past decade have forced Americans to become aware that Muslims have a very different concept of paradise for those who sacrifice their lives for Islam. Like the early Christian martyrs of the Roman Empire tribulations, they believe fiercely in the absolute certainty of the afterlife. Unlike these Christians, however, Muslims are convinced virgins await them in paradise. This awareness of Islam's ideology has led many Westerners to a radical reconsideration of their own longings for transcendence. Life on earth is so good for many in Western democracies that death is a real enemy, and heaven could hardly be better than earth.

Segal ends his long discourse on death and the afterlife in the world's different religions with the assertion that "our 'immortal longings' are mirrors of what we find of value in our lives." They are also based on what our forebears have told us to be true. They are not verifiable here and now; the dead do not return to tell us how the story ends. Therefore, since we on earth see "through a glass darkly," we are obliged to wait, like Paul told the Corinthians, until we can see "face to face: Now we know in part; but then shall I know even as also I am known" (1 Cor. 13:12).

See also: **Justice; Earthly Paradise; Temptation and Sin**

Bibliography

Alighieri, Dante. *The Divine Comedy.* Trans., Dorothy L. Sayers. New York: Basic Books, 1973.

Browne, Sir Thomas. *Hydriotaphia (Urn Burial).* In *British Poetry and Prose,* vol. I, ed. Paul Lieder, Robert Morss Lovett, and Robert Kilburn Root. Boston: Houghton Mifflin, 1950.

Chaucer, Geoffrey. *The Canterbury Tales.* New York: Modern Library, 1994.

Coleridge, Samuel Taylor. *The Rime of the Ancient Mariner.* In *Anthology of Romanticism,* ed. Ernest Bernbaum. New York: The Roland Press, 1948.

Crenshaw, James L. "Death." In *The Oxford Companion to the Bible*. New York: Oxford University Press, 1993.

DeVaux, Roland. *Ancient Israel: Its Life and Institutions*. Grand Rapids, MI: William B. Eerdmans Publishing Company, 1997.

Donne, John. *Devotions Upon Emergent Occasions* and *Holy Sonnets*. In *British Poetry and Prose*, vol. I, ed. Paul Lieder, Robert Morss Lovett, and Robert Kilburn Root. Boston: Houghton Mifflin, 1950.

Everyman. In *Religous Drama*, vol. 2, ed. E. Martin Browne. New York: Meridian Books, 1967.

Gaer, Joseph. *The Legend of the Wandering Jew*. New York: The New American Library, 1961.

Homer. *The Odyssey*. Trans., Robert Fagles. London: Penguin Books, 1996.

Kaufmann, Walter. *Tragedy and Philosophy*. Princeton: Princeton University Press, 1992.

Kohler, Kaufmann. "Immortality of the Soul." http://www.jewishencyclopedia.com/view.jsp?artid=11 (accessed December 20, 2004).

Plato. *The Republic and Other Works*. Trans., B. Jowett. New York: Anchor Books, 1989.

Poe, Edgar Allan. "The Masque of the Red Death." In *The Bible as/in Literature*, ed. James S. Ackerman and Thayer S. Warshaw. Glenview, IL: Scott, Foresman and Company, 1971.

Praz, Mario. *The Romantic Agony*. New York: Meridian Books, 1963.

Robinson, Marilynne. *Gilead*. New York: Farrar, Straus, Giroux, 2004.

Sartre, Jean Paul. *No Exit, and Three Other Plays*. Trans., Stuart Gilbert. New York: Vintage Books, 1955.

Segal, Alan F. *Life after Death: A History of the Afterlife in Western Religion*. New York: Doubleday, 2004.

Tennyson, Alfred Lord. *In Memoriam*. In *Victorian and Later English Poets*, ed. James Stephens, Edwin L. Beck, and Royall H. Snow. New York: American Book Company, 1949.

Last Days

Readings

Introduction

> Blow ye the trumpet in Zion, and sound an alarm in my holy mountain:
> let all the inhabitants of the land tremble: for the day of the Lord cometh,
> for it is nigh at hand; A day of darkness and of gloominess, a day of clouds
> and of thick darkness, as the morning spread upon the mountains:… A fire
> devoureth before them; and behind them a flame burneth: the land is as the
> garden of Eden before them, and behind them a desolate wilderness; yea, and
> nothing shall escape them. (Joel 2:1–3)

The prophet Joel calls the people of Judah to repentance with these words. He then
tells of the horsemen who will descend on the people like an invincible army. Then,

even the earth itself "shall quake before them; the heavens shall tremble: the sun and the moon shall be dark, and the stars shall withdraw their shining."

He sums up this frightening vision: "And the Lord shall utter his voice before his army: for his camp is very great: for he is strong that executeth his word: for the day of the Lord is great and very terrible; and who can abide it?" (Joel 2:11).

In both the Old Testament and the New, it is clear that time will have an end. That which God has created will finally cease to exist: the stars will dim, the sun will burn out, the grass will dry up, and all of the created world will come to an end. The manner in which this will happen is not at all clear. There are references to earthquakes, floods, wars, and pestilence. Throughout the scripture, some phenomena are repeatedly predicted to occur during the apocalypse:

1. The coming of the Redeemer
2. The Kingdom of God proclaimed
3. The New Covenant
4. The restoration of Israel
5. The outpouring of the Spirit
6. The Day of the Lord
7. The New Heavens and the New Earth (Hoekema, 11)

Some of these themes are also part of secular literature, which also considers the possibility that we all live "between the times." A number of writers have considered the end of the world, or the apocalypse. A number have also dealt with the forebodings of this great event, and the vision of the new creation that scripture promises.

Scripture

Since time began, humans have assumed that it will also end. Over and over, humans have believed that they are living in the Last Days. Certainly, those who experienced the Great Flood of Noah believed that all humans and perhaps the rest of the created world were destroyed. It was a enormous act of faith that Noah continued his search for evidence of dry land after the prolonged sojourn on the ark. The citizens of Sodom and Gomorrah must have believed that the fire which fell from the heavens was burning not just their cities, but all humankind. Because Lot's daughters thought everyone else was killed, that they were the last people left on earth, they took it upon themselves to repopulate the land through incest with their drunken father.

When the Babylonians swept down on the Israelites and leveled their cities and carried their people off into captivity, the Jews must have thought their country and their culture was forever lost. The prophets spoke of the Valley of Dry Bones, of the coming of the Day of the Lord. Joel's voice was an early warning to the people of Judah, but hardly the only one. Other examples include Zephaniah (1:14–15) and Isaiah 65 and 66.

The people of the New Testament inherited this tradition of the coming apocalypse, the great Day of the Lord, when all the forces of justice would finally be unleashed. For the disciples and many of those who followed Jesus, the Day of the Lord appeared to be at hand. They saw Christ as the Messiah, the Christian faith as the New Covenant, and anticipated the coming of the Kingdom of God, and the Last Judgment. Jesus, especially in his "Olivet Discourse" (Matt. 24:3–51; Mark 13:3–37; and Luke 21:5–36) describes graphically the end of the Temple, of Jerusalem, and the world. He speaks of the Judgment to come, of the separation of the sheep from the goats, of his coming again in glory, and of the resurrection of the dead. For these people, the Kingdom seemed to be at hand, probably in their lifetime.

All through the New Testament, with the awareness of the Redeemer's advent, Christians anticipated the coming of the Kingdom of God. Paul and other epistle-writers of the New Testament saw themselves living in the Last Days. They believed in the New Covenant based on the sacrifice of Christ for the remission of sins. The Spirit had come upon them from the day of Pentecost. The words of Acts 21:9 quote Joel: "And it shall come to pass afterward, that I will pour out my spirit upon all flesh; and your sons and your daughters shall prophesy, your old men shall dream dreams, your young men shall see visions." So many of the old prophesies were fulfilled within a few years of Christ's ministry that they had every reason to anticipate that God would bring down the kingdoms of the world and his justice would flow down upon them like a mighty river.

The prophet Joel also points to the rest of the story: "And I will show wonders in the heavens and in the earth, blood, and fire, and pillars of smoke. The sun shall be turned into darkness, and the moon into blood, before the great and terrible day of the Lord come. And it shall come to pass that whosoever shall call on the name of the Lord shall be delivered: for in mount Zion and in Jerusalem shall be deliverance, as the Lord hath said, and in the remnant whom the Lord shall call" (Joel 2:28–32). Thus, the believers awaited the Day of the Lord and the New Heaven and New Earth, the terrible judgment, and the deliverance of the remnant of the faithful.

The prophetic pronouncements all through the scripture follow a pattern that is difficult for moderns to follow. They are highly imaginative, with symbols appearing and disappearing, referring to specific contemporary people or kingdoms at one point, and to larger patterns at another. By creating a generalized description of an event, the prophet also provides a type of event, which may be used by other speakers for other events. Thus, in Jesus's conversation on the Mount of Olives, he may be referring to the past, the present, or the future, or all of them at once in a single speech. The *Day of the Lord* in the Old Testament often means the day when God will redeem his people and clear the way for their return to the Promised Land. For Christians, it assumes a different meaning, a happening at the end of time when the Lord will come to judge the just and the unjust (Bock 1999, 293–296).

Various New Testament epistles indicate that Paul and the other early Christians believed that the end of time was coming quickly. Paul writes to his good friend Timothy that the last days will be perilous times, filled with iniquity. He writes to the Thessalonians about the time when the evil will be punished "with everlasting destruction" and the Lord would return in glory and power" (2 Thess. 1:9). He assures these people that in those last days, the wicked will be revealed and the Lord will "consume with the spirit of his mouth, and shall destroy with the brightness of his coming" (2 Thess. 2:8). The letter is sprinkled with details of the Last Judgment and the Second Coming of Christ.

John's Revelation is the great vision of the final days, the wars and rumors of wars, the sign of the beast, the whore of Babylon, the anti-Christ, and the four Horsemen of the Apocalypse. Some of what is pictured in this magnificent apocalypse is historical, a memory of the events that occurred centuries earlier, some of it is much more recent, such as the abominations of Antiochus Epiphanes. Some points to the destruction of Herod's Temple in 70 A.D. or the eventual fall of the Roman Empire. Some of it is prophesy of the persecutions to come, the birth pangs of the new heaven and the new earth.

The Seven Great Signs (Rev. 12–14) include: the dragon's war against the son, the woman, and the woman's offspring; the beast from the sea and the beast from the earth; the Lamb on Mount Zion; angelic messages of judgment; the harvesting of the earth; and the reaping and judgment of the wicked (Ryken, Ryken, and Wilhoit, 638).

These signs of the times are the indications that the end is at hand. They have been periodic topics of concern among religious groups and in literature. Over and over, Christians through the centuries have interpreted the events of their day as signs of the end. Even today, there remains considerable disagreement regarding the nature and interpretation of these signs—all of which have proven fertile territory for writers. After the Battle of Armageddon, the earthquakes, floods, and pestilence, Revelation does conclude with the vision of the new heaven and new earth, God's sealing those who have been faithful to him, and the wedding feast of the Lamb. All of this gives the Last Days a quality of joy that is not common in other religions. One of the last lines in the book reads, "Even so, come, Lord Jesus."

Literature

Each culture and each century has had its own sense of impending doom, its own prophesies that plague or warfare or natural disasters will put an end to human life. The Greeks saw limits to their gods and to human life. Their mythology included stories of one generation of gods displacing another, casting them into Tartarus, and then sitting precariously on Mt. Olympus, frightened of the next generation that will surely cast them into utter darkness. In Aeschylus's *Prometheus Bound,* this is the belief behind the great argument between Prometheus (who knows the future) and Zeus (who is powerful but not omniscient). He is aware that Necessity foretells his doom, but is not informed about the details.

Like Plato, many peoples have believed in a circular pattern of history, with recurrent cycles of destruction and creation. By contrast, Bible history, from creation to the apocalypse is linear, with time bracketed by eternity. God was there at the beginning, he will be there at the end. He is the "Alpha and Omega." In between is the great story of God's deliverance of humankind. Revelation shows God still in control, as he deconstructs the heavens and the earth.

For the early medieval Germanic peoples, even the gods were expected to come to an end, in the Twilight of the Gods. Germanic myth assumed that this would be foreshadowed by a great winter that would last three years, with much suffering, wickedness, and warfare, when earthquakes would come, the sun would be darkened, and the monsters would be unleashed. "The armies of the gods and the giants would meet on a great plain for the final battle." The gods themselves would be destroyed in this conflict, leaving only the sons of the gods and Surt, the fire-bringer, who was destined to destroy earth and heaven with fire. Following this doomsday, would come the renewal of life, "when earth rises green and fertile from the sea, and the sons of the gods remember the past only as men recall evil dreams" (Davidson, 202). Apparently, the old world will be at an end, just as after Noah's flood, but the Germans believed that most of the gods will also be obliterated. The new world comes back to life, without mention of how it might be peopled.

The legacy of this vision is found in Anglo-Saxon poetry and prose, where it carries on into the stormy scenes that have been only faintly Christianized. When the Christian faith was first introduced to the Britons, King Edwin of Northumbria described the Germanic vision of life as the flight of a swallow through the king's hall on a winter night: "For a short time he is safe from the wintry storm, but after a little space he vanishes from your sight, back into the dark winter from which he came" (in the Venerable Bede's *Ecclesiastical History of the English People,* quoted in Lieder, 9). This is parallel to man's life on earth: we know nothing of what came before our life here or what is to follow.

In "The Wanderer," for example, the speaker, "weary of exile," trolls the waters of the wintry seas, fleeing Fate, mindful of misery, disasters, and the death of kin. His advice, as a "wise man," is to contemplate the world and expect doom:

> When I reflect on the fates of men—
> How one by one proud warriors vanish
> From the halls that knew them, and day by day
> All this earth ages and droops unto death,
> No man may know wisdom till many a winter has been his portion....
> A wise man will ponder how dread is that doom
> When all this world's wealth shall be scattered and waste...
> Wretchedness fills the realm of earth,
> And Fate's decrees transform the world.
> Here wealth is fleeting, friends are fleeting,
> Man is fleeting, maid is fleeting;
> All the foundations of the earth shall fail!
>
> ("The Wanderer," 49)

The poem ends with a pair of tacked-on lines about turning to God, but these appear to contradict the rest of the dirge, which attributes all of the world's woes to Fate, not God, and sees everything running down, without hope of a new creation.

Many years later, the world-weary nineteenth-century British poet Algernon Charles Swinburne was to find comfort in the idea that all the chaos and pain of earthly existence would finally be put to rest. In "The Garden of Proserpine," he admits that he is "tired of tears and laughter" and of "days and hours," of "every thing but sleep." In a gentle, rocking rhythm with musical rhyme, he lures the reader into his nihilistic vision:

> From too much love of living,
>   From hope and fear set free,
> We thank with brief thanksgiving
>   Whatever gods may be
> That no life lives forever;
> That dead men rise up never;
> That even the weariest river
>   Winds somewhere safe to sea.
> Then star nor sun shall waken,
>   Nor any change of light;
> Nor sound of waters shaken,
>   Nor any sound or sight;
> Nor wintry leaves nor vernal,
> Nor days now things diurnal:
> Only the sleep eternal
>   In an eternal night.
>
> (Swinburne, "The Garden of Proserpine," 703)

Swinburne, weary of life and of the assurances of Christianity, finds no solace in antique Greek gods either (not even in Proserpine, the goddess of springtime and rebirth). He prefers the gentle annihilation of the individual and the world.

Edgar Allan Poe, another nineteenth-century writer who found little comfort during his chaotic life in Christian thought, chose to portray the last days in less gentle terms. He pictures a pestilence, "The Red Death," which no person can escape. It sounds like one of the horsemen of the apocalypse, though more like the pale horse than the red one (Rev. 6:1–8). In this gothic short story, this American author takes his story back into an imaginary kingdom of Prince Prospero (using the name of Shakespeare's hero in *The Tempest*). The masked ball and the elaborate decoration of the rooms in his fabulous castle make this sound like renaissance Italy. The dance, as it turns out, becomes the dance of death, for no amount of wealth and preparation can protect a man from his doom. Like the biblical example of the coming of the end, the Red Death comes "like a thief in the night. And one by one, the revelers in the blood-bedewed halls of their revel, and died each in despairing posture of his fall." In the concluding lines, "the Red Death held illimitable dominion over all." The story reads like a fable, with none of the characters individualized, the whole setting and plot contrived and symbolic.

The story is a curiosity, hardly typical of American literature. A far more effective use of the apocalyptic symbolism is Katherine Anne Porter's famous story of the influenza epidemic at the end of World War I (1917–1918), which decimated the population. "Pale Horse, Pale Rider" (1939) is a prolonged set of visions, dreams, nightmares, which Miranda has as she weaves in and out of consciousness. The story describes this epidemic, which seemed particularly hideous at a time when the soldiers were preparing to go to the bloody front lines in France. The young soldier whom she loves is killed, not with bullets and gas, but with this plague. Porter intermingles the visionary quality of Revelation with the realities of actual life, chronicling a month in the life of a newspaper theater columnist in New York and her soldier lover, Adam.

A more recent novel, Marilynne Robinson's *Gilead* (2004) includes a powerful memory of the epidemic. The old pastor, who is in the process of dying, thinks about a sermon that he burned rather than preached to his congregation. He notes that the Spanish influenza was a terrible thing, which "struck just at the time of the Great War, just when we were getting involved in it. It killed the soldiers by the thousands, healthy men in the prime of life, and then it spread into the rest of the population." He notes that it was like the war, with one funeral after another. Rather than seeing this as a scourge of God, the pastor considers that it was a blessing, sparing the young men "the trenches and the mustard gas" and the "act of killing. It was just like a biblical plague, just exactly. I thought of Sennacherib." The burned sermon would have preached to the congregation that these deaths were a sign of the Last Days, "and a warning to the rest of us that the desire for war would bring the consequences of war, because there is no ocean big enough to protect us from the Lord's judgements when we decide to hammer our plowshares into swords and our pruning hooks into spears, in contempt of the will and the grace of God" (Robinson, 42). This old pacifist has seen enough of war to know its horrors and the lasting mark it leaves on people, but he decides this fire and brimstone sermon would hurt the gentle old people of his tiny congregation.

While Poe used the horrors of this plague for his exotic and romantic purposes and Porter used it to underscore the irony of death when the war was almost over, another writer found the plague a useful symbol of his philosophy. Albert Camus, an early twentieth-century French atheistic existentialist, in his famous novel *The Plague*, describes in hideous detail the city of Oran, which has been overrun by rats.

They have brought with them the bubonic plague. The doctor hero fights with all his strength against this epidemic, finally seeing it come under control after it has decimated the city's population. But at the end, he prophesies, "It's only a question of time. The rats will be back." In the long run, no amount of heroism or self-sacrifice can make much difference. Civilization is doomed, destined to be destroyed by inhuman forces. All we can do in the face of this ultimate destruction is to show a meaningless courage and accept the absurdity of the universe.

In scripture, plagues are most often portrayed as a part of God's plan. Certainly the plagues that strikes Egypt, one after another, reinforce Moses's demand that the Pharaoh let his people go. The famine and sickness that come with the prophesies in Revelation are also part of God's plan, along with the other catastrophes that lead up to the end of time. Poe and Camus, like many other moderns, use biblical imagery stripped of its underlying meaning.

William Butler Yeats, an Irish poet, enamored of both Irish folklore and Eastern mysticism, also mined the Bible for symbols and themes, but interpreted these according to far more eclectic strategies. A thoughtful and exciting writer, who packed his poems full of meaning, Yeats wrote one of the more famous prophetic poems about the twentieth century, which he called "The Second Coming." Rather than accepting the scripture's linear historical path, he pictured time and history as circular, turning in a "widening gyre." In this poem he employs the image of the falcon and the falconer for this purpose, indicating that the bird sails in circles, farther and farther from the falconer, until it can no longer hear his voice. Like modern humans, whirling about, the falcon sails away from God's controlling hand and voice, finally losing sight of God and of his path or purpose:

> Things fall apart; the centre cannot hold;
> Mere anarchy is loosed upon the world,
> The blood-dimmed tide is loosed, and everywhere
> The ceremony of innocence is drowned;
> The best lack all conviction, while the worst
> Are full of passionate intensity.

To the speaker, these all seem signs that the end of the world is imminent, perhaps the beginning of something new:

> Surely some revelation is at hand;
> Surely the Second Coming is at hand.

His speculation is interrupted by a vision of a vast image, "somewhere in sands of the desert" that resembles the famous Sphinx, a "shape with lion body and the head of a man." He ends the poem with these enigmatic lines prophesying the Second Coming:

> The darkness drops again; but now I know
> That twenty centuries of stony sleep
> Were vexed to nightmare by a rocking cradle,
> And what rough beast, its hour come round at last,
> Slouches toward Bethlehem to be born?

(Yeats, "The Second Coming," 184)

This conclusion hardly provides comfort to those facing the end of days. His "rough beast" echoes Revelation 11:7, "the beast that comes up from the abyss will wage war upon them and defeat and kill them. Their corpses will lie in the street of the great city, whose name in allegory is Sodom, or Egypt, where also their Lord was crucified" (*New English Bible* translation).

For Christians, the ending will have redemptive purpose. The world will not end with either a bang or a whimper, but with the return of Christ. In his poem, "The Hollow Men," T. S. Eliot portrays the apocalypse in a parody of the children's song, "Here we go 'round the mulberry bush." "The Hollow Men" was written in 1925, during a period of disillusionment between the great world wars of the twentieth century and before Eliot's conversion to Christianity. In the poem, Eliot describes a kingdom of the living dead. In the final stanzas of this painful song of life in the "valley of dying stars," Ezekiel's Valley of the Bones, the speaker cannot even recite the Lord's Prayer with meaning or accuracy.

Unlike Camus and Yeats, Eliot is groping toward a faith in orthodox Christianity rather than atheistic existentialism or occult eastern mysticism. This particular poem, nonetheless, describes beautifully the sense of desolation felt by many who witnessed the senseless slaughter, which destroyed an entire generation of young Europeans in the trenches of Europe,

This gloomy portrayal of destruction and despair can be contrasted to a brief poem called "Fire and Ice," by poet Robert Frost. A contemporary of Eliot, Frost spoke in a laconic New England dialect, In nine short lines, he surveys the two popular scenarios of the world's end. Although most would equate fire with weapons of mass destruction, Frost makes it more personal and passionate, noting that he would favor fire "From what I've tasted of desire." He then goes on to contemplate the possibility of a double destruction, noting that he has seen enough of hate, and that ice "would suffice." The comic rhymes, the simple language, and the clever summary of contemporary philosophy is refreshing. Frost brings the cosmic issues back to human flaws of desire and hate, issues over which people have some control.

Another American writer, Thornton Wilder, also turned the sense of approaching doom into comedy that relieved the mood and comforted the people. At the beginning of World War II, he wrote *The Skin of Our Teeth* (1942), a slapstick drama about the recurrent cycle of disaster and rebirth. In it, the characters are American versions of Everyman, his wife, his children, and his mistress. Sometimes they appear as Adam, Eve, Cain, and (oddly) the Sabine women. Sometimes they are Noah and his wife, preparing for the Great Flood (and taking the mistress along for the ride). The final act presents the warrior, Mr. Antrobus, home from the wars (any wars, Roman, Napoleonic, or European).

The play begins with the experience of Adam and Eve putting their lives back together after the expulsion from Eden and the death of Abel, though in Wilder's story, Cain remains with the family, which now includes a daughter and a mistress. It ends with a return to the first chapters of Genesis and a promise of a New Creation.

The drama, though filled with biblical allusions, is humanistic rather than scriptural in its point of view. The nature and resilience of humans rather than the will of God makes the repetitive pattern of destruction and rebirth possible. Although the characters acknowledge that the evil that motivates Cain somehow dwells deep in each person, it also reaffirms the persistence of humanity, the eagerness to make "something good out of this suffering." Antrobus tells his family that three things always seem to come together to preserve humanity: "The voice of the people in their confusion and their need," the family, and books. He asserts that life is a struggle, that "every good and excellent thing in the world stands moment by moment on the razor-edge of danger and must be fought for.... All I ask is the chance to build new worlds and God has always given us that." He ends this speech, and his role in the play by asking the audience to remember, during this time of war, "We've come a long ways. We've learned. We're learning. And the steps of our journey are marked for us here." At this point, he turns the leaves of a book on which are written a series of great philosophical thoughts, concluding with the phrase "In the beginning." *Skin of Our Teeth* was originally titled *The Ends of the Worlds*, reflecting this cyclic vision of history. Wilder does pay some incidental homage to God's role in all this, but assigns most of the responsibility for re-creation to humans.

Since the dropping of the Atom bomb, which ended the Japanese offensive in World War II, the Western world has been convinced that we will finally succumb to a man-made holocaust, fire rather than ice. Beyond those who fear this explosive apocalypse, there are the writers who believe in an ecological disaster. Many believe that humans are destroying the environment, and the world is hurtling toward a natural disaster: nuclear winter, global warming, or a world-wide plague. Fear has become pervasive and the sense of doom is palpable in much of modern fiction. Currently, many of the best sellers in the bookstores are devoted to the themes of Revelation, the signs of the times.

This particular trend in apocalyptic literature has been apparent for over half a century. Archibald MacLeish assumes in his "Epistle to Be Left in the Earth" (1952) that the end of the world is at hand. Rather than speculate as the reason or the means of the catastrophe, he considers the reactions of the last survivors as they escape the earth. This poem is a first-person narrative of the last days of the late, great planet Earth. He begins his free verse poem, "It is colder now," as if describing a world ended by ice a frozen earth, drifting off into space. The poem's title and tone identify this as the kind of letter left behind by survivors, trying to compress into a few lines the great truths they have discovered. The word *epistle* has biblical connotations, reminding the reader of Paul's messages, and even John's Revelation, which was an epistle to the seven churches. The ending suggests that the denizens of earth have lost their faith along the way: "Voices are crying an unknown name in the sky."

In 1971, Walker Percy, a richly philosophic Southern Catholic, also told a mad tale of the apocalypse in his novel, *Love in the Ruins*, subtitled "The Adventures of a Bad Catholic at a Time Near the End of the World." The novel describes America as a fractured country, divided by race, religion, politics, and class into warring factions. During "the Troubles," the whole social system is reversed, leaving urban guerrillas, called "the Bantus" in the big fancy homes in Paradise Estates, frittering away their leisure time playing golf and bird-watching. The flower children, who have fled to the swamps, have turned into killers. The white doctor is now refused permission to practice in the black hospital. He and his family live in the slave quarters, fish the bayou waters, and enjoy their happy simple life. The Church endures, with the priest repeating the familiar rituals and the penitent understanding the same need for acknowledging his sin and repenting of it. For all of its black humor, the book is a solemn warning to a country blessed with affluence and peace that "the center can-not hold," unless that center is the Rock, the Church, which Christ promised would prevail over powers and principalities and which has survived plagues, earthquakes, floods, and wars.

With his "lapsometer," this lapsed Roman Catholic views his world sympathetically, judging that it is troubled with "angelism, bestialism, and other perturbations of the soul." The intellectuals have become so abstracted that they lose their grip on life and nature. Dr. More, a comic descendent of the great English Catholic saint, Sir Thomas More, finds himself and preserves what little is left of his sanity by marrying Ellen, his Presbyterian nurse, who has a kind of Calvinist morality without the underlying faith, balancing his mysticism without morality. The story ends with More's return to the Church, to confession and mass, and to the marriage bed with joy and abandonment—the modern parallel to the wedding feast of the Lamb.

Some writers have gone beyond these signs of the end to consider the rest of the pattern of the promises of God in an eschatological hope of the resurrection of the dead. Here, they are considering a time of the Great Judgment, when the dead shall rise to a new life and a new body. A twentieth-century American writer, Richmond Lattimore, has written a sonnet entitled "Rise and Shine," in which he describes this great event in terms his own audience can understand. The trumpet will sound, and we must find our dentures. We will dress, assemble ourselves from the grave, and rise. Echoing Paul's proclamation of the death of Death, the victory over the grave, he exclaims, "We have won." He also echoes Ezekiel in his vision of the "valley of our bones" which will now rise up. Then we will "crawl like grubs from under stones" to reach out of the earth, "to scarf our loves in paradisial air."

Lattimore alludes to both scripture and earlier literature. In one of John Donne's Holy Sonnets, this seventeenth-century divine prophesies much the same event in far more elegant language, also using the Petrarchan sonnet form. Like Lattimore, he opens his poem with the trumpet call, then imagines people from all ages and nations, and looks forward to eternal bliss. His poem is compact and powerful, ending with an exhortation (typical of Donne's sermons) to repent, but making the repentance quite personal.

> At the round earth's imagined corners, blow
> Your trumpets, angels, and arise, arise
> From death, you numberless infinities
> Of souls, and to your scattered bodies go,
> All whom the flood did, and fire shall o'erthrow,
> All whom war, dearth, age, agues, tyrannies,
> Despair, law, chance, hath slain, and you whose eyes
> Shall behold God, and never taste death's woe.

This octave of address to the angels and hope for the resurrection of the souls from all ages, is then followed by this sestet of supplication:

> But let them sleep, Lord, and me mourn a space,
> For if above all those my sins abound,
> 'tis late to ask abundance of thy grace,
> When we are there; here on this holy ground,
> Teach me how to repent, for that's as good
> As if thou hadst sealed my pardon with thy blood.

(Donne, *Holy Sonnets*, VII, 487)

Conclusion

We all sense that death is inevitable. People die, trees die, rivers dry up, and earthquakes change the landscape. Certainly the earth itself is changing, perhaps dying. As sentient creatures, we are also determined to predict this conclusion to our world. The various hints, however cloudy, in the Bible have lured poets and prophets to proclaim that the end is at hand. History is full of predictions of the end of the world, with specific identification of signs that the late, great planet Earth is spiraling downward. Novels tell of the Rapture, when Christ will come to claim his own people, leaving behind all the others who are marked with the sign of the beast. Even within individual congregations of Christians, some believe that the Rapture will come before the next millennium, others believe that it will come later. Some believe that Christ will reign on earth for one thousand years; others think this is a symbol, not to be taken literally. Some ministers preach sermons on the specific dimensions of the New Jerusalem; others think this is a no more than a splendid promise of unimaginable bliss to come. No portions of scripture have raised more controversy than the scattered visions of the Last Days.

The old preacher in Ecclesiastes warns us that "no man knows when his hour will come." Jesus further warns that we do not know when the world will end. For most of humankind, it is enough to deal with life one day at a time.

See also: **Creation; Death and the Afterlife; Predestination and Free Will; Temptation and Sin.**

Bibliography

Baumbach, Jonathan. *The Landscape of Nightmare: Studies in the Contemporary American Novel.* New York: New York University Press, 1965.

Bock, Darrell L. *Three Views on the Millennium and Beyond.* Grand Rapids, MI: Zondervan, 1999.

Camus, Albert. *The Plague.* Trans., Stuart Gilbert. New York: Vintage Books, 1991.

Davidson, H. R. Ellis. *Gods and Myths of Northern Europe.* Middlesex, England: Penguin Books, 1964.

Donne, John. *Holy Sonnets.* In *The Renaissance in England: Non-Dramatic Prose and Verse of the Sixteenth Century,* ed. Hyder E. Rollins and Herschel Baker. Boston: D.C. Heath and Company, 1954.

Eliot, T. S. "The Hollow Men." In *The Complete Poems and Plays: 1909–1950.* New York: Harcourt, Brace & World, 1952.

Frost, Robert. "Fire and Ice." In *Modern American Poetry,* ed. Louis Untermeyer. New York: Harcourt, Brace and Company, 1950.

Hoekema, Anthony A. *The Bible and the Future.* Grand Rapids, MI: William B. Eerdmans Publishing Company, 1979.

Lattimore, Richard. "Rise and Shine." In *The Bible as/in Literature,* ed. James S. Ackerman and Thayer S. Warshaw. Glenview, IL: Scott, Foresman and Company, 1971.

Lieder, Paul, Robert Morss Lovett, and Robert Kilburn Root (eds.). *British Poetry and Prose,* vol. I. Boston: Houghton Mifflin, 1950.

MacLeish, Archibald. "Epistle from a Dying Planet." In *The Bible as/in Literature,* ed. James S. Ackerman and Thayer S. Warshaw. Glenview, IL: Scott, Foresman and Company, 1971.

Percy, Walker. *Love in the Ruins.* New York: Farrar, Straus, and Giroux, 1971.

Poe, Edgar Allan. "The Masque of the Red Death." In *The Bible as/in Literature,* ed. James S. Ackerman and Thayer S. Warshaw. Glenview, IL: Scott, Foresman and Company, 1971.

Porter, Katherine Anne. *Pale Horse, Pale Rider; Three Short Novels.* New York: Harcourt, Brace and Company, 1939.

Robinson, Marilynne. *Gilead.* New York: Farrar, Straus, Giroux, 2004.

Ryken, Leland, Philip Ryken, and James Wilhoit. *Ryken's Bible Handbook.* Wheaton, IL: Tyndale House Publishers, 2006

"The Seafarer," and "The Wanderer." In *British Poetry and Prose,* vol. I, ed. Paul Lieder, Robert Morss Lovett, and Robert Kilburn Root. Boston: Houghton Mifflin, 1950.

Swinburne, Charles Algernon. "The Garden of Proserpine." In *British Poetry and Prose,* vol. II, ed. Paul Lieder, Robert Morss Lovett, and Robert Kilburn Root. Boston: Houghton Mifflin, 1950.

Wilder, Thronton. *Three Plays by Thornton Wilder.* New York: Perennial Library,1985.

Yeats, W. B. "The Second Coming." In *The Collected Poems of W. B. Yeats.* New York: The Macmillan Company, 1959.

Selected Bibliography

Throughout the book, I have relied primarily on the King James Version of the Bible. I used primarily: *The King James Study Bible: King James Version.* Nashville, TN: Thomas Nelson Publishers, 1988. When I have relied on any other translation, such as the *New International Version,* or the *New English Bible* I have indicated so. The quotations from the Apocrypha are drawn from: *The HarperCollins Study Bible: New Revised Standard Version,* ed. Wayne A. Meeks. New York: HarperCollins, 1989. Most of the classic texts are available in many editions. These entries indicate the ones I have used, not necessarily the best available:

Ackerman, James S. and Thayer S. Warshaw. *The Bible as/in Literature.* Glenview, IL: Scott, Foresman and Company, 1971.

Adler, Mortimer J. *The Great Ideas: A Lexicon of Western Thought.* New York: Macmillan Publishing, 1992.

Aeschylus. *Orestia.* Trans., Ted Hughes. New York: Farrar, Straus and Giroux, 1999.

Aristotle. *The Works of Aristotle.* Trans., W. D. Ross. Chicago: Encyclopædia Britannica, 1952.

Alighieri, Dante. *The Divine Comedy.* Trans., Dorothy L. Sayers. New York: Basic Books, 1973.

Aristotle. *The Rhetoric and the Poetics.* Trans., Ingram Bywater. New York: The Modern Library, 1954.

Auerbach, Eric. *Mimesis: The Representation of Reality in Western Literature.* Trans., Willard R. Trask. New York: Jovanovich, 1982.

Augustine, St. *The Confessions.* Grand Rapids, MI: Baker Books, 2005.

Bernbaum, Ernest, ed. *Anthology of Romanticism.* New York: The Roland Press Company, 1948.

Bonhoeffer, Dietrich. *Creation and Fall: Temptation.* New York: Macmillan Publishing Company, 1959.

Brown, Colin, ed. *The New International Dictionary of New Testament Theology,* Grand Rapids, MI: Zondervan Publishing House, 1986.

Bunyan, John. *Grace Abounding to the Chief of Sinners.* New York: Penguin Classics, 1987.

———. *The Pilgrim's Progress.* New York: Pocket Books, 1957.

Calvin, John. *The Institutes of the Christian Religion*. Trans., Henry Beveridge. Grand Rapids, MI: William B. Eerdmans, 1990.

Campbell, Joseph. *The Hero with a Thousand Faces*. New York: The World Publishing Company, 1956.

Chaucer, Geoffrey. *The Canterbury Tales*. New York: Modern Library, 1994.

Coleridge, Samuel Taylor. *Biographia Literaria*. Online at http://www.gutenberg.org/etext/6081 (accessed September 12, 2006).

Creswell, Denis R. *St. Augustine's Dilemma: Grace and Eternal Law in the Major Works of Augustine of Hippo*. New York: Peter Lang, 1997.

Davidson, H. R. Ellis. *Gods and Myths of Northern Europe*. Middlesex, England: Penguin Books, 1964.

DeRougemont, Denis. *Love in the Western World*. Trans., Montgomery Belgion. Princeton, NJ: Princeton University Press, 1983.

DeVaux, Roland. *Ancient Israel: Its Life and Institutions*. Trans., John McHugh. Grand Rapids, MI: William B. Eerdmans Publishing Company, 1961.

Edersheim, Alfred. *The Life and Times of Jesus the Messiah*. Peabody, MA.: Hendrickson Publishers, 2004.

Edwards, Paul, ed. *The Encyclopedia of Philosophy* (8 volumes). New York: Collier Macmillan Publishers, 1967.

Eliot, T. S. *The Complete Poems and Plays: 1909–1950*. New York: Harcourt, Brace & World, 1952.

Fairchild, Hoxie Neale. *Religious Trends in English Poetry* (6 volumes). New York: Columbia University Press, 1968.

Ferguson, George. *Signs and Symbols in Christian Art*. New York: Oxford University Press, 1966.

Foerster, Norman and Robert Falk, eds. *American Poetry and Prose*. Boston: Houghton Mifflin, 1960.

Frye, Northrop. *The Great Code: The Bible and Literature*. New York: Harcourt Brace, 1982.

Fussell, Paul, *The Great War and Modern Memory*. New York: Oxford University Press, 2000.

Gilbert, Sandra M., and Susan Gubar, eds. *The Norton Anthology of Literature by Women: The Tradition in English*. New York: W.W. Norton, 1985.

Graves, Robert, and Raphael Patai. *Hebrew Myths: The Book of Genesis*. New York: McGraw-Hill Book Company, 1964.

Henry, Matthew. *Commentary on the Whole Bible*. Grand Rapids, MI: Zondervan Publishing House, 1961

Hoekema, Anthony A. *The Bible and the Future*. Grand Rapids, MI: William B. Eerdmans Publishing Company, 1979.

Homer. *The Iliad*. Trans., Robert Fagles. New York: Penguin Books, 1998.

———. *The Odyssey*. Trans., Robert Fagles. London: Penguin Books, 1996.

Lewis, C. S. *Reflections on the Psalms*. New York: Harcourt Brace and Company, 1958.

Lieder, Paul, Robert Morss Lovett, and Robert Kilburn Root, eds. *British Poetry and Prose*, vols. I and II. Boston: Houghton Mifflin, 1950.

Lovejoy, Arthur O. *The Great Chain of Being: A Study of the History of an Idea*. New York: Harper and Row, Publishers, 1960.

Lucretius. *On the Nature of the Universe*. London: Penguin Books, 1951.

Metzger, Bruce M., and Michael D. Coogan, eds *The Oxford Companion to the Bible*. New York: Oxford University Press, 1993.

Milton, John. *The Student's Milton*. Ed. Frank Allen Patterson. New York: Appleton-Century-Crofts, 1930.

Pagels, Elaine. *The Gnostic Gospels*. New York: Random House, 1979.

Plato. *The Republic and Other Works*. Trans., B. Jowett. New York: Anchor Books, 1989.

Praz, Mario. *The Romantic Agony*. New York: Meridian Books, 1963.

Ryken, Leland, Philip Ryken, and James Wilhoit. *Ryken's Bible Handbook*. Wheaton, IL: Tyndale House Publishers, 2006

Sayers, Dorothy L. *The Mind of the Maker.* Westport, CT: Greenwood Press, 1941.

Segal, Alan F. *Life after Death: A History of the Afterlife in Western Religion.* New York: Doubleday, 2004.

Shakespeare, William. *Shakespeare: Major Plays and the Sonnets,* ed. G. B. Harrison. New York: Harcourt, Brace and Company, 1948.

Shelley, Percy Bysshe. *Defense of Poetry.* In *Anthology of Romanticism,* ed. Ernest Bernbaum. New York: The Roland Press Company, 1948.

Sproul, Barbara. *Primal Myths: Creating the World.* San Francisco, CA: Harper & Row, 1979.

Stephens, James, Edwin L. Beck, and Royall H. Snow, eds. *Victorian and Later English Poets.* New York: American Book Company, 1949.

Thomas, Keith. *Man and the Natural World: A History of the Modern Sensibility.* New York: Pantheon Books, 1983.

Trawick, Buckner B. *The Bible as Literature: The Old Testament and the Apocrypha.* New York: Barnes & Noble Books, 1970.

Untermeyer, Louis, ed. *Modern American Poetry.* New York: Harcourt, Brace and Company, 1950.

Untermeyer, Louis, ed. *Modern British Poetry.* New York: Harcourt, Brace and Company, 1950.

Welty, Eudora. *Stories, Essays & Memoir.* New York: Library of America, 1998.

Index

About the Author

NANCY M. TISCHLER is Professor Emerita of English and the Humanities at the Pennsylvania State University. Her previous books include *All Things in the Bible* (2006), *Men and Women of the Bible* (2003), and *Student Companion to Tennessee Williams* (2000), all available from Greenwood Press.

DATE DUE

OCT '08